OUTDOOR LIVING SPACES

OUTDOOR LIVING SPACES

How to Create a Landscape You Can Use & Enjoy

SUSAN RADEMACHER FREY & BARBARA W. ELLIS

ILLUSTRATIONS BY KATHRYN D. KESTER

Rodale Press, Emmaus, Pennsylvania

Our Mission

We publish books that empower people's lives.

RODALE BOOKS

Printed in the United States of America on
acid-free ∞ paper

If you have any questions or comments concern-
ing this book, please write:
   Rodale Press
   Book Readers' Service
   33 East Minor Street
   Emmaus, PA 18098

Library of Congress Cataloging-in-Publication Data

Frey, Susan Rademacher.
   Outdoor living spaces : how to create a
landscape you can use & enjoy : featuring
hundreds of professional, practical design ideas /
Susan Rademacher Frey & Barbara W. Ellis.
         p.   cm.
   Includes bibliographical references and index.
   ISBN 0-87596-132-0   hardcover
   1. Gardens—Design.   2. Landscape
gardening.   3. Gardens.
   I. Ellis, Barbara W.   II. Title.
SB473.F833   1992
712'.6—dc20   92-17336
                              CIP

Distributed in the book trade by St. Martin's Press

2   4   6   8   10   9   7   5   3   1   hardcover

Executive Editor: **Margaret Lydic Balitas**

Senior Editor: **Barbara W. Ellis**

Associate Editor: **Jean Nick**

Production Editor: **Nancy J. Ondra**

Editorial Assistant: **James E. Farrell**

Photography Editor: **Heidi A. Stonehill**

Copy Manager: **Dolores Plikaitis**

Copy Editor: **Laura Stevens**

Editorial Production Coordinator: **Susan L. Nickol**

Editorial/Administrative Assistant:
Karen Earl-Braymer

Indexer: **Ed Yeager**

Art Director: **Anita G. Patterson**

Book and Cover Designer: **Linda Jacopetti**

Associate Designer: **Linda Brightbill**

On the Front Cover: Dappled shade, comfortable
chairs, and beautiful flowers all work together to
create an outdoor living space that's both welcoming and practical. Who could resist visiting this
simple space again and again, whether to chat
with a friend, read a book, or just enjoy the
outdoors? (Photograph by Balthazar Korab)

CONTENTS

CREDITS

About the Authors

Susan Rademacher Frey lives in Louisville, Kentucky, where she is the executive director of the Olmsted Parks Conservancy and assistant director of the Metropolitan Parks Department. She received a bachelor of arts degree from Miami University in Oxford, Ohio, and was the 1986-87 recipient of the Loeb Fellowship in Advanced Environmental Design from the Harvard Graduate School of Design. From 1984 to 1991 she served as editor in chief of *Landscape Architecture* and *Garden Design* magazines. She has lectured and written about landscape design for nearly 15 years. Two of her previous books are *Bold Romantic Gardens* and *Garden Design: History, Principles, Elements, Practice.*

Barbara W. Ellis is senior editor of garden books at Rodale Press in Emmaus, Pennsylvania. A lifelong gardener, she received a bachelor of arts degree from Kenyon College in Gambier, Ohio, and a bachelor of science degree in horticulture from The Ohio State University in Columbus, Ohio. She is the editor of several Rodale Press books, including *Rodale's Illustrated Encyclopedia of Gardening and Landscaping Techniques, Rodale's All-New Encyclopedia of Organic Gardening,* and *The Organic Gardener's Handbook of Natural Insect and Disease Control.* She is a former editor and publications director of *American Horticulturist* magazine, the publication of the American Horticultural Society. She lives in a 200-year-old stone farmhouse in Alburtis, Pennsylvania, and gardens on 9 acres.

About the Designers of the Gardens

Richard Haag is a landscape architect in Seattle and a professor of landscape architecture at the University of Washington, College of Architecture and Urban Planning. Through his firm, Rich Haag Associates, he has designed a range of outdoor living spaces, from private gardens to public parks, for more than 30 years.

Sheila Lynch is an environmental master planner and holds a bachelor's degree in environmental design and a master's degree in landscape architecture from the Harvard Graduate School of Design. Her firm, Sheila Lynch and Associates, in Cambridge, Massachusetts, develops environmentally sound landscape designs for public projects and for individuals.

W. Gary Smith is a registered landscape architect and an assistant professor of landscape design and construction at the University of Delaware in Newark. He lectures extensively on using native plants in garden design.

Sherry Wheat is a landscape architect with the Dekalb parks department on the outskirts of Atlanta. She holds a master's degree in landscape architecture from the University of Pennsylvania in Philadelphia and owns her own design firm specializing in creating planting plans to please wildlife and people, for single homes or whole developments.

C. Colston Burrell is a horticulturist, garden designer, and photographer based in Minneapolis. He has a master's degree in horticulture and is pursuing a second master's in landscape architecture. His firm, Native Landscapes, specializes in landscape restoration and in the innovative use of native plants and perennials. He also teaches classes in ecological garden design and lectures throughout the United States on growing and propagating native plants.

Carol Shuler is a landscape architect, horticulturist, and plant ecologist. She is president of C. F. Shuler, Inc., a Scottsdale, Arizona, design firm that specializes in innovative and environmentally sensitive designs for private and public outdoor spaces, planned communities, golf courses, and highways.

Bruce Carnahan has a master's degree in landscape design from the Conway School of Landscape Design in Conway, New Hampshire. His firm, Bruce Carnahan Landscape Design, Inc., in Louisville, Kentucky, specializes in residential gardens, especially perennial gardens and water gardens.

Gael Dilthey holds a degree in ornamental horticulture from the University of Wisconsin-Madison. She is a landscape specialist for the city of Milwaukee, where she has championed the use of perennials to replace some of the city's annual plantings. She also designs perennial plantings for private gardens.

Timothy Steinhoff is a professional horticulturist who received his early training at the Royal Horticultural Society's Wisley Garden. He is currently the landscape curator of Montgomery Place, a 400-acre historic garden estate on River Road in Annandale-on-Hudson, New York. He has designed and maintained numerous public and private gardens in the New York area, and has taught and lectured extensively.

Michael McKinley is a garden photographer and designer based in Point Richmond, California. He has a master's degree in landscape architecture from the University of California, Berkeley. He is the co-author of a number of books published by Ortho, including *All about Perennials, All about Annuals*, and *All about Shrubs,* and the author of *How to Attract Birds to Your Home.*

About the Illustrator

Kathryn D. Kester is a designer based in Philadelphia. She has a bachelor's degree in plant science from the University of Delaware in Newark and a master's degree in landscape architecture from the University of Pennsylvania in Philadelphia.

INTRODUCTION

The book you hold in your hands is a guide to the most exciting, creative, intimidating, and complex part of gardening: designing your own garden. In *Outdoor Living Spaces* you'll find all the tools you need to create your own landscape design — from gathering ideas and inspiration to drawing plans and installing your garden.

In the pages that follow, you'll discover a host of examples and ideas to guide you, but you won't find endless rules to follow and principles to adhere to. That's because *Outdoor Living Spaces* isn't a typical book about design. Instead, it's a guide to help you discover what *you* enjoy and want most in your garden — not what someone else says you should want.

Through text, illustrations, photographs, and examples, you'll learn how to design a garden that's beautiful and useful. Above all, you'll learn how to create one that's tailor-made to suit you, your family, and your property.

Here's a brief overview of what you'll find in each part of the book:

Part 1, "Landscapes for Living: Getting from Fantasy to Fact," provides an overview of general design concepts and also introduces the design process.

Part 2, "A Gallery of Gardens: Ten Designs for Outdoor Living," presents the stories of ten gardens and their owners. In each chapter, you'll learn about the features that make the garden special, and in the process, you'll discover ideas to use in your own garden. In addition to "before" and "after" drawings of each property, there's a color painting to show what each garden looks like, and plenty of information on what inspired the design, what each family wanted their garden to become, what problems the design solves, and ideas for adapting the design to your own region, and much more.

Part 3, "Creating Your Own Outdoor Living Spaces: A Step-by-Step Guide," shows you how to discover what you truly want and really need in your garden — and how to turn that knowledge into concepts you can use to guide your design. You'll also learn how to map your property, develop a framework for the outdoor living spaces you'd like to have in it, select plants, and develop a plan for installing your garden.

Undoubtedly, as you read this book, you'll discover that there are as many ways to design a garden as there are gardeners. And that's just as it should be, for every person is unique — as is every property. We hope this book will guide you through the process and help you discover and design the garden you've always wanted. Happy gardening!

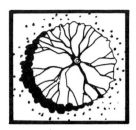

PART
1

LANDSCAPES FOR LIVING
Getting from Fantasy to Fact

Who hasn't dreamed of having a garden that's a pleasure to explore, tend, and enjoy all year long? But how do you go about creating one? It can be hard enough just to find the right planting combination for a shady, dry spot under a tree, but thinking about designing an arbor leading from the garage to the kitchen door or making changes such as developing a shrub border or planning a water garden can be downright intimidating.

Whether you've thought about creating a private shady nook where you can sit and read or a sunny patio with a water garden surrounded by colorful perennials, it's hard to know how to get from garden fantasy to fact. You may begin to wonder if you have the skills, knowledge, and cre-

◀

Outdoor living spaces don't need to be complicated or expensive to be effective and welcoming. In fact, sometimes it's just a matter of recognizing opportunity. A vine-covered arbor, loads of colorful geraniums, and comfortable furniture transform this simple corner into an inviting alcove.

ativity it takes to design your garden. Rest assured that you do. You carry within you a native genius for garden making. This book aims to help you discover that gift and show you how to use it.

Outdoor Living Spaces is a guide to help you create the garden you've always dreamed of: Use it like a helping hand as you work through the design process—from discovering what you really want and need in your garden to drawing the final plans and installing it. In the pages that follow, you'll find all the encouragement and inspiration you need to start your design and take it to completion.

But before you start your own design, there are a few basic principles to keep in mind. They'll guide you through the process and help you get the most out of your garden.

Principles to Get You Started

Fortunately, a garden doesn't have to be big or expensive to be great. It need only be intriguing, meaningful, and memorable. Just imagine a tiny courtyard garden in the French Quarter of New Orleans. You might catch a tantalizing glimpse through a dark and cool entryway and see a fountain with a splash of water playing in the sun. It's surrounded by the hot pinks and oranges of impatiens lighting up the shadows. There's no doubt that even such a simple garden has all the character it needs to lure you back to it again and again.

So how can you make your own garden into one that's intriguing, meaningful, and memorable? You'll be well on your way if you keep three basic ideas in mind as you develop your design: character, connection, and change. In part 3 of this book, you'll find information that will show you how to use these principles in your own design.

Character

A memorable garden expresses your personal style as well as the character of

T. L. Gettings/Rodale Stock Images

▲ *Beds of impatiens and other groundcovers surround this simple sitting area, nestled on the edge of a bank under the the arching branches of nearby trees. Rustic furniture and flagstone paving create an appealing outdoor room that is loaded with character. The clump of gnarled tree trunks, at left, serves as a landmark while luring visitors out to enjoy the terrace.*

your site and its region or locale. You can express your personal style in many ways: You may want to display a collection of weather vanes, create a crazy-quilt garden filled with flowering herbs, design a kitchen garden with specialty vegetables, or grow an impeccably groomed croquet lawn. Your garden is a place to accommodate your special tastes and favorite activities.

You could express the character of your site by using native stone to build walls and terraces or by opening up views or highlighting what's unique and attractive about your lot. Gardens that express local character might include the pickets that fence a New England dooryard, the art deco tiles of a Miami swimming pool, or the pungent aromas and subtle textures of a desert courtyard in New Mexico, where a string of red chili peppers hangs by the door. All are ways to celebrate the character of the region in which you live.

Connection

An intriguing garden contains a variety of spaces that are linked together and that lure you from one part to another. For example, the sight of a wood-chip path that disappears behind a rhododendron might tempt you to leave the back porch and walk through a fernery sprinkled with wildflowers. From there, the path might lead to a sunny patio where you can sit, rest, and enjoy the garden. Perhaps you'll discover a turtle sidling under a clump of perennials or catch sight of birds nesting in the shrubs that screen the patio from the sights and sounds of the outside world.

When you design every space with care, from the front walk to the lowly alley gate, you can create a garden that will invite you and your guests to explore it time and again.

Change

A meaningful garden is always changing and evolving. Perhaps your star athlete grows up and the basketball court becomes the foundation for a screened-in teahouse. Or you develop a passion for water lilies and replace a sunny lawn with a new pond. Or an old tree succumbs to a wind storm and a formerly shady bower is now a sunny opportunity.

Change is always afoot in a garden because nature never runs out of surprises, and neither do you. Plants grow and change from day to day and year to year, and your interests and needs change as well.

Gardens that are meaningful aren't installed overnight and then kept perfect by a maintenance service. The relationship between an active gardener and a changing landscape is like the relationship between two people in a running conversation. You develop areas and fine-tune the plants and materials they feature, and the garden changes and develops according to your current interests and outdoor activities. An effective design will provide a framework within which your garden can evolve over time.

Piecemeal Landscapes

Unfortunately, our society teaches us to see our landscapes as a kit of loose parts rather than as a single interconnected whole. Most gardens are made up of a collection of objects: plants used as specimens or planted in scattered beds; production gardens for vegetables, cut flowers,

Jerry Pavia

and herbs; and structures such as tool-sheds, cold frames, greenhouses, compost bins, and doghouses. Here you have a patio, there a walkway. Such landscapes take shape in fits and starts like an old house with addition upon addition tacked one upon the other. The result is a piecemeal garden that's made up of totally unrelated elements arranged with no apparent order, all of which are visible at first glance. Piecemeal landscapes aren't intriguing, meaningful, or memorable.

The typical suburban backyard is the perfect example of such design—or lack of design—with shrubs outlining the perimeter and everything from terrace to compost heap visible at a glance. This type of arrangement generally doesn't provide much privacy. And since you can see everything from the back door, it also fails to create any compelling relationships between the parts of the garden. There's no intrigue and no reason to explore the garden—no half-hidden views or secret spaces to discover. As a result, the garden becomes a picture to look at (and most likely, an unattractive one at that) rather than a place to enjoy and spend time in.

Effective Design

The term *design* sometimes implies a master stroke, as if there is one comprehensive solution that resolves all prob-lems in a pleasing and useful way. Don't be misled by that concept. You're not looking for a garden that comes in a standardized, ready-to-assemble kit. Good design takes thought and time.

An effective design and a thoroughly satisfying garden start out as a creative idea that grows out of a knowledge of both who you are and what you want in a garden. You must take into account an understanding of exactly where you are making your garden (your site and its region) and your design resources. In part 3 of this book, you'll learn how to identify and use your patterns of daily and seasonal living as well as your individual needs, tastes, and memories in your design. You'll also learn to use characteristics of your site—such as its history, traces of previous gardens or buildings, views, and biological networks of soil, water, light, plants, and wildlife—to inspire and guide your design. Learning more about yourself and your place, and using that knowledge to develop your design, will lead you to a garden that is not only a place to labor in and admire, but also a place to live in, alone or in the society of family, friends, and wildlife.

An effective design not only helps you translate your dreams into reality, it also solves functional problems in your landscape. For example, the design in "Rejuvenating an Older Garden: New Plants and Terraces" on page 134 uses a series of

◀

This path proves that in a garden, getting there can be half the fun. Who could resist exploring it? The exuberant display of flowers that edge it includes white callas as well as pink clematis, hardy geraniums, and pinks (Dianthus spp.). At the end, the path dips out of sight, connecting the spaces of the garden and luring visitors to discover what's in store beyond the bend.

terraces not only to create beds for colorful perennials but also to eliminate steep, difficult-to-mow slopes on two sides of the property. An effective design also takes into account existing site features, boundaries, zoning or other municipal codes, available materials, ecology, time, and budget.

Through a garden, you also can consciously join with nature's living system. The way you use water, for instance, is

▶

Understanding both why you want a garden and how you want to use it is crucial to effective design. This space seems tailor-made for reading, visiting with a friend, or just relaxing during a quiet moment to enjoy the lavender and other herbs that surround it. The arbor, which echos the shape of the bench, is covered with sweet autumn clematis (Clematis paniculata).

Pamela Harper

▲ *Plantings as rich as the ones surrounding this backyard lawn aren't installed overnight. Instead, they develop over time—as plants grow and bloom and new specimens are added. Here, the result is a rich array of roses, annuals, and perennials that provide vibrant color and interesting texture. Trees and shrubs provide privacy along with colors from bright green to burgundy.*

more crucial when you consider its role in the local environment. And the way you design a boundary fence becomes a social act since it affects the relationship between your property and your neighbor's. Even providing for a place to recycle kitchen and garden wastes can benefit you and the community around you. Thoughtful design is a way for you to contribute deliberately to the health of our communities and, by extension, our planet.

Awakening Your Creativity

Where do you discover the creative ideas to guide you? In part 3, you'll find a host of ideas for unlocking your creativity. In fact, creativity—and the act of coming up with a creative idea around which to develop a garden—is often just a matter of recording and mulling over your thoughts and ideas. Here are some suggestions to help guide you in that process.

Pamela Harper

▲ *Ideally, a garden works with nature's living system rather than against it. A design can incorporate nesting sites and food plants to attract native birds, or plantings of flowers to lure butterflies—just as the fragrant white blossoms of garlic chives (Allium tuberosum) have attracted this buckeye.*

All too often, gardens are long on work to do and short on ▲
spaces to sit. A comfortable bench in a quiet spot—this one is
nestled under a magnolia tree and surrounded by spring flowers—is
a perfect place for jotting down your thoughts in a garden
journal. It's also an ideal place to develop new design ideas or
just to enjoy the sights and sounds of your garden.

Walter Chandoha

Record Your Thoughts

Begin now to keep a garden idea journal. In this case, you don't want a pristine book filled only with artfully written prose; a small spiral-bound notebook filled with scribbled words and phrases is fine. Write whatever comes to mind as you read this book and study the design concepts it contains. In addition, go into your garden and write. Visit gardens around

you, too. Write about different sounds that wind makes. Make a note when you realize that you really don't enjoy looking at the neighbor's satellite dish. Try writing first thing in the morning before you've spoken or heard a word. Sketch what your mind's eye sees. Describe a problem and imagine its solution. All these notes will help you focus your thoughts. As time passes, your journal will hold your memories and inspirations and will be a record of your explorations and the actions you take. It will contain no wrong entries—just many options and ideas for you to refer back to and choose to keep, build on, or ignore.

Collect and Consider Ideas

Imagining gardens and mulling over ideas is a good way to start the process of designing. So often books will try to simplify this process by telling you to start with "planning," as though creating a garden is an entirely rational process. Although analysis, strategies, and step-by-step plans do play crucial roles, they must follow from your design inspiration and ideas. Your dreams will run the gamut from practical needs, such as an area for composting or trash cans, to fantasies, such as a moon-viewing platform.

It will also help you to reach out to family, friends, and neighbors for ideas, as well as local garden associations, botanical gardens, nursery retailers, professional designers, national hotlines, magazines, and books. All of these sources are valuable, as are your memories of a gardening grandmother's way of rooting rose slips, or the peaceful retreat you often enjoy in a neighbor's gazebo, where your conversations are cooled by the breeze of an overhead paddle fan and refreshed by the trickling sound of a nearby fountain.

Make friends with time. As a gardener, you're always living partly in the future—waiting for trees to grow and perennials to fill out. You'll always be planning and thinking about what will happen next, so be patient and take time to dream about the garden you'd love to have. The great English gardener Vita Sackville-West imagined her now-famous White Garden—an ethereal garden in gray, green, and white—in her mind's eye long before she began to make it. As she wrote in a newspaper column,"It is, in fact, nothing more than a fairly large bed, which has now been divided into halves by a short path of grey flagstones terminating in a rough wooden seat. When you sit on this seat, you will be turning your backs to the yew hedge, and from there I hope you will survey a low sea of grey clumps of foliage, pierced here and there with tall white flowers."

Plan

Analysis and planning come into play once you know your heart's desires. Planning is your bridge from dreams to reality. As the English gardener Marion Cran writes, "Once the plan is made, the comfort of it is a thing to lean upon. To know the pattern which it has to cut makes the cutting-tool work glibly. There is another comfort in a plan—half-way through the terracing, leveling, pond-formation, or whatever operation may be in progress, it is my own experience that the spirit quails. Everything looks hideous, impossible, and squalid. A glance at the plan, so formal, so neat, and so assured restores confidence in a wonderful way, and makes the labour of construction once more an act of joy."

A good garden design will bring together your own imagination and abilities to create the spaces in which you want to live. Even more exciting, a well-planned design will actually save you time and effort in the long run, because it is a strong framework within which you can constantly experiment with changing tastes and lifestyles. One impulse purchase or a lengthy

A plan will help translate good ideas into an effective design for outdoor living. It will help you identify all the details you need to keep in mind when implementing your design, and help you budget the time, effort, and money you have available. Perhaps more important, it will help ensure that the creative ideas that inspired the design don't get lost in the process.

J. Michael Kanouff/Rodale Stock Images

absence will not ruin it. Every good design starts with patient observation. Know yourself and your place, and let the two work on each other, telling you what to do.

Pitfalls to Avoid

While you can learn about designing wonderful spaces and details from lavish gardens at historic American homes—like Dumbarton Oaks in Washington, D.C., or California's Filoli—it can be very hard to translate their designs into a form that will suit your own home and outdoor living spaces. Ultimately, it's futile to model your own garden after any other. Anyone who has ever taken a photograph to a hair stylist knows that it's next to impossible to re-create the effects with different hair and facial features. Gardens work in much the same way. With the infinite variety of physical conditions, architectural character, and personal taste, why even attempt a clone? Truly memorable gardens are places of character, fitted to their particular landscape.

Amid all the media hype and "off the rack" garden styles that you can get from computer programs and pattern books, it's all too easy to go "shopping without a list," meaning without a clear design that's based on your style, what you already have, and what you really need. Another pitfall is mistaking an expensive garden for a good garden. As gardening in America enjoys a golden age of popularity, too often gardens degenerate into an empty status symbol of wealth and taste rather than a creation that is a personal statement about a gardener's style and relationship with the land. Impulse shoppers

usually come home with back-of-the-closet items they rarely use. An "off the rack" garden will never have the custom-fitted feeling that one you designed especially to fit your needs and the character of your site does.

Finally, don't fall into the trap of letting your garden become an ideal image that you dream about but never realize. Your image of your ideal garden is probably most vivid in the winter, when you mull over catalogs and books. Then as spring overwhelms your senses and the work of simply keeping up with plant growth takes more time than you can give, the image fades from view. Why is this a problem? It shows the garden as a thing apart—an object of fantasy, which can never be realized. It reveals the reality gap between thinking and doing, and that's where design falls apart. Learn to use the design process outlined in this book to make your wish for your ideal garden come true. Your design isn't something that you will be able to roll out suddenly to instantly transform your yard. Instead it will give you a direction to work toward and goals to attain.

Creating Livable Landscapes

As you read this book, you'll discover that *Outdoor Living Spaces* isn't about planting front yards and back yards, or locating flower beds and swing-sets. Instead, it's about seeing the entire landscape that surrounds your home as a connected sequence of spaces, or garden rooms, that are all designed as a unified composi-

Jerry Pavia

Livable landscapes start with a design that encompasses your ▲ entire property. The design links one part to the next in a sequence of spaces you'll want to use and enjoy. In this garden, it's easy to see how tempting it would be to wander out of the sunroom, into the garden, and up the stone steps to explore the rock garden that wraps around the house.

tion. It's also about learning to use design to create a garden with outdoor spaces that's more than just a picture to look at. That's because whether you inherit a garden from previous owners or start from scratch, your challenge as a designer is to make a garden you'll want to live in, with areas that you and your family can use and enjoy for a wide variety of activities.

Space and Design

Space and design are unfamiliar concepts that may seem vaguely threatening at first. But they're easier to understand than you might think. Space is the one element that flows throughout the landscape; design is how you choose to define it. In Far Eastern traditions, space is actually viewed as a living substance that con-

Pamela Harper

▲ *Although surrounded by walls, this outdoor room is closely linked to the garden beyond. The arched doorway frames a view that's flooded with light and bright with colorful flowers. Pots of foliage plants and flowering annuals strengthen the link between this shaded sitting area and the garden beyond.*

nects all things. The Japanese have a word for it—*ma*—and space in a Japanese garden is not seen as empty, but as a tangible volume somewhat like water or gas. You can "see" space when smoke rises from a fire pit or when fog lies along the hollows of the earth.

When children play house, the first thing they do is mark off the spaces they'll be playing in by outlining the walls and doors with their toes in the dirt. They have

an unerring instinct not only for the need to organize the spaces but also for the size of a comfortable space. Using design to establish and organize the spaces in your garden and connect one to another in a logical and comfortable manner is the key to a successful garden, too. Through your design, you shape space in your landscape into areas for the activities you would like to have room for, including everything from growing vegetables or making compost to entertaining friends, bird-watching, or playing sports.

It helps to think of outdoor living spaces as you would the rooms of your home. Your home is a personal expression of your taste and your needs. Each room, or separate space, supports a different aspect of your life, including eating, resting, playing, and socializing. These activities guide your design choices for each space, including furnishing, lighting, materials, equipment, and so forth.

Like your house, your garden is an important part of your life that should express your taste and your needs. There's one important difference, though: Your garden doesn't come with ready-to-occupy rooms with walls, ceilings, and floors that you can simply furnish and decorate. That's why garden design is so much harder than

Joanne Pavia

Shrubs form the "walls" of this outdoor room, and an arched rose ▲ *trellis forms the doorway, but it's easy to see the space they create. Plants form the furnishings, including roses, foxglove, and an orange-fruited calamondin (× Citrofortunella mitis). Cheery blue Dalmatian bellflowers (Campanula portenschlagiana) carpet the ground along the path that leads to the lawn beyond.*

SEEING SPACES

Training yourself to sense space is fun because all your senses, not just sight, get into the act. Smell, touch, and hearing can also tell you a great deal about space once you start paying close attention. In fact, the first step in this activity of discovering space is to slow down and attune yourself acutely to what's going on around you.

Sensing Space

Find something fragrant (or smelly!) and then move away from it until you pass out of its "zone of scent." Or late in the day, find a masonry wall that faces west and has been soaking up the sun all afternoon. You'll feel the heat radiating out into nearby space. Move in and out of this warm space until you can draw a line in the air with your finger to mark the edge of this space. Walk under a tree when the wind is blowing its leaves and hear the rustling sound rise, then sharply fall off as you leave the vicinity of the tree. Once more, walk in and out of this sound space until you can draw a line in the dirt with your toe to show the edge. You can try all kinds of variations with shadow, hose spray, or whatever occurs to you.

Drawing Space

Drawing is another way to see space anew. One exercise is to draw an edge where a thing meets the space around it, like two pieces of a jigsaw puzzle. Allow a half-hour of relaxed drawing time. Choose something simple at first, like a leaf from your garden. Tape some plain paper to a board or table, position your pen or pencil on the paper, and then turn away so you can't see what you are drawing. Draw as slowly as your eyes move along the edge between the air and the leaf. It doesn't matter if your drawing turns out to look nothing like the leaf—what's important is that you see the edge of the object you are draw-

---

interior design. You must build the garden from the ground up. Remember playing house? Designing your garden is all about dividing up the spaces, deciding how they are connected, and then furnishing them with plants and other materials.

When you design your garden to create outdoor living spaces, you don't erect walls around all the different areas, of course. There are a wide variety of ways to distinguish rooms or spaces in a garden that range from obvious and unmistakable to subtle. Hedges and shrub borders are among the most obvious examples. On the other hand, the deeply shaded area under a tree can become an alluring space that's unmistakably distinct from the hot sunny area around it.

For some exercises that will help you visualize space in your garden, see "Seeing Spaces" above. Reading about the gardens that you'll find in part 2 of this book may also help you understand what it means to organize space in a garden. For example, in "The Small Garden: Rooms to Grow In" on page 33, Jeanne and Bill used a

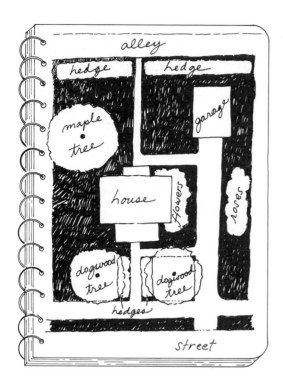

ing as its own thing—the meeting line between object and space.

The second exercise will help you to see the shape of space. On a fresh sheet of paper, outline some part of your landscape as though you are looking down on it from a hot-air balloon. Within this "frame" draw the outlines of each object—house, picnic table, flower bed, hammock, tree, doghouse, whatever. Next, fill in all the open space with your pen or pencil to make it seem real and solid, leaving the objects blank. Now you can see that space connects everything—it's equal in substance and importance to the things it surrounds. Architects call this a *figure-ground* study.

How do these exercises relate to design? Becoming more sensitive to space and the ways it can be defined will make it easier for you to recognize potential spaces in your garden. It will also help you see interesting opportunities for dividing up the space in your garden and organizing it in your design.

simple grid to divide the space in their nearly empty lot into a series of rooms. A combination of vine-covered trellises, shrubs, trees, and changing paving patterns establishes the boundaries between the rooms in their garden.

Making Your Design Work

Unity is the root of a great garden. It comes from developing a central creative idea that will guide and inspire you as you make your design—from selecting plants and materials to establishing the spaces

you develop and the transitions between them. In part 3, you'll learn how to identify the concepts or ideas you want to guide your design and how to use them to create a pleasing and unified garden. For examples of the ideas that guided the designs in part 2, see the "Key Concepts" boxes in each chapter.

Linking House and Garden

Whatever kind of garden you design, it should encompass your house, because your house is part of your garden. As you

develop your design, consider how you can enjoy your garden from indoors as well as what your house looks like from the garden. Is it easy to move from indoors out into the garden? Do the plants around your house simply overwhelm it? Or are they boring and dull, and make your house look that way, too? Think about what parts of the garden you can see from indoors and what views you might enjoy seeing. For example, if you spend time every day at your kitchen sink, why not design a view you can enjoy out the window while you work?

You'll also find opportunities for using plantings around your house to create spaces such as patios or terraces that strengthen the link between house and garden. If you're having trouble imagining how a house and garden can work together, look through the gardens in part 2. All are closely linked to the houses they encompass, and you'll find numerous examples of ways to link the two.

One simple factor you should take into consideration is how easy it is to walk between house and garden. You'll find several of the gardens in part 2 include such improvements. For example, in "From Bare to Beautiful: Foresting a Courtyard" on page 60, the final design features new French doors that make it possible to move directly from the breakfast room into the garden. In "Reclaiming a Suburban Ranch House"

◀

on page 118, the design features a new landing, designed as part of a new system of terraces, outside the back door to make it easier to get in and out.

Design for Movement

Remember the principle of connection? Consider how you will move through your garden, not just what it looks like. What will lure you from one place to the next? How fast will you be walking, and where will you want to pause or sit and rest? The experience of entering and moving through a garden's spaces is like a dance—think of design as garden choreography. For example, if you have to climb a hill to reach the front door, a series of steps and landings will allow you to rest along the way; an interesting shrub or well-framed view will provide entertaining excuses to pause.

Transitions between spaces are a way to connect the garden and control how you and your visitors will move through it. Like frames in the landscape, transitions attract your attention and then lure you to explore what lies just out of sight. For example, say you come upon a glimpse of a lily pond through an arch in a hemlock hedge. You can't simply stand back and admire the scene; you have to step through the arch and become a part of the next space. Each transition holds the memory of the place you've just come from and the

An effective design encompasses the house and is attractive and enjoyable from both outdoors looking in and indoors looking out. There's no doubt this house is part of its garden. Pink-flowered mandevillas cover the walls, and plantings frame the French doors. A well-designed entryway provides a convenient and efficient link between house and garden.

anticipation of what's ahead. For this reason, they heighten your senses and are a vital element that helps hold the design together.

Consider Scale

To be successful, a garden design must be balanced. Each element needs to fit comfortably into the scene when viewed from within or from the next space. For example, an imposing row of tall, dark

▶

Transitions between parts of a garden unify the design and encourage visitors to move through a garden's spaces. This rose-covered archway links two outdoor rooms. The sights and sounds of the fountain, along with anticipation of what lies beyond, form a strong connection that encourages visitors to explore the garden.

Karen Bussolini

▲ *Paths that wind out of sight have natural appeal that literally pulls visitors from one part of a garden to another. This path skirts an informal pond edged with a thick planting of shrubs and trees. From this vantage point, visitors catch a glimpse of the bright orange and yellow blooms of Exbury azaleas. This alluring path promises many more surprises beyond the bend.*

evergreens towering around a house dwarfs the house and seems to glower at the rest of the landscape.

Humans should fit into the garden comfortably, too. As you make your design, consider what will make you and your guests comfortable in your garden. What's a comfortable spacing for stepping stones? How high should branches overhanging a path be? What is the comfortable distance for a seated conversation? Try to design spaces that are comfortable to you. For example, a cozy bench under a tree, with small herbs and flowers strewn about its legs, provides an open invitation to sit down and enjoy. Another aspect you'll want to consider is the width of the paths in your garden. Some people prefer to have wide paths so they can stroll side-by-side with friends. Others like narrow paths that bring them in close contact with plants growing along the edges.

A design can also gently force a visitor to pay attention. An excellent example of this is the Japanese technique that places stepping stones at distances and angles just awkward enough to require the stroller's attention to every step. This subtle exaggeration of the human scale draws the individual into the ground plane, and thus readies him or her for contemplation and meditation.

No matter how small, a garden needs to relate not only to human scale but to the magnificent scale of the out-of-doors, ◀

or the overall design will lose its unity. The great expanse of sky overhead makes everything below it shrink in proportion. Often, the secret of balancing a design is to increase the proportions, and use bold architecture and simple contrasts. As the great American landscape architect Thomas Church once said, "When in doubt, make it larger."

Ecological Values

As you plan, build, and live in your own garden, remember that conscientious gardeners are stewards of the land. Consider the obvious ecological choices: Make compost to recycle precious nutrients, use natural fertilizers and pest management techniques, and design plantings to match natural rainfall. As you develop your garden, you can also find out about the not-so-obvious issues, such as new products made of recycled plastics or the disposal of paint or even the source of that teak bench you want to buy—did it come from an endangered rain forest?

In addition to caring for plants, animals, and water, stewardship gardening implies the constant activity of recycling through composting and soil rejuvenation. Your garden can be a focus for your values and can reinforce your intentions and choices about economy and respect for life's balance. It is also a place of family cooperation and storytelling, where traditions of living with nature can be passed from generation to generation.

Well-designed spaces are comfortable for people as well as plants. Paths and steps should provide stable footing so exploring the garden is an enjoyable experience. Here, well-designed stone steps, accented by ferns, lead from one garden space to another. A lush border of ornamental grasses dotted with bright yellow ligularias frames the space above.

ECOLOGY: GETTING IN DEEP

Your garden is an ecological system. It is a magnificent machine in which plants convert the sun's energy—its light—into food. This food supports the plants as well as the living creatures along the food chain, including you if you harvest herbs, fruit, or vegetables for your table. And it's part of the larger ecosystem of your city and countryside.

Deep Ecology is a term coined by the Norwegian philosopher Arne Naess in 1973 for a spiritual approach to "living as if nature mattered." In Deep Ecology, the world of all living things, including human beings, has central value. We are citizens of that biological world, but we're *not* its conquerors. Aldo Leopold, the ecologist and author of *Sand County Almanac* (1949), defined this ecocentric position when he said, "A thing is right when it tends to preserve the integrity, stability, and beauty of the biotic community. It is wrong when it tends otherwise."

Deep Ecology is based on the following principles:

- Harmony with nature
- The intrinsic worth of all nature
- Simple material needs
- The limited supplies of the earth
- Appropriate technology
- Recycling
- The diversity of bioregions and minority traditions

How could these principles apply to your garden design? First and foremost, you'll want to deepen your knowledge of the place in which you live. Find out, for instance, what native plants grow in your region, where your water comes from, where your garbage goes, which birds are migrating and which are residents, how Native Americans lived there—their seasonal rituals, plant uses, and totem animals.

The more you know about your site, the more inspired and appropriate your own garden will be. Look for ways that your design can reflect, rather than reject, its native environment. An effective design can also be practical, save water, recycle wastes into organic nutrients, and exist in partnership with nature. The garden will mean more to you, your family, and your friends as it contributes to the well-being of the larger environment and all its living creatures.

Make Your Spaces Come Alive

Once you've decided on the framework for your garden and the spaces you want to create, it's time to make them come alive by adding plants, color, fragrance, and texture, as well as details like sculpture and furniture. Like the spaces themselves, the "furnishings" you select

A riot of flowers and foliage transforms what could have been an uninteresting area into an attractive space. The pair of perennial borders, which feature peonies, pinks, hardy geraniums, and a host of other spring-blooming perennials, are in scale with the space available and don't overwhelm it. Vines trained on the fence add to the lush effect.

for your garden rooms will be guided by the central concepts or ideas that inspired your design and guided it from the start. For more on the process of identifying these ideas, see "Identifying Your Key Concepts" on page 248.

There are many ways to bring life to your outdoor living spaces and make them unique. Your use of plants and plant combinations, color, fragrance, texture, light and shadow, and water will express the unique character of your garden and create a garden that you'll want to visit again and again. Details like sculpture, benches, arbors, and other accessories also help to add a personal touch to your garden. For

Jerry Pavia

▲ *Selecting plants that will thrive with the natural rainfall, soil, and weather patterns of your yard is a great way to design a garden that will thrive. This foundation planting, which captures the feel of a desert oasis, features the flat, spiny pads of beavertail cactus* (Opuntia basilaris) *and pinkish-purple-flowered moss verbena* (Verbena tenuisecta).

more ideas on making your outdoor living spaces come alive, see "Furnishing the Spaces" on page 277.

Getting from Fantasy to Fact

Now that you have a general idea of the possibilities and the process, it's time to start the journey from garden fantasy to fact. Keep the principles of character, connection, and change in mind as you start the step-by-step process of designing your garden. Part 3, "Creating Your Own Outdoor Living Spaces: A Step-by-Step Guide," begins on page 183. There you'll find loads of ideas and suggestions to guide you on everything from discovering what you really want in your garden to map-

Jerry Pavia

This lively garden has loads of features that keep it exciting all ▲ year long. Brick paving adds color, texture, and a sense of movement to the design and connects the garden to a sitting area just beyond the house. The beds in this plant-lover's garden are chock-full of flowers and foliage. They feature a wide variety of groundcovers, perennials, ferns, and evergreens. The water garden is overflowing with plants as well.

ping the property and furnishing the spaces. You'll find the garden stories in part 2 will be an invaluable source of inspiration along the way. They not only illustrate basic principles of design, but also provide a wealth of ideas you can use when you make your garden. And when you are ready to start thinking about what plants you want to grow, check Appendix B on page 312. There you'll find annotated lists that can help you choose the right plants to furnish your outdoor living spaces. You're at the starting point of an exciting process that will uncover your native genius as a garden maker and lead you toward a garden that is uniquely yours.

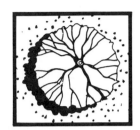

PART 2

A GALLERY OF GARDENS
Ten Designs for Outdoor Living

Designing your own garden can be exciting, inspiring, and fun, but it can also be intimidating and overwhelming. Whether you're starting with a nearly empty lot, a previously owned garden that's terribly overgrown, or just a design with outdoor spaces that don't suit your needs, it's hard to know where to start. Where is the best place to plant the new shade tree you want? Which plants need to be removed and which can be salvaged? Where would a patio and a vegetable garden best fit in? The number of questions alone can be intimidating. That's where design comes in. A thoughtful design will not only answer questions about what goes where, it will also help you shape your property into outdoor living spaces that are uniquely suited to you and your family.

◀

A design that suits your needs and those of your family provides room for outdoor activities you enjoy. This shaded garden features separate areas for sitting and outdoor dining. The two spaces are distinguished by a step between them as well as different styles of furniture. Trees surrounding the area provide privacy and meld the house into the garden.

Every garden design is a kind of renovation project, unless you're starting from a completely blank slate. You probably wouldn't remodel a room in your home without a plan that answered basic questions—such as who wants to use it, what kind of construction is required, and what types of furniture you will need. You shouldn't try to design your garden without a plan either. But where do you start?

Ten Garden Stories

What better way to learn about design than to take a close look at how other homeowners have worked through the process? To give you an idea of how many different ways there are to design and develop a garden, we asked ten innovative garden designers and landscape architects from across the country to design gardens. Each of the ten chapters that follow tells the story of a garden and its owners. Although all of the gardens are unique, each demonstrates how the dreams and needs of a family were merged with the character of their property to yield a wonderful and satisfying landscape.

These gardens will show you how other homeowners came up with their own lists of needs and wants and carried out their ideas. In each story, we walk you through the garden, discussing its layout, construction, and the experiences it makes possible. The detailed "before" and "after" drawings, as well as the watercolors of the finished landscapes, will make it easy to imagine what the property looked like at the start and what it has become.

All the homeowners and designers used the same basic design process. They started by deciding what they wanted and needed in their garden and by learning about what their site had to offer. Although the owners and their sites and gardens are all different, they share certain values: They want to take good care of the natural environment; they want more spaces for a variety of outdoor activities; and they want more privacy while showing a friendly face to the community.

Once these homeowners knew what they wanted and what their site had to offer, they developed key concepts that guided the overall design. Each chapter has a box entitled "Key Concepts for a Successful Design" to highlight some of these all-important principles. You'll find many more ideas when you read the text and study just what each garden is all about. You can read more about the overall design process each of them used in part 3, "Creating Your Own Outdoor Living Spaces: A Step-by-Step Guide" on page 183.

To make it easier to see how these gardens developed and how they satisfied the aspirations of their owners, we've presented all of them as if they were completed. That way you can see the entire process.

Of course, no garden is ever complete, and these are no exceptions. Their owners love to garden and want to be free to add plants, rearrange them, and replace them altogether. They also wanted designs that can grow and change as they do. For this reason, you'll find that each chapter presents ideas for how the garden could grow and change over the years.

Ideas for Every Garden

Whether you call them case studies or just stories about gardeners and their gardens, these chapters are designed to show how people made gardens that fit their lives and their land. Don't try to find the story that matches your family and situation in this section of the book. This gallery of gardens is designed to give you lots of ideas, along with a feeling for the possibilities that exist. Each design contains many ideas that you'll find useful, no matter where you live. You'll also find solutions to problems—common and otherwise.

It's also not a good idea to look for the "right" design for your plot of land, because there isn't one. That's true for these ten gardens as well. But there is an inevitable design. It is found in the way your hands, mind, and heart shape the place where you live. Think of these chapters as a place to look for ideas that will inspire you. In these stories, you'll find loads of ideas and design principles that make outdoor spaces more appealing. These examples show just some of the possibilities; you'll undoubtedly come up with many more.

Once you're overflowing with ideas, you'll be all ready to start the process

yourself. Part 3, "Creating Your Own Outdoor Living Spaces: A Step-by-Step Guide"
on page 183, will tell you how.

A Guide to the Gardens

To get you started, here's a bite-size
look at the ten gardens. Some gardens
may suit your fancy—and your site—more
closely than others, but you'll find great
ideas you can use in all of these stories.
You'll see that recycling everything from
garden waste to old fences is part of design
thinking, as is the connection between house
and garden and the distinction between
private and public areas. Let the story of
each garden become part of your thinking
and you'll become a garden maker, too—
whether or not you decide to work with a
designer as most of these homeowners did.

Use this guide to see which ones you'd
like to read first, but you'll want to read
them all eventually. After all, you don't
want to miss the great ideas they have to
offer. So just settle back, enjoy the stories
of these gardens, and think about what
ideas might be right for yours.

**The Small Garden: Rooms to Grow
In.** Designing a garden takes thought, but
it can also take courage. That's especially
true when you're faced with nothing but
an empty space. Landscape architect Richard Haag helped homeowners Jeanne and
Bill organize the space in their small garden so they'd have room for all the outdoor
activities they loved. To design the garden's all-important framework, Haag used
a grid—a technique that's practical for a
garden of any size. Efficient use of space,
a flexible plan, and a variety of garden
"rooms" are other key elements of this
successful design. Page 33.

**Converting a Farmstead for Work and
Play.** Landscape architect Sheila Lynch
helped Bonnie and Charles highlight the
unique character of their Vermont farmstead and create outdoor spaces for their
entire family. To help link the garden to
the land and create a memorable landscape,
she used signs of the land's history as a
farm—hedgerows and old stone walls, for
example—as integral parts of the design.
New terraces for taking in the view, paths
for wandering through the property, plenty
of space for wildflowers, and a vegetable
garden that breaks out of the conventional
rectangular-bed mold all add up to a landscape that Bonnie and Charles will never
tire of. Page 45.

**From Bare to Beautiful: Foresting a
Courtyard.** Sheila and Terry's now-lush
garden started out as nothing more than a
hot, sunny concrete courtyard. Landscape
architect W. Gary Smith transformed it in
short order into a forestlike oasis with
plenty of shade and irresistible appeal.
Efficient use of space, a cool spot for a
beloved dog, ingenious recycling, and a
two-phase plan for implementing the garden make this a design that's as practical
as it is beautiful. Page 60.

**A Woodland Garden: Spaces for Peo-
ple and Wildlife.** People and pets are not
the only creatures who get to live in gardens. Karen and Henry wanted a beautiful garden that is as friendly to people as
it is to birds, butterflies, and other wildlife. Landscape architect Sherry Wheat
helped them to develop a plan that welcomes a host of wild creatures to share
their outdoor living spaces. It provides
plenty of appealing places for people, too,
along with an attractive setting for the
house. Page 74.

Joining Forces: Perennial Gardens and Prairie Plantings. A nearly featureless lot can be an intimidating design challenge. Landscape designer C. Colston Burrell developed a plan for Susan and David's midwestern property that combines conventional flower and food gardens with a low-maintenance prairie planting of native wildflowers, trees, shrubs, and grasses. Shade, privacy, places to explore, and room for children to play outdoors are features of this garden. Page 89.

Celebrating a Desert Landscape. Desert plants and plenty of privacy are just two of the features of Patrice and John's practical yet alluring Arizona landscape. Along with landscape architect Carol Shuler, they've created a water-wise garden that's uniquely suited to their site and ideal for the climate. The plan features desert wildflowers, shrubs, and trees that will tolerate the harsh conditions and also uses the land's natural drainage patterns to advantage. Other elements of this intriguing garden include private spaces in the front yard and a design that links house and garden into a harmonious whole and also brings in nearby scenery. Page 104.

Reclaiming a Suburban Ranch House. Overgrown, neglected plantings are a far-too-common sight in suburbs across the country. Elizabeth and Matthew wanted a new "public" face for their ranch house that was colorful, neat, and appealing. Designer Bruce Carnahan helped them achieve this goal and much more. He helped them convert the old garage into an apartment with a separate entrance and landscaping, and located a new garage near the back of the property. In addition, a new driveway and front entrance make it easier to accommodate guests and provide much-needed off-street parking. Better yet, new terraces and plantings in the backyard create private spaces for work and play. Page 118.

Rejuvenating an Older Garden: New Plants and Terraces. Steep, unmowable slopes and a garden overwhelmed by plants were among the challenges Phyllis and Norman faced in their older garden, located in Milwaukee. Garden designer Gael Dilthey helped them create a landscape that not only is easier to maintain, but also features places for plants, plenty of storage for garden equipment, and private outdoor areas for sitting. Page 134.

A Country Garden: Privacy and Pathways. Screening the sights and sounds of neighbors and a nearby state highway were at the top of Timothy Steinhoff's agenda. As owner and designer of this garden, he also wanted places to collect and grow a host of plants, room for a kitchen garden, and interesting places to explore throughout the property. He developed a design that met all his needs and also hearkens back to the rich garden history of the Hudson River Valley where he lives. Page 151.

Sharing Space: Turning Two Yards into One Garden. Margaret and Steven are neighbors who came up with a unique solution to creating their ideal outdoor living spaces: With the help of landscape architect Michael McKinley they turned their two tiny lots into a single garden with space they share. A handful of design tricks make the garden seem larger than it is. They now enjoy an edible landscape with plenty of herbs, fruits, and vegetables to harvest; a shared utility area; private patios near each house; and completely secluded secret gardens where they can get away from it all. Page 169.

THE SMALL GARDEN:
ROOMS TO GROW IN

All too often, gardeners with new homes face an empty rectangle for a backyard. When Jeanne and Bill moved into a condominium in a planned community near Seattle, they faced not only a bare lot but a small one. The question before them was how to create an inviting and livable outdoor area where they could enjoy a wide range of activities. Landscape architect Richard Haag helped them to develop a garden with room for everything from berry picking and beekeeping to growing herbs and flowers or just relaxing by a cozy fire.

The Place and the People

The cool, wet Pacific Northwest offers a wonderful climate for growing just about anything. Its forests are magnificently layered with evergreen trees towering over several layers of deciduous trees and shrubs. Ferns and huckleberries form an evergreen understory, and a lush carpet of mosses and fungi covers the forest floor. Gardens in the Pacific Northwest are the closest you can come to English gardens in America. Yet, as everywhere else, developers are carving up land on the outskirts of Seattle, leaving it barren. Jeanne and Bill agreed that they wanted their backyard to be anything but a barren, anonymous space. Their desire was for a yard that was an extension of the living space in their condominium—a place where they could entertain or just relax. They also

wanted their yard to celebrate in greenery the lushness of a fine Pacific Northwest garden.

Starting from Scratch

Jeanne and Bill's condominium came with a standard-issue, 50×50-foot square, absolutely bare lot with a shared wooden

KEY CONCEPTS FOR A SUCCESSFUL DESIGN

Making a small space seem larger. Efficient use of space is one of the key elements of this successful design. This garden also illustrates other techniques used to make a small space seem larger: creating hidden and partially hidden views, adding a variety of heights and levels, and forced perspective.

Developing a flexible plan. The individual areas within this garden can change and develop according to the owner's time, budget, and needs.

Using a grid. A grid is a valuable, easy-to-use design tool that helps to define spaces and create an effective framework for a garden design.

Creating views from indoors. This garden is beautiful from indoors and out. The designs for the two "ells" on either side of the house are especially effective because they create attractive views into areas that might otherwise be boring and unattractive.

fence. As in many such developments, the architect created a sense of privacy by varying the depth of the individual units. This staggered arrangement created two narrow "ells" of yard, one on either side of the back of the condominium. These often end up as neglected, wasted space. Fortunately, when a garden starts out as a blank slate, such awkward spaces can be used to best advantage.

Like thousands of Americans with grown children, Jeanne and Bill had recently moved from their suburban acre into this community. Their lifestyle may have changed, but their values had not. As active gardeners, they wanted to re-create the feeling of their wide-open suburban property. While their "old place" wasn't designed as a whole, there was plenty of room for different activities. In their new garden, they still wanted to keep bees and harvest fruit; they wanted some lawn and the sound of water. They dreamed of transforming the bare backyard into an alluring area for outdoor living—one that seemed larger than it really was.

All in all, they wanted a garden that was both productive and ornamental—and easy to convert to play space for grandchildren as they come along. They saw the need for careful planning if they were going to have their heart's desire in such a small space.

Getting from Fantasy to Fact

Because Jeanne and Bill wanted to use their garden for so many different activities, a flexible design that could accommodate changes in activities, needs, and gardening ability was essential.

A Flexible Framework

While the word flexible may suggest little or no design, in fact a flexible garden design starts with a strong framework. Within this framework, various elements are designed so that they can be changed, expanded, reduced, or combined as changing circumstances require. By making changes within the basic framework of such a design, it's possible for the owners to adapt the garden to their changing needs over time without having to start from scratch again and again.

A well-designed garden can accommodate changing gardening interests. For example, the space left vacant by a waning interest in roses can be filled by a new sunken pool and bog garden to satisfy an emerging interest in water plants. Or an outgrown swing-set and sandbox area can give way to a new sitting area— all without changing the basic framework of the design. While it isn't always possible to anticipate or plan for specific changes, a flexible plan makes it possible to adapt to them gracefully. For example, at a later time Jeanne and Bill can convert the steps in this garden to a ramp that will accommodate a wheelchair or a walker because the original design is of generous proportions.

Designing with a Grid

Probably the easiest way to create a flexible design or framework is to start with a grid, which is formed by sets of parallel lines drawn at right angles to each other. Graph paper is a common example of a grid. When landscape architect Haag designed this garden, he drew the grid over the garden plan to divide the yard into areas or spaces. Because of its square shape, the yard for this condominium was ideally suited to a design based on a grid.

The result was nine squares plus two ells, one on each side of the house. Haag treated each square as an outdoor room. A series of garden rooms designed for specific purposes surrounds the central lawn. The actual sizes of the rooms vary a bit to create a larger central lawn, which unifies the whole garden.

Over time, the design or function of any of these rooms can change without radically affecting the others. Yet the rooms are related to each other; each is assigned a use that complements that of its neighbors. For example, the fire pit, lath house, and the section of lawn at the far end of the garden between the lath house and the orchard are each complete and self-contained spaces for sitting. But because they are side by side, they can also serve as a continuous space for entertaining large groups of people.

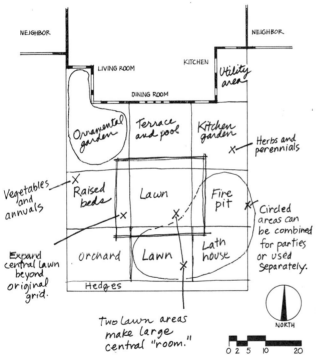

Using sets of parallel lines, landscape architect Richard Haag divided the lot for this condominium into a grid of nine squares. Then he sketched in the uses of each area, and adjusted the sizes of the squares or "rooms." Using a grid is an easy way to establish a framework for any landscape design, whether for an entire yard or a portion of one.

Creating a Comfortable Landscape

At its most fundamental level, Jeanne and Bill's garden represents the primal landscape of woodland clearing and watering hole. Human beings, like other animals, feel most comfortable when they are in a protected place, like a woodland edge, from which they can look out over a landscape around a watering hole. It's a kind of hide-and-seek, says Haag, an ancient game of protecting our backs and looking for opportunities that are basic to our psyches. It is a habit that may go all the way back in memory and instinct to humanity's emergence in the African savanna.

In this design, the terrace, fountain pool, lawn, and surrounding plantings fulfill these primal needs. Although the terrace is a mere 18 inches above the lawn, *(continued on page 40)*

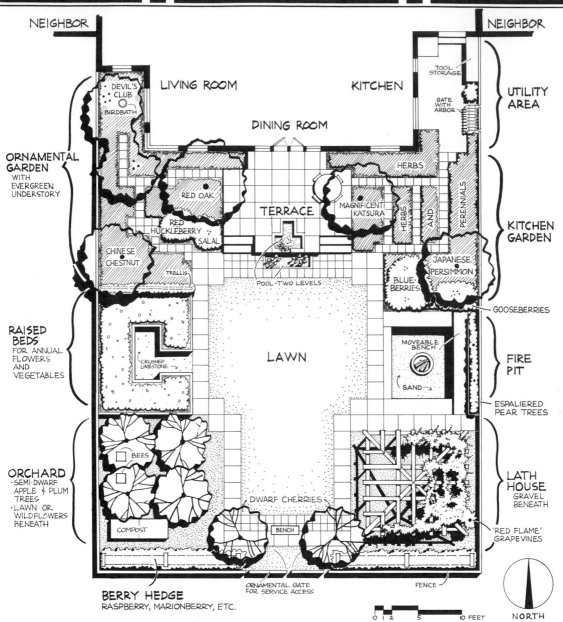

NEIGHBOR

NEIGHBOR

LIVING ROOM

KITCHEN

TOOL STORAGE

UTILITY AREA

DEVIL'S CLUB

BIRDBATH

GATE WITH ARBOR

DINING ROOM

ORNAMENTAL GARDEN
WITH EVERGREEN UNDERSTORY

RED OAK

HERBS

TERRACE

MAGNIFICENT KATSURA

HERBS

AND

PERENNIALS

KITCHEN GARDEN

RED HUCKLEBERRY

SALAL

CHINESE CHESTNUT

JAPANESE PERSIMMON

TRELLIS

POOL—TWO LEVELS

BLUE- BERRIES

GOOSEBERRIES

RAISED BEDS
FOR ANNUAL FLOWERS AND VEGETABLES

CRUSHED LIMESTONE

LAWN

MOVEABLE BENCH

FIRE PIT

SAND

ESPALIERED PEAR TREES

ORCHARD
· SEMI-DWARF APPLE & PLUM TREES
· LAWN OR WILDFLOWERS BENEATH

BEES

DWARF CHERRIES

LATH HOUSE
GRAVEL BENEATH

COMPOST

BENCH

'RED FLAME' GRAPEVINES

BERRY HEDGE
RASPBERRY, MARIONBERRY, ETC.

ORNAMENTAL GATE
FOR SERVICE ACCESS

FENCE

0 1 2   5   10 FEET

NORTH

Although the basic grid design is still apparent in this overview, it's obvious that this yard is much more inviting than the nine simple squares might indicate. Garden "rooms" designed for specific purposes or activities surround the central lawn. Plants, trellises, terracing materials, activity centers, and garden furniture make maximum use of space in this small yard. And just as important, owners Jeanne and Bill can develop each square as time and budget permit.

PLANTING NOTES

Both the ornamental and kitchen gardens provide an attractive view from inside the house. The trees, shrubs, groundcovers, and bulbs in the ornamental garden are reminiscent of the native forest floor of the Pacific Northwest. Herbs such as chives, lavender, oregano, rosemary, sage, and silver thyme planted in beds just outside the kitchen are handy for cooking. Perennials are interplanted with the herbs to provide flowers for the dinner table. The magnificent katsura tree provides shade for an outdoor eating area. A Japanese persimmon tree, along with 'Oregon Champion' gooseberries and several cultivars of blueberries, adds fruit to the kitchen garden. A small spray of water dances in the pool on the terrace between the ornamental and kitchen gardens. Just below, old world arrowhead (*Sagittaria sagittifolia*) surrounds a second pool, which is level with the lawn.

This yard also features fruit trees and shrubs in various parts—not just the orchard. Dwarf 'Seckel' and 'Anjou' pears are espaliered along the fire pit. 'Red Flame' grapes clamber over the lath house, and dwarf 'Montmorency' sour cherry and 'Lambert' sweet cherry flank the back gate. A kiwifruit vine twines over the trellis that separates the raised bed area from the ornamental garden.

Trees and Shrubs

Castanea mollissima (Chinese chestnut)
Cercidiphyllum magnificum (magnificent katsura)
Gaultheria shallon (salal)
Leucothoe fontanesiana (drooping leucothoe)
Oplopanax horridus (devil's club)
Quercus rubra (northern red oak)

Vaccinium parvifolium (red huckleberry)

Groundcovers and Bulbs

Galanthus elwesii (giant snowdrop)
Gaultheria procumbens (wintergreen)
Hyacinthoides non-scriptus (English bluebell)

Perennials

Allium giganteum (giant onion)
Anemone × *hybrida* (Japanese anemone)
Aster novi-belgii (New York aster)
Bellis perennis (English daisy)
Chrysanthemum × *superbum* (Shasta daisy)
Coreopsis grandiflora (tickseed)
Crocosmia × *crocosmiiflora* (crocosmia)
Crocus vernus var. *neopolitanus* (Dutch crocus)
Dianthus caryophyllus (florist's carnation)
Hemerocallis 'Stella de Oro' ('Stella de Oro' daylily)
Lycoris squamigera (magic lily)
Papaver orientale (Oriental poppy)
Sedum × 'Autumn Joy' ('Autumn Joy' sedum)
Zantedeschia aethiopica (calla lily)

Orchard and Berry Hedge

'Cascade' blackberries
Dwarf 'Italian' and 'Damson' plums
Marionberries ('Marion' blackberries)
'Perfection' currants
Raspberries
Semidwarf 'Spartan' and 'Criterion' apples

Orchard Underplanting

Ajuga reptans (ajuga)
Bellis perennis (English daisy)
Crocus spp. (crocuses)
Galium odoratum (sweet woodruff)
Narcissus spp. (daffodils)
Primula auricula (auricula primrose)

A simple design transforms what was once a barren, square yard into an attractive outdoor living space that is an extension of Jeanne and Bill's condominium. From left to right: a garden of perennials and herbs by the kitchen door, a fire pit for festive occasions, a lath house for private moments, a sitting area near

an access gate, a small orchard of semidwarf trees, raised beds for annual flowers and vegetables, and an ornamental garden. The varying heights of the "rooms" add visual diversity while making a small yard look larger.

it's high enough to provide a vantage point overlooking the whole garden. People also feel most comfortable when they can walk directly from inside the house to the outside without having to step down, so the terrace is built on the same level as the indoor spaces.

Making More Space

One way to make a small space seem larger is to create hidden and partially hidden areas. Here, the partially hidden raised beds, fire pit, and secluded areas suggest a hide-and-seek idea that creates unseen spaces to explore. These spaces draw visitors into the garden.

Developing the vertical dimensions of a garden is also a critical factor in making a small space seem larger. A level garden without varying heights of plants or structures is flat, like a carbonated drink that has lost its bubbles. The addition of even one step, or a simple arbor, will make a space seem much larger.

It is possible to make a small space look larger by varying the surface and level of the ground. In this garden, the three balanced pairs of spaces on either side of the central lawn create varying heights in the design. Flanking the main terrace, the ornamental garden and the kitchen garden are paved like the terrace, but on the same level as the lawn, orchard, and lath house. The next two spaces, the sunken fire pit with its sandy floor, and the raised beds flanked by crushed limestone, balance each other. It appears as though the earth has been dug out of the left side and piled up on the right. In the garden's far corners, the lath house with

its gravel floor, and the orchard trees underplanted with wildflowers add balance to the design.

Strong transitions between each section of the garden expand the overall sense of space by separating and connecting at the same time. For instance, a fountain "encloses" the edge of the upper terrace while bringing the long vista across the lawn into focus. The T shape of the upper pool, which mirrors the outline of the yard, strengthens the view. (A circular pool would also work as an effective contrast to the garden's many rectangles.) On either side of the pools, wide steps lead graciously down to the central lawn, which serves as a playing surface for croquet or badminton. Pavers frame the lawn, which is surrounded by a series of more intimate spaces designed for specific purposes.

Using Paving Patterns

The color, texture, and size of the paving plays an important role in telegraphing the use of each space and integrating the overall design. On the upper terrace and along both sides of the lawn, large 2 × 2-foot pavers create a central frame for the garden. Haag selected smaller, 1 × 1-foot pavers for areas of potentially high traffic near the house.

All pavers are cast-in-place concrete. That means the concrete was poured into square, wood-edged forms built in place. Mixing cinders (also known as expanded shale aggregate) into the concrete lightens the weight of the pavers and gives them an earth tone.

The wooden forms, made of alder wood or poplar, will rot out in a year's time, making space for strips of grass to grow in the joints. Grass will soon edge the smaller pavers so that they will look like lawn from a distance. While the pavers will still be a useful walking surface, the intimate spaces of the garden won't appear to be overwhelmed by hardscape, the term designers use to refer to the constructed, nonplant parts of a landscape such as paving, walls, steps, and lighting.

Crushed limestone in the vegetable garden creates a more casual effect. It binds together well and doesn't get into shoes or scatter across the pavement and grass as loose gravel does. The fire pit, which is usually used for sitting rather than walking, features loose sand for a soft, beachlike effect. The far corners of the garden get the least foot traffic and can have less-resistant carpeting. The wildflower meadow under the fruit trees is soft and cool to look at or walk in. Under the shade of the lath house, the gravel is cool and yielding and makes a gentle sound when walked on.

Linking House and Garden

All three spaces closest to the house—the upper terrace and the flanking pair of paved spaces—are strongly linked to indoor living spaces through expanses of glass and easy access. Inviting views of these spaces seem to enlarge the indoor areas, and also entice Jeanne, Bill, and their guests out into the garden. These areas closest to the house are most appropriate for plantings that offer rich detail but may require higher maintenance than other areas. This type of layout, often used in Japanese gardens, makes sense because visitors to the garden will see and enjoy areas close to the house or along heavily traveled paths more often than remote parts of the garden. It's also easier to remember to keep up with routine maintenance of such areas.

To the west of the upper terrace is the

It's possible to create a view even in the smallest space. The view from the living-room window is a birdbath and devil's club underplanted with low shrubs and a variety of groundcovers—the once-dominant privacy fence now simply fades into the background. Who wouldn't enjoy looking at a panorama of birds and plants, accented by the woolly blossoms and bright red berries of the devil's club?

ornamental garden, which includes the ell outside the living-room windows. The design creates a deep view from the living room into a softly naturalistic space reminiscent of a northwestern forest. Several trees wrap the corner of the house, and underplantings of evergreen shrubs and groundcovers drift informally across the neat pavement. This area also provides climate control by shading the living areas from the afternoon sun.

Herbs and perennials in rectangular planting beds on the east side of the upper terrace are visible from a kitchen window. A path leads around the side of the kitchen into the other ell, which is used for tool storage. Since this area is visible from the kitchen, Haag framed a gate to the neighboring property with an arbor to create visual interest.

Places for Plants

Other structures sprinkled throughout Jeanne and Bill's garden create not only a strong sense of organization, but also more space in which to grow plants. Trellises for vertical gardening enclose the raised bed for annual flowers and vegetables on two sides. Gourds thrive on these trellises because they're open to maximum sun. The section of trellis against the fence, which receives morning sun only, is suitable for raising sweet peas (*Lathyrus odoratus*). The trellis framework is 3½-inch-square cedar posts that cross on a 2-foot-square grid. Each spring, Jeanne and Bill staple new netting onto the frame.

Four semidwarf fruit trees fill the gar-

IN ANOTHER PLACE

The design strategy that landscape architect Richard Haag created for the yard of Jeanne and Bill's condominium would also be suitable with little change to a detached home with a similarly shaped yard. Even with a radically different lot shape, such as a wedge, the idea of subdividing the space into even-sized areas using a grid would still be a useful starting place. Using a grid is especially helpful if you're trying to fit many types of plants into a little area. Plant choices would vary from region to region. For example, you might have an orange grove in southern California, peaches or apples in Indiana. The woodland space that provides a fantasy view from the living room could become a semitropical jungle in southern Florida or an alpine rock garden in Colorado—each inspired by distinctly local flora and fauna.

den's southwest corner and create a small orchard. Underplanted with wildflowers and native grasses, this is an area of intense natural activity, with a pair of beehives and a compost bin representing parts of the garden's life cycle. Jeanne and Bill set up the birdhouse so that the rich droppings fall directly into the open-topped compost bin. Birds also help control the population of insects. Here in the orchard, a section of fence disappears behind a mixed hedge of raspberries and marionberries.

A Room for Resting and Relaxing

Tucked between the orchard and the lath house is an inlet of lawn. Two trees frame a seating niche that is the focal point of the long view from the house and upper terrace. Because the lawn narrows by 8 feet at the far end, the view from the terrace appears deeper and the bench seems farther away. This illusion is an important drawing card, designed to entice visitors from spaces close to the house out into the "far reaches" of the garden. Once here, guests find that the bench is a pleasant place to read; also, it is easy to move it into another space in the garden. An ornamental gate set in the back fence allows for service access if need be. It's topped with an arbor to augment the view from the terrace as well as match the side gate by the kitchen.

Next to the lower lawn is another seating area. Because the lath house is a room of its own, it is the most private and special "getaway" that the garden offers. Haag designed the lath house to be built in two phases, according to the lifestyle and finances of Jeanne and Bill. In its early years, the lath house will function as an open, wooden structure, supporting grape vines and having a gravel floor. Years from now, as their finances dictate, they plan to enclose the roof and sides with translucent material, such as tempered glass, and add French doors to open on both sides to the lower lawn and the fire pit. A bench for shade-loving plants, a ceiling fan, and paving will upgrade the interior.

A Room for Celebrating with Friends

What could be more attractive in the cool, damp climate of the Pacific Northwest than a cozy space warmed by a fire? Adding to the magic of the fire pit are the sound and sight of running water on the main terrace so close by. People have always gathered around fire for protection, feasting, and telling stories. In this garden, it's a place to feel romantic or festive, to sip Sunday-morning coffee or to toast marshmallows—whatever suits the moment.

The pit is designed to provide benches for seating on all four sides. On three sides, the benches are fixed in place. The step down into the pit, located on the side nearest the lawn, can be covered by a bench that slides over from the far side. The sliding bench fits over the bench on the side nearest the fence. In addition to providing additional seating, the sliding bench can be tilted so that one end goes down into the sand, making it into an incline board for sit-ups or sunbathing.

The fire pit is a flexible space that Jeanne and Bill can modify as the needs of their family change. A beach umbrella or a play structure can transform the pit into a play area for grandchildren. The fence behind the pit is ideal for training fruit trees, but it is equally appealing as a place to mount a blackboard. That's easy to do with a sheet of plywood and three coats of blackboard paint. Chalk paintings can create a changing mural that washes off in time. Ultimately, when the space is no longer needed as an activity space, it will be ideal as a planting bed.

NOTES FROM THE DESIGNER

"Keep it simple," suggests Richard Haag, when constructing various elements of your landscape. He urges simplicity in function. For example, the Seattle-based landscape architect likes an ornamental pool to drain easily. He uses a friction-seated overflow—just one tapered pipe that fits snugly into another one—that you can pull out to drain the pool with gravity providing the power. For a fountain spray in a small pool, he usually puts on a good bronze hose nozzle that can be adjusted for different effects. Simplicity is also good for economics. "When I'm working with lumber," says Haag, "I don't like to exceed 16 feet because you start paying a premium for longer boards. I try to keep everything within the normal lumberyard dimensions."

Haag has a favorite building material, too. "Always use the softest paving material that you can get away with," he advises. "I oppose great oil slicks of asphalt and big slabs of concrete. When you want to make a change, you have to bring in a jackhammer. Generally, I use unit pavers, like brick, leveled on pea gravel or sand, which allows the rain and air to go down and around and under them."

Looking to the Future

One advantage of a comprehensive garden plan like this one is that Jeanne and Bill can develop one square at a time, perhaps one square per season. They can set the unit paving (precast concrete, cast-in-place concrete, brick, or stone) on sand so that it is easy to take up, stack, or rearrange at a later date.

Building a pergola next to the house and over the upper terrace is a part of Haag's plan that Jeanne and Bill will defer in order to economize. When it comes time to build it, they will use wood that matches the simple cedar members and joinery of the lath house and arbors in the rest of the garden. They plan to make the pergola shorter than the terrace, so that it doesn't block views across the yard. The pergola, designed with the sun angles in mind, will act as a summer sun screen for the dining room and as a sun gatherer in winter, when sun angles are lower and deciduous vines are bare.

As this couple ages and perhaps one of them begins to use a walker or a wheelchair, they may replace one set of terrace stairs with a ramp. And since it is likely that lawns will be less important to them at this stage in their lives, they may expand and widen the paved areas. Raised beds will also become more useful than ever and perhaps even replace the fire pit. ◆

CONVERTING A FARMSTEAD FOR WORK AND PLAY

This old farmstead, located in Vermont's Green Mountains, is home to Bonnie, Charles, and their two children. The family moved here recently from the city to enjoy the peace and health of country life. Bonnie and Charles knew they wanted the stone walls, hedgerows, and other traces of the land's past life as a farm to figure prominently in any plan for the property. Landscape architect Sheila Lynch's design is closely linked to the landscape and its history and uses these features to best advantage. To augment the site's natural beauty, Lynch added many native trees, shrubs, and groundcovers.

Lynch's design for this property turned it into an adventure playground for both adults and children. Wildflower meadows, woods, and streams provide a multitude of spaces for camping, playing fantasy games, riding horses, building "forts," and bird-watching. There are also terraces for relaxing and taking in the view. A sculpture/food garden with fruits, vegetables, herbs, and flowers is practical while inspiring.

The Place and the People

Views are one of Vermont's greatest assets. The view from the top of one rolling hill always leads to another. Even though they're called the Green Mountains, and are quite greenly wooded close up, the atmosphere shades them from purplish to light blue in the far distance. The four seasons are especially dramatic, too. An

KEY CONCEPTS FOR A SUCCESSFUL DESIGN

Highlighting the landscape. A unique site deserves a unique plan; this design uses stone walls, hedgerows, and other signs of the land's rich history as a farm as key elements. A pair of terraces behind the old farmhouse provides comfortable, people-size places for enjoying the out-of-doors and also frames the breathtaking scenery nearby.

Creating public and private spaces. Plants can effectively define the boundaries of outdoor spaces. In this garden, plantings of birches not only define a private, crescent-shaped terrace but also separate this private space behind the house from the public spaces—namely the studio and driveway. A strip of densely planted groundcovers completes the separation between public and private spaces.

Planning for low maintenance. Native plants, environmentally sound principles, and a basically simple approach to design add up to a manageable landscape. For example, the native grasses and wildflower meadows in the front and side yards not only are pretty to look at but also require little maintenance because they're naturally adapted for this area. Once seeded and established, they need only annual mowing and occasional rejuvenation.

Using old-field succession. One approach to a lot that contains a pasture or old farm field is to simply allow it to revert to forest. Low maintenance and a wildlife-friendly habitat are among the dividends to this approach.

extreme climate—ranging from bitter cold winters to midsummer highs that rival those anywhere in the United States—brings marvelous springs and fabled fall colors.

Vermont's southern region, where this old farm is located, is characterized by its forest of Eastern white pine and other evergreens mixed with deciduous birches, oaks, hackberry, red maple, and sugar maple. Although many trees contribute to the rich autumn colors, among the most colorful are yellow birch, brilliant yellow in the fall; red maple, which turns crimson; and sugar maple, which provides vibrant orange-yellow hues.

Although it seems as though the forests are eternal, it was not always so. The Europeans who settled here hundreds of years ago heavily farmed the region, despite its poor, acidic soil. These thrifty settlers neatly stacked the glacial rocks that littered their fields into the handsome stone walls that are now a signature of the region. Then, after the Erie Canal opened, many people abandoned vast acreages of New England—and even whole towns—for the greener, less rocky pastures of the West. The abandoned farms gradually gave way to the process of old-field succession, as trees started to take over the uncultivated fields.

A Site with a History

Bonnie and Charles's old farmstead told the story of just such a history. Ten acres in all, the property was gently sloping and drained by two streams that join in the woods. Fragments of stone walls were a reminder that the woodland along the west property line was farmland in the 1800s. A horse stable and paddock were tucked between fields and woodland, a couple of fields had been kept in corn and hay, and stone walls set off a cow pasture on the north slope across the stream. A managed woodlot along the southern property line provided previous owners with woodstove fuel for decades and harbored rare pink lady's slipper orchids (*Cypripedium acaule*), which Bonnie and Charles have vowed to protect and preserve.

It was obvious to a keen observer that the woodlot was an open field long ago. Unlike the majority of the trees, which seemed to reach for the sky, a few of the oldest trees had wide, spreading branches. These so-called wolf trees grew in the first stages of the woodland's retaking of the open field. With plenty of sunshine and no competition from taller trees, they grew thick trunks and spreading branches.

Just about the only ornamental planting was an overgrown border of sweet mock orange (*Philadelphus coronarius*) and deutzia (*Deutzia* sp.) planted along the west side of the house to screen the view, dust, and odors of the working part of the farm. Probably planted in the 1800s, this border had become ugly and unruly beyond all salvation.

The plain wooden farmhouse, situated in a traditional cluster with a barn and garage, was at the end of a long, straight driveway. A handsome old tree hydrangea (*Hydrangea paniculata* 'Grandiflora') anchored the center of the turnaround. Lilacs along the south side of the barn, badly afflicted with powdery mildew, showed where an outhouse once stood. (Lilacs were traditionally planted near outhouses to counteract the odor.)

At the driveway entrance was a magnificent white spruce (*Picea glauca*)—a landmark traditional to the region. Sugar maples that have often been tapped for sap, the makings of maple sugar, lined part of the two-lane road along the front of the property.

It's possible that contemporary housing—perhaps cluster development—will be built both across the street and north

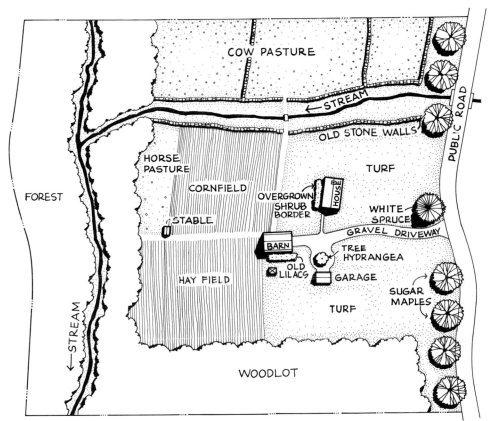

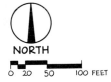

This old farmstead in Vermont's Green Mountains, loaded with character right from the start, offered plenty of inspiration for designing spaces for enjoying the outdoors. Fields of corn and hay, a forest and woodlot, and timeworn stone walls that crisscrossed the property surrounded the frame farmhouse and barn. To make the property both usable and beautiful, landscape architect Sheila Lynch needed to create a design that would link the house, grounds, and surrounding scenery and also highlight the history of the land.

of the farm as the local housing market changes.

Design for Living

Bonnie and Charles moved to the Vermont countryside from Boston in order to lead a healthier life. It's a familiar way of life to Bonnie, whose grandparents were farmers. Despite growing up in town, she has fond memories of childhood days spent exploring her grandparents' farm. As a financial consultant, Bonnie can take advantage of electronic communications to continue her career from this rural location.

Like his wife, Charles grew up in a small town near Boston. He prefers lots of space and solitude for his work as a sculptor and craftsman; also, a rural location is more affordable for a full-time artist. This property appealed to him because of the spacious barn, which was suitable for conversion to a studio, and the availability of good granite from local quarries.

Bonnie and Charles favor cleaner air and the "school of nature" for raising their two preteen children, both of whom are excited about having space for horses of their own. Although the children are old enough for unsupervised play, their parents are concerned about safety along the busy county road.

Now in their middle years, Bonnie and Charles plan to live here for 20 or 30 years, investing slowly and carefully in the landscape. They wanted the property to give a feeling of overall privacy, so they can feel surrounded by nature in all seasons. Both also have an abiding interest in ecology and enjoy learning about the farm's ecosystem, its seasonal cycles, and its wildlife.

Although intrigued with the region's agricultural history, they expected to manage the woodlot and grow feed for the horses without aggressive farming practices. Low maintenance is crucial because the property must be able to survive when they take a vacation or visit relatives in Boston. Mostly, they wanted to manage nature with a light hand in order to conserve natural resources while feeding the horses, supplying produce to the family table, and enjoying the property to its fullest.

Already fairly capable and knowledgeable about gardening, they planned to have an edible garden that is beautiful and organic. Charles wanted to display outdoor sculpture and furniture in a garden setting for sales to clients. The family's "wish list" of spaces also included an open, sunny sitting area and a ferny woodland glade. A place to swim was important, too. Bonnie wanted to be able to escape from her computer and fax machine to a private retreat—a place for meditation. Finally, they felt the garden should provide a four-seasons outlook from the house, while making the most of the hazy mountain view.

Getting from Fantasy to Fact

Here is a case where the most obvious asset—the mountain view—could easily overwhelm any design concept for a series of outdoor living spaces. The most important element facing landscape architect Sheila Lynch was how to fit this family into such a grand scale without diminishing them or the view. Her design for Bonnie and Charles's property maintains the spirit of the place—the breathtaking view and the reminders of early farms and stalwart farmers—while making spaces for family and friends to enjoy the land.

Because this property is so large, the main outdoor living spaces are bold in design and play very specific roles. The design provides areas where the family's own interests come first. Turf and granite terraces near the house set the stage and are the main places for gathering with family and friends or just relaxing and taking in the view. Wild areas provide space for walking, swimming, and observing nature. Utter quiet and privacy prevail at the woodland swimming hole. The sculpture garden not only serves to showcase Charles's sculptures for his clientele but also meets the family's need for fruits, vegetables, herbs, and flowers.

Linking House and Garden

The strength of Lynch's design pivots on two semicircular terraces that connect the family's domestic spaces and the larger natural spaces beyond. Lynch replaced the overgrown border of mock orange and deutzia that once grew against the west side of the house (thus blocking the view of the fields and mountains beyond) with a grassy terrace of closely mown native grasses. This large lawn terrace meets the west edge of the house and allows a clear view and easy passage from inside to outside.

The lawn terrace is a huge recreation room for the house, embraced by curving arms of birches. It's scaled for lawn games and picnics and would also be a good place for a swing-set or play structure, perhaps crafted in Charles's studio. The contrast between the smooth, level grass of the terrace and the complexly textured view across the meadows is striking. There, rows of blueberries call out the topography and draw the eye to the horse pasture, woods, and distant mountains beyond.

Beyond the lawn terrace, a smaller granite terrace mirrors the shape of the lawn and the birch crescent and forms an overlook. This paved semicircle, lushly edged with ferns and perennials, is a comfortable spot for formal entertaining. It also serves to draw people out into the landscape and away from the house, where patios are so often located. From the granite terrace, a wide and grassy path follows the gentle, rolling slope down through the meadow, into the woods, and across the stream.

An old pathway that ran from the barn (now the studio) north to the stream and the cow pasture beyond was used to define the boundary for the new lawn terrace. A lowbush blueberry hedge now follows the old pathway to separate the wildflower meadow from the lawn. The same line forms the junction between the lawn and the mirroring granite terrace.

Setting the Stage

The distant mountains are not the only feature of the view from the back terraces; a view is made up of all that you can see, including the foreground. To link the two together, this design features four wildflower meadows laid out to follow the undulating contours of the slope. When seen from the house and upper garden terraces, these contoured meadows accent

(continued on page 54)

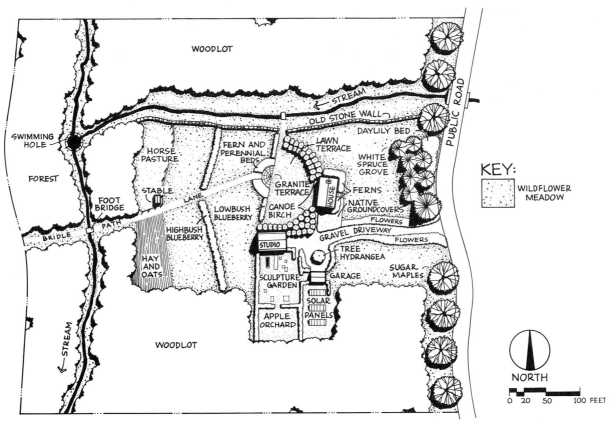

WOODLOT

STREAM

OLD STONE WALL

PUBLIC ROAD

SWIMMING HOLE

DAYLILY BED

FERN AND PERENNIAL BEDS

LAWN TERRACE

HORSE PASTURE

WHITE SPRUCE GROVE

FOREST

GRANITE TERRACE

FERNS

STABLE

HOUSE

LANE

NATIVE GROUNDCOVERS

FOOT BRIDGE

CANOE BIRCH

LOWBUSH BLUEBERRY

FLOWERS

PATH

GRAVEL DRIVEWAY

BRIDLE

HIGHBUSH BLUEBERRY

FLOWERS

STUDIO

TREE HYDRANGEA

SUGAR MAPLES

HAY AND OATS

GARAGE

SCULPTURE GARDEN

SOLAR PANELS

STREAM

APPLE ORCHARD

WOODLOT

KEY:

WILDFLOWER MEADOW

NORTH

0　20　50　　100 FEET

Crescent-shaped terraces for taking in the scenery behind the house, blueberry hedges bordering wildflower meadows, and a new lane leading to the forest are among the elements that make this design compelling. The sculpture garden doubles as a vegetable and herb garden, and the new grove of trees along the road provides much-needed privacy. Birch trees enclose the private lawn terrace and separate it from the driveway. The former cow pasture north of the house, now a woodlot, provides rich wildlife habitat.

PLANTING NOTES

Native plants form the backbone of this garden landscape. Those plants that aren't native, such as the daylilies, flowering bulbs, and wintercreeper (*Euonymus fortunei*), will adapt well to the site and thrive with little care.

Groundcovers and Ferns

Adiantum pedatum (northern maidenhair fern)
Asarum canadense (Canada wild ginger)
Cornus canadensis (bunchberry)
Dennstaedtia punctilobula (hay-scented fern)
Dryopteris spp. (wood ferns)
Matteuccia struthiopteris (ostrich fern)
Polystichum acrostichoides (Christmas fern)
Thymus spp. (thymes)

Shrubs

Clethra alnifolia (summersweet)
Kalmia latifolia (mountain laurel)
Rhododendron prinophyllum (rose-shell azalea)
Rhododendron viscosum (swamp azalea)
Vaccinium angustifolium (lowbush blueberry)
Vaccinium corymbosum (highbush blueberry)

Trees

Acer saccharum (sugar maple)
Betula papyrifera (canoe birch)
Carpinus caroliniana (American hornbeam)
Cornus florida (flowering dogwood)
Populus alba (white poplar)
Populus nigra 'Italica' (Lombardy poplar)
Populus tremuloides (quaking aspen)
Quercus palustris (pin oak)
Tsuga canadensis (Canada hemlock)

Perennials and Bulbs

This design features flowers that echo the natural colors of the landscape—primarily blues and purples. In spring, bulbs such as snowdrops, snow crocus, grape hyacinths, daffodils, and wood hyacinths in shades of white, blue, and purple appear in great sweeps between the house and the road. Later in the year, the informal perennial border along the driveway sports white, blue, and purple flowers such as forget-me-nots, irises, and asters.

The roadside planting of daylilies features pale yellow and soft rose tones. The beds overlooking the reflecting pool in the sculpture garden run toward vibrant yellows.

The ferns and flowers in the terrace border are ideal because of their care-free habits and visual interest throughout the seasons. Bright, cheerful bulbs welcome spring, and white, blue, and purple flowers grace the terrace all summer long. As fall approaches, however, the native foliage starts to turn the myriad of yellows, pinks, oranges, and reds of the New England fall, and the border reflects these colors with asters, chrysanthemums, and coneflowers.

Terraces don't need to be hard-surfaced to be compelling. The lawn terrace behind the house is perfect for taking in the breathtaking view of the Green Mountains beyond the edge of the property. Unlike a typical concrete patio or wooden deck, this semicircular terrace, enclosed by plantings of birch trees, is a fine spot for much more than just sitting—it's suitable for active recreation like sports, outdoor dining, and family gatherings.

Beyond it, a granite terrace surrounded by beds of perennials contrasts with the soft turf and beckons visitors farther from the house. Once there, they can wander along the new lane toward the forest or just enjoy the wildflower meadows and blueberry hedges that echo the shapes of the mountains and help pull them into the garden.

the distant hilly horizon, visually connecting the foreground to the hazy mountains beyond.

Blueberry bushes divide the meadows, and in fall when their foliage turns, they create sinuous red stripes on the landscape. The meadows' role in the overall design—to link the garden to the mountain view—calls for a wildflower seed mixture blended in blues and purples that reflect those of the mountains themselves.

Separating Public and Private Spaces

The crescent-shaped planting of canoe birches (*Betula papyrifera*) that encloses the lawn terrace serves as an architectural extension of the house. This planting gives form to the lawn terrace behind the house while protecting this private space from the more public areas of the studio, driveway, and beyond.

On the north side of the crescent, the birches are planted in a double row along a line that extends from the northwest corner of the house all the way to the old stone wall by the stream. The double row arrangement forms a delightful passageway: One way to stroll from the house to the north meadow is through the shady tunnel formed between the two rows of arching birches to the opening in the stone walls along the stream.

Between the house and the studio, in the southern half of the crescent, the birches are planted in a mass. Because birches are so thin, a massed planting or a double row gives more body to the design. (The only birches planted in a single line are those along the studio wall that complete the southwestern end of the crescent.) This massed planting follows the advice of Vermont landscape architect Daniel Urban Kiley, who says that one of anything looks measly.

A wide strip of densely planted, native groundcovers along the driveway helps separate the house and private garden spaces from the semipublic studio area. Yet it's also important to knit the structures—in this case the house and the barn—to the overall site. The birch trees solve this problem by creating a "transparent wall" that connects the barn to the house and, between the slim trunks, allows glimpses of the terrace from the parking area.

A Woodland Retreat

Lynch's design calls for a new lane to run from the granite terrace west past the stable and into the forest beyond. In the woods, just beyond the meadows and stable, is a sturdy footbridge, wide enough to ride across. It connects the lane through the meadows with a bridle trail leading off the property to trails throughout the local woods. The footbridge is very simple and unobtrusive. Made of wood, and without railings, it looks more like a raft that got washed up along the stream.

A short walk upstream brings the swimming hole into view. This space is a total retreat from the civilized world. Here, a simple circle in the woods becomes a magical place of literal immersion into nature. Located where the two streams come together, the pool's basin is made of black river stones tightly embedded in concrete to make a soft edge and give the pool the effect of a deep, dark mirror. Ruined stone walls lead the way out of the woods to the strip of meadow along the stream and the horse pasture.

From Farm to Forest

The design calls for the pasture north of the stream to go through old-field succession. Old-field succession is the name for the natural process that reforests a man-made field left to its own devices. First, scattered trees and shrubs will sprout up in the field among the grasses and other plants. Thickets of red maples will soon join the first trees. Within 30 years, a thick woodland of tall trees will cover the site. If left unharvested, trees in this midmature-forest stage will periodically blow down or be struck by lightning, creating holes in the leafy canopy overhead. Light streaming in through the holes will foster the next generation of trees—oaks and other hardwoods—that will eventually grow up and replace the earlier trees to form a fully mature forest. The species that make up this final stage will remain constant over time, and the forest will have reached its climax. Eventually, the only sign of the land's one-time life as a farm will be the stone walls that crisscross the forest floor.

Bonnie and Charles plan to enjoy observing this gradual transformation of pasture into woodland. The benefits are twofold: This land will become a rich wildlife habitat as well as a screen to block out the eventual development of the neighboring property.

Creating a Friendly Face

In front and on both sides of the house, a wide fringe of care-free hay-scented ferns (*Dennstaedtia punctilobula*) ties the house to the surrounding meadow without obscuring it. Although the family never uses the formal front door, as is typical of households throughout New England, a gap in the fernery is a visual nod to the architectural detail.

This is a neighborly design that shares a little bit of mountain view with people passing by on bicycles and in cars, and allows glimpses down along the stream without sacrificing the family's privacy. The landmark white spruce at the driveway entrance is the anchor for a thickly planted new grove that will fill in the gap directly in front of the house between the existing sugar maples. This grove will also screen out any future development across the road, while protecting the children from venturing too close to the traffic. Rather than completely screening the roadway, as with a thick hedgelike planting across the entire road frontage, it's more friendly to create pleasant but limited views into the property. Toward the north corner, the spruce grove curves away from the road, echoing the line of birch trees along the terrace. A daylily planting, which is both attractively simple and easy to care for, enhances the view from the road past the spruce grove.

The entire front and side yards are a managed meadow, seeded with a mixture of native grasses and wildflowers. Along the gravel driveway, naturalized bulbs and perennials sprout up in purple and blue hues to complement the distant view of the Green Mountains. A loosely composed flower border, about 2 feet deep, consists of such plants as forget-me-nots (*Myosotis* spp.), irises, and asters to extend the color play from spring through fall.

The Sculpture Garden

Visitors and clients alike may park at the barn or in the driveway circle. The sculpture garden is well screened with Canada hemlock (*Tsuga canadensis*) hedges, although taller sculptures might peek intriguingly over the top. A low groundcover of wintercreeper (*Euonymus fortunei*) signals the entrance between two staggered hedges that overlap to form an entranceway between them. Gravel covers the ground in the most formal areas of the sculpture garden nearest the barn. Drought-tolerant native grasses serve as groundcovers in the middle portion, while the apple orchard in the farthest section rises from a low-cut wildflower meadow.

This design provides privacy but also allows a friendly glimpse of the house and mountains from the road. An informal planting of perennial bulbs borders the driveway and adds color to the scene. The perennials blend with the wildflower meadow that serves as a front lawn.

IN ANOTHER PLACE

This old farmstead is essentially a setting typical of the whole Appalachian chain. All along the Appalachian mountains there are sites that have similar rolling hills with layered views and homestead patterns. The locale, the view, and the topography give this area a distinctive feeling, and the design strives to complement these natural features. In West Virginia, for instance, this design would work well with different plant species. Redbuds (*Cercis* sp.) or river birch (*Betula nigra*) could replace the canoe birch (*B. papyrifera*), which does poorly outside of New England. The spruce grove would become Virginia pine (*Pinus virginiana*). Of course, the wildflower mix in the meadows would change according to local soil and climate conditions. The sculptured Canada hemlock (*Tsuga canadensis*) hedges would change to boxwood (*Buxus* sp.), although the blueberry hedgerows bordering the meadows would stay the same. All in all, the basic design forms respond to the same rounded mountains and rolling floor.

Of course, not all properties have such panoramic vistas to take advantage of, but yours may have other "borrowed scenery" that can be worked into your garden design. For example, planting a few strategically located shrubs on your property could frame a nice view of a neighbor's perennial bed while screening their parked car. Or perhaps thinning some trees from a hedgerow will open glimpses of a pleasing expanse of meadow on the next lot.

The entire sculpture garden is a piece of art in its own right. Raised beds, in whimsical geometric shapes like triangles, are reminiscent of a maze or a patchwork quilt. Perennials and vegetables fill the planting beds, which are edged with local granite. These shaped beds also create innumerable niches and backdrops for sculpture. A non-sculptor might use a garden like this to display a collection of weather vanes, birdhouses, whirligigs, or even purchased sculptures.

A reflecting pool, lining up with the studio door, is a dramatic spot for a standing sculpture. Display sites, such as the niche at the far end of the orchard, are also included in the design. Carefully planned views and interesting angles make even this small garden a rewarding place to explore.

Looking to the Future

A landscape of this scope comes to pass in numerous phases, depending on family energies and budget. For Charles, certainly the sculpture garden is a top priority, since it is an important aspect of selling his work and thus feeding the family from the proceeds. It is also wise at an early stage to establish the white spruce grove, which screens the road, as well as the birches—at least those between the studio and the house—to give the family some privacy as soon as possible. For safety reasons, the swimming hole might wait until the children are older, although the clearing could be opened up for a handsome bench or camping spot. It takes a few years to establish the structure of such

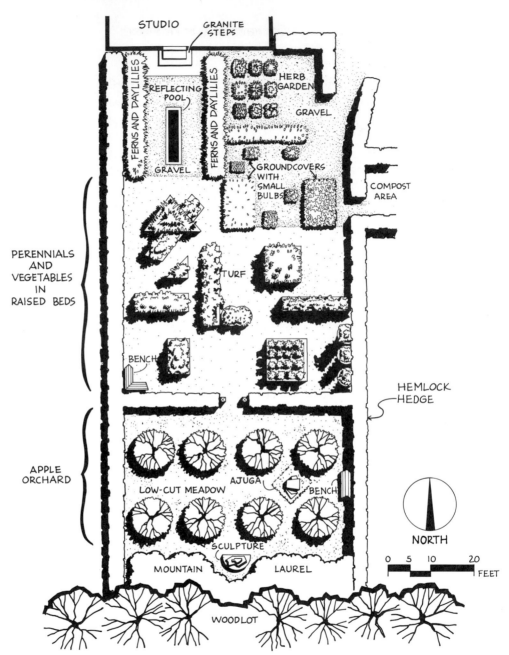

STUDIO   GRANITE STEPS

FERNS AND DAYLILIES

REFLECTING POOL

GRAVEL

FERNS AND DAYLILIES

HERB GARDEN

GRAVEL

GROUNDCOVERS WITH SMALL BULBS

COMPOST AREA

PERENNIALS AND VEGETABLES IN RAISED BEDS

TURF

BENCH

HEMLOCK HEDGE

APPLE ORCHARD

AJUGA

LOW-CUT MEADOW

BENCH

NORTH

SCULPTURE

MOUNTAIN

LAUREL

0 5 10 20 FEET

WOODLOT

Vegetables, herbs, groundcovers, and apple trees fill the sculpture garden, which homeowner Charles uses to display his work. This lighthearted treatment adds lots of appeal to what is all too often a mundane part of a garden. The enclosing hemlock hedges create the feel of a secret garden, which could be used in many different ways. The area could become a purely ornamental garden with beds of perennials and annuals or be used to display a collection—of roses, herbs, or dwarf conifers or even birdhouses, weather vanes, or antique sundials.

NOTES FROM THE DESIGNER

As a landscape architect who is also an environmental activist, Sheila Lynch is continually working to increase her knowledge of the native materials and habitat of New England. She advises people, wherever they live, to use native plant species because they can handle the extremes of climate, support wildlife, and look appropriate in terms of color, texture, and form. Native plants are the best choices for a low-maintenance landscape.

When plants have bad reputations, it's often due to unwise choices. In the case of birches, many people have trouble with borers because they select European white birch (*Betula pendula*) instead of the canoe birch (*B. papyrifera*). Not only is the native birch happy in Vermont soil and relatively problem-free in the right conditions, it's a marvelous presence in all seasons. The foliage is fresh green in spring, rich green in summer, and bright yellow in fall; in winter, the white trunks are ethereal. In all seasons, whether the foliage is present or absent, native birches add an elegant white architecture to the landscape.

Farther south, where canoe birch wouldn't be as happy, river birch (*B. nigra*) is a good choice because it is heat-tolerant, disease- and borer-resistant, and native as far south as Florida. While the species has attractive rust-colored bark that peels and flakes, the cultivar 'Heritage' features pale, salmon-colored bark.

Another word of advice from Lynch: When you find a plant you like, don't buy just one. "I advise beginners who are starting their own designs to go with plants that you like, but to use lots of each kind to form spaces." The wonderful exception to this rule is the old tree hydrangea she saved in the Vermont farmstead design. She allows that "There's still a place for such a thing as a specimen."

a large landscape, but building upon the old framework gives the family a head start on a new homestead.

A Question of Management

How self-managing can these outdoor living spaces be? Overall, a design like this, which has a simple and restrained approach to nature and relies on native plants and environmentally sound practices, can be low-maintenance (after the initial planting). In this case, the old-field woodlot is simply harvested of fallen and dead wood for the family's wood stoves. The meadows, once seeded and established, need only annual mowing and an occasional rejuvenation with new seeds. The horse pasture will be left completely to its own devices.

In a way, the design's success depends on learning to prefer the subtle beauties of a plant's entire life cycle—from unopened bud to faded seed head—to the large and showy effects of heavily managed perennial borders or the neatly mown lawns characteristic of so many American gardens. ◆

FROM BARE TO BEAUTIFUL: FORESTING A COURTYARD

Sheila and Terry's small, barren courtyard in their center-city Philadelphia home had nothing to lose and everything to gain from a bit of garden-design sleight of hand. This space lacked *everything* essential for an appealing outdoor living space. Inspired by the peaceful, wild woodlands of Pennsylvania, landscape architect W. Gary Smith worked with Sheila and Terry to create the illusion of a private natural retreat in a very small space. But the transformation of the garden was more than just illusion; it's now a cool, green oasis for its owners and their dog, Emma, to enjoy.

The Place and the People

Philadelphia is renowned as a city of trees and proud horticultural tradition. But like every city, it has its share of bleak pavements, with a surprising number of them in private yards.

Sheila and Terry's former concrete desert, located behind their three-story townhouse in a late-nineteenth-century neighborhood, was an uninviting space. The L-shaped courtyard, roughly 200 square feet, wrapped around a solarium breakfast room with a glass wall. In the middle of summer, there was almost no shade, and the sun pounded down on the cracked concrete. In addition, there were absolutely no plants to shade the broken concrete,

and no air circulation either. The courtyard was very dusty and hot. Several neighboring houses overlook the space, which was screened by a partially rotted, 6-foot-tall redwood fence. A little wooden gate opened to the alley right outside the kitchen door.

KEY CONCEPTS FOR A SUCCESSFUL DESIGN

Creating a forest. In a small garden, a design calling for a forestlike planting may seem like an unlikely idea. But that's just what provides this tiny garden with desperately needed shade and transforms it into a lush, inviting oasis.

Using space efficiently. Efficient use of space is crucial in any small garden, but even gardeners with large lots have a thing or two to learn from this space-saving design, which includes a forest, sitting area, and storage and utility area.

Recycling. Recycling is good for the environment, and it's also economical. This design demonstrates some ingenious recycling ideas such as donating discarded plants and materials to a community garden.

Planning and implementation. For any gardener on a budget, developing a plan for phasing-in a garden is a practical, dollar-wise approach. This two-phase plan illustrates how to implement a design over time.

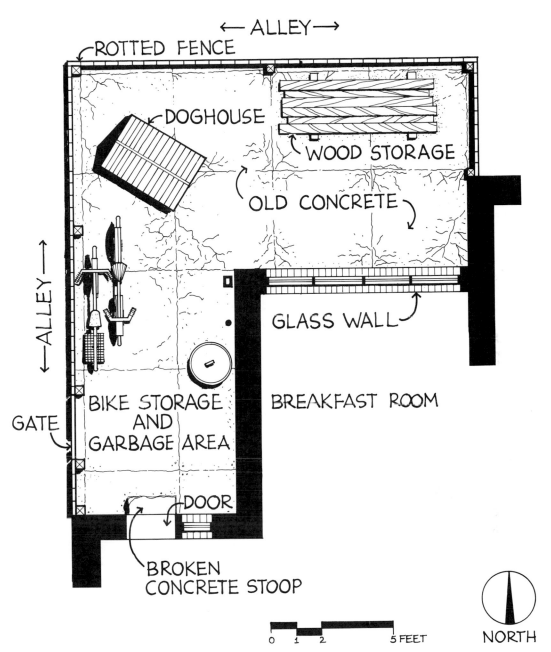

← ALLEY →

ROTTED FENCE

DOGHOUSE

WOOD STORAGE

OLD CONCRETE

← ALLEY →

GLASS WALL

BIKE STORAGE
AND
GARBAGE AREA

BREAKFAST ROOM

GATE

DOOR

BROKEN
CONCRETE STOOP

0 1 2   5 FEET

NORTH

An urban backyard with cracked concrete, a rotted fence, and a stack of redwood boards left over from an interior renovation was an unlikely place to start a garden, to say the least. Yet this tiny, L-shaped lot had nothing to lose and everything to gain from a wholesale renovation. Trees, new paving, and some ingenious recycling have turned this barren backyard into a lush, green oasis for its owners and their beloved dog to enjoy.

A stack of 1×4-inch redwood boards saved from the remodeling of an interior room of the house was about the only asset in this yard.

A Crystal-Clear Agenda

Sometimes a clear set of inherent constraints makes a very challenging design problem seem easier. In this case the constraints were small size, a dog, hot sun, and especially, two people who knew what they needed and wanted. This couple, in their mid forties, are devoted to their Akita dog, Emma. Emma stays in the yard while they're at work, and during the first year after they moved to Philadelphia, she suffered from the heat and boredom of spending her days on a concrete slab. Above all, Emma and her people needed a cool, shady retreat in order to enjoy this small space.

Sheila and Terry wanted a quiet oasis in which to unwind at the end of the day and enjoy each other's company. While they are interested in plants and have some do-it-yourself skills, they didn't want to be slaves to the garden. It was also important to them to hold down costs by developing the garden in phases. Their desire was for a strong plan to which they could add plants and ornaments such as interesting sculptures over the years.

Their immediate wish list included a place to sit, some sort of water feature, and storage for bicycles, compost, trash cans, and recycling bins. They also needed to screen the yard from the sun and from neighbors looking down into it. In addition, the fence needed to be repaired; it was so decrepit that it could have fallen over the next time Emma leaned against it.

Plan for a Private Oasis

Landscape architect W. Gary Smith chose Pennsylvania's woodlands as a model for this urban garden and treated the space much like a clearing in the forest. In a forest clearing, tulip trees (*Liriodendron tulipifera*) commonly fill in gaps created when older trees are downed by lightning or wind. During the first stage of a natural process called succession, as many as 50 tulip-tree seedlings can sprout up in such a chance clearing. Within a few years, however, competition thins out the trees naturally, and the next stage of succession is under way.

This natural life cycle inspired Smith's two-phase design. Since rapid shade was the motivating force for implementing the garden design, it called for planting fast-growing trees—tulip trees and a red maple. These quickly grow up—instead of out—as they compete with each other for light. Within a year, they established a high canopy and forestlike environment for Emma and her owners.

Phase one also called for installing cobblestone block (brick-shaped pieces of granite) paving and a small garden pool. During this stage of the garden, all of the beds were planted with a single groundcover; in this case, fast-growing, easy-care common periwinkle (*Vinca minor*).

After five years, Sheila and Terry began phase two by removing a few of the now-tall trees so the tops of the remaining ones could spread out. Removing a few trees also made room for understory layers of smaller trees and shrubs. Sheila and Terry also added a wider variety of paving, groundcovers, bulbs, and flowers. During

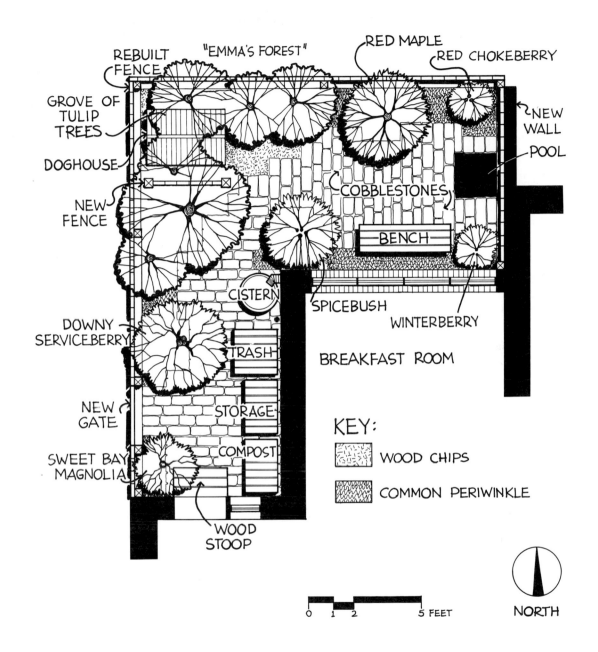

REBUILT FENCE

"EMMA'S FOREST"

RED MAPLE

RED CHOKEBERRY

GROVE OF TULIP TREES

NEW WALL

POOL

DOGHOUSE

NEW FENCE

COBBLESTONES

BENCH

SPICEBUSH

WINTERBERRY

CISTERN

DOWNY SERVICEBERRY

TRASH

BREAKFAST ROOM

NEW GATE

STORAGE

KEY:

SWEET BAY MAGNOLIA

COMPOST

WOOD CHIPS

COMMON PERIWINKLE

WOOD STOOP

0 1 2   5 FEET

NORTH

At the end of phase one, the no-longer-barren backyard featured cobblestones, efficient storage space, and a new grove of tulip trees that, along with a red maple, provide all-essential shade. A rebuilt fence, plantings of shrubs and groundcovers, and a new lily pool completed the first part of the transformation from bare to beautiful.

this second phase, French doors were added to the breakfast room to give the garden a "front door."

Getting from Fantasy to Fact

There are three major spaces in this garden, and deciding where to locate them was a matter of straightforward reasoning for Smith. The storage and utility space, which needs easy access to the alley west of the courtyard and house, is the best use of the area right outside the kitchen door. "Emma's Forest" is located in the outside corner, where it can be screened from view from the kitchen door and is hard to see from the breakfast-room windows. Finally, to provide a pretty view from indoors, it made the most sense to locate the sitting area and pool right outside the breakfast room.

Renovated fencing and new paving and plantings throughout the garden unify these three areas, despite the fact that they are used for distinct purposes.

Out with the Old, In with the New

The first step in implementing this design was dismantling the old fence and piling it temporarily out of the way. Then Smith hired a contractor to break up and haul away the cracked concrete slabs.

During phase one, a resilient layer of wood chips was used to cover the area around Emma's house, making it a comfortable surface for her while preventing a muddy area from developing. In the central area of the garden, cobblestones laid in sand replaced the cracked concrete to form a solid but easily removable paving. To help give the garden a natural, rustic feeling, Smith selected cobblestone paving that was eroded—notched in and out—for this little woodland retreat. Sheila and Terry planted the remaining unpaved space with common periwinkle.

Renovating the Fence

The existing fence was an eyesore from inside and out, and in imminent danger of falling down. The supporting posts had rotted off at ground level, and the bottom 6 inches of the prefabricated redwood panels were also rotted.

Rather than discarding the fence and putting up a totally new one, Smith's design called for some creative recycling. The unrotted sections of the old fence posts were put aside to be used for building the storage bins and a phase-one bench. The rotted bottom edge of each panel was cut off, and a new edge made from some of the stockpiled 4-inch redwood boards. New pressure-treated fence posts were installed, and the shortened panels mounted on the outside. The loss in height was made up by topping the fence with a strip of lattice.

The new posts and lattice are stained light gray to complement the weathered dark brown of the older panels. Emma's doghouse, too, is screened with a low, gray lattice fence. A native sweet autumn clematis vine (*Clematis paniculata*) softens that screen, while Virginia creeper (*Parthenocissus quinquefolia*) ranges along the lattice at the top of the tall fence.

This renovation was an economical move, only requiring new posts, standard off-the-shelf lattice, a can of stain, and a few nails. It also saved the cost of having the old fence hauled away, a budget item that's easy to overlook until you are standing over a huge pile of debris that the regular trash pick-up won't take.

While the large scale of the overhanging tree canopy connects the garden to the neighborhood, the renovated fence will make it as beautiful to look at from outside as it is inside. The fence doesn't have a wrong side, because the posts are part of its design. Usually fence posts are set on the outside, with the facing boards on the inside, so the right side forms a background for the garden. However, in this case the posts are designed to stand out as vertical gray lines against the dark brown panels of the recycled redwood. These con-

Although the tulip trees in "Emma's forest" were still small at the end of stage one, the shade they provided was a welcome relief. These are fast-growing trees, and planting them close together forced them to grow up instead of out to provide a forestlike appearance in only a few years. Shrubs and ground-hugging common periwinkle softened the scene and reduced the amount of paving, thus reducing reflected heat. A simple bench outside the breakfast room provided a spot to sit and enjoy the new plantings.

trasting strips make a visual play on one of the garden's main attributes—the vertical lines of tree trunks—and contribute to the creation of a "forest."

Building a Storage and Utility Space

Sheila and Terry ingeniously used recycled materials to create a storage area that is attractive, utilitarian, and economical. They salvaged the old fence posts to use as the structural members of the storage bins for compost and recyclables—as well as the phase-one bench in front of the breakfast-room windows. The stockpiled 4-inch redwood boards came in handy as the tops and sides of the bins. The only new material needed was the hardware.

Above the storage units, Sheila and Terry's bicycles hang from hooks on the brick wall of the house, where they are somewhat sheltered by the roof overhang. Sheila and Terry used recycled redwood to build new kitchen steps to cover the broken concrete stoop. To conserve water, they also installed a cistern to collect water from the downspout for use in watering the garden.

Adding Life to the Garden

The power of this predominantly green garden comes from its developing forest structure of vertical tree trunks and soft understory plantings. But it is also animated as color, fragrance, and flowers mark the passing of the seasons.

A sweet bay magnolia (*Magnolia virginiana*), planted between the kitchen door and the garden gate, is a delight throughout the year. This is a rewarding small tree in any garden, maturing at about 20 feet in northern areas (about 60 feet in the South). It has an attractive multi-stemmed habit and long oval leaves that are glossy olive-green with silvery undersides. Better yet, its large, creamy-white flowers appear sporadically all summer and are extremely fragrant. Sheila and Terry walk by the tree frequently and enjoy the fragrance. On the other side of the gate, a downy serviceberry (*Amelanchier arborea*) bears delicate white flowers in spring followed by edible blueberry-like fruits in summer.

Within view of the breakfast room, a spicebush (*Lindera benzoin*), red chokeberry (*Aronia arbutifolia*), and winterberry (*Ilex verticillata*) provide food, cover, and perches for birds in the garden. In the fall, the tulip trees and spicebush turn a cheerful yellow. After the leaves fall, bright berries cling to the shrubs well into the winter and look especially lovely when accented by a light snow.

A Place to Sit

In phase one of the design, the route to the sitting area was out the kitchen door, past the storage bins, down a little woodland path, around the corner, and into the main part of the garden. The recycled redwood bench faced away from the house, toward the red maple, the clambering Virginia creeper, and the dense green carpet of common periwinkle. Both the route and the orientation of the bench made that section of the garden seem like a destination far from the house. A small, new garden pool, located against the masonry east wall of the garden, was added to enliven the sitting area.

The Oasis Matures

About five years after the initial planting, the garden had become a wonderful oasis. The trees spread their shading branches over the formerly barren space, and mature vines clambered everywhere. Instead of a hot and barren concrete desert, this yard had become an inviting garden room that was an enjoyable living space in any season.

As planned, Sheila and Terry had some of the original trees removed at the beginning of phase two to allow the remaining ones to spread out. This also made room for the new shrubs and small trees such as a mapleleaf viburnum (*Viburnum acerifolium*), which completed the understory that had been developing over the last few years. During phase one, Sheila and Terry had planted spring-flowering bulbs and wildflowers, along with shade-loving perennials such as astilbes, hostas, and ferns, among the groundcovers. Together, they form a rich ground layer of plants, like that of a forest floor.

Installing the garden in phases allowed Sheila and Terry to add features as time and money permitted. They replaced the redwood bench during phase two with a Victorian-style cast-iron bench and chair.

They also installed a lion-mask fountain above the little garden pool. A recirculating pump keeps a small stream of water falling from the lion's mouth into the little pool. The east wall of the garden, behind the pool, is covered with cream-colored stucco that's partially screened with redwood fencing. To mount the fountain in an attractive setting, Smith left a portion of the stucco behind the pool

(continued on page 72)

IN ANOTHER PLACE

The techniques used in a tiny garden such as this one can be useful no matter what the size of your garden may be. Use every inch of space to its best advantage whether you have a courtyard or a country estate. Locate plants with the most pleasing effects where you will see them often. In this garden, a fragrant sweet bay magnolia (*Magnolia virginiana*), planted between the kitchen door and the garden gate, is located where it can be enjoyed whenever anyone goes in or out.

If you prefer a more formal design, you could use the forest idea, but express it differently, and still borrow the structure of a quick canopy and rich underlayers. For a formal design, the same plants would be arranged symmetrically. Two rows of four tulip trees, for instance, would extend along the seating space. The paving would have a very regular edge and would be made of brick or concrete pavers instead of cobblestone, to give a sense of polish.

You don't have to have a tiny garden to benefit from implementing it in phases. In fact, this strategy is probably even more useful in larger gardens, where the work and expense may be hard to manage all in one season.

This type of garden can't be created all at once. It takes time to develop the rich sequence of layers that create a forestlike effect. Each layer is planted in its turn, as the one before it grows up to give the next shade. The time restraints of waiting for the layers to grow also has an added benefit: It helps spread the work and expense of developing the garden over a number of years.

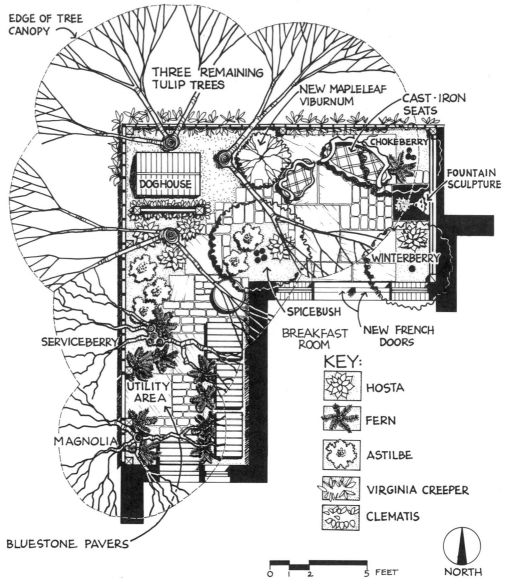

EDGE OF TREE CANOPY

THREE REMAINING TULIP TREES

NEW MAPLELEAF VIBURNUM

CAST·IRON SEATS

CHOKEBERRY

FOUNTAIN SCULPTURE

DOGHOUSE

WINTERBERRY

SPICEBUSH

SERVICEBERRY

BREAKFAST ROOM

NEW FRENCH DOORS

UTILITY AREA

MAGNOLIA

BLUESTONE PAVERS

KEY:

HOSTA

FERN

ASTILBE

VIRGINIA CREEPER

CLEMATIS

0 1 2   5 FEET

NORTH

Removing trees is an unlikely step to take to develop a mature garden, but that's just what it took to reveal the final form of this tiny lot. Sheila and Terry removed all but three of the now-grown tulip trees to open up space for more shrubs and an enlarged sitting area. A rich array of ferns, hostas, and other shade-loving perennials and groundcovers now carpet the yard, while bluestone pavers interspersed between the cobblestones add texture and color to the scene.

PLANTING NOTES

By the end of phase two, the courtyard had been transformed into a forest in miniature. Native plants form the backbone of the garden. Tulip trees (*Liriodendron tulipifera*) provide the primary shade as well as a foliage canopy for privacy. Understory trees and shrubs were selected for all-season interest, so that spring flowers, fall and winter berries, and ornamental bark provide a tapestry of color and texture. Vines soften the fence and screen around Emma's doghouse, and add to the green canopy. The lush and varied layer of perennials, wildflowers, and groundcovers provides a wealth of color and texture that adds immeasurable appeal to the garden. And the wide range of spring- and fall-blooming bulbs adds yet another dimension of seasonal interest to this space.

Understory Trees and Shrubs

Amelanchier arborea (downy serviceberry)
Aronia arbutifolia (red chokeberry)
Ilex verticillata (winterberry)
Lindera benzoin (spicebush)
Magnolia virginiana (sweet bay)
Viburnum acerifolium (mapleleaf viburnum)

Vines

Clematis paniculata (sweet autumn clematis)
Parthenocissus quinquefolia (Virginia creeper)

Perennials and Wildflowers

Aquilegia canadensis (wild columbine)
Astilbe × arendsii (astilbe)
Astilbe chinensis 'Pumila' (Chinese astilbe)
Epimedium grandiflorum (long-spurred epimedium)
Hosta plantaginea (August lily)
Hosta sieboldiana (Siebold's hosta)
Hosta ventricosa (blue hosta)
Mertensia virginica (Virginia bluebells)
Phlox divaricata (wild blue phlox)
Phlox stolonifera (creeping phlox)
Tiarella cordifolia (Allegheny foamflower)

Ferns

Matteuccia struthiopteris (ostrich fern)
Onoclea sensibilis (sensitive fern)
Osmunda cinnamomea (cinnamon fern)
Osmunda regalis (royal fern)
Polystichum acrostichoides (Christmas fern)

Bulbs and Groundcovers

Anemone blanda (Grecian windflower)
Asarum europaeum (European wild ginger)
Chionodoxa luciliae (glory-of-the-snow)
Colchicum autumnale (autumn crocus)
Crocus sativus (saffron crocus)
Crocus speciosus (showy crocus)
Cyclamen hederifolium (hardy cyclamen)
Eranthis hyemalis (winter aconite)
Fritillaria meleagris (checkered lily)
Galanthus nivalis (snowdrops)
Iris reticulata (reticulated iris)
Muscari armeniacum (grape hyacinths)
Scilla sibirica (Siberian squill)
Vinca minor (common periwinkle)

Lush flowers and foliage, efficient storage, and new French doors leading directly from garden to breakfast room add up to an appealing yet practical urban oasis. A fountain sculpture provides the soothing sound of cascading water, and trees provide

dappled shade to suggest a woodland retreat far removed from the chaos of city life. Berry-bearing shrubs, including spicebush, red chokeberry, winterberry, and sweet bay magnolia, provide food for birds that visit the garden.

NOTES FROM THE DESIGNER

It is important to remember that this garden is not a forest. Though it may have many attributes of a natural ecosystem, any garden requires your time and energy to keep the system in balance. With that in mind, it's crucial to get an accurate reading of how much energy you really want to put into your garden's care, and not to design beyond your means. This is another good reason to install the garden in phases.

As a professional landscape architect, W. Gary Smith likes to "get the ecosystem rolling, help the owners to understand what the system is about, and get them actively involved in having a relationship with that system." When someone asks him if a garden is going to involve maintenance, his answer is simple: "A garden is the expression of your relationship with the earth. How many relationships have you ever been in that haven't required some form of caring? Relationships aren't maintenance-free, and neither are gardens." Maybe that's the best definition of maintenance—your relationship with the garden.

"People are very thing-oriented," says Smith. "And a garden is not a collection of things." It's a natural desire to want to buy things to put in the garden before you actually have the garden, but Smith advises saving the embellishments for later. "First get the garden's basic structure going—plant the trees, install the fence and paving—or else it ends up as a hodgepodge collection of stuff. Plus the ornate or interesting things can be expensive, so why not save them for later?"

uncovered, and framed it with the same stained lattice used atop the fence. The lattice forms a decorative appliqué against the wall and also frames the fountain, which can be seen and heard both inside and out. Repeating the colors and textures of the wooden fence helps tie this area to the rest of the garden.

Using Paving Patterns

In phase two, Sheila and Terry also added large bluestone pavers to extend the seating area. Inserted among and replacing some of the cobblestones, the bluestone pavers provide contrasting texture and color. The combination of pavers adds interest to the entire paving scheme. Like boulders in a stream, the bluestone pavers mark landings and turning points in the garden: one at the alley gate, two where you turn the inside corner, and several forming an island running between the French doors and the seating area. The cobblestones are now secondary: They seem to flow between the pavers and planting beds like the current of a stream and connect these areas. The resulting pattern adds life and movement to this tiny space.

Linking House and Garden

As you design your yard, it might be wise to emulate Sheila and Terry's two-phase plan. Not only did their plan help them budget time and money, they also saved something wonderful for phase two, so they'd be sure to carry out the entire plan. In phase two, they installed French doors in the breakfast room, which brought about a direct connection between outdoor and indoor living spaces. This all-important change means their garden is immediately accessible as an extension of

The new French doors that lead directly from the breakfast room into the garden create an entirely new perspective on the design. They allow owners Sheila and Terry and their guests to walk right out into the "forest clearing" where the comfort of a shaded sitting area, the aroma of flowering shrubs, and the soothing sounds of flowing water wait to greet them.

their home. They and their guests no longer have to travel through the utility and storage space to enjoy their yard. And another small but nice benefit of this two-phase approach was that everything they removed from their yard in phase two, such as plants small enough to transplant, the redwood bench, and the cobblestones, was recycled to the community garden three blocks away.

Looking to the Future

Once phase two was completed, Sheila and Terry's garden required surprisingly little maintenance. As the tulip trees grow, the couple might decide to prune off a few branches to let a bit more sunlight into the garden or to deal with stray limbs that might touch the house. The shrubs may also need occasional trimming to prevent them from blocking the paths and doors.

While space is somewhat limited, Sheila and Terry will still keep looking for small, interesting garden ornaments. Besides that, the couple can just sit back and enjoy the peace and privacy of their little woodland retreat. ◆

A WOODLAND GARDEN:
SPACES FOR PEOPLE AND WILDLIFE

Karen and Henry knew their wooded, semi-rural property outside Atlanta had the potential to become an inviting place for enjoying the out-of-doors. There were some obstacles, though. The house sat uneasily on the site, and the property was cut off and unappealing from indoors. The boundaries between house and forest were abrupt and unnatural looking.

In the few years they had been living in the house, Karen and Henry had become dissatisfied with the abrupt transition between the house and its surrounding landscape. They wanted to be able to enjoy the property to its fullest, but another problem was that much of the surrounding woodland was completely inaccessible due to rampant vines and shrubs. The house also lacked a welcoming, friendly looking entrance.

They turned to landscape architect Sherry Wheat, who developed a design that makes the most of the site. It provides plenty of hospitable outdoor spaces for people, and the house now fits comfortably into the surrounding forest. Karen and Henry have spotted numerous birds and other animals on their property — including cardinals, downy woodpeckers, cedar waxwings, common flickers, crows, doves, robins, mockingbirds, blue jays, and tufted titmice, along with squirrels and other small mammals. Wheat's design provides plenty of features that in years ahead will encourage even more birds, butterflies, and other wildlife to make this wooded property home.

The Place and the People

Located at the end of a cul-de-sac, this 2-acre property was clearly part of a

---

KEY CONCEPTS FOR A SUCCESSFUL DESIGN

Developing a yard friendly to wildlife. This property is not just beautiful to look at, it's also an ideal habitat for birds, butterflies, and other wildlife. Adding a new forest edge area rich with plants for food and shelter makes this an especially attractive home for wild creatures.

Developing a yard friendly to people. This design provides for a variety of new places to enjoy the outdoors, whether sitting and talking or enjoying the abundant wildlife. These new places include attractive entry and pool terraces, a woodland clearing, and a private nature trail.

Unifying parts of the landscape. Key repeated elements, such as trellis styles and paving patterns, help unify the parts of this large garden. The designer also uses plants to mark passages between parts of the garden and soften the transition between the house and surrounding woodland.

Creating a welcoming entry. Neat but low-maintenance plantings add an appealing public face to this home.

forest habitat that extended beyond its boundaries. It's fair to say that native habitat usually loses out when an area is developed. We don't have to look as far as the Amazon to see serious deforestation and habitat loss. In Atlanta, real estate development is so intense that an estimated 50 acres of native woodland are bulldozed daily. Add to that the perception that a native landscape takes too long to grow, and you can see what a struggle it is for wildlife to survive. Karen and Henry's goal was to reverse this trend on their own property.

The site for the house and driveway was literally carved into a north-facing hillside. Stone retaining walls surrounded the modern, two-story stone and wood home on three sides. The property sloped steeply up to the southwest boundary, which was about 20 feet above the yard. This portion of the property had probably been farmed at one time, but was now covered with pine forest.

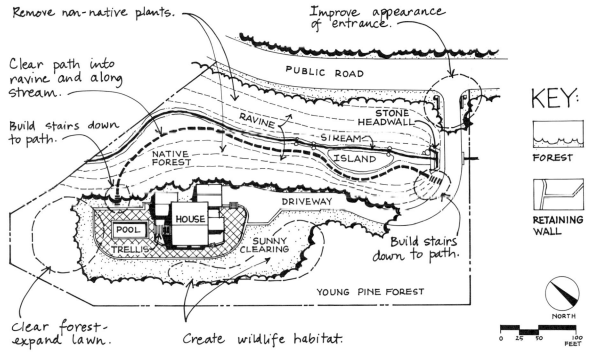

This wooded lot outside Atlanta, Georgia, had all the ingredients for an appealing landscape, but it had its share of problems, too. The ravine on the property boasted a beautiful forest, but it was clogged with a nearly impenetrable tangle of weedy vines and shrubs. To show designer Sherry Wheat what they wanted, owners Karen and Henry started by sketching some of their ideas onto their plan. In addition to wanting to clear a woodland walk through the ravine, they wanted plants to attract butterflies, a path from the front terrace to the pool behind the house, and a more attractive entrance to the property.

On the side nearest the ravine, which ran along the northeast side of the property, the land sloped abruptly down to a stream at the bottom, about 20 feet below the yard. It then climbed back up to the northeast boundary along the road. Down in the ravine was a dense hardwood forest overrun with aggressive plants. This unnaturally thick vegetation provided good cover not only for desirable wildlife but also for poisonous copperhead snakes.

Room for Improvement

Before Wheat's plan for Karen and Henry's yard was implemented, the house was essentially an island within its stone retaining walls. From indoors, there were good but limited views into the surrounding woods through large windows. Although several patios and a trellis helped strengthen the relationship between indoors and out, there was no friendly transition from human area to wild area. Even the stone veneer on the house was overbearing.

The lack of comfortable spaces around the house was another problem. Karen and Henry enjoyed entertaining family, friends, and business associates but seemed to need more lawn to accommodate large groups comfortably. They also wanted the pool terrace to seem brighter and more intimate—perhaps with the addition of attractive paving. The front-entry area needed to be more welcoming as well.

Karen and Henry knew the site offered a lot, and they suspected that it just needed to be developed and enhanced. They didn't want to spend a lot of time pruning and planting; they'd rather take advantage of native plants and natural growth cycles so they can spend most of their time just enjoying the landscape.

They also wanted to enjoy the forest more fully. As nature-lovers, they wanted to attract birds, butterflies, and other wildlife. To do this, they needed to provide a habitat for many more species. They also needed access to more of the property, both physically and visually. They wanted to be able to stroll through the ravine, descending into it near the rear of the property, and eventually emerging somewhere along the driveway. They also wanted to increase the seasonal interest of the landscape.

Getting from Fantasy to Fact

Put a bird-loving, leisure-loving couple together with a wooded site and it's clear that this place should remain a natural landscape. For Wheat, improving the quality of life for the people and wildlife who live here was only a matter of revealing the native landscape and gently enhancing it.

Designing for Wildlife

Any landscape that attracts a wide variety of birds and other animals must meet the following four basic needs of native creatures:

1. Seasonal food sources. Seeds, nuts, berries, fruit, and edible flower buds must be available year-round.

2. Water. Wildlife requires year-round access to water. Potential sources include small pools, birdbaths (special heating elements are available to keep them from freezing in winter), and a trickling brook.

3. Cover. Cover is necessary for breeding, nesting, shelter, safety, and feeding.

Ideally it should include varied, clumped plantings and areas of fallen branches and tree trunks.

4. Territory. Wildlife needs space or range in which to live. As a general rule, the more sources of food and water available to wildlife in an area, the less territory they need. Wildlife roams beyond property lines, so cooperative management with neighboring landowners is always a good idea.

A Rich Transition

The area between a clearing and the surrounding woodland is a rich habitat that naturally supports an abundant variety of plants and wildlife. Because Karen and Henry's home is already located in a woodland clearing, developing a wildlife-friendly "clearing edge" was fairly easy. Their plan calls for adding plants that provide new food sources—seeds, berries, and flowers—as well as essential shelter and nesting sites. The existing stream is already a very good water source, which also is attractive to wildlife.

When planning any natural landscape, Wheat also takes a look at what animal species are missing that should be present. *(continued on page 82)*

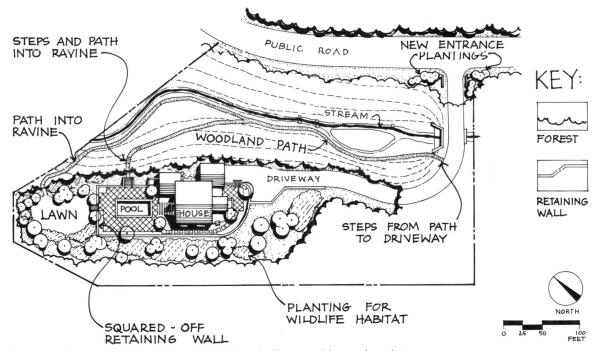

Native shrubs and trees that provide shelter and bear berries, nuts, and seeds form the backbone of the new plantings for this wildlife-friendly design. The woodland path is now a reality, and Karen and Henry spend many happy hours strolling leisurely through the now open woodland and watching for wildlife.

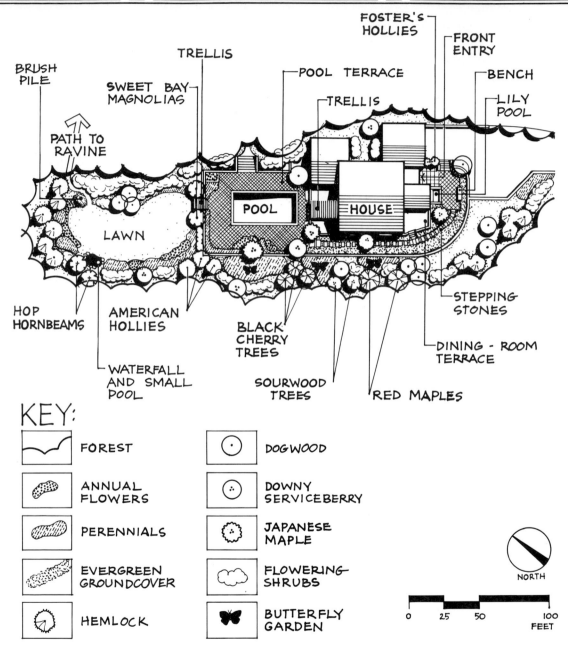

BRUSH PILE

PATH TO RAVINE

SWEET BAY MAGNOLIAS

TRELLIS

FOSTER'S HOLLIES

FRONT ENTRY

POOL TERRACE

TRELLIS

BENCH

LILY POOL

POOL

HOUSE

LAWN

HOP HORNBEAMS

AMERICAN HOLLIES

WATERFALL AND SMALL POOL

BLACK CHERRY TREES

SOURWOOD TREES

RED MAPLES

STEPPING STONES

DINING - ROOM TERRACE

KEY:

FOREST		DOGWOOD	
ANNUAL FLOWERS		DOWNY SERVICEBERRY	
PERENNIALS		JAPANESE MAPLE	
EVERGREEN GROUNDCOVER		FLOWERING SHRUBS	
HEMLOCK		BUTTERFLY GARDEN	

NORTH

0 25 50 100 FEET

The new, welcoming entry terrace features smart new paving and a lily pool. From there a path leads around the house, past the butterfly gardens to the pool terrace, which is a bright and lively area for entertaining friends. Beyond the pool terrace, a new lawn area has been carved out of the woodland. Here, a brush pile and a small pool provide water and shelter for wildlife.

PLANTING NOTES

This garden features a host of plants selected especially for their value to wildlife. In addition to the plants suggested by landscape architect Sherry Wheat, Karen and Henry kept some existing plants that would provide food and shelter for wildlife. Oaks (*Quercus* spp.), beeches (*Fagus* spp.), and hickories (*Carya* spp.) provide all-important nuts for squirrels and other wildlife. Here are some of the other wildlife-friendly plants on the property.

Trees with Berries

Amelanchier arborea (downy serviceberry)
Cornus florida (flowering dogwood)
Crataegus mollis (downy hawthorn)
Ilex × *attenuata* 'Foster #2' (Foster's holly)
Ilex opaca (American holly)
Magnolia virginiana (sweet bay)
Prunus caroliniana (Carolina cherry-laurel)
Prunus serotina (black cherry)
Vaccinium arboreum (farkleberry)

Shrubs with Berries

Aralia spinosa (devil's-walking stick)
Aronia arbutifolia (red chokeberry)
Callicarpa americana (beautyberry)
Cornus amomum (silky dogwood)
Ilex verticillata (winterberry)
Ilex vomitoria (yaupon)
Rhus copallina (shining sumac)
Sambucus canadensis (American elder)
Vaccinium corymbosum (highbush blueberry)
Viburnum acerifolium (mapleleaf viburnum)
Viburnum dentatum (arrowwood viburnum)
Viburnum rufidulum (southern black haw)

Evergreens for Shelter

The property features a number of evergreens that provide winter color as well as cover and nesting sites for birds. These include American and Foster's hollies, yaupon, and farkleberry. Hemlocks are also important wildlife plants. Birds eat the seeds and depend on their dense foliage for cover. For this reason, Karen and Henry added both Canada and Carolina hemlocks (*Tsuga canadensis* and *T. caroliniana*).

Plants for Color and Fragrance

There's no lack of color in this garden, even though much of the area is shady. Perennials such as daylilies, hostas, and species planted to attract butterflies provide plenty of interest. A number of trees and shrubs also add color and fragrance. These include trees such as flowering dogwood, red buckeye (*Aesculus pavia*), sourwood (*Oxydendrum arboreum*), and Carolina silverbell (*Halesia carolina*). Blooming shrubs include common witch hazel (*Hamamelis virginiana*), Florida pinxter azalea (*Rhododendron canescens*), and oakleaf hydrangea (*Hydrangea quercifolia*). Several shrubs on the property are prized for their wonderful fragrance. These include Carolina allspice (*Calycanthus floridus*), sweet pepperbush (*Clethra alnifolia*), sweetspire (*Itea virginica*), and spicebush (*Lindera benzoin*).

Flowering vines add color, nesting sites for birds, and fragrance to the scene. Cross vine (*Bignonia capreolata*) and trumpet vine (*Campsis radicans*) bear orange-red blooms that are attractive to hummingbirds. Carolina jasmine (*Gelsemium sempervirens*) bears fragrant yellow flowers. Wisteria's (*Wisteria* sp.) lavender blooms are also fragrant.

The new lawn area beyond the pool terrace resembles a forest clearing. A variety of shrubs and trees flourish in the dappled shade, and the sights and sounds of birds make this a peaceful retreat from the rest of the world. Looking back toward the pool

and house beyond, visitors are treated to a pair of trellises covered with the bright blossoms of flowering vines. Shiny-leaved sweet bay magnolias frame the view to the back door and help link the house with the landscape.

Here, for example, butterflies are conspicuously absent. They need a sunny area and a variety of flowering shrubs, perennials, annuals, and vines for food. Wheat's plan calls for areas that meet these requirements. And although many bird species are already present on the site, the plan will help attract new species and encourage those already there to stay year-round.

Setting Out a Welcome Mat

Plantings that will attract wildlife can also create an inviting setting for the house. The surrounding forest, with its tall trees and shady canopy, already creates plenty of space and atmosphere around the house. But the transition between the woods and the clearing around the house is so abrupt that it seems like the area has very large walls—which is one way of describing the edge of the woods. To soften this transition and bring these "walls" down to human scale, Wheat created a new, in-between edge of smaller-scale plants. In some cases, all that needs to be done to soften the transition is to "select" for a particular plant by removing other plants. For example, there are already native ferns growing along the driveway. When other plants are removed, the ferns will thrive. Once established, they'll soften the transition between the driveway and the natural forest.

Wheat also designed new areas where Karen and Henry can enjoy the out-of-doors. These include a new lawn designed as a quiet space away from the house and closer to the forest, and a winding path through the ravine.

Creating a Welcoming Entry

An attractive entranceway is a welcoming signal for guests and neighbors alike. A formal planting along the road or the driveway, which runs between the ravine and the house, would be out of place, but a neat, naturalistic planting makes the entrance to the property look loved, cared-for, and appealing. The flowering dogwoods (*Cornus florida*) and Carolina hemlocks (*Tsuga caroliniana*) planted in this area not only provide food and shelter for songbirds and other creatures, but also help suggest a garden setting while requiring little maintenance—just what Karen and Henry were looking for. Several kinds of hostas planted as groundcovers are neat and attractive throughout the growing season, and they attract butterflies when in flower.

To make the entrance even more attractive, some trees, shrubs, and undergrowth were removed along the driveway to create views into the woods. A stretch of summer-blooming daylilies announces arrival at the house. A couple of cars can pull off to the left at a 60-degree angle, out of the way of cars entering or leaving the garage. A pair of glossy dark green Foster's hollies (*Ilex* × *attenuata* 'Foster #2') next to the garage does double duty in this design. The hollies screen the garage from the front door and form one side of a gateway for the steps up to the entry terrace from the parking area. An existing 20-foot-tall flowering dogwood tree forms the other side of the gateway. Its limbs are pruned up so that they don't interfere with the driveway. On the other side, they arch over the entry terrace and separate it from the driveway.

Planning Pathways

The entry terrace feels like a foyer to the garden and is also a crossroads for people coming from the front and back. It's paved in a diagonal pattern that makes the space seem larger. The diagonal paving pattern also helps direct visitors to the front door. A wooden bench across from the house is a welcoming feature—a good place to take off your muddy boots after a walk through the ravine, or an equally nice spot to chat with a neighbor. The bench is set into a niche, making it seem more intimate and keeping it out of the traffic pattern.

Wheat added a new lily pool and fountain on the entry terrace, using the high stone facade on the house as a backdrop. The pool makes the stone facade less overpowering and creates a pleasant place to stop and linger. The pool edge is raised so visitors can sit and dangle their fingers in the water and watch the fish dart to and fro; the fountain provides a quiet trickle. The day the pool was filled, butterflies and dragonflies showed up almost as if by magic.

Karen and Henry wanted a connection between the parking area and entry terrace and the pool terrace in the backyard. To make sure visitors wouldn't be con-

Butterflies galore will float and weave over this dazzling array of sweet-smelling flowers. This garden features some of the best plants for attracting butterflies, including butterfly weed, bee balm, and butterfly bush. This garden feeds birds, too—trumpet vines attract hummingbirds, and a host of seeds and berries flourish in this sunny hillside garden.

A HAVEN FOR BUTTERFLIES

Landscape architect Sherry Wheat's plan includes a rich assortment of plants designed to attract butterflies. Many are common garden plants; others, native wildflowers. All have nectar-rich flowers. Common garden flowers that attract butterflies include alliums (*Allium* spp.), butterfly bushes (*Buddleia* spp.), daylilies (*Hemerocallis* spp.), gayfeathers (*Liatris* spp.), and bee balm (*Monarda didyma*). The brightly colored blossoms of wildflowers planted in the garden also attract a host of butterflies. These plants include well-known butterfly weed (*Asclepias tuberosa*), threadleaf coreopsis (*Coreopsis verticillata*), pale coneflower (*Echinacea pallida*), purple coneflower (*E. purpurea*), wild bergamot (*Monarda fistulosa*), Joe-Pye weed (*Eupatorium purpureum*), thin-leaved coneflower (*Rudbeckia triloba*), goldenrods (*Solidago* spp.), and New York ironweed (*Vernonia noveboracensis*). *Aster grandiflorus* (a large-flowered native aster), *Penstemon smallii* (a native pink-purple penstemon), mountain mint (*Pycnanthemum* spp.), and moss verbena (*Verbena tenuisecta*) are equally attractive but less well known.

fused by mixed messages, the path that leads around the house is distinctly less formal than the front entry. The solid paving of the front terrace gives way to stepping stones that lead around the house to the side entry by the dining-room terrace and back to the pool terrace. This gives visitors a clear message that one direction is more formal and important than the other. A multi-stemmed Japanese maple (*Acer palmatum*) planted at the corner of the house encloses the entry terrace and forms a gateway to the informal side entry. It also provides privacy to the dining-room terrace just around the corner.

A Side-Yard Walkway

The stepping-stone path around the side of the house creates a pleasant corridor from the entry terrace to the dining-room terrace and around to the pool terrace behind the house. Evergreen groundcovers and pine-straw mulch carpet the ground around the stepping stones to create a foresty feeling. Trees planted at intervals above the retaining wall and pruned to arch overhead give a sense of walking through woodland doorways.

Located about halfway along this walkway are two bay windows on the side of the house. In the wider space between the windows, Wheat planted a downy serviceberry tree (*Amelanchier arborea*). The serviceberry brings the woods in close to the house and, from inside the house, frames the view of a butterfly garden above the retaining wall and across the path. The butterfly garden is in a sunny spot and is loaded with plants known to attract butterflies, including the aptly named butterfly bush (*Buddleia* spp.).

As the path approaches the pool terrace, Wheat used larger flagstones and set them closer together. This announces arrival at the pool terrace and smooths the transition to its solidly paved expanse.

A Bright and Lively Terrace

The pool terrace is the main place where Karen and Henry gather with friends and family in the garden. This is an area for restful activities like sitting and sunning as well as dining, entertaining, and of course, swimming. But it's also a crossroads: Visitors can walk from the pool terrace to the back lawn or ramble down to the ravine. New greenish bluestone paving spruces up the area and complements the tan stone walls around the terrace. The colors brighten up the space and reflect the surrounding woods. Wheat used a diagonal paving pattern like that used on the entry terrace to unify the overall design and signal that this, too, is an important area where lots of activity takes place.

Originally, the area around the pool inside the retaining wall was much too large and undifferentiated to be a comfortable place for people to gather. Wheat modified the area by squaring off a curve in the retaining wall to better define the terrace. To create an opening to the new back lawn, she removed a section of the wall altogether. Wheat also added planting beds along the edges of the terrace to add color to the area. The retaining wall serves as a background for these beds, which Wheat designed with varied widths to create interest and soften the edges of the terrace. Located on the same level as the terrace, these beds may be planted with vegetables along with annuals and perennials for cutting.

Although the forest surrounds the pool terrace with its tall wall, this is a bright, sunny spot, where water and pavement color bring lots of light into the area. It is very much a "built" space that contrasts with the shady and wilder forest around it. A trellis links the pool terrace to the back of the house. Wheat designed a new trellis using the same style to create a transition from the pool terrace to the lawn beyond it. Using too many types of materials in a design is a pitfall, which leads to a garden that looks more like a mishmash than a unified whole. In this case, using the same style of trellis in both places helps unify the area.

A New Woodland Clearing

The trellis serves as a doorway from the more architecturally designed space around the pool into the more natural space of the lawn behind it. Two sweet bay magnolias (*Magnolia virginiana*) frame the trellis and strengthen the sense of two separate rooms or spaces. When you walk out onto the lawn, there's a real sense of being in nature. Compared to the scale of the trees, it's small enough to make you feel like you're in a little opening in the forest.

SAVE THAT DEAD TREE!

Do you want to attract nuthatches, flickers, and woodpeckers? These species will home in on a garden that provides a *snag*—a dead tree that's still standing. In fact, one snag or more per quarter acre is ideal, so think before you remove dead, standing trees. This garden's design incorporates an existing snag near the lawn, blended into the new edge plantings. If you have no standing dead trees, you can erect old trunks of trees and other timbers with holes cut out for suet, although these would be more like artificial feeding areas. If you do have a dead tree, what better fate could it have than becoming the centerpiece of a new wildlife area in your garden?

This lawn area is carved sinuously out of the woodland, its curving shape a soft contrast to the rectangular pool terrace, which is almost the same size. The lawn is a dramatic yet comfortable space that links the surrounding property to the more formal areas around the house. A look back toward the pool terrace reveals a dramatically formal architectural view. At the far end of the lawn a trail leads into the forest, luring the visitor to explore the wilder reaches of the property.

The curving outline of the lawn has several benefits, in addition to its soft contrast with the terrace. It provides more interesting views, because the curves conceal some things from view and make the lawn area look more open-ended than it really is. The curves also provide a larger area of edge habitat for wildlife. Yet another benefit comes from creating a longer edge for planting shrubs and perennials—the greater the diversity of vegetation, the greater the diversity of wildlife.

Another element in this area that attracts wildlife, especially chipmunks and rabbits, is the brush pile. It's hidden behind three flowering dogwoods and set back within a curve so that Karen and Henry won't have to look at it all the time. Just a dash across the lawn from the brush pile, a small pond provides wild residents with a source of water. It's important that these two features—home and water—are close to each other.

The pond is set underneath two American hop hornbeams (*Ostrya virginiana*) whose arching branches are a lookout spot for birds jumping back and forth from the protecting trees to the pond. Birds are also attracted to the sound of a waterfall, quietly trickling from massed boulders at the highest edge of the pond, powered by a recirculating pump. The rough fieldstones have pits and pockets that collect rain water, making little puddles where birds and butterflies can drink, bathe, and flutter around. About 2½ feet deep, the pool has hidden ledges to provide a variety of depths for potted water-loving plants. Rocks on the bottom provide warm habitats for overwintering goldfish, while rocks just below the surface are good places for birds to stand and bathe.

A Woodland for Wildlife and Rambling

The design calls for a pleasant woodland nature path along the stream from the pool terrace to the driveway. This part of the design will highlight one of the property's best features: the existing forest, which is a diverse mix of trees and shrubs. Majestic hickories, oaks, beeches, and tulip trees form a canopy overhead. Southern magnolias and American hollies provide evergreen foliage. Understory trees include flowering dogwoods and Carolina silverbells.

Before they could enjoy strolling through this beautiful natural area, Karen and Henry had to tackle the impenetrable tangle of exotic and aggressive species that clogged the ravine, especially at streamside. The principal plants that they needed to remove included honeysuckle (*Lonicera* spp.), muscadine grapes (*Vitus rotundifolia*), poison ivy (*Rhus radicans*), Russian olive (*Elaeagnus angustifolia*), greenbrier (*Smilax rotundifolia*), and bamboo. Privet (*Ligustrum* sp.) was an especially big problem. Although a useful garden plant, privet has spread rampantly in the South, taking over floodplains and forests and shading out native species.

IN ANOTHER PLACE

While many older suburban neighborhoods were planned around wooded areas and waterways, where a variety of wildlife live, few modern developers plan for such "wasted" space. In newer developments, it's often up to the property owners to develop a place where wildlife can live in harmony with humans.

You don't have to design a garden that looks naturalistic in order to provide all the elements that wildlife needs. If your tastes are formal, or your place already has a more architectural plan, you could fit new plants and water features into a balanced and regular layout. Many of the plants that provide food and cover for birds, such as flowering dogwood (*Cornus florida*), are already considered important to gardens for their ornamental value alone. And a pool can be rectangular and edged in beautifully cut limestone without compromising its utility for drinking and bathing. At the other end of the spectrum, you could completely avoid grass in your "woodland clearing" by using leaf mulch and low-growing wildflowers or ferns as groundcover.

Wherever you garden, it's a good idea to learn about the plants and animals native to your area before you begin. In addition to local field guides, there are many sources of information on landscaping for wildlife. One of the best is the U.S. Department of Fish and Wildlife, at both the national and regional levels. Other government agencies, such as your state's Department of Natural Resources and local extension services, publish guides and run workshops. There are also national organizations with local chapters and excellent publications, like the Nature Conservancy, the National Wildlife Federation, the Audubon Society, and the Sierra Club. Also check into wildlife programs offered by local universities, wildlife preserves, state parks, and bird-watching clubs.

The initial clearing-out was done in the spring. Karen and Henry had the trees and shrubs pruned as needed to open up views into the ravine and make room for a streamside path. They also began a program of selective clearing. Non-native species were pulled out, cut back, and their roots were dug up and removed. In all, six truckloads of brush were hauled out.

Unfortunately, many of the weeds clogging the ravine are rampant, difficult-to-control woody plants that can easily come back from the roots. That's why an annual program of spring and fall cleanup is on Karen and Henry's calendar. Poison ivy is a good example. Once it has been cut back and the roots have been dug up as much as possible, it's not unusual to find it growing back again in a few months. Heavy beds of poison ivy will take two or three years of checking on and removing repeat growth to prevent its return. After the first few years, once the major cleanup has been accomplished, Karen and Henry will continue their spring and fall cleanups in order to watch for new unwanted plants that sprouted from seeds brought in by wildlife, wind, and water.

There's a delicate balance between clearing for human access and leaving enough habitat for wildlife and plants. Along the path where Karen, Henry, and their guests are going to walk, they've removed logs in order to make it easier to stroll along and also to deny snakes a hiding place. In most of the forest, however, where they'll look but not walk, old logs and other organic matter such as leaves and twigs are left in place. As they decay, they'll supply the natural recycling process on the woodland floor that eventually nourishes growing plants.

At the southeast end of the ravine, new stairs complete the path through the ravine and form a pleasant walking loop to the driveway. There's not much space between the ravine bottom and the driveway, and it would have been easy to damage the steep slope with the heavy construction required to build a solid stairway. Fortunately, a flight of stairs can be tied into the old, but reasonably sound, headwall of stone and concrete where the driveway crosses the stream.

As Karen and Henry had hoped, the ravine is a perfect place to enjoy nature close up. They are aware, however, that not all wildlife is desirable. To discourage poisonous copperhead snakes from living in the ravine, they have carefully removed their favored hiding spots. Fortunately, the more Karen and Henry use their new nature path, the more the snakes are apt to move elsewhere.

Looking to the Future

Designing outdoor living spaces to attract wildlife opens a new door to understanding the natural world. Karen and Henry's yard and garden have become a habitat they share with other creatures, not just keep for themselves. It's no longer a place simply to maintain, but a place to manage. Although they started out wanting to have lots of birds to watch and feed, they quickly learned that management

NOTES FROM THE DESIGNER

"I try to plant the way nature plants," says Sherry Wheat. The Atlanta-based landscape architect particularly likes to plant multi-stemmed trees wherever she can for a more natural feel. "A tree that hasn't been bred and hybridized to stand straight might arch over a space instead of looking like a lollipop in the landscape."

Her training in ecological design at the University of Pennsylvania showed that nature does not space trees 15 or 20 feet apart as designers usually do. Instead, nature plants that same tree species two and three feet apart, to grow together in clumps. Sherry says, "I find that approach to planting creates wonderful spaces and opportunities for interaction. I try to use the clumps, gaps, and drifts of plants in nature as my point of departure." For inspiration, she drives up into the mountains to look at old highway cuts where plant succession is creating exquisite mosaics.

means encouraging certain animals and discouraging others. They've found it's a fascinating learning experience to see wildlife respond to the conditions created by plant choices and arrangements—especially in the rich, new forest-edge area Sherry Wheat has created. In the long run, observing the plants and wildlife—and their relationships with one another—will be Karen and Henry's strongest management tool, for it will give them the information they need to continue to improve their woodland home—both for themselves and for the wildlife with which they live. ◆

JOINING FORCES: PERENNIAL GARDENS AND PRAIRIE PLANTINGS

When Susan, David, and their two children moved to their new home west of Minneapolis, the yard didn't have much to offer. The developer had seeded their nearly bare landscape to keep the soil from washing away, but that was about it. The only trees on the property were a row of Norway pines (*Pinus resinosa*) along the state highway that ran next to the northwest lot line. There weren't any plantings at all around the house, which was exposed to neighbors on three sides.

Susan and David knew they wanted—and needed—a landscape that was more interesting and exciting. The nearly bare slate that confronted them was daunting, to say the least. They had dreams of room for lawns, flowers, vegetables, and fruits, along with room for the children to play and explore. Both were quite interested in the plants native to the region and hoped they could restore some of the property with wildflowers and other plants. In addition, they wanted to add to the row of Norway pines on the rear lot line to block the house from the northwest winds and to screen the sights and sounds of the adjoining state highway.

Designer C. Colston Burrell created a plan for Susan and David that included the conventional lawn and garden areas they wanted. As for the rest of the property, he transformed it into a rich and diverse natural landscape reminiscent of the vast prairies that once stretched across the Midwest. The design celebrates the native wildflowers and grasses of the prairie, and also has places to play, paths to explore,

KEY CONCEPTS FOR A SUCCESSFUL DESIGN

Minimizing maintenance with a native landscape. Designing and planting a yard that features native wildflowers and other plants can require lots of time and effort. The owners will reap the benefits over the long run, however: Their prairie landscape needs only one mowing a year and little other annual care because the plants are all adapted to the local soil and climate. The native trees and shrubs on the property will also thrive with little maintenance.

Combining styles in a single design. This garden combines areas with two distinct styles—formal and naturalistic. Rather than blending the two together gradually, this design features a sharp dividing line between the two, which creates an attractive contrast that highlights the features of each area.

Using architectural clues to design a garden. One way to link a house and garden is to repeat clues gleaned from the architecture of the house. This design repeats the shape of the arched windows on the front and back of the house, and the end result is a pleasing, unified garden.

Planting a prairie. This design celebrates the natural prairie vegetation of the Midwest. To ensure the long-term success of the new landscape, the seed mixes sown throughout were carefully matched and custom-mixed to fit the soil and moisture conditions available on each part of the property.

and private, screened areas for outdoor activities near the house. The yard and garden are now beautiful to look at from indoors, too. Native trees and shrubs around the property form the backbone of this design—especially in the shelterbelt that now screens the highway and winter winds.

The Place and the People

This new house is located near the southern edge of a 2-acre lot west of Minneapolis. Until the developers moved in, the land had been a farm field. Susan and David moved here when it was still a new subdivision. The gently rolling contour of the property added some interest to the site, especially in front where the driveway swings around a knoll. There's a knoll in the backyard, as well. The developer had seeded most of the lot with a pasture mix of alfalfa and timothy to keep the rich loam soil from washing away. He seeded annual ryegrass around the house for the same reason.

A Prairie Heritage

Before settlers began farming the Twin Cities region, it was a region of woodlands and prairies. The prairie plant communi-

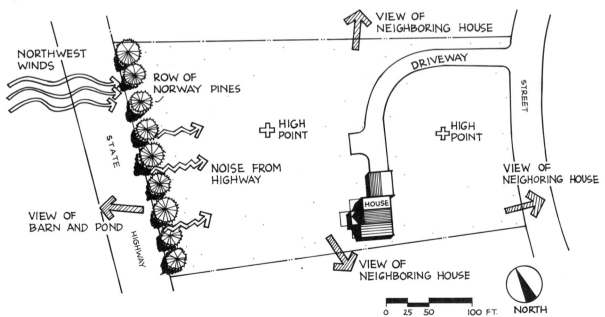

This property, west of Minneapolis, is part of a subdivision carved out of farmland. The developer had seeded the lot with a pasture mix of alfalfa and timothy, as well as annual ryegrass, but had done little else to improve the property. Its attributes included gently rolling contours and an unlimited opportunity for design. At the rear of the property stood a row of Norway pines, planted to deflect highway noise and chilling winds.

ties were made up primarily of grasses but also had a rich mix of wildflowers, including such well-known garden flowers as pasque flower (*Anemone patens*), butterfly weed (*Asclepias tuberosa*), and black-eyed Susan (*Rudbeckia hirta*). Other areas of the prairies were dotted with islands of oak trees; these sections were referred to as savannas.

A prairie is much more than a random collection of native grasses and wildflowers: It is a community of plants that belong together and are uniquely suited to the soil and climate of a particular area. A prairie community can be described as dry (xeric), moist (mesic), or wet (hydric). These descriptions refer to more than just average precipitation: The soil itself is another determining factor. Most dry prairies have gravelly or sandy soil. Dry prairies generally have lower-growing plants than the moist or wet prairies, which more commonly have loam soils. The prairies of this portion of Minnesota range from dry to moist.

The particular plant community once found in this area was unique, because the Minnesota River acted as a barrier to the introduction of some plants from the more southern and western prairies. The river also blocked wildfires that burned their way across the landscape. Fire is essential to the health and stability of native prairie plant communities. As the plants burn, they release vital nutrients that feed the soil and the new growth that follows on the heels of the fire. Native prairie species adapted to survive these periodic wildfires, which kept most woody trees and shrubs from invading these vast grasslands.

On all of Susan and David's property, only one small hollow hadn't been farmed.

Here, a few native prairie plants had survived, including panicled aster (*Aster simplex*), spotted Joe-Pye weed (*Eupatorium maculatum*), and boneset (*Eupatorium perfoliatum*). These few species were but a small sampling of the diverse range of species that had once covered the region.

Strong Design for New Gardeners

Susan and David were very enthusiastic about developing their new yard, but they didn't bring much hands-on gardening experience to the project. While they expected to learn as they went along, they wanted a strong design that wouldn't falter due to an occasional misjudgment or time shortage. They looked forward to doing as much of the work themselves as possible. After all, they had moved to this subdivision to have lots of outdoor space to play and learn about plants and gardening. On the other hand, they didn't have countless hours to spend weeding and fussing.

Although they realized that formal gardens meant more maintenance, they wanted a conventional garden and lawn around the house, with places for children to play and spaces for vegetable and perennial gardening. They also needed trees and shrubs to screen neighbors and provide shady places to relax outdoors. On the other hand, they wanted to restore most of their land to a near-natural condition: They hoped one day to be able to enjoy prairie plants native to the region. Naturalistic areas would not only provide their grade-school children with places for adventuring, they would also require little maintenance once established.

Getting from Fantasy to Fact

Combining a formal, conventional garden with wild, natural areas in the landscape presents a unique design challenge. How could two very different types of landscape be brought together so they added up to a satisfying whole? Burrell decided the answer was not to blend one into the other, but to design a strong, clear edge where the two styles meet and contrast with each other.

A Unifying Theme

Burrell used the arched windows on the front and back of the house as an architectural clue to the design of the garden. The division between the formal lawns and gardens, and the prairie beyond is a sweeping curve based on these arched windows. An arched arbor, which is the main gateway between the formal gardens behind the house and the backyard prairie, also echoes the arched windows. The same curving theme reappears in the horseshoe-shaped council ring near the back of the property.

Susan and David's available time dictated that the design be phased-in over a few years. They concentrated on the lawn and formal garden areas around the house during the first phase. After that, they began the process of planting and developing the prairie and the shelterbelt along the back of the lot.

First Steps

The first thing Susan and David planted was a grove of four bur oaks (*Quercus macrocarpa*) on the knoll in front of the house. Bur oaks are prairie natives that would naturally have grown on such a knoll. Here, in addition to forming the beginnings of a natural-looking prairie island, the grove acts as a distinctive landmark for the house. The trees also form a privacy screen and a gateway where the driveway curves under them. Susan and David planted two more bur oaks along with a northern red oak (*Q. rubra*) between the house and the south property line. These shade the patio and main deck. They also screen them from the view of a neighbor, who gladly gave permission to plant the oaks on the property line.

During phase one, Susan and David also replaced the annual ryegrass cover crop that the developer had seeded around the house. They selected a slow-growing, drought-resistant lawn grass that was well adapted to their area. Since they felt it would be too much if the prairie came right up to the house, Burrell's design called for a conventional lawn as a buffer around the house, both in front and in back.

Susan and David also added plantings at the front of the house, along with a new paved front walk so visitors could easily travel from the parking area to the front door. A formal planting of perennial flowers intermixed with native prairie plants, located inside the walkway along the house, makes for a cheerful and welcoming front entrance. A small semicircle of lawn reaches out beyond the walkway to the edge of the prairie.

Burrell used native shrubs throughout the property, and the foundation plants around the entry area were no exception. Clumps of black chokeberry (*Aronia melanocarpa*) frame the front door. A planting of smooth sumac (*Rhus glabra*) and wild plum (*Prunus americana*) wraps around the southeast corner of the house. These plantings soften the hard architectural edges of the house and help tie it to the site.

Areas for Games and Gardening

The lawn behind the house is quite a bit larger than the one in front: It's extensive enough for playing games like soccer and volleyball. Because the land slopes away from the house, Burrell had to fill in

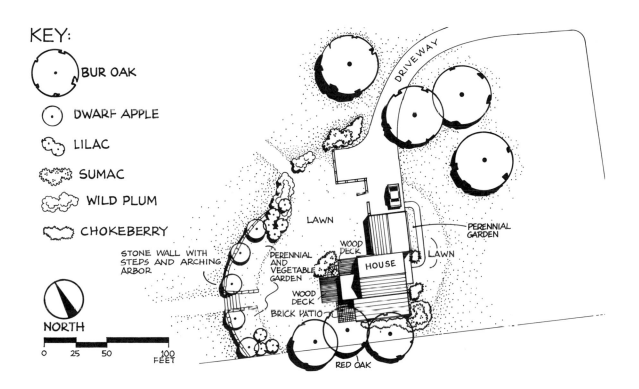

For the owners of this midwestern garden, designer C. Colston Burrell combined a conventional garden—planted in flowers, vegetables, and lawn—with natural areas. He used a two-phase plan to make the project more manageable for the owners. In phase one, shown here, he developed the area around the house by planting shrubs, a grove of bur oaks, and a garden filled with flowers, fruits, and vegetables surrounding a lawn in back. Burrell used an arched window on the house as inspiration when he designed the shape of the stone wall that divides the conventional garden from the natural areas.

the area to form a nearly level lawn. A retaining wall made of limestone marks the sweeping curve that divides the formal lawn and garden from the prairie beyond. The retaining wall is a ha-ha wall, which means it's built into the slope and is only visible from below. Susan and David can't see it when they look out from the house, but looking at it from the back, toward the house, it's easy to see how it separates the wild and tamed spaces of the garden.

A semicircular garden bed, located just inside the retaining wall, also mirrors the shape of the arched windows on the house that link this design together. It's planted with five dwarf apple trees, with dwarf lilacs anchoring the ends of the bed. The lilacs give way to low, mounded thickets of wild plums (*Prunus americana*) on the north end. In between, there's plenty of room for flowering perennials and annual vegetable crops such as tomatoes, chard, eggplant, and peppers. Together, these plantings form a garden that's both beautiful and productive. An in-ground irrigation system in the bed guarantees regular watering.

Both the retaining wall and the garden bed are cut by limestone steps that lead to the prairie. A vine-covered arbor marks the cut and forms an inviting gateway. The arbor also echoes the arched shape essential to the design.

There is a gap in the thicket of wild plums at the north end of the bed that forms a second gateway to the prairie. To the right of this gateway is an opening where the prairie meets the lawn. Prairie grasses spill over onto the edge of the lawn and among the shrubs, giving this area an informal character. A taller thicket of smooth sumac and black chokeberry along the driveway turnaround completes the sweeping arc of the back lawn.

Places to Sit

Susan and David wanted plenty of areas near the house to sit and watch their children's athletic antics on the lawn or enjoy the view of the garden and prairie. For this reason, wooden decks on two levels and a brick patio hug the back of the house.

The upper deck opens off the family room and is the main crossroads between house and garden. Susan and David can look out the kitchen windows and see the deck and the adjacent lawn area. In summer, they often put an inflatable pool on the lawn in view of the kitchen so the children can splash happily while still being close by.

A semicircular flight of steps descends from the upper deck to the large lower one. This is the most heavily used of the three seating areas, perhaps because it's surrounded on three sides by grass and shrubs, and seems to belong more to the garden than to the house. The whole family enjoys this deck for eating fresh-air meals, relaxing with friends, and watching the sun set over the prairie.

The decks also serve a second function; they were an effective way to deal with the sloping ground next to the house. At the base of the circular stairs that connects the two, Burrell also added a clump of smooth sumac on one side and a dwarf lilac on the other to help hold the sloping ground.

Susan and David asked for a brick

patio at the southwest corner of the house, because they feared that the sight of too much wooden deck would be oppressive. Situated two steps below the large deck, it is a quiet, secluded spot, partly screened by the house and shaded by the oak trees. Glass doors open from the patio to the den on the lowest level of the house for easy access.

Moving Out to the Prairie

Once phase one was complete, Susan and David were ready to move out from the house and start developing the prairie areas Burrell had designed for them. Here in its native setting, a prairie landscape offers many advantages—both practical and ethical. A prairie's requirements for water, care, fertilizers, and chemicals are nearly nonexistent here in the Midwest—after a few years of work to help it get established, anyway. It attracts wildlife and plays a part in preserving the seed bank of native plants. It is also astonishingly and subtly beautiful year-round. Susan and David find that one of the best ways to appreciate its delicacy is to explore it. They enjoy getting as close as possible to each flower and curious seed.

Planting a Prairie

During phase one, Susan and David did one thing that helped get the areas that were to be planted in the prairie ready for seeding: They patrolled regularly and removed annual weeds before they went to seed. In one instance, Susan collected 11 bags full of a persistent and prolific weed just before its seed dropped. Otherwise its seed would have germinated like crazy when the field was plowed to sow the prairie. Susan and David's regular patrols significantly reduced the amount of weeding that was necessary to ensure the survival of new native prairie plant seedlings.

In early spring once they were ready to plant, they had the areas that were to be seeded in prairie plowed and harrowed to make a fine seedbed. Then Susan and David broadcast each area with a mixture of seeds selected especially for the site. All the seed mixes used on the property had quick-germinating annual ryegrass added to prevent erosion and suppress weeds. Once the prairie plants started to grow, Susan and David mowed the heads off the rye. That way it wouldn't produce much seed, but it would still hold the soil.

Burrell was careful to choose the right mix of plants for each area—based on soil moisture and the ultimate plant height he was looking for. He also wanted to ease the transition between Susan and David's yard and the closely cropped turf of their close neighbors. To make sure neighbors didn't view the new prairie as simply tall and unkempt, he wanted to avoid having a sharp line between it and neighboring lawns. For this reason, Burrell planted much of the front yard with shorter plants that typically are found in dry-prairie areas where the soil is in transition from sandy to loamy. In back, he used a more typical mix of taller prairie plants that would grow well on the loamy soil of the site.

Native grasses form the backbone of all the mixes Burrell used. These include sideoats grama (*Bouteloua curtipendula*), little bluestem (*Schizachyrium scoparium*),

(continued on page 100)

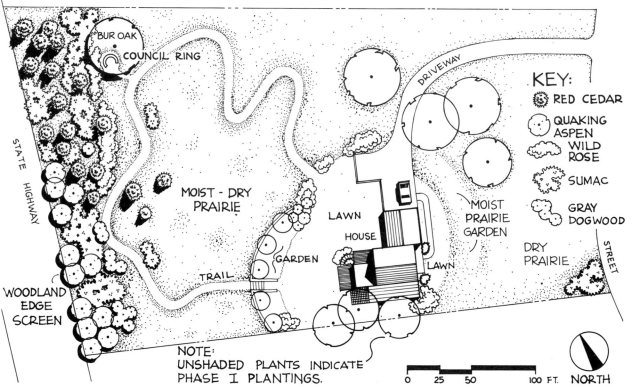

BUR OAK

COUNCIL RING

STATE HIGHWAY

MOIST - DRY PRAIRIE

TRAIL

WOODLAND EDGE SCREEN

DRIVEWAY

KEY:
RED CEDAR
QUAKING ASPEN
WILD ROSE
SUMAC
GRAY DOGWOOD

LAWN
HOUSE
GARDEN

MOIST PRAIRIE GARDEN

LAWN

DRY PRAIRIE

STREET

NOTE:
UNSHADED PLANTS INDICATE PHASE I PLANTINGS.

0   25   50   100 FT.   NORTH

Phase two of this garden called for a denser, wider shelterbelt to screen the sights and sounds of the state highway—as well as the stiff northwest winds. The trees and shrubs in the shelterbelt are all native and will thrive with little care. On the rest of the property, Burrell seeded plantings of native grasses and wildflowers to re-create the prairie communities that once dominated the area. Once established, they'll require little annual care. A trail through the new backyard prairie provides plenty of opportunity for enjoying the plants up close.

PLANTING NOTES

When re-creating a native ecosystem, especially a prairie, it's important to select the correct species and types of native plants for the site. Designer C. Colston Burrell took a careful look at the landscape and the soil, and then chose plants that would thrive in the conditions available. He developed four separate mixes—two for the front yard and two for the back. Native grasses form the backbone of all four mixes. These include sideoats grama (*Bouteloua curtipendula*), switchgrass (*Panicum virgatum*), little bluestem (*Schizachyrium scoparium*), and prairie dropseed (*Sporobolus heterolepis*).

Short-Prairie Mixes

The front yard was seeded with mixes of shorter plants so the yard would blend more effectively with neighbors' yards. He seeded a number of wildflowers throughout the area, because they would grow well in both the drier and moister portions of the yard. These included lead plant (*Amorpha canescens*), long-headed thimbleweed (*Anemone cylindrica*), heath aster (*Aster ericoides*), stiff coreopsis (*Coreopsis palmata*), purple prairie clover (*Petalostemon purpureum*), and black-eyed Susan (*Rudbeckia hirta*).

The land nearest the road and on the knoll in front was the highest and best-drained part of the property. Here, he seeded the basic grass mixture combined with a variety of native prairie wildflowers. Many of these are also familiar garden plants, including pasque flower (*Anemone patens*), white sage (*Artemisia ludoviciana*), butterfly weed (*Asclepias tuberosa*), and dotted blazingstar (*Liatris punctata*). The mixture also included some less well known prairie natives such as field pussy-toes (*Antennaria neglecta*), azure aster (*Aster azureus*), long-plumed purple avens (*Geum triflorum*), downy phlox (*Phlox pilosa*), and gray goldenrod (*Solidago nemoralis*).

For the moister, low-lying areas in front of the house he planted little bluestem, Kalm's brome (*Bromus kalmii*), and prairie dropseed. To round out the short moist-prairie mixture, he added prairie onions (*Allium stellatum*), smooth aster (*Aster laevis*), Virginia mountain mint (*Pycnanthemum virginianum*), and golden Alexanders (*Zizia aurea*).

Tall-Prairie Mixes

The land behind the house ranges from moist to dry, depending on the location. Here, to capture the true feel of a tallgrass prairie, Burrell used somewhat taller plants that were well suited to all but the very lowest, and therefore most moist, areas. For the backyard he augmented the basic grass mixture with towering big bluestem (*Andropogon gerardii*) and Indian grass (*Sorghastrum avenaceum*). He added some taller species to the wildflower mix used in front as well, including wild bergamot (*Monarda fistulosa*), stiff goldenrod (*Solidago rigida*), and hoary vervain (*Verbena stricta*).

The moist, low-lying areas of prairie behind the house are sown with tall grasses, including big bluestem, switchgrass, and Canada wild rye (*Elymus canadensis*). The moist prairie areas are especially vibrant. They're planted with spotted Joe-Pye weed (*Eupatorium maculatum*), wild bergamot, stiff goldenrod (*Solidago rigida*), Canada goldenrod (*S. canadensis*), New England aster (*Aster novae-angliae*), and Maximilian sunflower (*Helianthus maximiliani*).

Dwarf apple trees, colorful flowers, and productive vegetables form a pleasing medley above the retaining wall that separates the formal and wild parts of this landscape. Looking back from the prairie to the house, it's easy to see that the arched arbor repeats the shape of a window on the house. The arbor serves

as an ornamental door, linking the lawn and gardens to the prairie below. A second arbor marks the edge of the driveway. This once-bare landscape now boasts a pleasant patio shaded by a red oak, plenty of lawn for children to play on, and plants that provide color galore throughout the season.

and prairie dropseed (*Sporobolus hetero-lepis*). Each area—the dry to moist areas in the back along with moister, low-lying areas in front and back—was seeded with a slightly different mix.

Prairie plants are slow to establish, and the year after planting was the hardest for Susan and David. Regular weeding is critical at this stage to help the desirable prairie plants get established. If the weeds got out of hand, Susan and David could have mown over the whole prairie (with their mower set at its highest level) once or twice a year. This would keep the weeds from going to seed and would reduce future weed problems. By the third year, the prairie had really begun to take hold. Since then, it has become more interesting and diverse every year.

A Prairie Trail

Burrell knew Susan and David wanted to be able to enjoy their new prairie firsthand. For this reason, he designed a meandering trail through the prairie and past the new woodland shelterbelt at the back of the property that provides plenty

Visitors who walk through the arbor and pause at the top of the stone steps are treated to a panoramic view of the prairie and shelterbelt beyond. Clumps of smooth sumac, with red candlelike seed clusters, and Eastern red cedars punctuate the landscape. Once visitors descend the steps into the prairie, the tassels of native grasses like big bluestem wave overhead, and the mown trail lures them on to explore the rolling landscape.

of opportunity for experiencing the plants and animals found there.

The trail begins on the lawn behind the house, where the steps cut through the arching retaining wall and garden bed. From atop the steps, a barn and lake are visible in the distance across the highway, which is completely screened from view by the new woodland shelterbelt.

Once visitors pass under the arbor and descend the limestone steps, they become totally immersed in the unique experience of a tallgrass prairie. The trail enters the prairie at a low point, and the barn and lake are immediately hidden from view. In the height of summer, the tassels of big bluestem (*Andropogon gerardii*) can reach 7 feet or more; they and other prairie grasses and wildflowers block out everything but the sky.

The mown trail follows the lay of the land as it winds through the prairie grasses and wildflowers and back toward the woodland shelterbelt. (Mown paths work better in a grassland than wood chip or compost ones, which would encourage weed seeds to germinate and grow.) The land rises gradually to the right; the moist area to the left of the trail is planted with moisture-loving natives such as Maximilian sunflowers (*Helianthus maximiliani*), Kansas gayfeathers (*Liatris pycnostachya*), and prairie coneflowers (*Ratibida columnifera*).

Plants for a Native Shelterbelt

Burrell replaced the Norway pines along the rear property line with a variety of native trees and shrubs more appropriate to the site. Eastern red cedars (*Juniperus virginiana*), which provide an evergreen screen, and clumps of quaking aspen

IN ANOTHER PLACE

Organizing a landscape that begins as a nearly empty slate can be a challenge. Here the designer used the arched shape of windows on the house as inspiration for the lines he drew across the land to divide areas and organize the garden. A design for a property like this one could also draw on the shape of the house, natural landforms, or an attractive view for inspiration.

Developing destinations in a landscape—in this case a prairie trail and "council ring"—is an effective way to get the most out of a piece of property. Whether the destination is a bench near the back corner of a yard, or a trail through a forest, meadow, or prairie, it provides a reason for getting out into the landscape and enjoying the garden close up. Without the trail that designer C. Colston Burrell created for this prairie landscape, for example, it would be just a picture to look at, not a place to live in and enjoy.

You could re-create a native prairie throughout much of the Midwest. Gardeners living in other parts of the country can create a similar effect, and reap similar benefits, by turning to grassland areas found in their own regions for inspiration—an eastern meadow, for example. Wherever you live, selecting plants native to your area is the best place to start. Don't be fooled by the prepackaged mixes that promise effortless results. Instead, look to local wildflower societies, natural areas, or local seed sources for the best mix for your property. You can even grow a small patch of prairie or meadow plants if that's all you have room for. For a more gardenlike feel, try planting extra wildflowers up front where you can enjoy them.

(*Populus tremuloides*) form the tallest part of the screen. The evergreens form a visual barrier from the highway, while the rustling foliage of the aspen provides soothing "white" noise to mask the sounds of the traffic. Both species can reach 90 feet at maturity. Gray dogwoods (*Cornus racemosa*) and smooth sumac (*Rhus glabra*) fill out the shelterbelt, while wild roses (*Rosa* spp.) thrive in the edge between the trees and the prairie.

Even before Susan and David formally planted the woodland shelterbelt, a few of each of these species sprung up voluntarily. The final plan combines both planted specimens and self-sown ones.

At the edge of the woodland, the trail swerves right, and from here it's possible to look back across the lower prairie to the retaining wall, arbor, and house beyond. Then the trail continues, meandering along the edge between the prairie and woodland.

The Council Ring

The trail begins to climb a small hill near the back corner of the property. Just before it turns back toward the house, a side trail branches away to the left. This leads to a "council ring" nestled just below the crest of the hill, under a bur oak planted just to shade it. The ring features a horseshoe-shaped bench made out of pieces of limestone left over from building the retaining wall.

Susan and David find this secluded destination a perfect place for holding informal family meetings. The tradition of a special, neutral place for discussions can be traced in both Scandinavian and Native American culture. The children also love to use the ring as part of their fantasy games—such as pretending to be lost pioneers—because it seems so remote.

Burrell decided to locate the council ring at the farthest corner for several reasons. He knew it would be most effective if it seemed like destination of its own—remote and removed from the everyday world. Locating it away from the house at the end of a meandering path also makes the property feel larger. It also seems more private set into the far side of the knoll. Although this put it rather close to the highway, it's 20 feet higher and thickly screened by trees, so noise isn't really too much of a problem.

Beyond the council ring, the trail winds along a ridge to the top of the backyard knoll, where the prairie spreads out on all sides. From here, the trail snakes along the descending contours of the land back toward the plum gateway and the lawn.

Looking to the Future

Susan and David watch their prairie from day to day and year to year. They mow it once a year in late winter or early spring so they can enjoy the colors and textures of the dried grasses and other plants through the winter months. They're not the only ones who enjoy the prairie. It's also a rich source of food for birds and other wildlife throughout the year.

The family will continue to weed out invasive, non-native plants from time to time. In addition, they plan on seeding in and plugging in nursery-propagated native wildflowers that either haven't become well established or that they'd like to have more of.

One maintenance chore they won't have is watering. Since the plants in nearly all

NOTES FROM THE DESIGNER

"There's so much misinformation given about prairies," says Minneapolis-based designer C. Colston Burrell. One of the worst misconceptions is that planting a prairie—or a meadow, for that matter—takes no more effort than sprinkling a can of premixed seeds on bare soil. Prairies and meadows grown from site-specific seed mixes take quite a bit of maintenance in the first few years (mainly in the form of careful weeding), until they've become established. After that, they require little more than an annual mowing to control weeds. Most of the prepackaged meadow mixes, on the other hand, require a lot of maintenance to look their best. They're only suited for growing like annuals—in a conventional prepared bed that's replanted every season or two. These mixes generally consist primarily of flowers, many of which are not native, and usually don't contain the array of native grasses that's an essential part of a meadow or prairie.

For best results, Burrell recommends making a site-specific mix of species, as he did for Susan and David. "Prepackaged mixes are, at best, regional," he says. "And in that case, you're wasting money on plants that aren't suited to your site."

To make a mix especially for your own site, start by making a list of plant species that will thrive in the soil moisture, light level, and exposure that you have available. In addition to looking at what's growing on your own property, Burrell recommends looking for nearby sites that are similar to your own. For example, if you have a dry, sandy hillside, look for plants growing on a similar site; plants you find growing in a moist bottomland won't be appropriate, regardless of how close they are growing to your property. Natural areas that have similar conditions are ideal. Identify the plants there and add them to your list. Then order seed of the individual species from a nursery specializing in native plants. (See Appendix C on page 330 for addresses. Local botanical gardens or arboreta are also good sources of native plants.) You may be able to collect seed of common grasses and wildflowers, but be sure to get the property owner's permission. Once you have all the types of seed you need, prepare the soil, mix the seed, and sow as Susan and David did.

Whether you're growing a meadow or prairie garden, Burrell warns clients not to expect a solid mass of color all season long. "A meadow is a beautiful and wonderful thing, richly carpeted with grasses and plants that come and go. It's very subtle." Natural landscapes like this one are best appreciated by watching them change day to day and season to season—as flowers bloom, seed heads appear, and grasses ripen.

of their landscape are native, they're well adapted to the local conditions and will thrive even if left to respond to the whims of weather. Even the lawn is seeded in drought-tolerant grasses.

Neighbors have already noticed the advantages Susan and David are enjoying from their prairie plantings. Already, a few have expressed interest in creating common areas of prairie along property lines and in the farther reaches of their lots. Over time, Susan and David hope more neighbors will want to create and nurture their own native landscapes. ◆

CELEBRATING A DESERT LANDSCAPE

The owners of this acre of desert near Phoenix knew the property had loads of potential when they first saw it. With their children grown and gone, Patrice and John had been looking for a home that could suit their dream of lots of private space set within the austere beauty of the desert they'd come to love. This place was just what they were looking for: It combined a contemporary-style home with a natural desert landscape crossed by two shallow washes, which fill briefly after sudden desert rainstorms. It also commands a spectacular view of the rolling desert beyond its boundaries.

The Place and the People

Patrice and John wanted a landscape that celebrated the area's rich native plant and animal life. The whole neighborhood has a desert flavor (there are progressive deed restrictions that ensure desert-style architecture and vegetation), and they wanted their property to blend with the local landscape.

They hoped their modern home could become the center of a lush but low-maintenance oasis that provided a variety of comfortable outdoor living spaces. For them, the ideal design wouldn't reveal everything at once; instead, it would provide intriguing views, places to explore, and of

KEY CONCEPTS FOR A SUCCESSFUL DESIGN

Creating private spaces in the front yard. Plantings and a gentle, newly created rise screen the front of this desert house to create private spaces near the front door. Enhanced plantings along the driveway make the trip from street to door almost like a journey into the wilderness.

Designing with native plants. In this garden, plantings that feature desert natives illustrate why using native plants makes so much sense. The garden celebrates the colors and textures of the native landscape and requires a minimum of maintenance.

Accepting natural drainage patterns. This design accommodates the land's natural drainage patterns and keeps them intact, thus preventing problems each time it rains. Working with the natural pathways by which water drains off the land, such as the washes on this property, is vital to the success of any design.

Using design to unify a garden. Repetition of elements helps unify this garden. Boulders on the terraces repeat the shapes of nearby mountains and a series of lines echo the shape of the house to link the two together. Building elements such as the pinkish cinder block used in the house and throughout the garden also unify the design.

course, areas to rest and relax. They wanted to attract rabbits, ground squirrels, lizards, and birds to the garden. In addition, they wanted to take advantage of panoramic views of the surrounding countryside, while screening themselves from the sights and sounds of neighbors. Other needs included guest parking, a vegetable garden, and a dog run.

Landscape architect Carol Shuler helped them accomplish these goals. Plantings of desert-adapted plants and gentle sculpting of the land combine to create a private yet open landscape in which to live. She also developed a design that would use water wisely—an all-important factor in this arid area.

A Plan for Desert Rains and Washes

Many people who aren't familiar with the American Southwest imagine a bleak and barren desert right out of an old western. They expect painted mesas, sagebrush, and the occasional cactus. In fact, America's deserts are quite varied. The Arizona upland section of the Sonoran Desert, where this garden is located, is a surprisingly lush region, which has many trees and large succulent plants that retain water. The plants in this desert landscape provide a continually changing panorama of colors and forms.

The Arizona upland has three rainy seasons a year. From July through September, monsoons come out of Mexico, delivering high-intensity rains that fall and then rush off the land in a very short time. These are very spotty storms, with one city block getting rain while the next one

stays dry. In the fall, from September through November, coastal influences bring more-damaging storms, which cover the whole area with heavy rainfall for several days. From December through April, rainstorms come from the west or northwest. Total annual rainfall varies widely from place to place depending on the proximity of a site to mountains that catch rain clouds. Phoenix gets 6 to 7 inches; Tucson gets about 1 foot; while Carefree, which is right up against the mountains, averages 17 to 18 inches. In this region, knowing the average rainfall a site receives is an especially important part of a successful design.

The lay of the land is characterized by the washes, or dry stream beds, that cross it. Think of a wash as a creek-in-waiting for the next storm. When rains do come, washes carry a great deal of water off the land in a very short period of time. For this reason, property owners are prohibited from disrupting the system of washes. Usually it's acceptable to divert a wash within one's property, but the places that it enters and exits the property must remain the same. That way, the natural system of washes will continue to work from one property to the next.

The presence of washes on and around Patrice and John's suburban acre dictate everything from the location of the house to the planting plan. The house sits on a *bajada*—a rolling plain of alluvium (sand and gravel) that has washed down over the eons from the mountains. Clumps of native trees, including palo verde (*Cercidium floridum*), and saguaro cacti (*Carnegiea gigantea*) mark the front of the property. Two shallow washes, 3 to 4 feet deep, run diagonally across the long, rectangular lot, dividing it roughly into thirds. A driveway dips across these washes and loops in front of the house. Just off the property's northeast corner is a much bigger wash, about 20 feet wide and 20 feet deep, with a sandy bottom. Neighboring houses are located as far away as possible from this wash, because it's such a major drainage-

way. This deep wash also creates a nice vista from the back of the house.

Patrice and John's modern, angular house, designed by a follower of Frank Lloyd Wright, is built of pinkish concrete block in two sizes for a patterned surface, and has a flat roof. It's situated very close to the rear property line to avoid the washes in front. This leaves little space behind the

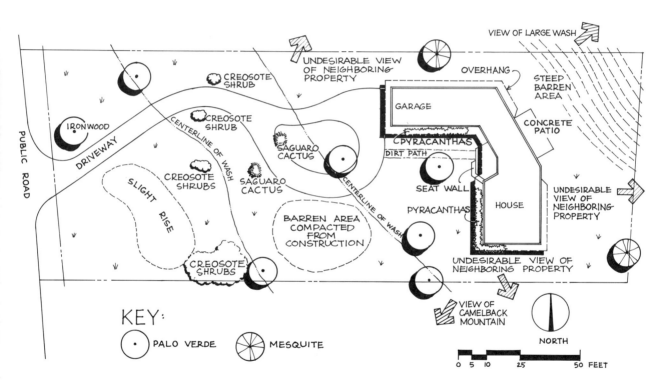

This suburban acre of high desert, located near Phoenix, Arizona, had lots of potential, but it had its share of problems, too. The lot was sparsely covered with native shrubs and trees and crossed by two shallow washes. The modern, angular house (built in the style of Frank Lloyd Wright) needed shade and plantings to provide privacy from close neighbors. It's also located close to the rear property line, which left a nearly barren backyard that was steep and unusable. The backyard overlooks not only an unattractive house but also a deep wash, and there's a spectacular view of Camelback Mountain in the distance.

house for private areas. A small slab of plain concrete served as a patio, and the area had no shade at all.

In front of the house, a dirt path led to the front door and a few pyracanthas (*Pyracantha* spp.) grew at the base of the house. South of the driveway was a barren area of ground, probably where construction equipment and materials were located while the house was being built. Patrice and John wanted to screen the neighboring houses on either side, which are set forward on their lots, to provide more privacy.

Getting from Fantasy to Fact

All along, Patrice and John planned on a head-to-toe renovation of the property. They added a master bath and a breakfast area to the house, and the excavation from this addition provided fill dirt to use elsewhere on the site.

Outside, they wanted to enhance the desert landscape around them. They knew they wanted to spruce up the entry of the house and add new patio areas, including a private, walled-off one adjacent to the new bathroom for sunbathing. Although it was hard to imagine that the small space behind the house could accommodate a swimming pool and spa, they wanted room to float two rafts and relax in the water. Developing the backyard made it important to screen a small, dark-pink, fifties-era house just over the rear property line. They also took advantage of the opportunity to open up the view across the large wash beyond the rear of the property.

Tough Plants for a Tough Place

Native plants form the backbone of all the plantings that Shuler designed for Patrice and John's house because they flourish in this harsh climate. Desert natives thrive in the existing soil, which is alkaline and made up primarily of decomposed granite, without supplemental fertilizer or organic matter. For this reason, they're the perfect choice for desert plantings—especially low-maintenance ones. Yet it's only recently, thanks to the efforts of conservationists, nursery owners, and designers like Shuler, that people are beginning to want to live in the midst of a natural-looking desert landscape. All too often, landscapes in this arid region are planted with water-guzzling lawns and other plants unsuited to the natural conditions of the area.

In addition to native plants, Shuler selected species from arid regions of Australia, Africa, and Mexico that will grow well in the Sonoran desert without becoming invasive. Regardless of origin, all fit in with the color, texture, and scale of the desert. In color, desert natives tend toward the cooler tones of olive, blue-green, and gray—all colors that reflect the heat. Most arid-zone plants have small, fine leaves, with a leathery or waxy coating, so they lose very little moisture to evaporation. The leaves of some species turn during the day, so the edge of the leaf is always toward the sun. This adaptation also reduces moisture loss.

Although the maximum height for trees is only about 20 feet, they're used
(continued on page 112)

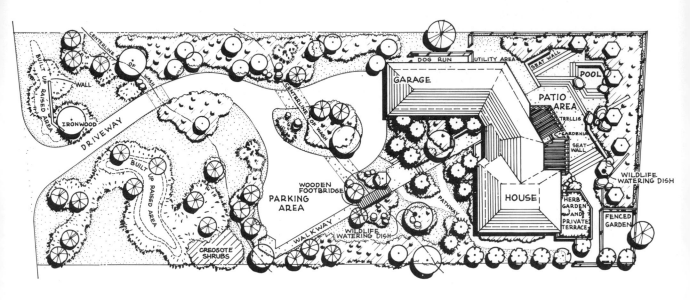

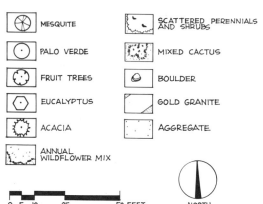

⊕ MESQUITE		SCATTERED PERENNIALS AND SHRUBS
⊙ PALO VERDE		MIXED CACTUS
✿ FRUIT TREES		BOULDER
⬡ EUCALYPTUS		GOLD GRANITE
✲ ACACIA		AGGREGATE
ANNUAL WILDFLOWER MIX		

0 5 10   25   50 FEET

NORTH

Landscape architect Carol Shuler's plan for this lot made the
most of the desert landscape and created a uniquely beautiful
garden. New parking spaces for visitors and an intriguing walkway to the front door created a welcoming entrance. In back,
the steep slopes were transformed into a series of patios and
terraces with a small pool for cooling off during the day. There's
plenty of shade, too—from both drought-tolerant trees and a
vine-covered trellis in back. Plantings of drought-tolerant trees,
shrubs, perennials, and wildflowers screen views of neighboring
houses and provide a rich desert setting.

PLANTING NOTES

Patrice and John's property features a wide variety of native and drought-adapted plants. Because of their interest in ethnobotanical species, Patrice and John chose many plants that were used by Native Americans for food, fiber, and medicine. For example, plantings of saguaro cacti (*Carnegiea gigantea*) on either side of the driveway provide magnificent gateposts halfway to the house. Native Indians ate their red, egg-shaped fruits. Saguaros are also important shelter and food plants for wildlife. Another edible cactus is blue-blade (*Opuntia violacea* var. *santa-rita*), which is a purplish form of the familiar prickly pear. It yields edible pads featured in Mexican cooking.

Pendulous yucca (*Yucca recurvifolia*) represents a genus of plants of great importance to desert Indians, who used the leaves, flowers, and roots of many different yucca species. The leaves provided fiber for baskets and sandals; the flowers could be cooked and eaten, or fermented to make a drink; and the roots served as a soap.

Ocotillo (*Fouquieria splendens*) is yet another ethnobotanical. Native Americans ate its flowers and seedpods and used the flowers to make drinks. In addition, the bark yielded a wax and the powdered root, a wound dressing.

Many legumes, or pea relatives, do well in poor desert soils. Some feature fragrant flowers and sweet edible pods and seeds. The garden includes palo verde (*Cercidium floridum*), western honey mesquite (*Prosopis glandulosa* var. *torreyana*), and several different species of cassia (*Cassia* spp.), a large genus of non-native perennials, shrubs, and trees.

Other tough, desert natives on the property include quailbush (*Atriplex lentiformis*), a silvery-gray shrub that bears large quantities of small, edible seeds, and creosote bush (*Larrea tridentata*), an aromatic shrub with yellow flowers and olive green leaves. Coyote brush (*Baccharis pilularis*) is a valuable groundcover: It forms a dense evergreen mat of bright-green leaves on plants 1 to 2 feet high.

Flowers for Color

The garden includes a variety of drought-adapted flowers, such as evening primroses (*Oenothera berlandieri* and *O. caespitosa*), which produce fragrant 2- to 4-inch white flowers that open in the evening and turn rosy pink as they age. Bright scarlet firecracker penstemon (*Penstemon eatonii*) and a native rose-colored penstemon (*P. parryi*) bear vibrant 3-foot spikes of flowers and attract hummingbirds. Sweet marigold (*Tagetes lucida*) bears small, brilliant gold flowers. Cape weed (*Arctotheca calendula*), a South African native, adds a gray-green carpet of leaves throughout the year and 2-inch yellow daisies in spring.

Plants for Near the House

Patrice and John delight in their native desert landscape but wanted to surround the house with more lush-looking but still drought-resistant plants. Green groundcovers such as creeping fig (*Ficus pumila*) and 'Hahn's Self-Branching' English ivy (*Hedera helix* 'Hahn's Self-Branching') are used in shady areas near the house for a cool-looking carpet. The exotic flowers of Barbados pride (*Caesalpinia pulcherrima*) and bird-of-paradise (*Strelitzia reginae*) add a tropical air to the patios.

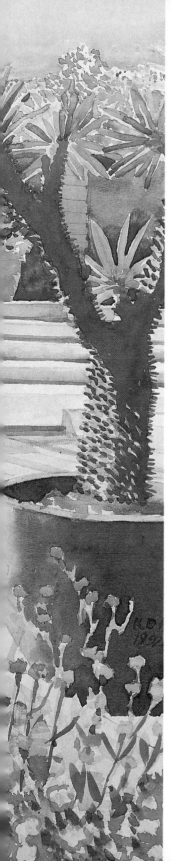

*The once-barren backyard has been transformed into a verita-
ble oasis. The pool, set near the bottom of the slope so it would
be natural-looking, is surrounded by terraces. Rocks and plants
set among the terrace walls repeat the shapes and colors of the
landscape beyond the boundaries of the property. They're especially effective at bringing the view of Camelback Mountain into
the garden. Water trickling off a cluster of boulders into the pool
produces a gentle, relaxing sound. The lines of the terraces also
echo the architectural style of the house, thus linking the two. The
lush green foliage and fragrant yellow flowers of Carolina jasmine clamber across the trellis over the patio to shade the sitting
area beneath.*

throughout this design as they would be in any garden: to add interest, to provide shade for people and smaller plants, and to screen undesirable views. Western honey mesquite (*Prosopis glandulosa* var. *torreyana*) and palo verde (*Cercidium floridum*) are two trees native to the Sonoran desert that Shuler included. She also planted willow acacia (*Acacia salicina*) and two members of the vast genus *Eucalyptus,* red cap gum (*Eucalyptus erythrocorys*) and swamp mallee (*E. spathulata*), all native to Australia.

Ocotillo (*Fouquieria splendens*) is an especially interesting native species that Shuler included. It's a showy, drought-deciduous native that looks like a clump of long, spiny sticks (up to 20 feet tall) stuck in the ground. Drought-deciduous plants, of which there are many, drop their leaves if the soil gets too dry. But it's not a disaster—new ones will grow when conditions become favorable. Ocotillos drop their leaves in dry seasons, only to leaf out three days after a summer monsoon. They bloom in spring, whether they have leaves or not, bearing spectacular 8- to 12-inch-long panicles of red flowers at the tip of each branch.

Shuler's plan also accommodates Patrice and John's interest in native ethnobotanical plants—plants collected and used by Native Americans for cooking, medicine, and crafts. For this reason, the design calls for agave and yucca, the leaves of which were peeled and dried to make cordage and cloth. Patrice and John also enjoy clumps of a salvia used as a substitute for oregano. As they restore disturbed parts of their lot, they want to incorporate even more of these fascinating plants. They've found it's interesting and fun to know the uses of native species; these plants are also essential ingredients in the regional cuisine of the area, which Patrice and John enjoy.

One plant you won't find in Shuler's design is lawn grass; a lawn simply needs too much water. A garden without a lawn may seem strange to visitors from areas where water isn't at such a premium, but here it makes absolute sense. Actually the decomposed granite soil here doesn't require a vegetative groundcover; the soil holds water quite well and cools roots without an additional layer of mulch. It is handsome in color and texture, and Shuler used its color to advantage throughout the design. Bare earth is visible in many parts of the garden except those close to the house, which Shuler wanted to be very lush and full.

A New Entry: Welcoming Yet Private

The areas in front of the house had not been restored since the house was constructed some 30 years ago. Patrice and John planned their remodeling and garden improvements so they could coordinate the two efforts. For example, they used the fill dirt from the excavation to build up a gentle rise over sparsely vegetated areas near the street and south of the driveway. They then planted it with palo verde and mesquite trees. The planted rise gives extra emphasis to the first wash and suggests a transitional "wall" between the street and the interior of the property. On the other side of the driveway, a second built-up rise continues the suggestion of a wall.

Knowing that it would be impossible to see the house once the new plantings were established, Patrice and John decided they'd need a landmark by the street. Shuler designed a 3-foot wall, built of the same cinder block as the house, for house numbers and a mounted mailbox. In fact, Shuler used the same cinder block throughout the garden for every new wall—a repeating detail that helps unify the whole garden.

Guests walking up to the front of the house can enjoy the shade of palo verde trees flanking the walk and take a close-up look at clumps of agave and evening primrose. The new entranceway also provides a semi-private terrace in the front yard. It's a perfect spot for sitting and watching the birds and other wildlife that come to drink from a small pool installed just for them under one of the palo verdes.

A Desert Drive

Driving into this designed landscape is like driving off the road into the desert—except that you don't need a four-wheel-drive vehicle. The illusion begins with the driveway paving itself, which is packed, decomposed "gold granite" that matches the color of the soil. Regular driving to and fro over the driveway keeps the granite packed and prevents it from becoming a muddy track. The sections of driveway that dip down through the washes are protected from erosion with concrete paving; ⅜-inch aggregate mixed into the concrete gives it a neat, pebbled look that blends well with the packed granite driveway. Boulders and massed plantings at strategic points mark the lane.

To reinforce the illusion of the driveway being a natural track through the desert, it's important to keep it as narrow as possible. Instead of widening the driveway so that cars can pass and guests park, Shuler suggested using the construction-damaged area to the right of the loop as a guest parking area. Aggregate concrete paving defines the edge of the parking area and serves as a walkway toward the house.

From the parking area, visitors cross the wash nearest the house on a wooden footbridge that leads to a landing. Here, the path from the parking area joins up with the path leading from the driveway turnaround to the house. This landing is a kind of crossroads where the flow of foot traffic from both parking areas comes together before proceeding toward the front door. From this point, you can also turn off onto a packed granite path leading around the side of the house.

IN ANOTHER PLACE

This garden isn't just about desert plants: It's a garden that celebrates the natural landscape of a particular region of the country. Wherever you live, native species are wonderful choices for your garden because they're adapted to the naturally occurring soil and weather patterns. Similar gardens in the Mojave or Chihuahuan deserts would feature different native species than those used in this Sonoran garden but would share the benefits of a water-saving landscape that thrives in the harsh desert conditions. Planting native species also makes it possible to echo the character and beauty of the surrounding landscape. It can also encourage local wildlife to take advantage of newly restored habitat and make a garden their home. Although gardens in other parts of the country—the Rocky Mountains, Midwest prairie states, or an Eastern deciduous woodland, for example—would all look different from this garden, they would share the advantages of a native land-scape. See Appendix C on page 330 for ideas on where to get more information on the native plants in your region.

By incorporating the two washes in the front yard into this design, landscape architect Carol Shuler accommodates—and in fact takes advantage of—the natural pathways by which rainwater drains off the land. Wherever you garden, it's always a good idea to know how and where rain drains off your yard—even if it means prowling around your yard with an umbrella during a rainstorm. Watching water flow off the land may help you uncover the reason one corner of the basement is always wet, or why a particular corner of the property is unusually wet or dry. Once you know where the water flows naturally, you can take steps to redirect it, if necessary. Mulching and eliminating areas of compacted soil are two other useful ways of managing water flow: Both will increase the amount of water that soaks into the soil and therefore stays on your property.

First-time guests discover a pleasant progression of spaces as they walk toward the house. As the path passes under a large, arching palo verde tree, it begins to feel more enclosed. Closer to the house, the path widens into an inviting terrace framed by a wall that doubles as a seat. The seat is a good place to watch wildlife drinking at a little nearby watering hole or to sip a morning cup of coffee while reading the paper in the shade.

The quarry tile landing at the front door, which is two steps up from the terrace, has another seat-wall. This was part of the original construction, and its angled design inspired the design of the lower seating area. The area feels surprisingly private, even though it's in what's traditionally called the front yard, because these front spaces are well screened and far from the street.

Building an Inviting Oasis

Shuler's plan for Patrice and John's once-barren backyard transformed it into an area with an inviting assortment of outdoor living spaces and pleasant vistas. Instead of a sun-baked concrete patio and conflicting views of neighboring homes, they now have an enlarged and improved rear patio, a pool, a series of private and semiprivate terraces, and an unobscured view of Camelback Mountain.

A Pleasant Transition

The greatly enlarged patio behind the house is now partially shaded by a trellis. The patio extends quite a ways beyond the outer edge of the trellis roof, but the covered portion of the patio seems as much indoors as out. This eases the transition between the two spaces, making the new outdoor spaces more inviting and thus encouraging visitors to explore them.

The trellis provides shade but isn't dark or oppressively heavy. Its structure is quite open, while it serves to shade the large east-facing windows from the early morning summer sun. The wood, which is stained a warm, light gray, blends with and complements the pinkish cinder block. Underneath the trellis, a gardenia (*Gardenia jasminoides* 'Veitchii') in a planter fills the air with heady perfume and invites guests to linger and enjoy.

Planting beds extend along the house and under the edge of the trellis at both ends. These connect the patio with the garden and add interest outside the breakfast-room windows.

The pool area is surfaced with "cool deck" paving. It is cool to walk on because its irregular surface keeps feet from making complete contact, and its porous surface absorbs water that cools the pavement as it evaporates. Narrow strips of redwood dividers provide an interesting contrast to the cool deck paving. Upper levels are paved with exposed aggregate accented by redwood dividers.

Linking with Lines

Shuler's design for the backyard creates strong links between the house, the site, and the views beyond. The straight edges of the patio, steps, and lower terrace walls echo the strong architectural lines of the house. The lines created by these structures divide the outdoor spaces from each other—the patio area from the pool, for example. They also guide the eye toward compelling views and interesting elements. The strips of exposed aggregate paving were designed with the angular theme of the patios and terraces in mind, as were the expansion joints in the pavement. The expansion joints were designed to accent different features, such as pots overflowing with bright seasonal flowers and large potted agaves. Patrice and John also find that the scored lines help break up the monotony of the large expanse of pavement.

Boulders at the ends of retaining walls seem to bring the mountains onto the terraces. They also ease transitions from one line to the next. One wall "slides" into a boulder and the next wall emerges from behind it. The boulders counter any heavy architectural feeling the terrace may have because of its expanse of paving. Finally, the native boulders tie the backyard to the distant mountains by repeating their textures, shades, and shapes.

The Essential Pool

The swimming pool is located near the bottom of the sloping backyard, down several steps below the terraces behind the house. It fits comfortably and naturally here, especially because we all know subconsciously that in nature water settles to the lowest point. Its location at the bottom of the terraces also makes the pool a pleasant getaway, which it would not be if it were smack-dab against the house.

To increase the feeling that the pool is a remote getaway, Shuler carefully designed plantings to frame an attractive view of Camelback Mountain from the pool terrace. There's an additional advantage to locating the pool below the level of the main patio: Looking south from the main patio you can see unattractive houses built on the lower slopes of the mountains beyond; they're out of sight from the lower pool terrace.

The pool is just large enough to float two rafts in as Patrice and John had planned. A bench around the pool below the water line is a nice cool place to sit and relax after a day in the hot sun. Water trickling over a cluster of rocks and falling into the pool is reminiscent of a natural spring. Patrice and John find it delightfully relaxing to listen to the soft, melodic trickling sound that the water makes as it falls from different heights and ripples over the rocks.

Other Special Spaces

Directly off the new master bathroom is a private sunken terrace enclosed by a high cinder-block wall. A glass, floor-to-ceiling window and sunken tub in the bathroom give Patrice and John a luxurious

NOTES FROM THE DESIGNER

"One of my pet peeves is home entries," says landscape architect Carol Shuler. "Many of them are so awful and uninviting. In my part of the country, if an entry doesn't look shady, you don't want to go up to the front door."

Shuler also likes entries to be exciting and contain hidden surprises. "Even in a small front yard, you can still use the idea of a staged entry to the house, so that a visitor's arrival unfolds through a series of events." In this design, visitors are treated to a desert journey on the way to the front door. They can't see the house from the road, and as they turn onto the driveway it seems as if they've left civilization altogether. Then, on the path to the front door they cross a bridge over one of the washes before they finally arrive at their destination.

One way to ensure that your landscape will appear natural, she advises, is to "augment the natural grade and blend in with the environment." In this design, the shape of the land undulates with its washes to form the base of the design layout. Native materials such as crushed granite and native desert plants blend in with the property's surroundings, linking the garden to the nearby landscape.

sensation of bathing outdoors. The terrace also provides a secluded spot for sunbathing. Not far from the kitchen, the terrace also provides a sheltered site for an herb garden. Traditional culinary and medicinal herbs are grown here, while ethnobotanicals are allowed to grow in the natural landscape areas of the desert garden.

Tucked into the southeast corner of the property is a fenced vegetable garden. Sometime in the future, a greenhouse will share the space to extend the gardening season year-round.

Pool equipment and the air conditioner are located out of sight around the northeast corner of the house. A dog run takes up the rest of the narrow strip of land between the north wall of the house and the property line. This area is quite comfortable for Patrice and John's dogs: They can get some winter sun on either end when they want it, and there's lots of shade from the house and a huge western honey mesquite tree (*Prosopis glandulosa* var. *torreyana*) on the neighboring property. The dogs live indoors most of the time but stay comfortably in their run when Patrice and John are away or have guests.

Chain-link fencing is used for the garden and dog run, and it's virtually invisible save for the pipe rail on top. The new fencing was sprayed with a commercial oxidizing agent to turn it a mottled brownish gray color that disappears into the landscape. This product was also used to disguise newly placed rocks and concrete since it darkens the surface. The concrete and rocks that form the waterfall into the pool were sprayed with it, making the concrete blend into the surroundings.

Looking to the Future

This kind of garden landscape can only get better. Trees and shrubs will fill in and mature, and perennials and annuals will spread, eventually covering the damaged areas of the yard. Patrice and John will need to pay close attention to which plants keep seeding. Native penstemons are gorgeous but not long-lived, so it's important to make sure they self-sow if they are to continue from year to year. On the other hand, some of the other wildflowers seeded along the washes have been far too proficient at self-sowing—every seed seems to germinate. Patrice and John will need to keep them under control to prevent them from squeezing out the others.

Patrice and John are conscientious stewards of their land and enjoy examining it close up. They look forward to watching the garden mature and are excited by each new bird or animal attracted to the newly restored habitat they've created. Patrice and John plan on doing the pruning and some of the routine care themselves, but a gardener comes once a month to help with maintenance. Now and then, they add a plant as the spirit moves them. Even though this is a native landscape, it's still designed for a pleasing composition. Patrice and John know what spaces they want to keep open and what views are valuable. In some parts of the garden, they have lots of latitude to add plants and let new ones volunteer; in others, the structure needs to be maintained.

Although an automatic underground irrigation system extends throughout the garden, one thing Patrice and John won't need to do very often is water: Nearly all of the plants in their desert garden will thrive with whatever rainfall is available. The vegetable garden and certain ornamental plantings—such as the gardenia in the patio planter—will need regular watering to maintain them, but that's a small price to pay for living in a desert oasis. ◆

RECLAIMING A SUBURBAN RANCH HOUSE

When Elizabeth and Matthew bought this overgrown suburban ranch house, the yard looked just like thousands of neglected, poorly designed landscapes found all over the United States. Overgrown shrubbery completely obliterated the front of the

house. Beyond mowing whatever grass chose to grow, little maintenance had been done to the yard for 20 years. And the existing plantings provided absolutely no privacy from close neighbors—in front or back.

From the moment that Elizabeth and Matthew set eyes on the yard, they saw its potential but knew this landscape needed a face-lift. In addition to removing the overgrown foundation plants and making other improvements to the garden, they wanted to convert the attached garage into a semi-independent apartment. They planned on building a new garage away from the house. They wanted a lush and livable landscape around their new home—especially with private areas in the backyard. They also realized that the house needed a welcoming, but somewhat screened, front lawn and entry area.

Designer Bruce Carnahan helped give this ranch house its much-needed face-lift. It now has an attractive new public "street-side" face. He also added a series of comfortable and useful areas beside and behind the house—and created more privacy than Elizabeth and Matthew ever thought they would have on this small suburban lot.

The Place and the People

Folks around Louisville, Kentucky, often say that if you don't like the weather, just stick around and it'll change tomorrow.

This is not an easy part of America to garden in. The weather can rapidly plunge to well below zero in winter or zoom above 100°F in summer. There's not much insulating snow in winter, which is often dry and has breezes that rob the ground of moisture. A particularly harsh winter comes every decade, damaging or killing broad-leaved evergreens, especially azaleas (*Rhododendron* spp.), hollies, and southern magnolias (*Magnolia grandiflora*).

The easy way out is to get central air-conditioning, spend the summer indoors, and ignore the landscape altogether. The previous owners of this one-story ranch house must have done just that. The yard had been left pretty much untouched over the years. It featured the standard mix of drastically overgrown yews (*Taxus* sp.) and junipers along the front, along with some overgrown crab apples, once planted for spring color. There was, however, a nice

Overgrown foundation plantings weren't the only problem to overcome on this typical suburban lot. Its new owners, who wanted to make room for a new garage and driveway, were faced with overgrown, unhealthy trees, ugly views from the backyard, an unappealing front entrance, and a busy street that was hard to turn onto. The backyard lacked privacy, and it didn't provide any reason to get out and enjoy the outdoors because it featured little more than weed-infested lawn.

hardwood shade tree in front—a pin oak (*Quercus palustris*). The rest of the plantings seemed to consist of whatever else had volunteered and hadn't gotten mown down over the years.

Most of the neighbors haven't done much better with the plantings around their homes. The property in back has an old, rusty steel storage building and a section of dated chain-link fence with green plastic slat inserts. Another section of plain chain link runs along part of the west property line.

Making a New House into a Home

New transplants from the Carolinas, Elizabeth and Matthew have a family that's in transition. They have only one child still at home—a daughter who is attending the local university. Since this is the last major move the family expects to undertake, they have persuaded Matthew's widowed mother to accompany them—with promises of separate quarters.

This house was ideal for them, because the attached garage could be converted into an attractive suite for Matthew's mother. There was also plenty of room on the property for building a new garage. Locating the new garage was a key problem to solve with this new landscape design.

Another problem concerns the driveway: In the few months the family has lived here, they've all developed a healthy respect for the busy road out front. There's a lot of fast-moving traffic that makes it hard, and at times frightening, to pull out of the driveway.

The family also missed the lush garden they'd enjoyed in the moist and mild Carolinas. In conversations with local gardeners, they discovered that many of their old favorites wouldn't survive Louisville's fickle climate. They wanted to start out with a conservative planting plan using plants they know will survive. They'll use these to create private and appealing outdoor spaces in which to entertain new friends. After that, they plan on experimenting with more tender species as they get to know the local conditions and the microclimates around their property.

Getting from Fantasy to Fact

All too often, storage and parking areas for cars take over the landscape—especially with all the comings and goings of an extended family like this one. But this design uses these spaces to advantage: The new driveway and garage are the backbone for organizing all the new spaces the family needs.

The most important decision was to locate the garage in the southwest corner of the property. There, it screens the neighbor's rusty shed and also begins to enclose and frame the backyard's open space. The driveway's new contours were then used to inspire the shape and flow of new outdoor spaces in both front and back. To satisfy the family's nostalgia for the greenery of the Carolinas, Carnahan engulfed the outdoor living spaces with a series of lush, informal plantings.

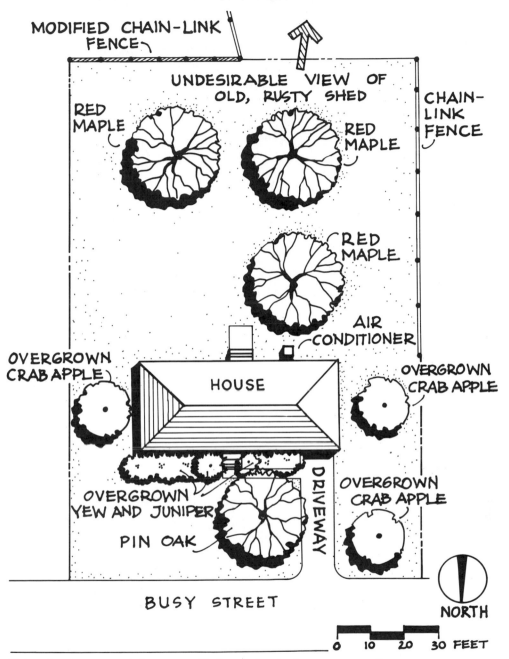

MODIFIED CHAIN-LINK FENCE

UNDESIRABLE VIEW OF OLD, RUSTY SHED

RED MAPLE

RED MAPLE

CHAIN-LINK FENCE

RED MAPLE

AIR CONDITIONER

OVERGROWN CRAB APPLE

HOUSE

OVERGROWN CRAB APPLE

OVERGROWN YEW AND JUNIPER

PIN OAK

DRIVEWAY

OVERGROWN CRAB APPLE

BUSY STREET

NORTH

0 10 20 30 FEET

This suburban ranch house, with its neglected, overgrown foundation plantings and patchy lawn, could be found in just about any city in the country. Designer Bruce Carnahan knew that a new, more welcoming street-side face would give this unkempt-looking house, located in Louisville, Kentucky, much more appeal. The large shade tree near the driveway—a pin oak—was one of the few attractive features on the property.

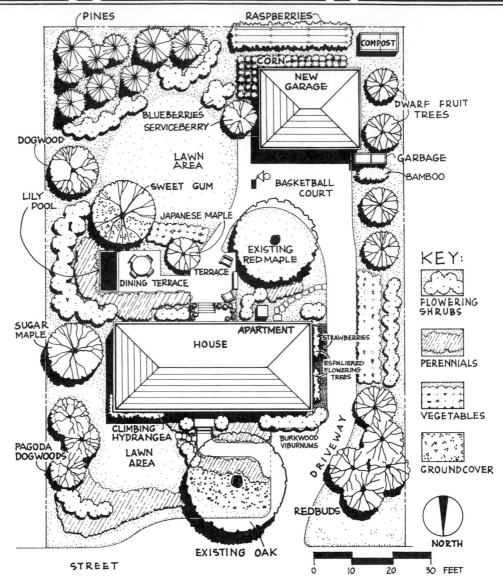

PINES
RASPBERRIES
COMPOST
CORN
NEW GARAGE
DWARF FRUIT TREES
BLUEBERRIES
SERVICEBERRY
GARBAGE
DOGWOOD
BAMBOO
LAWN AREA
SWEET GUM
BASKETBALL COURT
LILY POOL
JAPANESE MAPLE
EXISTING RED MAPLE
TERRACE
DINING TERRACE
APARTMENT
SUGAR MAPLE
HOUSE
STRAWBERRIES
ESPALIERED FLOWERING TREES
CLIMBING HYDRANGEA
BURKWOOD VIBURNUMS
PAGODA DOGWOODS
LAWN AREA
REDBUDS
DRIVEWAY
EXISTING OAK
STREET

KEY:
FLOWERING SHRUBS
PERENNIALS
VEGETABLES
GROUNDCOVER

NORTH
0   10   20   30 FEET

This design provides newfound privacy in the backyard for owners Elizabeth and Matthew. The new terraces behind the house
are surrounded with shrubs and trees, making them a private
oasis perfect for a host of outdoor activities. A bubbling fountain
in the lily pool off the dining terrace helps mask the noise of cars
on the street. The backyard is enclosed by a miniature woodland of pines and other shrubs on one corner and the new
garage on the other. This practical design also provides room for
vegetables and fruit, a compost bin, a basketball court, and
even necessities like garbage cans.

PLANTING NOTES

Elizabeth, Matthew, and designer Bruce Carnahan agreed they wanted to stick to tried-and-true plants—those nearly guaranteed to thrive—for forming the backbone of this design. This is an especially useful approach for selecting major plants that require some investment, such as trees and shrubs, because it reduces the risk of losing a valuable specimen.

Trees and shrubs native to the area provided a good start on their plant list. They also used another technique for identifying safe, reliable species: They scoured the immediate area looking for old, already-proven plantings. An area garden yielded *Miscanthus sinensis* (eulalia grass), *M. sinensis* 'Gracillimus' (maiden grass), *M. sinensis* 'Zebrinus' (zebra grass), and *Phalaris arundinacea* var. *picta* (ribbon grass), and the garden's owner was more than happy to part with divisions. She also gave them a rooted piece of an evergreen bamboo. In shady areas, Elizabeth and Matthew's garden also features native species of ferns along with tough and hardy hostas, bearded irises, and daylilies to provide spots of color and contrast.

Trees and Shrubs

Acer palmatum (Japanese maple)
Acer rubrum (red maple)
Acer saccharum (sugar maple)
Amelanchier canadensis (shadblow serviceberry)
Cercis canadensis (Eastern redbud)
Chaenomeles speciosa (flowering quince)
Cornus alternifolia (pagoda dogwood)
Cornus florida (flowering dogwood)
Cornus sericea (red-osier dogwood)
Liquidambar styraciflua (sweet gum)
Liriodendron tulipifera (tulip tree)
Myrica pensylvanica (bayberry)
Pinus nigra (Austrian pine)
Quercus palustris (pin oak)
Rhododendron 'P.J.M.' hybrids ('P.J.M.' hybrid rhododendrons)
Rhododendron spp. (azaleas)
Viburnum × burkwoodii (Burkwood viburnum)
Viburnum trilobum (American cranberrybush viburnum)
Viburnum wrightii (leatherleaf viburnum)
Weigela florida (old-fashioned weigela)

Not only is this garden beautiful, but it produces bounty for the table as well. Highbush blueberries (*Vaccinium corymbosum*) mark the edge of the back lawn, and raspberries form a living fence along part of the rear property line. Strawberries serve as a groundcover between the house and the driveway, and there's also room for growing vegetables and cut flowers.

Removing the overgrown shrubbery that blocked the front of this suburban house made a dramatic improvement. The house now has a welcoming appearance. A bed of groundcovers and shade-loving perennials replaces the patchy lawn under the pin oak, while plantings of shrubs and trees screen the neighboring houses without being unfriendly. The newly widened driveway lip

makes it easy to merge with oncoming traffic. The transformation is apparent from indoors, too. Instead of dingy, dark rooms with windows blocked by overgrown evergreens, this design lets light into the house and creates views from indoors. The view toward the street is softened by the pagoda dogwoods, leatherleaf viburnums, zebra grass, and perennial flowers.

Separating Public and Private Spaces

The front and back yards in this garden are decidedly different. While the backyard is reserved for the family's private use, plantings in front are designed for good connections with the outside world. In front, plantings are set back slightly from the lot lines and are surrounded with lawn. That way, they blend with the yards on either side, which are both well-manicured greenswards. Keeping plantings away from property lines is an excellent good-neighbor policy, especially in the front yard. It maintains a friendly continuity with neighboring properties, which may be an especially valuable bit of diplomacy for newcomers. Neighbors who are dedicated "lawn people" may not want plantings that shade their grass or compete with it for water—and people have been known to lop off overhanging branches!

Designing a Friendly Entrance

A driveway is often the single most intrusive element on a landscape. For this reason, it's important to integrate it into the overall design as logically and as gracefully as possible. Elizabeth and Matthew's new driveway has a special feature that makes it a little easier to enter and leave the busy road on which they live—Carnahan widened the lip of the driveway in front of the house along the road. This makes it safer and easier to exit from the driveway onto the street. The lip is also handy for delivery vehicles pausing in front of house. (Before you plan such a lip of your own, be sure to check local restrictions that may govern curb cuts.)

Although the main driveway curves around the house, for convenience there's a guest parking space located in front where the old driveway used to enter the garage. Burkwood viburnums (*Viburnum* × *burkwoodii*) screen the view of any parked cars from the apartment.

Guests who arrive are welcomed by a double-wide sidewalk landing along the driveway. Even after the sidewalk narrows to 50 inches, it's still wide enough for two people to walk shoulder to shoulder. It's also wide enough to accommodate the southern custom of the long good-bye, which can add a half hour to a visit as hosts accompany guests to the door, to the porch, and to the car, chatting all the way.

The new front walk is located farther out from the house than the original one. That leaves room for attractive low plantings along both sides of the walk in the shade of the handsome existing pin oak. Shade-loving hostas, ferns, mixed perennials, and groundcovers make the walk to the front door pleasant and appealing. These shade-loving plantings are work-saving, too. They flourish with little care, whereas the lawn grass they replaced under the pin oak had to struggle in the shade for survival. Elizabeth and Matthew also have less lawn to mow and no longer have to trim around the base of the tree.

Groundcovers to the left of the front door enclose the walk, but a stepping-stone path through this planting provides a shortcut for the family and the mail carrier to the lawn area beyond. Good planning nearly always accommodates shortcuts like this one. It's inevitable that family and visitors alike will use such pathways, and plantings that are in the way will ultimately suffer from careless trampling. Carnahan has ensured that this area will remain neat and that plantings won't be damaged, by adding just a few stepping stones.

Carnahan selected a climbing hydrangea (*Hydrangea anomala* subsp. *petiolaris*) to plant on the northeast corner of the house. There, it will clamber around and soften the corner without blocking the shortcut to the next-door neighbor's house. Nor does it take away valuable space from the front or side lawn. This slow-growing species can be kept under control quite easily and will provide white flowers in early summer and attractive, reddish peeling bark throughout the year.

Altogether, the front garden offers a colorful gift to the street, instead of the bland, anonymous overgrown foundation plantings that once made the house so unappealing. Plantings on either corner of the lot help to enclose the front and add to the appeal—both from the street and because of the additional privacy provided in front and on the side. A grove of eastern redbuds (*Cercis canadensis*) beside the driveway gently separates Elizabeth and Matthew's lot from the lot next door. The grove also suggests a boundary between the driveway's public and private areas, which lie beyond the house. A planting of pagoda dogwoods (*Cornus alternifolia*), mixed flowering shrubs, and perennials serves a similar purpose on the other side of the lot.

These plantings have a couple of other benefits, too. They're attractive to look at from inside the house, and they also help cut down on noise from the street beyond.

New Privacy in the Backyard

While it's considered neighborly to have front-yard plantings that blend in with adjoining yards, the backyard is widely acknowledged as private space. It's quite acceptable to completely enclose it. In this backyard, the lawn is surrounded by plantings to provide privacy and create a lush feel.

Connecting Inside and Out

Like many suburban houses, this one is built on a raised foundation, which means that a few steps are needed to get from the back door to ground level. Ideally, however, people are most comfortable when they can walk directly from inside the house to the outside without having to step down. Keeping the transition from inside to out on the same level also makes the strongest connection between house and garden.

To accomplish this, Carnahan added a landing and terrace at the same level as the back door. (A porch or deck could serve the same function in another situation.) This provides room to negotiate the door, especially when lugging a bagful of groceries, balancing a tray of appetizers, or using a cane or a walker.

The main terrace and landing are the same width and appear as one space, although they're on two levels. This all-important space connects the house to a variety of new outdoor rooms that compensate for the fact that, every so often, the house just isn't big enough. The new spaces in the backyard provide for a much greater range of activities than the nearly barren rectangle Elizabeth and Matthew had started with. During a family party of

20 people, for instance, four people can play bridge on the dining terrace by the lily pool, and the kids can skate on the driveway without disturbing the group on the terrace. Others can shuck corn on the main terrace, play croquet on the lawn, or play basketball in front of the garage.

All these activities are manageable because the outdoor spaces are clearly defined and room-size. Instead of walls, vegetation bounds each space. Gaps in the upright plantings become windows that frame views from one space to the next. For example, guests seated on the dining terrace can look through a gap between a sweet gum (*Liquidambar styraciflua*) and a Japanese maple (*Acer palmatum*) to the lawn beyond. Glimpses of the garden beyond help lure visitors out into the yard to explore.

Designing for Comfort

Another strategy for making the man-made structures look as if they belong in the landscape is to use human-size materials. The landing is built of 2×4-inch treated wood because its width is about the same as a person's foot. Likewise, the walks and terraces are paved with individual bricks, laid one by one, that are made to fit the grip of a human hand. Bricks also relate to the size of a person's foot. This tactic produces a subtle feeling of comfort that "this place was made for me because it fits," as landscape designer Bruce Carnahan likes to say.

Movable furniture is another key element that helps make visitors feel comfortable and at home in a garden. It's a fact of human nature that many people

TAKE ADVANTAGE OF MICROCLIMATES

"Gardening is forcing nature's hand," says designer Bruce Carnahan. If you're not satisfied with the safest plant choices for your climate and you want to plant things that are marginally hardy, you have to learn how to read your microclimates—the specific conditions of light, moisture, soil, wind, elevation above sea level, and so forth in various parts of your property. You can measure all these conditions by taking soil tests and using tools like a rain gauge, thermometer, light meter, and even a wind sock. In fact, exploring your yard for microclimates is part of doing a good site analysis before designing.

Once you understand each microclimate, you can exploit it. For example, Elizabeth and Matthew found that rhododendrons need protection from drying winter winds to do well in their area. They've accommodated these much-loved shrubs by planting them in protected locations and choosing cultivars that are both winter-hardy and heat-tolerant. Other spots you might want to look for include a cool area for a summer patio or a south-facing brick wall to protect a frost-tender peach tree. Don't forget to look for a shady spot for a hammock, too!

like to move a chair a few inches when they sit down. For this reason, building fixed furniture, like benches built into deck rails, can be a mistake; guests will probably be more at ease in individual chairs. While there is a permanent wooden frame on the edge of the main terrace for a hanging swing, the swing itself moves naturally when someone sits there.

A Space for Outdoor Dining

Although both terraces are on the same level, the dining terrace seems more secluded by virtue of the narrow passageway between the two spaces. A Japanese maple divides the two, gently screening one terrace from the other and creating the feel of two distinct outdoor rooms.

A simple, rectangular lily pool on the dining terrace is the garden's one formal element. A bubbling fountain, which produces soothing background noise that helps drown out sounds from the surrounding neighborhood, makes it even more pleasant to dine there. The pool is framed with

Owners Elizabeth and Matthew can enjoy the privacy of the new dining terrace whether they're enjoying a quiet dinner on a summer evening, playing cards, chatting with friends, or just sipping iced tea on a hot afternoon. The sound of moving water from the fountain and glimpses of goldfish create a special allure. And although the terrace is surrounded by plantings of arching grasses, flowering shrubs, and perennial flowers, it doesn't feel cramped or closed off from the rest of the yard.

cut limestone to establish a crisp edge and make an attractive link to the surface of the surrounding pavement. Brick, concrete, or cut wood would also work for a formal pool such as this one. Native rocks are ideal for creating a more naturalistic pool with a free-form shape.

Paths for Connecting

The Japanese maple that divides the two terraces does double duty, as it also marks a transition from the terraces to the lawn. The path leading from the main terrace toward the garage narrows as it passes the Japanese maple on one side and an existing red maple (*Acer rubrum*) on the other. It gradually widens again to open out into the driveway turnaround, which currently serves as a basketball court. The path eases the transition between the quiet, semi-secluded terrace and the backyard lawn and basketball court/turnaround — two large spaces designed for more active pursuits. A multi-trunked shadblow serviceberry (*Amelanchier canadensis*) alongside the garage marks the end of the walkway from the terrace. It provides four-season interest with its white spring flowers, black summer fruit, bright fall color, and interesting winter bark. It also helps soften the bulk of the new garage.

The basketball hoop is expressly for Elizabeth and Matthew's daughter, who is attending school on an athletic scholarship. Although it could have been located on the garage, it serves as a convenient marker of the shift from path to turnaround. More important, Elizabeth and Matthew wanted to avoid broken garage windows and circular scuffs on the garage's paint.

The pole can be easily removed at a later date, since it's attached at ground level to a threaded pipe.

Throughout this design, Carnahan has used paths that are quite fluid, meaning they expand and contract in width. Even the driveway, which is essentially a wide path, has a fluid, changing width. All too often, walkways are designed with the same width from start to finish. Allowing the walkway to be fluid, to expand and contract in width according to its function, eases transition between areas and produces a more visually interesting result.

Tying In the Garage

The new garage encloses the backyard and screens the rusty shed over the rear lot line. It also provides space for two cars and a small workshop. Although the garage and the house are separate buildings, Carnahan used the design of the garage to link the two. For this reason, the garage has a hip roof and white siding that matches the house. It's almost as if part of the house has been broken away and pushed to the back corner.

The garage is also the focus of produce gardening, with room for vegetables along the outside rear wall (they planted corn the first year) and raspberries filling in the gap in the neighbor's fence. Carnahan provided space for composting in the back corner of the lot behind the garage and dwarf fruit trees along the west property line. Along the driveway, exclusively for the use of Matthew's mother, is more space for raising vegetables and cut flowers. Stepping stones lead from the driveway to her private rear door, so she can come and go as she pleases.

IN ANOTHER PLACE

This design for a suburban lot in Louisville, Kentucky, has ideas to offer gardeners in any part of the country. There are literally hundreds of thousands of houses across America with overgrown, unattractive foundation plantings, any of which would benefit from a similar face-lift. Choosing new plants native to the area or adapted to the local climate, soil, and site, is always the best place to start. That way, the end result is a landscape that looks at home in the region and thrives with little care. In the Midwest, for example, a patch of native prairie might be used in the front bed. In the Northeast, canoe birches (*Betula papyrifera*) and native flowering shrubs would do well. In arid areas, patches of raked stones and islands of native plants could replace lawn areas.

If you have a garage that's totally out of character with the house, whether in architectural style or building materials, yet you don't have the luxury of designing a brand-new one, don't despair. Instead of a major architectural renovation, there are economical ways to get the two to blend. Paint color is perhaps the simplest. New coordinated shutters, flower boxes, windows, dormers, or doors can also tie house and garage together. Another option is to erect an outer wall of lattice and grow a wallpaper of flowering or fruiting vines over the walls of the garage.

While the new driveway and garage called for in this garden are investments that are easily recouped, a family that expects to move again within two years should be leery of making big changes. Any improvement to the garden (and the house) should be something that you really want or must have, or that will improve the site and property values, so that you'll be able to recover the investment. The more individualized a garden is, the less able someone else will be to move into it and enjoy it. The lily pool, for instance, could be a real drawback for a family with toddlers, whereas the expanded back deck and terrace is an obvious improvement because it adds beautiful and usable living space.

Adding a Backyard Forest

A miniature forest of thickly planted pines, azaleas, and rhododendrons encloses the southeastern corner of the backyard to provide complete privacy. This planting is like bringing a little bit of the Carolinas to Louisville, but it also screens the ugly, plastic-slatted fence along the rear lot line.

Because they want to continue their good relations with close neighbors, Elizabeth and Matthew have been careful to keep everyone informed during the entire renovation process. They understand it's important not only to communicate with neighbors before making changes, but also to visualize the design from the outside in, to get an idea of what the neighbors will be looking at.

So far, their efforts have been well worthwhile. They took the time to walk neighbors through the design to make sure everyone knew what was going to happen. And they've been tactful, too. To the neighbor who owns the now-screened plastic-slatted fence they explained, "We just moved from the Carolinas and we really missed the woodland." This particular neighbor, who is retired, was excited that the family was developing the garden. He got a vicarious thrill out of watching new plants go in, and it has had an impact on his space, too. Elizabeth and Matthew have made every effort to make sure that the neighbors will be as happy as they are with the new plantings.

Construction Priorities

Elizabeth and Matthew implemented much of this design in one fell swoop, soon after they bought the property. Since they had planned all along to convert the existing garage to an apartment right away, coordinating the new garage and driveway construction at the same time seemed to make the most sense. That way, they could get the mess and disruption over all at once. While they were in the midst of heavy construction, they also added the new front walk and pathways throughout the garden, along with the terraces and the landing at the back door, because these changes made it so much easier to come and go.

Once all the heavy construction was over and the bones of the garden were in place, Elizabeth and Matthew planted their backyard forest. They wanted it started as soon as possible so they could benefit from the much-needed privacy it provided in

NOTES FROM THE DESIGNER

Bruce Carnahan prefers to choose native trees that are tried-and-true. "You can experiment with the smaller stuff, especially perennials, because they are going to get frequent attention as you move them around to develop that ultimate composition. But trees are a bigger investment in money and long-term commitment." He often finds it necessary to remind people that "perennials are not forever." While they'll last for a long time, at least a few years, the light conditions are going to change as trees grow, so the perennials underneath are going to have to change, too. Bruce says, "If you're into gardening, you're into commitment, and you'll find another place for them. Just like bubble-gum cards, you can trade 'em with your friends."

Before you start any property renovation, the Louisville-based designer advises you to make a list of things you do and do not like. This applies whether you're going to have a professional develop your design or do it yourself. Starting with a list makes for clear communication up front, and ensures that you won't forget anything. It also helps avoid pitfalls and the need for major changes later. A list will ensure that you get a better job from a professional, and for the do-it-yourselfers, it makes even more sense. This way you'll solve the problems you're concerned about, and the design will fit together all the spaces you dream of having.

the backyard. They added other plants— such as the ones that screen the front of the house—as budget and time permitted.

Looking to the Future

Once their daughter moves away from home, Elizabeth and Matthew plan to remove the basketball hoop and use the space for containers of colorful annuals.

Elizabeth and Matthew haven't yet decided whether or not they want to fence in their backyard. Depending on whether they get a dog, want to keep neighborhood pets out, or need to safely contain a grand-child, they can add sections of chain link to the neighbors' existing sections along the property lines. A gate across the drive-way beside the house could be operated by remote control, just like a garage door, to open and close on command.

Chain link can be renewed and im-proved dramatically by electrostatic painting. This technique, performed by qualified contractors, is a matter of charg-ing the metal surface to attract and help the paint adhere. They could paint the fence black (with the adjoining neighbor's permission) so that it would "disappear" by fading into the background. Another option for camouflaging an ugly bound-ary fence is to cover it with vines. It's best to discuss any such changes with your neighbor first to avoid a range war. ◆

REJUVENATING AN OLDER GARDEN: NEW PLANTS AND TERRACES

Developing an inviting garden can be a challenge on a small lot—especially a corner one. When Phyllis and Norman moved to this older bungalow in Milwaukee, they were confronted with countless factors to consider and problems to overcome. The house sported a mishmash of overgrown, poorly maintained plantings. The entrance and "public" spaces generally needed to be spruced up to make them more attractive and inviting. The yard was very steeply sloped up from the sidewalk to the main level of the yard. Visitors approached the front door via a decrepit set of steps that led up from the corner of the lot.

They hoped they could create private space for outdoor dining and other activities on the lot and also screen unattractive views—all without offending the neighbors. Finally, they needed a space-efficient way to carve out utility areas for composting, a recycling bin, and trash cans.

Phyllis and Norman knew that what they wanted from this property was a tall order. Garden designer Gael Dilthey helped them realize their dreams, transforming a garden beset with problems into an attractive and usable space they could garden in and enjoy.

The Place and the People

Located not far from Lake Michigan, Phyllis and Norman's home is in an older Milwaukee neighborhood of bungalow

> ## KEY CONCEPTS FOR A SUCCESSFUL DESIGN
>
> **Terracing to tame steep slopes.** The steep slopes on two sides of this house were nearly impossible to mow and gave the house an uncomfortable, "too tall" look from the street. They've been replaced by easy-to-care-for terraced beds filled with colorful perennials, herbs, and flowering shrubs.
>
> **Making room for storage.** It's often hard to find room for a storage and utility area, especially on a small lot like this one. This design features a neat, space-efficient storage and utility corridor along with an attractive new shed that does double duty as a screen for the side-yard terraces.
>
> **Renovating an older garden.** One all-important step in fixing up an overgrown garden like this one is looking at the plants with an unsentimental eye. Before this plan was implemented, the designer removed many ugly, overgrown, and unhealthy shrubs and trees that were crowding the lot.
>
> **Making private spaces close to the street.** On a corner lot, it's particularly difficult to carve out private space. This design uses a combination of plantings, a shed, and the trickling noise of a fountain to block the sights and sounds of the street and close neighbors.

houses and steep lawns. It's a good spot for gardening, because the lake makes the climate milder. Unfortunately, the lot itself was full of problems. Located on a noisy

134

street, it's only 45 × 60 feet. Like many houses in the neighborhood, it had awkward, difficult-to-mow slopes along the street frontages—the result of a street-widening project years earlier. On two sides, the land slopes abruptly from the house down nearly 6 feet to the sidewalks, leaving 45-degree slopes that were spottily covered with grass but impossible to mow. An overgrown honeysuckle hedge held the steepest part of the slope with its thick root system, but Phyllis and Norman found that they still had to scrape washed-down soil off the sidewalk periodically.

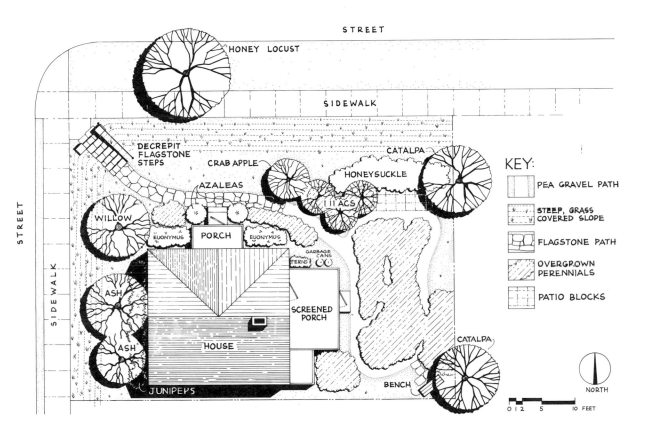

STREET

HONEY LOCUST

SIDEWALK

STREET

SIDEWALK

DECREPIT FLAGSTONE STEPS

CRAB APPLE

CATALPA

HONEYSUCKLE

AZALEAS

LILACS

WILLOW

EUONYMUS

PORCH

EUONYMUS

GARBAGE CANS

FERNS

ASH

SCREENED PORCH

ASH

HOUSE

CATALPA

BENCH

JUNIPERS

KEY:

	PEA GRAVEL PATH
	STEEP, GRASS COVERED SLOPE
	FLAGSTONE PATH
	OVERGROWN PERENNIALS
	PATIO BLOCKS

NORTH

0 1 2   5   10 FEET

Cluttered, overgrown, and unappealing were the watchwords for this corner lot. Its owners grappled with steep, grass-covered banks on two sides that were nearly impossible to mow, and the side yard was so cluttered with rampant perennials that it was hard to take a step in any direction. Sickly, overgrown trees, decrepit steps, and little privacy completed the less-than-promising picture. In addition to wanting to solve these problems, homeowners Phyllis and Norman wanted to have storage and utility space along with areas for gardening and sitting outside.

A Need for Renovation

Almost two-thirds of the property was right out front and visible from the street. Although the house is set back 20 feet from one sidewalk and 10 feet from the other, it overwhelmed the lot, looming two stories high. Foundation plantings of overgrown euonymus (*Euonymus* sp.) in front of the house, not to mention the steep lawns, only accentuated its uncomfortable stance. The foundation plantings also obscured the house's handsome facade of local stone.

Decrepit stone steps with a rusted, broken railing lead from the front corner up to the house. Not only were the steps too narrow, but over the years they had sunk and were cracked and dangerously tilted. Rakishly slanted stone pillars marked either side of the bottom step. In fact, Phyllis and Norman's homeowner's insurance company required them to replace the steps.

At the house level, a flagstone path that was hard to shovel in the winter led to awkward steps at the front door. Water draining from the porch-roof gutter ran over the path, making it especially dangerous when it froze in winter.

Plantings on the property weren't in much better condition. The main privacy plantings along the front of the lot were the overgrown honeysuckle (*Lonicera* sp.) hedge that merged with a thicket of shabby, powdery-mildew-prone lilacs with poorly colored flowers. The lilacs had overwhelmed a lopsided, poorly blooming crab apple nearby. The roots of a corkscrew willow (*Salix matsudana* 'Tortuosa') on the west side of the lot interfered with the sewer line. Two mountain ash trees (*Sorbus* sp.) next to it suffered from fire blight.

Privacy was at a premium on this small corner lot: Phyllis and Norman have neighbors very close on both sides. In fact, the house is situated only 3 feet from the rear property line. The only area they could develop into private outdoor living spaces was the side yard beyond the

The street-side view of Phyllis and Norman's house highlights some of the problems that needed solving. The dilapidated steps were unsafe, and the lopsided stone pillars were an eyesore. In addition, the steep, grassy banks created an unflattering setting for the house, which seemed to tower above the street. Unkempt trees and foundation plantings completed the less-than-appealing picture.

screened porch. However, the side yard had been so overplanted by the zealous gardener who used to live there that it was almost impossible to take a step in any direction. Paths of loose pea gravel looped through the area but were too narrow and overgrown to use. The only space for sitting was a small area paved with ugly patio blocks. Clearly, the entire property was suffering from the good intentions of a gardener with great enthusiasm but no plan.

Agenda for Change

Phyllis and Norman are an active couple who enjoy gardening and cooking together. When they first moved into this house, they concentrated on making improvements to the house, inside and out. Soon after moving in, they dressed up the second story's aging stucco with new vinyl "cedar" shakes. They also replaced the downstairs windows and reused the screens to enclose a side porch. Once they had completed the improvements they had planned for the house, they turned their attention to its setting. Their four major goals for the garden are described below.

1. A handsome appearance. They wanted the garden to present a bright and showy face that complemented the house and balanced its tall, narrow proportions. They also wanted to accomplish their renovation and still provide attractive, or at least neat, views from neighboring properties.

2. Comfortable private space. They needed to carve out private spaces to make a "backyard" where there was none. They wanted a peaceful, cozy outdoor room that

worked equally well as a place to sit alone, garden, or entertain guests. By the same token, they wanted to, in a pleasant way, discourage unwanted visits from the four neighbor children and their dog.

3. Room for plants. As devoted gardeners, they preferred a wealth of sunny, colorful plants and as little grass to mow as possible. They especially wanted room to grow a variety of perennials, herbs, and flowering shrubs.

4. Practical paths and storage areas. They had loads of practical improvements on their list. They needed steps and walkways that would be easy to shovel when it snowed, and they wanted to somehow fix the steep, impossible-to-mow slopes that were on two sides of the lot. They also needed a staging area—a work space and storage area where all the behind-the-scenes activities that support daily life go on. With no room for a garage, they needed places to put everything from wheeled trash carts to the aluminum extension ladder.

Getting from Fantasy to Fact

Designer Gael Dilthey developed a plan that solved all the many problems of this small corner lot. A series of terraces along the street sides of the lot are at the heart of her solution. Altogether, these plant-filled terraces eliminate the steep lawns and make the house appear to sit more gracefully on the lot. The terraces also provide all-important spaces for growing plants: They're now filled with a host of colorful, sun-loving perennials, annuals, herbs, and flowering shrubs. A new set of steps, designed as an integral part of the terraces, replaced the old, dilapidated ones.

As for the side yard, it became the main outdoor living area once the old, overgrown plantings were renovated and the area was screened to provide a bit of privacy. Dilthey added two terraces and a small lily pool so there would be space for a variety of activities. The narrow strip of land along the back of the house was transformed into a neat and tidy storage and utility corridor. A new shed at the rear corner of the lot adds even more storage space.

Step One: Out with the Old

When they began this project, Phyllis and Norman found out firsthand that it can be a liability to inherit someone else's garden. Their yard had a lot of very common plants, many of which were not good cultivars. Disease, poor maintenance, and overcrowding had also taken their toll. Gael Dilthey was able to look at the yard with an unsentimental eye and evaluate the quality of the existing plants. Then she chose which to save or relocate, and which to discard. This is an invaluable step in any renovation—especially of an older garden.

On the west side of the house, the diseased mountain ash trees and the corkscrew willow, whose roots were wreaking havoc with the sewer line, were among the plants that needed removing. Dilthey also decided some of the plants were worth saving: These she dug and moved to a holding bed so they'd be protected during the construction of the garden. The holding bed, located against the house's west end, was crescent-shaped and outlined in native stone.

After removing or transplanting many of the existing plantings, the major goal for phase one of this renovation was to build the terraces that would begin eliminating the awkward slopes along both streets. Then Phyllis and Norman planned on planting groundcovers and shrubs in the new terraces to make the street-facing sides of the house more attractive.

New Use for an Age-Old Technique

Terracing is an age-old technique for turning steep slopes into productive land. Here, it's used in much the same way—Dilthey's terraces convert the sloping side yards into areas that provide Phyllis and Norman with much-needed room to grow plants and experiment with different plant combinations.

From the beginning, Phyllis and Norman planned on building the extensive system of terraces themselves. All the terrace walls are built of native stone laid without mortar, so as they settle they will have a natural look. Unmortared stone walls will also be easier to repair.

Terracing can be backbreaking work, so Phyllis and Norman decided to tackle the transformation of their lot in two phases to divide the effort into manageable chunks. They built the required terraces slowly and cautiously, giving themselves time to learn how to handle the stone and develop the strength they'd need. They found the hand-laid walls became a sculpture that evolved as they progressed. As the terraces and the rest of the garden took shape, they allowed themselves the freedom to adjust the design to accommodate new ideas for the shape and spacing of the terraces.

The terraces along the west side of the property and the two lower terraced beds on the north side got phase-one priority because they reduced mowing chores and made the house's setting so much more attractive. They also provided much-

needed gardening space. In all, the phase-one stonework required 25 to 30 tons of stone. Since much of it is laid flush with the ground level along the sidewalk, however, the end result doesn't give the impression of immense quantities of stone.

As Phyllis and Norman built the walls, they planted perennials in the crevices between the stones and on top of the wall to hold the soil. These include creeping

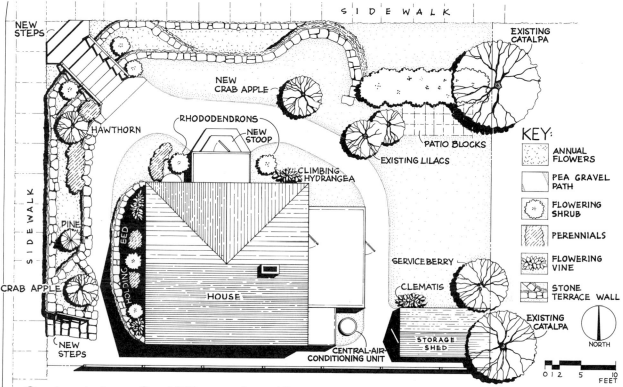

Garden designer Gael Dilthey replaced the steep, unmanageable slopes with a series of plant-filled terraces enclosed by hand-laid stone walls. Since owners Phyllis and Norman wanted to build and plant the garden themselves, Dilthey developed a two-phase plan to make the workload manageable. In phase one, they built the stone terraces along the north and west sides of the property and replaced the unsafe steps at the corner of the property. They also added a new pathway to the front door and a new stoop to provide easier access to the house.

sedums (*Sedum* spp.), hens-and-chickens (*Sempervivum* spp.), rock cresses (*Arabis* and *Aubrieta* spp.), bellflowers (*Campanula* spp.), and creeping thymes (*Thymus* spp.). As soon as they finished a terrace, they filled in behind it with soil to create a level planting bed. Then they planted it with annuals to hold the soil and get some much-deserved immediate gratification. They waited a season or so to plant perennials, after the soil settled and had been adequately conditioned with compost, with pH adjusted as necessary, and protected and enriched by a cover crop.

New Front Steps

Phyllis and Norman had the old, decrepit set of steps from the sidewalk to the house replaced during phase one, too, because they had been so dangerous. The steps remained at the corner of the lot because it's convenient to park on either street. The new steps were designed as an integral part of the terracing system. They link the terraced slopes that stretch along the sidewalk on either side of the corner. In addition, they act like a gate into the garden and are a welcoming landmark for the house.

The design of the new steps, along with the planting around them, introduces the garden's overall character and mood: The steps have an extremely simple and open design, an indication of the garden's charm. Cedar railings match the house shingles in texture and color. At the same time, they make the massive steps seem lighter and less of a climb. Pots of annuals decorate the ends of the treads. The treads are boxed in with landscape ties and filled with aggregate concrete, which was washed while still wet to expose the pebbles for a close match to the texture of the pebbled walks.

In phase one, Phyllis and Norman planted two new trees at either end of the terrace on the west side of the house to provide a privacy screen. A crab apple (*Malus* × *zumi* var. *calocarpa*) overhangs the walkway and stone steps leading to the storage corridor at the back of the lot, while a thornless cockspur hawthorn (*Crataegus crus-galli* var. *inermis*) stands near the front steps. In between, a Swiss mountain pine (*Pinus mugo*) and transplanted irises are the first permanent elements of the plantings. At the front steps, a few special plants were added right away to underline the appeal of the new renovated garden. Two pink 'Bonica' shrub roses flank the steps on the first terrace up from the sidewalk. A goldflame honeysuckle (*Lonicera* × *heckrottii*) and a tree peony (*Paeonia suffruticosa*) are planted opposite each other on the next terrace level.

Practical Paths and Places

Phyllis and Norman replaced the old flagstone pathways near the house with packed pea gravel. They also extended the system of pathways so they could reach planting beds on all sides of the house. The new paths were created by pressing pea gravel saved from the previous garden's backyard walks into a base of mixed recycled materials—primarily crumbled asphalt and broken concrete—with a roller to hold it firmly in place. They liked the softer feeling and the textural contrast it provided against the native stone of the house and terraces. Packed pea gravel also covers the ground along the new storage and utility corridor.

SIDEWALK BORDERS

Phyllis and Norman created a flower border between the sidewalk and the street on the north side of their house. Not only did this eliminate more lawn that needed mowing, but it also adds to the new colorful and friendly exterior of the house. The city of Milwaukee owns this 8 × 40-foot strip, but property owners are required to maintain it. Since the city can tear it up at any time for access to underground utilities, Phyllis and Norman use the area to test new plants. They don't think gardening along this strip is too big a risk, because they view the plantings as experimental. Any plants growing there that they value will eventually be absorbed into the garden proper.

To make this experimental area more attractive, Phyllis and Norman built a low wall of leftover stone around the existing honey locust tree (*Gleditsia* sp.) near the street. They then planted the new bed with daylilies. On the northwest corner, where people sometimes cut across the grass, they extended the sidewalk with stone paving. Along the west sidewalk, they used sections of brick alternated with planting spaces for annuals to fill in the 1-foot-wide curbside strip.

Phyllis and Norman also improved the area around the front door during phase one. The old front steps had been very awkward: To open the door and walk through, it was necessary to stand a step or two below the door. The new front steps have an angled design with three-sided steps, leaving more room to step to the side to get around the door. To give a unified feeling, the new steps are made of the same materials as the ones coming up from the sidewalk.

They also removed the overgrown and ailing foundation plantings. Two new lavender-pink flowered 'P.J.M.' hybrid rhododendrons flank the new steps. They're planted far enough away to provide plenty of room around the door, even after the plants are mature.

A Storage and Utility Area

When they began work on the much-needed new storage area, Phyllis and Norman started by adding a back fence along the lot line. At 4 feet, the gate and new back fence is tall enough to keep out kids and dogs, and short enough to be friendly. The fence is constructed of rough-cut, 1 × 4-inch cedar boards used in a board-on-board pattern to let air circulate. A major problem was the window wells from the basement that were sited along this narrow area; the solution was to cover them with wooden grates to provide safe footing. They planted a 'Snowmound' nippon spirea (*Spiraea nipponica* 'Snowmound') by the new gate that secures the storage area at the back corner of the house.

The new space-efficient design allows room for storing a recycling bin and a garbage cart. An aluminum extension ladder hangs from the fence posts, and flowerpots are stacked on the ground. Phyllis and Norman even made their own compost bins out of wheeled plastic garbage cans with holes punched in the sides and bottoms. To turn the compost, they can easily wheel the cans out of the narrow space, turn them on their sides, and roll them to mix up the materials. At the end of the storage corridor, they found room for a gas grill.

A New Shed

The new shed was built in the rear, southeast corner of the lot, at the end of the storage corridor. It not only provides all-important storage space for bikes and tools, it also forms part of the screen that encloses the private areas in the side yard from neighboring properties.

Phyllis and Norman wanted their new shed to be both attractive and practical, and the design they came up with complements the house and adds charm to the garden. The shed is covered with panels of cedar grooved to look like siding; the color matches the cedar shingles of the house. Two casement windows, six panes each, are mounted side by side with a long window box underneath. The window box is planted with red, pink, and white begonias to match the one above the front door of the house. A pink clematis (*Clematis montana* var. *rubens*) clambers up a trellis at the shed's corner.

Creating an Outdoor Retreat—Phase Two

The main focus of phase two was to transform the side yard into a private area for outdoor activities. They started by completing the stone terrace along the upper walk by the house. Then they worked out toward the new private terraces in the side yard. In all, phase two required 10 more tons of native stone.

Screening Sights and Sounds

Screening the side yard—both from the street and from adjoining neighbors— was the all-important priority of phase two. To begin the enclosure of the back of their lot, during phase one Phyllis and Norman had planted an apple serviceberry (*Amelanchier* × *grandiflora*), in front of the new shed at its far corner. This spring-flowering shrub softens the edge of the shed and helps screen the private, side garden area from backdoor neighbors. A Japanese stewartia (*Stewartia pseudo-camellia*) added along the east property line during phase two also helps screen the side yard from neighbors. It also bears beautiful white flowers in summer and has attractive peeling bark that adds winter interest to the garden.

Once they removed the old, ugly honeysuckle hedge, along with the mildewed lilacs and lopsided crab apple, Phyllis and Norman realized that managing sound was as big an issue on their lot as managing sight. They hadn't realized just how much street noise these plants had blocked. To block the sights and sounds of the street, Dilthey designed a planting that combines a mixture of evergreen and deciduous trees and shrubs. These provide attractive flowers, ornamental bark for winter interest, and a host of leaf colors and textures. Most important, they provide a sound and sight barrier to make the new side-yard terraces more appealing.

Evergreens such as dwarf Canada hemlock (*Tsuga canadensis* 'Compacta') and dwarf Japanese yew (*Taxus cuspidata* 'Nana') provide year-round color and form the backbone of this screen. A 'Shasta' doublefile viburnum (*Viburnum plicatum* var. *tomentosum* 'Shasta') offers spectacular white flowers in spring. It is underplanted with a ground-covering layer of 'Beacon Silver' spotted lamium (*Lamium maculatum* 'Beacon Silver'). Rockspray cotoneasters (*Cotoneaster horizontalis*) cascade down the slope. A coppery-orange-flowered witch hazel *(Hamamelis × intermedia* 'Jelena') adds blooms to the scene in winter to early spring. And the coppery, peeling bark of a paperbark maple (*Acer griseum*) on the edge of the terrace adds color and texture throughout the year.

Side-Yard Terraces

Visitors can reach the side-yard garden simply by following the walk that leads from the front. The garden is within easy reach from indoors, too. Phyllis or Norman can pop out the porch door to harvest herbs or vegetables growing nearby. A climbing hydrangea (*Hydrangea anomala* subsp. *petiolaris*) planted on the corner of the house eases the transition to the side yard.

As the front walk turns the corner to the side yard, it widens into a paved niche designed for a container garden. Phyllis and Norman love this small, sunny spot and use it to grow pots of brightly colored annuals, herbs that are either tender or invasive (such as scented geraniums and spearmint), and vegetables.

Just beyond the container garden, a set of semicircular steps descends to a grass terrace used for sitting, dining, or outdoor entertaining. The steps are built

of native stone mortared in place. The terrace, which is a pleasant spot for barefoot picnicking, offers the garden's only lawn grass. Here, grass is a soft, cool alternative to the paved surfaces elsewhere but still is easy to cut quickly with a push mower.

The grass terrace is a favorite place for indulging the great American pastime of watching the traffic cruise by. Now that they can see out more easily than the passersby can see in, Phyllis and Norman enjoy it all the more. A new crab apple and a threadleaf Japanese maple (*Acer palmatum* 'Dissectum') block the view of eastbound travelers. The low, flowing branches of the Japanese maple gracefully frame the stone steps that are tucked into the hillside and form a shortcut from the yard down to the sidewalk. The mixed planting of shrubs and small trees that encloses the side yard from the front screens the area from traffic and the adjoining neighbor.

Above the grass terrace is a smaller terrace that features a lily pool with a fountain. The pool is located on the edge of the upper terrace, so the water's surface is at about the same height as the table on the grass terrace. Phyllis and Norman enjoy watching the fish dart about the pool and trailing their fingers in the water while they sit and talk. For parties, they float lights among the 'Fabiola' waterlilies (*Nymphaea* 'Fabiola'), which have pink flowers with yellow centers. Blue-and-white Japanese irises (*Iris ensata*) nod over the edges of the pool. The trickling water of the fountain helps mask the noise from the nearby street.

(continued on page 148)

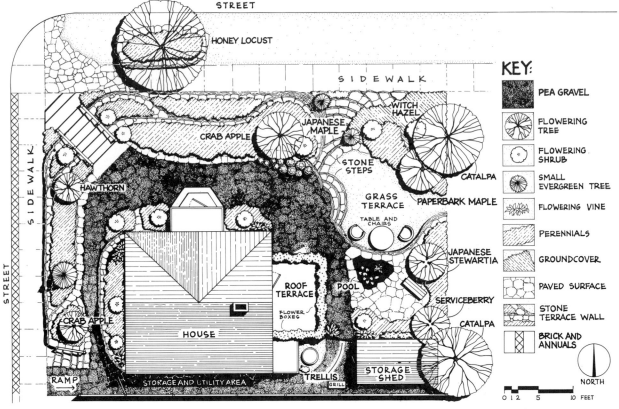

STREET

HONEY LOCUST

SIDEWALK

KEY:

PEA GRAVEL

FLOWERING TREE

FLOWERING SHRUB

SMALL EVERGREEN TREE

FLOWERING VINE

PERENNIALS

GROUNDCOVER

PAVED SURFACE

STONE TERRACE WALL

BRICK AND ANNUALS

CRAB APPLE

JAPANESE MAPLE

WITCH HAZEL

STONE STEPS

CATALPA

GRASS TERRACE

PAPERBARK MAPLE

HAWTHORN

TABLE AND CHAIRS

JAPANESE STEWARTIA

STREET

SIDEWALK

ROOF TERRACE

POOL

SERVICEBERRY

FLOWER BOXES

CATALPA

CRAB APPLE

HOUSE

STORAGE SHED

RAMP

STORAGE AND UTILITY AREA

TRELLIS
GRILL

NORTH

0 1 2   5   10 FEET

Phase two of this project transformed the side yard into a comfortable and private series of outdoor living spaces. Two terraces—one a casual grass terrace and the other paved, with a small lily pool—provide a choice of spots to sit and enjoy the yard. They've also added a roof terrace above the screen porch. Carefully placed trees and shrubs, as well as the storage shed, screen the side yard from neighbors and the street, yet make it possible to see out and watch the passing cars.

PLANTING NOTES

Dilthey included a wide range of plants to fill this garden with bold, cheerful colors, interesting textures, and a variety of forms so that it would be attractive throughout the year.

Flowers for Spring Color

Spring-flowering trees include white-flowered apple serviceberry (*Amelanchier* × *grandiflora*) and thornless cockspur hawthorn (*Crataegus crusgalli* var. *inermis*). A redbud crab apple (*Malus* × *zumi* var. *calocarpa*) bears pink buds followed by clouds of white flowers. Pink-flowered rhododendrons, white-flowered 'Shasta' doublefile viburnum (*Viburnum plicatum* var. *tometosum* 'Shasta'), and 'Snowmound' nippon spirea (*Spiraea nipponica* 'Snowmound') add to the show.

Throughout the garden, spring-blooming perennials and bulbs add a rainbow of colors.

Color and Texture for Shade

Much of this lot is in dappled shade, but a host of ferns and hostas with a dazzling array of blue, green, yellow, and bicolor leaves add color and texture. They also help hide the fading foliage of spring bulbs and wildflowers. All summer long, impatiens light up the shade, too. 'Beacon Silver' spotted lamium (*Lamium maculatum* 'Beacon Silver'), a groundcover with tiny pink flowers and silver leaves edged in green, cascades down the bank below the patio.

Two 4- to 6-foot-tall, white-flowered native wildflowers light up the shade in summer as well: goat's beard (*Aruncus dioicus*) and black snakeroot (*Cimicifuga racemosa*).

A Waterfall of Color

The stone walls are planted with creeping and trailing perennials that provide a lively show from early spring through frost. These include creeping phlox (*Phlox subulata*), pinks (*Dianthus* spp.), bellflowers (*Campanula* spp.), creeping thymes (*Thymus* spp.), and creeping baby's breath (*Gypsophila repens* 'Rosea') along with clumps of hens-and-chickens (*Sempervivum* sp.).

Summer Flowers

This garden has plenty of color through the summer and into autumn when some gardens seem to take a vacation. Vines and trees—along with lilies, irises, roses, and other summer-flowering perennials—add to the show. These include yellow-and-pink-flowered goldflame honeysuckle (*Lonicera* × *heckrottii*) and a climbing hydrangea (*Hydrangea anomala* subsp. *petiolaris*), which has white flowers. The Japanese stewartia tree (*Stewartia pseudocamellia*) bears white flowers with yellow centers.

Winter Interest

In winter, plants with attractive peeling bark add texture and color. These include Japanese stewartia, with blotches of silver-gray, mauve, and rich brown; paperbark maple (*Acer griseum*), with peeling orange-brown new bark; and climbing hydrangea, with red-brown peeling bark. There are also flowers for winter: In late winter, the bright-orange flowers of 'Jelena' witch hazel (*Hamamelis* × *intermedia* 'Jelena') light up the landscape.

The now-transformed garden is as inviting from the street as it is
fun to explore. The plant-filled terraces are alive with the brilliant
colors of perennials, trees, and shrubs. A new curbside planting
adds color and eliminates the need to mow the strip of lawn

between curb and street. The new front steps, framed by two shrub roses, are the gateway to the garden, which has an outward focus that provides a friendly landscape for the neighborhood and a pleasing setting for the house.

The pool terrace is paved with native stone. A wooden bench on the terrace next to the pool is a good spot to sit privately and enjoy the garden. This is the garden's innermost private space: A Japanese stewartia planted along the lot line near the pool creates an overhead canopy. Its multistemmed trunk visually separates the pool and grass terraces. Behind the bench, black snakeroot (*Cimicifuga racemosa*), a sum-

mer-flowering perennial, fills in to the property line. The ground is covered with a planting of mixed hostas, the leaves of which conceal the fading spring foliage of Virginia bluebells (*Mertensia virginica*) and mixed daffodils. Impatiens, ferns, and bleeding heart (*Dicentra spectabilis*) also give color and texture around the terrace edge. A 'Northern Lights' azalea, planted at the corner of the shed nearest the house, en-

The roof terrace above the screen porch was one of the last improvements that homeowners Phyllis and Norman added to their garden. It provides a bird's-eye view of the side yard along with a view of Lake Michigan in the distance. Window boxes inside the railing surround the terrace and provide color all season long.

IN ANOTHER PLACE

Stone terraces are only one of many ways to eliminate a steep slope that's hard to mow. You can fashion terraces from many types of building materials, including railroad ties, landscape timbers, or even brick. It's a good idea to match the style of the material to the style of your garden. For example, brick may be more appropriate for a formal garden than rustic railroad ties. Another option is to replace grass on a sloping site with a low-maintenance ground-cover such as ivy, hostas, or daylilies, which will hold the bank but not require mowing.

Terraces have many other uses in a garden, too. They're a great solution if your yard slopes up to the street, rather than down. In this case you have the perfect place for a handsome terraced garden display that you can enjoy from indoors or out. If your entire property is sloped, adding a series of terraces or a retaining wall and doing some regrading can give you a flat bit of lawn or a patio area to enjoy

closes the terrace space while screening the storage and utility area from view.

Completing the Enclosure

Across the path from the pool terrace, a bed filled with yellow-flowered buttercups (*Ranunculus* sp.) softens the base of the screened porch. Dilthey buried a drainage pipe under the path to channel rainwater from the porch downspout to a gravel dry well beneath the pool terrace. To separate the pool terrace from the storage and utility area, Dilthey added a narrow trellis on the rear corner of the porch. This trellis matches the one mounted on the shed, and together the two frame a solid cedar gate. The gate and trellises, along with the solid wall on that end of the screened porch, help mask noise from the central-air-conditioning unit. A second clematis clambers up the trellis and across a timber that spans the arched gateway to meet the first one, which was planted alongside the shed during phase one. These vines add a charming air to the transition between the terrace and the storage and utility area.

Saving the Best for Last

Phyllis and Norman saved an exciting part of this renovation for last, so they'd have something to look forward to: They built a deck on the roof of the screened-in porch to capture a view of Lake Michigan. To do this, they removed the porch roof and installed a "flat" roof with a pitch of 1 inch to every 2 feet for good drainage. Next they added a rubber liner to the roof and a level wooden deck above. Planter boxes on all three sides form a railing, and cascading vegetation disguises the gap between roof and deck. Plantings in these boxes change from season to season and year to year, but Phyllis and Norman generally plant a mixture of vegetables such as cucumbers and tomatoes with geraniums and trailing annuals.

Looking to the Future

Since Phyllis and Norman don't want to repeat the mistakes of the overzealous

NOTES FROM
THE DESIGNER

Gael Dilthey finds that it's easy to dispose of unwanted materials when neighbors and strangers take an interest in garden redesign projects. In one instance, a large stockpile of soil that was raked down a regraded hill to the sidewalk and shoveled to curbside quickly disappeared after she put up a "Free Soil" sign. On the other hand, when material like stone or mulch was delivered and unloaded in an area that was accessible to the public, she used a friendly sign to let people know that it was "For Our Garden" to dissuade scavengers.

When renovating a garden beset with unhealthy and overgrown plants, Dilthey feels strongly that sorting out the plantings is an essential first step. With a renovation as extensive as this one, it's best to move the "keepers" into a nursery bed where they can be held out of the way until the newly designed spaces are ready to accommodate them. It's equally important to discard plants that can't be salvaged. These include disease-ridden plants, overgrown specimens far too large for the site, and badly pruned plants that no longer have ornamental value. Otherwise, they'll always mar the design and take up room that a prettier plant could occupy.

Trees and shrubs too large to move can be roped off for protection. However, if the renovation calls for any grade changes, as this one did, it's important to remember that trees and shrubs must remain at the same depth. Piling soil on the roots or taking it away can be fatal, so if at all possible, avoid grade changes that might endanger plants you want to preserve.

gardener who originally owned their home, they're careful about picking and choosing the plants they add to their garden. That way, they can be sure the design will continue to make sense and the garden won't get out of hand. To make sure the trees and shrubs that screen their yard stay dense and attractive, Phyllis and Norman prune them annually in late winter.

They both love to garden and want to continue to have room for lots of different perennials and other plants. For this reason, they're continually on the lookout for plants that are flourishing and those that aren't. Since they don't have room for rampant, invasive plants, they're especially careful to control any overly vigorous specimens they see. ◆

A COUNTRY GARDEN: PRIVACY AND PATHWAYS

Timothy Steinhoff is both owner and designer of this property in New York's Hudson River Valley. He originally bought it as a weekend refuge from the hustle and bustle of New York City but has since come to live here full time.

Even when it was still just a weekend retreat, Tim knew that creating a feeling of privacy and seclusion was high on his list of priorities. Although the house is in the middle of a good-size lot, it seemed far too exposed to neighboring houses and a busy, noisy state highway—especially when deciduous trees lost their leaves for winter. Tim wanted to be able to ramble about the property and enjoy the landscape in relative privacy. He also wanted to block the noise from the nearby highway.

A gardener by both hobby and profession, Tim also wanted plenty of space to indulge his passion for gardening and plants. The area has a rich gardening history and tradition, which Tim found fascinating. He wanted his property to reflect this legacy.

The Place and the People

Tim's 3.2-acre country retreat is shaped somewhat like a piece of pie. The widest part of the wedge is located along the noisy state highway to the southeast, and the lot narrows sharply to the back. A haphazard complex of buildings in the middle of the lot includes the house, a barn, two sheds, and a summer kitchen. The property is located on a rolling hillside,

KEY CONCEPTS FOR A SUCCESSFUL DESIGN

Developing and controlling views. Plantings that screen the sights and sounds of an adjacent highway and close neighbors are essential to making this garden a wonderful place to live. In addition, the design uses the plantings and topography of the garden to develop attractive views within the property and scenery beyond its borders.

Creating pathways through the landscape. This is a garden with few formal pathways but many places to explore. The plantings that screen the highway and close neighbors also create a private inner world for the owner to enjoy. Destinations in the garden—such as a looping trail around the pond, a bench under an apple tree, or a fragrant border behind the house—provide places to go and things to see.

Taking inspiration from local traditions. Local history and tradition played an important role in inspiring the design of this garden. Although it isn't a historical re-creation, it uses ideas and principles developed in the nineteenth century that are still apparent in gardens in New York's Hudson River Valley. Views from one part of the garden to another and the new driveway plantings are just two of the elements that hearken back to the historic gardens of the area.

Places for plants. This design provides plenty of room for trees, shrubs, vines, perennials, and any other plants the owner wishes to collect, yet it provides a framework for displaying them in an attractive and appealing way.

which rises toward the northwest. Below the house, near the widest part of the lot and the road, stand the remnants of a valley orchard. In back, there are westward views of the Catskill Mountains. In the winter, a glimpse of the Hudson River opens to the north.

The house, sold as the "ultimate fixer-upper," sits close to the west property line. It's a mid-nineteenth-century house that combines wood frame and fieldstone. The fieldstone walls are built into the slope of the hillside, and the house fits snugly into the landscape. At the front, the house is two stories high, with two doors opening onto the first-floor porch. Living and dining take place on this level. The basement, one step down, is accessible through a low door. From the back, the house appears to be only one story, although this is actually the upstairs. A side door opens from a second-floor sitting room toward the west property line.

Initially, the landscape around the house was so exposed to neighbors and the adjacent highway that Tim found he tended to stay close to the house. At least there it felt a little bit private. He wanted to enhance the rural character of his property and at the same time create areas where he could garden or sit in peace and quiet. In addition, he wanted to develop areas and plantings that would give him reason to get out and ramble through the landscape and enjoy it firsthand. Since he also often has weekend guests, he wanted to design a garden for their enjoyment as well.

Using a Rich Local History

Tim wanted his Hudson River Valley property to reflect the fact that it is lo-

cated in one of America's cradles of garden history. American landscape gardener Andrew Jackson Downing, the son of a nurseryman, grew up along the Hudson among the estates first settled by the Dutch. Downing, who read widely about gardening and architecture, eventually settled along the Hudson himself and designed his own garden. He wrote the first important book by an American on garden design—*A Treatise on the Theory and Practice of Landscape Gardening*, published in 1841. Downing defined ideals of home landscape design that still influence us today, and which Tim followed to develop his own property. Many of the images Downing drew upon were reminiscent of the estates he knew along the Hudson.

In his writings, Downing described two types of landscape gardens, the "beautiful" and the "picturesque." Both were considered artistic embellishments of nature. Downing's beautiful landscape was a highly manicured expanse with undulating sweeps of neatly mown lawn, mature clumps of trees, magnificent single (specimen) trees, and a beautiful pond surrounded by flowers and shrubs. Today, suburban landscapes with flowing, free-form expanses of lawn accented by a specimen tree and curving beds of shrubs and flowers echo Downing's beautiful landscape. Downing's picturesque landscape was characterized by a woody glen or a valley draped with vines and studded with clumps of trees. A cottage-style house set in a wooded landscape would be the modern version.

The Hudson Valley was, and is, teeming with the gardens of Downing's followers and the nurseries that supplied them. One famed advocate was the painter Frederic Church, whose home, Olana, stands today as an outstanding example of the landscape garden. The Olana Scenic District, where Tim's garden is located, is a spectacularly beautiful area that features panoramic vistas spanning as far as 50 miles in clear weather. The climate is wonderful for fruit growing, which was extremely important to nineteenth-century American horticulture. (Downing also wrote books on fruit growing that are still respected today.) Orchards like Tim's still pattern the landscape.

The Hudson Valley's estates, many of which are open to visitors, often combine elements that are both "beautiful" and "picturesque." Along the country roads, it's easy to spot landscapes that feature rolling lawns, placid lakes, and artistically planted groves of trees—planted in odd numbers of plants, never even. Although he has replaced sweeping expanses of manicured lawn with rough-cut meadows, Tim's property also has elements of both landscape styles.

Getting from Fantasy to Fact

Tim wanted the interior of his garden to seem like a world unto itself. For this reason, he designed plantings of strategically placed trees and shrubs to protect the property from the sights and sounds of the busy highway, neighbors, and potential nearby development. He also used the property's rolling landscape to advantage: Not only did it allow him to develop beautiful views from one part of the garden to another, but he could also make the most of views beyond the garden's boundaries.

The design features elements of Downing's beautiful and picturesque landscapes—including an isolated cottage, open spaces, and scattered remnants of an old orchard. However, the end result is not a historic re-creation; it's a garden that suits Tim's own needs. He combined a new pond below the house, handsome groves of trees, rough-cut meadows, and rustic structures into a garden that seems far removed from the everyday world. He has plenty of places to enjoy the out-of-doors in private as well as places to garden, entertain, walk, or just sit and enjoy the scenery.

Manageable Development

To make developing the garden more manageable, he decided which areas were most important to him and planted them first. In many cases, he was content to buy small trees and shrubs and wait for them to grow.

Although he had a general plan for his property, Tim took a very informal approach to the design of specific plantings. He installed the design in phases. Plantings around the house and barn—especially those that screened the house—got top priority. He waited for phase two to add the pond and plantings in the valley below the house.

He left most of the nitty-gritty details of "what to plant where" for when he was actually ready to develop an area. That way, he could develop the garden as time and money allowed. It also left him free to experiment with plant combinations and make room for new plants he wanted to grow.

In areas where he wanted quick screening, he planted large, fast-growing perennials such as ornamental grasses to give him the privacy he wanted until trees and shrubs formed a more permanent barrier. Ornamental grasses such as eulalia (*Miscanthus sinensis*) and fountain grass (*Pennisetum* spp.) provide fast and full effect. Among the many other plants he has found useful for this purpose are plume poppy (*Macleaya microcarpa*), which is an 8-foot-tall perennial, and Ural false spirea (*Sorbaria*

sorbifolia), a vigorous 10-foot-tall shrub. Before he planted the fragrant border on the northwest side of the house, he planted the area with easy-to-grow cosmos 'Sensation', bronze fennel (*Foeniculum vulgare* var. *purpureum*), and 'Victoria' mealy-cup sage (*Salvia farinacea* 'Victoria'). In the front of the barn, he used white-flowered sunflowers (*Helianthus annuus* 'Italian White').

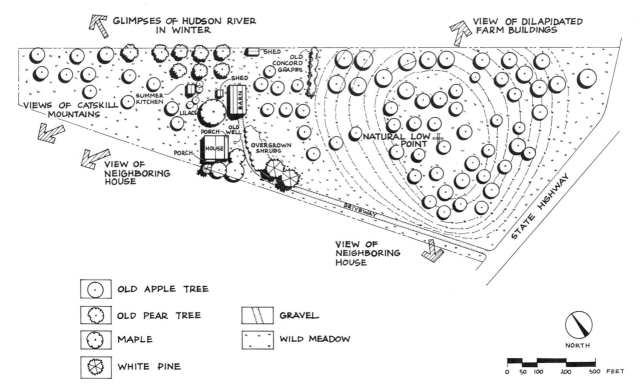

When Timothy Steinhoff purchased his 3.2-acre property in New York's Hudson River Valley it was a far cry from the secluded country retreat he had dreamed of. Much of the land was covered with an abandoned orchard. The farmstead featured a fieldstone and frame farmhouse, a barn, a summer kitchen, and a couple of old sheds. Although the property afforded views of the Hudson River and Catskill Mountains, it was also completely open to a noisy highway and several neighbors. A straight driveway led directly to the house, and there was no place for visitors to park.

Practical Privacy

One of the first improvements Tim made was to relocate the driveway. Originally, the long, straight gravel driveway led along the west lot line and curved below the front porch into the barn. There weren't any convenient places for guests to park. The new driveway runs partway up the lot line and then curves along the hill below the house toward the center of the property. Relocating the driveway accomplished a dual purpose: It made room for a planting that screens the house from the highway, and it made the entrance to the property more attractive.

Tim planted a dense evergreen barrier along the section of the old, abandoned driveway below the house. The planting is comprised mostly of pyramidal-shaped junipers and 'Techny' American arborvitaes (*Thuja occidentalis* 'Techny'). Fortunately, a contractor who was installing a new septic field agreed to dig large planting holes in the gravel driveway, so Tim could plant fairly large specimens for instant results. Tim also planted lavender- and purple-flowered butterfly bushes (*Buddleia* spp.) for added color. In addition to screening the sights and sounds of the highway from the house, this planting also hides the neighboring residence located near the base of the driveway.

Surprisingly, the new driveway is an element that hearkens back to the historic Hudson River Valley gardens Tim used for inspiration. In a traditional landscape garden, the horse and buggy trip through a property to the house was an essential part of the overall design. Visitors were meant to experience the landscape. This meant a winding, leisurely approach through a parklike setting that featured trees and a lake, with occasional glimpses of the distant manor house. Tim's design captures the essence of that experience. The new driveway winds along a simple curve that makes the most of the shifting valley topography. Along the way, guests enjoy pleasant views of the new pond, the old orchard, groves of trees, and the house.

Arrivals and Parking

The new driveway design provides space for everyday parking a short walk from the house. Guests find there's an ample parking area near the end of the drive just below the barn. The parking area also provides all-important room for a turnaround. To make sure it was big enough, Tim measured it with his van, which is about the largest vehicle he expects to have to accommodate. He also checked the dimensions against a reference book used by professional designers and architects—*Architectural Graphic Standards*—and confirmed they were generous, which is what he wanted. On the outer edge of the turnaround, the land falls off toward the valley. Tim was careful to build up this edge but also to grade it gently. That way, drivers know they're approaching the edge, and no one will get hung up if they drive off it.

Enclosing a Grassy Courtyard

Tim developed a border of shrubs, trees, and perennials to screen the parking
(continued on page 160)

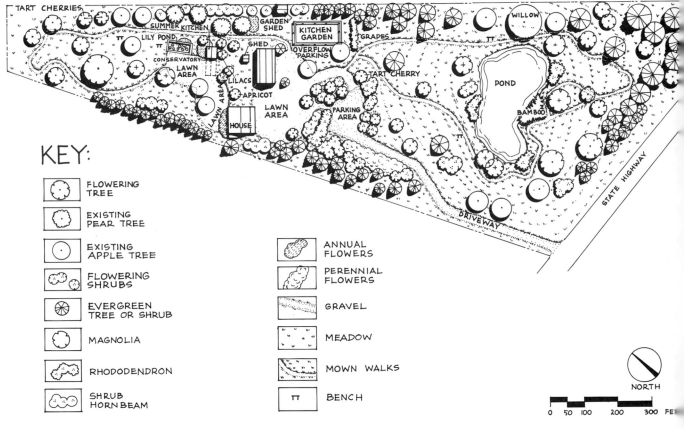

KEY:

- FLOWERING TREE
- EXISTING PEAR TREE
- EXISTING APPLE TREE
- FLOWERING SHRUBS
- EVERGREEN TREE OR SHRUB
- MAGNOLIA
- RHODODENDRON
- SHRUB HORNBEAM

- ANNUAL FLOWERS
- PERENNIAL FLOWERS
- GRAVEL
- MEADOW
- MOWN WALKS
- BENCH

NORTH

0   50 100   200   300 FE

The biggest change that phase two brought to the property was a pond in the valley below the house. Plantings around it screen the state highway, and owner Timothy Steinhoff maintains an informal mown path through the area so he can ramble about the property and enjoy the plants close up. Behind the barn, he added a lily pool, which also makes a pleasant destination on a summer afternoon. It is rectangular and therefore much more formal than the natural-looking earthen pond in the valley. Trees and shrubs around the edges of the property have transformed it into a private country retreat.

PLANTING NOTES

Timothy Steinhoff is a plantsman at heart, and this garden is his collection. Part of the design's charm comes from the rich diversity of plants he has woven into its fabric. Ancient apple and pear trees throughout the garden bear witness to the property's previous life as an orchard. Tim preserved the healthiest ones and added an apricot tree and some 'North Star' tart cherries to provide more fruit for the table and additional spring bloom.

By planting a wide variety of trees and shrubs—both species and cultivars—Tim was able to extend the bloom season and add considerable interest to the garden. For example, the earliest-blooming shrubs on the property are witch hazels (*Hamamelis* spp.), which bloom anytime from January to March. Tim has planted three different witch hazels to light up the late-winter landscape: *Hamamelis* × *intermedia* 'Jelena' and 'Diane', and *H. mollis* 'Pallida'. And Tim selected several clematis (*Clematis* spp.) vines to provide color from late spring to summer throughout the property. Cultivars 'Ramona' and 'Nelly Moser' bloom in late spring, while 'Mrs. Cholmondeley' is a summer-flowering cultivar.

Tim has planted an array of trees and shrubs that provide year-round color and interest. The following are among the most outstanding.

Shrubs for Spring Bloom

Rhododendron schlippenbachii (royal azalea)
Rhododendron vaseyi (pinkshell azalea)
Syringa vulgaris (common lilac)
Viburnum plicatum var. *tomentosum* 'Shasta' ('Shasta' doublefile viburnum)

Trees for Spring Bloom

Cornus kousa var. *chinensis* (Chinese dogwood)
Magnolia denudata (Yulan magnolia, formerly *M. heptapeta*)
Magnolia 'Elizabeth' (*Magnolia acuminata* × *M. denudata* hybrid magnolia)
Magnolia × *loebneri* 'Leonard Messel' ('Leonard Messel' Loebner magnolia)
Magnolia × *soulangiana* 'Coates' ('Coates' saucer magnolia)
Magnolia virginiana (sweet bay)

Trees and Shrubs for Summer Bloom

Aesculus parviflora (bottlebrush buckeye)
Buddleia davidii 'Nanho Purple' and 'Black Knight' (orange-eye butterfly bush)
Buddleia × 'Lochinch' ('Lochinch' hybrid butterfly bush)
Cotinus coggygria (smoke tree)
Hydrangea paniculata 'Tardiva' (panicle hydrangea)
Magnolia sieboldii (oyama magnolia)
Oxydendrum arboreum (sourwood)
Sophora japonica 'Regent Strain' (Japanese pagoda tree)
Sorbaria sorbifolia (Ural false spirea)
Stewartia koreana (Korean stewartia)

Trees and Shrubs for Screening

Carpinus betulus 'Fastigiata' (upright European hornbeam)
Euonymus europaea (European spindle tree)
Ilex pedunculosa (long-stalk holly)
Picea omorika (Serbian spruce)
Picea orientalis (oriental spruce)
Pinus strobus (Eastern white pine)
Thuja occidentalis 'Techny' ('Techny' American arborvitae)
Tsuga canadensis (Canada hemlock)

Who could resist taking a stroll around the pond and through the meadow and plantings that surround it? Junipers, pines, and spruces screen the highway and make the garden more private, and flowering shrubs and perennials add color and seasonal interest. Owner Timothy Steinhoff maintains a mown path around the pond so he can enjoy walking through the meadow, but he doesn't keep it in the same place from season to season. Instead,

he selects a new direction whenever the spirit moves him. That way, he can take advantage of shrubs that are in bloom or a particularly attractive view back across the pond to the house and garden. Redesigning the path not only lets him easily get close to plants he wants to enjoy, it also keeps the stroll around the pond interesting because it's always changing.

159

area from the house. The planting also encloses the grassy area between the front porch and the barn. A mature Eastern white pine (*Pinus strobus*) anchors the planting, which also includes European hornbeam (*Carpinus betulus*), butterfly bushes (*Buddleia* spp.), long-stalk hollies (*Ilex pedunculosa*), and 'Pallida' Chinese witch hazels (*Hamamelis mollis* 'Pallida'). Tim also added plantings of perennials.

The grassy courtyard this planting

outlines is the most important living space of the entire property. It's a peaceful and private space, where Tim can enjoy breakfast and bask in the morning sun. He also gardens intensively here; lush plantings of perennials and flowering shrubs are a testament to his efforts.

The courtyard also provides plenty of room for entertaining. The barn has sliding doors on the south side that can be pushed back. Tim pulls a large, old apple-

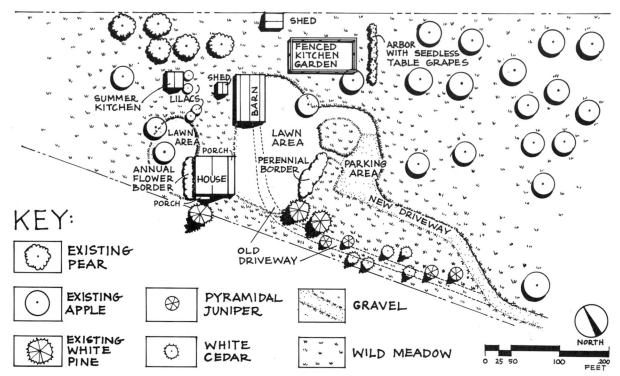

A two-phase plan was an obvious choice for a property as large as this one. Owner/designer Timothy Steinhoff started the renovation by redesigning the area around the house. He first relocated the driveway to provide an area for visitor parking and to make way for a planting of trees and shrubs on the old driveway to screen the highway. He also created a sunny lawn area around the barn planted with beds of perennials and shrubs, and fenced in a kitchen garden.

sorting table out of the barn and uses it as a buffet table. On evenings with a full moon, the area between the house and barn is a wonderful place for an outdoor supper and visiting with friends.

There's also extra parking for parties on the tough old sod among scattered orchard trees on the side of the barn that faces the parking area. Guests parking here are treated to a colorful, long-blooming border of perennials and shrubs planted alongside the barn. The border is framed on the corner nearest the house by a late-flowering cultivar of white-flowered panicle hydrangea, *Hydrangea paniculata* 'Tardiva', and long-stalk holly (*Ilex pedunculosa*). A clump of Adam's-needle (*Yucca filamentosa*) sits on the far end. In between is a rich assortment of blue- and yellow-flowered plants, including *Nepeta sibirica*, *Coreopsis verticillata* 'Moonbeam', 'Vanilla' torch lily (*Kniphofia uvaria* 'Vanilla'), *Aster × frikartii*, *Cosmos bipinnatus* 'Seashells', and *Artemisia ×* 'Powis Castle'.

The barn itself is "upholstered" with climbing flowers. Its silvery gray siding is a perfect foil for clear, light colors like those of pink-flowered 'New Dawn' roses and blue-flowered 'Ramona' clematis. Because it's so dry under the barn's deep eaves, the climbers are actually growing on a trellis set several feet out from the barn. The trellis wood is stained to blend in with the barn.

Tim enjoys this space in front of the barn regularly. Most of the time, when no cars are parked here, it's grand to walk underneath the limbed-up trees of the orchard or to drag a chair out under them for reading. It's also part of the view from the front porch, where he takes almost every warm-weather meal.

Tim used the plantings in front of the barn to enhance the long view north to the boundary of the property. An 8-foot-wide grass swath runs between the border in front of the barn and the orchard trees across from it. Just across from the far corner of the barn is another panicle hydrangea, planted on the southeast corner of the kitchen garden. It suggests a gateway and pulls visitors toward an interesting old shed, which is used to store large equipment. The shed, which has a dusty-pink door and an overhang, has a mildly exotic, Mexican flavor.

The Kitchen Garden

The 50 × 25-foot kitchen garden lies to the right of the long view past the barn. Although it's a mecca for those who love to cook and eat, Tim added wire fencing to keep unwanted foragers at bay. Along the west edge is a framework for growing hops (*Humulus lupulus*), which Tim uses in home-brewed beer. The framework, along with a planting of hornbeams (*Carpinus betulus*), also screens the view of the dilapidated farm buildings on the neighboring property.

Along the southeast side of the kitchen garden, Tim grows grapes. He replaced the old 'Concord' vines that were growing here with new seedless table grapes. The grapevines double as a boundary between upper garden areas and the plantings in the valley below.

Since there are lots of produce stands and pick-it-yourself farms in the area, Tim uses the kitchen garden only to grow crops that are unavailable locally or that are particularly good when just picked. These include peas, 'Yellow Finn' potatoes, salad greens, and tomatoes. Perennial crops include asparagus, raspberries, 'Canada Red' rhubarb, and such herbs as thyme, tarragon, chives, oregano, and sage. Each year, Tim plants a few new things, like popcorn, just for fun.

The kitchen garden also features a block of cutting flowers. Here, they're easy to tend, and picking them won't spoil the display in the rest of the garden. Among his favorites are sweet peas, pot marigolds (*Calendula officinalis*), blue-flowered centaureas (*Centaurea* sp.), cosmos, and zinnias.

Places to Ramble

From the very beginning, Tim wanted to be able to ramble around the property and explore it at will. This is a garden to be walked through and enjoyed firsthand rather than viewed from afar. Both the upper garden—the area around the house and barn to the northwest corner of the property—and the stroll garden around the new pond were designed with these explorations in mind. In both areas, informal, looping pathways lure owner and visitors alike out to explore the property. Because of their meandering nature, these pathways also make the lot seem larger than it is.

Most designs use physical links such as steps or paved pathways to connect one part of a garden with another. In Tim's garden the connections are largely visual. Glimpses from one area to another are the connecting force that leads visitors through the landscape.

The design uses plantings of trees and shrubs as well as the topography of the land to create a sense of discovery and lure visitors on to explore more of the garden. Carefully created views are part of the overall experience. For example, from the lawn in front of the house, visitors get a glimpse of the swath of grass and the plantings around the barn and kitchen garden. Once they've walked along to see these plantings up close, they catch a glimpse of the kitchen garden and shed beyond it. From the kitchen garden, they can see up the hill toward the plantings near the back of the property.

The pond in the valley has a similar allure. From some spots it's hidden from view because it's tucked into the hill below the house. Each glimpse of it lures visitors onward. Ramblers who make it to the far side of the pond are treated to a beautiful view back across the water to the house.

Tim's garden is the exception to the rule that well-defined and paved traffic patterns are crucial to a successful and functional design. The views that lead visitors through the landscape change from season to season: spring bulbs emerge, trees leaf out, perennials bloom, fruit ripens, and fall color arrives. All these events create new places to investigate, and the places Tim wants to walk will change accordingly. While over time he'll discover paths he repeatedly takes from place to place, he doesn't intend to add preplanned pathways. That way, he can continue to explore at will.

The Upper Garden

The area behind the barn and adjacent to the back of the house features a summer kitchen, a new lily pool, and a variety of plantings that link the area together. Tim designed the area so each part could be enjoyed individually, but views toward the back of the property and elements of the garden encourage visitors to wander on an informal loop through the area.

Once visitors pass the barn and kitchen garden, they catch sight of a lovely view up the gentle incline that leads to the back of the property. Just beyond the summer kitchen is a level place that Tim decided was perfect for a lily pool. Set like a mirror into the mown grass, the pool is a formal, 10 × 20-foot rectangle bordered with slate set in sand.

Tim didn't want the area to look crowded, so the pool is surrounded by an expanse of grass. Although he planted both pink and white waterlilies in the pool, he was careful not to overplant, because he wanted the surface of the water to reflect the sky and shifting clouds. For this reason, a full two-thirds of the water surface is

The placid mirror of the lily pool provides a central focus for a delightful retreat beyond the summer kitchen. To conceal the north wall of the old building, owner/designer Timothy Steinhoff added a rose- and clematis-covered trellis flanked with hollyhocks, asters, anemones, and many other flowers. Water lilies and darting fish add color and movement to the still water, and the stately foliage planted at the northeast edge of the pool and summer kitchen garden suggest the edge of this outdoor room.

open to the sky. This also makes it easier to watch the fish, which Tim added to eat mosquito larvae, darting about beneath the surface.

There's a bench at one end of the pool that's a perfect spot for enjoying the lush plantings set against the summer kitchen. These include asters (*Aster* × *frikartii*), 'September Charm' Japanese anemones (*Anemone* × *hybrida* 'September Charm'), and 'Moonbeam' coreopsis. The summer kitchen doesn't have windows on the north side, so Tim added a trellis to create a perception of depth and make the pool area more attractive. It's covered with 'New Dawn' roses and two cultivars of clematis— 'Mrs. Cholmondeley' and 'Nelly Moser'.

The west side of the summer kitchen has a many-paned glass wall. To frame it, Tim planted clumps of deep red snapdragons and light pink and buff single-flowered hollyhocks (*Alcea* sp.), which are survivors of a garden abandoned here over a decade ago.

Tim didn't want to have to skim petals and leaves off the surface of the pool, but he did find room for two magnolia trees nearby—*Magnolia* × *loebneri* 'Leonard Messel' and *M.* × *soulangiana* 'Coates'. To the north, an old apple tree encloses the space around the lily pool. It has a bench underneath, and the tree has been pruned to make an arched canopy over it. Apple and pear trees, remnants of an old orchard row, draw visitors uphill toward the back of the property. In spring, drifts of flowering bulbs decorate the meadow under the orchard. Tim only mows this area twice a year.

From the rear of the property in winter the Catskill Mountains and the Hudson River are visible. Tim screened the western view, which may be marred by development in the future, with a northern red oak (*Quercus rubra*) and 'Techny' American arborvitaes planted all along the property line to the house.

A Border for the House

From the lily pool, visitors loop past a couple of old apple trees that indicate a natural path that leads back through the heart of Tim's ornamental garden on the north side of the house. This is the only regularly mown lawn on the property. The lawn sets off a fragrant border against the house that's planted with daphnes (*Daphne caucasica* and *D.* × *burkwoodii* 'Carol Mackie'), roses, lavender, peonies, and tuberoses (*Polianthes tuberosa*) grown as annuals.

On the west side of the house, there's a porch and entry to the upstairs sitting room. Located on a steep slope and only 12 feet from the property line, the entrance faces west and was originally awkward to use. To make it easier to get from house to garden, Tim moved the porch railing to open up an exit to the north, directly into the back garden.

In the narrow boundary strip along the west side, Tim created a planting that screens the house from the nearby property. He combined a densely branched, vase-shaped cultivar of shrubby European hornbeam—*Carpinus betulus* 'Fastigiata'—that holds its leaves all winter, with *Fargesia murielae*, which is a very hardy evergreen, clump-forming, noninvasive bamboo with purple-streaked stems. Together they form a soft screen that doesn't appear to box in the house. Yellow-flowered Chinese witch hazels (*Hamamelis mollis*

IN ANOTHER PLACE

Every part of the country has its own traditions of landscape design that you can research and translate into your own outdoor living spaces. A visit to your local library or a nearby historic site or botanical garden should provide a wealth of ideas to consider. You may also uncover clues to local garden styles by just taking a Sunday bike ride to look at gardens in nearby neighborhoods.

However, the ideas of nineteenth-century designers like Andrew Jackson Downing are invaluable far beyond the Hudson River Valley. Designing a garden that features artistically planted groves of trees, carefully planned views, and exciting places to stroll through and enjoy close up is a great idea no matter where you live. This garden's designer, Timothy Steinhoff, also used an almost-forgotten technique that nineteenth-century designers excelled at: Using trees and shrubs to signal special places or transitions in a garden. For example, Tim used two clumps of giant rhubarb (*Rheum palmatum* 'Atrosanguineum') to mark a gateway into the area around the lily pool—one at the corner of the summer kitchen and the other at the corner of the lily pool. In front of the barn, he used two 'Tardiva' panicle hydrangeas (*Hydrangea paniculata* 'Tardiva') to create a gateway leading toward the kitchen garden. A row of orchard trees also forms an informal allée—a grassy corridor between lily pool and kitchen garden. Using plants in this manner is green architecture, and in a casual garden, it can be quite enough to make the landscape memorable.

These ideas aren't just useful for large gardens, either. Even in a tiny town garden, it's possible to use planned views and destinations to create a garden that's intriguing enough to explore again and again. A path that slips out of sight behind a shrub is enough to lure you out into the garden. If the path leads to a bench nestled among ferns and wildflowers in a secluded corner, there will be reason enough to visit the spot again and again. And in a small garden, you could use clumps of smaller plants— such as perennials or smaller ornamental grasses—to mark special places. For example, clumps of golden lemon thyme (*Thymus* × *citriodorus* 'Aureus') on either side of a path could mark the entry to a tiny herb or rock garden.

'Pallida') brighten up the area in late winter when they bloom. Patches of early spring bulbs and groundcovers also add color and interest early in the season.

Linking House and Garden

Views from inside the house out to the garden are an important way that Tim linked the two areas together. Upstairs, three large north-facing windows overlook the fragrant border against the house. East-facing rooms, both upstairs and down, have wonderful views as well. Tim mounted flower boxes below the barn's second-story windows; they're virtually at eye level from the house. The boxes are wrought-iron cages, 44 inches long. Each year, they're lined with moss and embedded with seed-lings all over the entire surface. They cas-cade with color and texture, giving the courtyard between house and barn a luxuriant, romantic feeling. Each year Tim plants them with a new medley of annuals.

Design for Seasonal Change

There are also views from the house into the triangular area between the house, barn, and summer kitchen. Views from the house into this less manicured area change through the seasons. It is mostly designed as a space to look across or as a shortcut around the back of the barn to the kitchen garden. There's a small gabled shed in the middle of this area where fruit boxes were once stored. One of Tim's cats has already claimed it as a refuge where she spends the day, so the shed stays put for now; eventually he'll remove it.

The grassy area to the left of the shed is planted with two lilacs (*Syringa vulgaris*) and an apricot tree (*Prunus armeniaca*). In spring, it's a woodland scene with drifts of bulbs, bleeding hearts (*Dicentra spectabilis*), Virginia bluebells (*Mertensia virginica*), foxglove (*Digitalis purpurea*), columbines (*Aquilegia* spp.), and sweet rocket (*Hesperis matronalis*). As summer comes on, the space quietly shifts to green, with occasional color from lilies, astilbes, and Japanese anemones (*Anemone* × *hybrida*).

When planting this area, Tim dis-covered a long-buried walkway that he promptly excavated. The concrete walk runs directly from the front porch to the barn's far end, where wildflowers shield a new compost bin. This unexpected walk-way immediately became a useful short-cut from the house to the grass ramp that goes up the hill or down to the kitchen garden. There's a clump of *Rudbeckia nitida* 'Herbstsonne' on either side of the walk at the end. This tall perennial bears bright-yellow daisylike flowers with greenish cen-ter cones. They provide a strong seasonal accent in late summer when they bloom—without all the work of formal planting beds.

Creating a Stroll Garden

Undoubtedly, the changes Tim made in the valley in front of the house were the most dramatic. The valley is part of the watershed for the whole area, and parts of it were always underwater during peri-ods of heavy rain. Before he added the pond, each spring two or three of the "geri-atric" orchard trees succumbed to the wet soil. He designed the new pond so that it would lie naturally in the valley's low point. In fact, he used the outline of the spring high-water mark to determine the shape of the pond.

Tim only needed to remove a hand-ful of the old apple trees before having the pond dug. The finished pond is clay-lined and between 12 and 14 feet deep to help to resist growth of algae. Because the valley drops 20 feet from north to south, there's an earthen dam on the southeast end where the driveway enters the property. Tim stocked the pond with fish and enjoys swimming in it.

Planning Informal Pathways

The valley features an informal walk-ing circuit, or stroll garden, around the pond. To lay it out, Tim simply mows a swath through the meadow and around the pond. The path itself is like a playground. He can cut it differently each time he mows. That way, he's free to develop new viewpoints every month by bringing the path closer to something that's in flower or playing with how it traverses the valley slopes.

The walking circuit threads among groves of evergreens and deciduous trees and shrubs that Tim planted in the Hudson River Valley's landscape gardening style. These groves create an ever-changing series of views, alternately hiding parts of the garden and revealing new places to wander as visitors stroll around the pond. Groves of trees planted in this manner act as islands on the landscape; they need plenty of open space around them for best effect. It's interesting to note that from the 1840s to the First World War, gardeners very consciously planned and planted such groves, although today people take them for granted—thinking that they occur naturally.

The groves of trees Tim planted also have an essential screening function, for they block undesirable sights beyond the property itself—most important, the busy state highway. Tim planted Japanese pagoda trees (*Sophora japonica*) to screen power lines along the road and a house on the opposite side of the valley. This is a fast-growing, long-lived tree that also provides beautiful flowers at summer's end. To conceal another house just over the line, he planted a weeping willow (*Salix* sp.) just above the pond's eastern shore along with a grove of oriental and Serbian spruces (*Picea orientalis* and *P. omorika*) at the brow of the hill.

In true landscape-gardening tradi-

NOTES FROM THE DESIGNER

"I've rarely worked for a client who wanted any bright colors, especially orange or red," says Timothy Steinhoff, but he feels that a landscape as green as New York's Hudson River Valley needs vivid hues in addition to pastels. Tim's plan for his own garden is a tapestry of all the rich colors like apricots, maroons, and violets that he seldom gets to use.

All too often, in Tim's experience, people plant new shrubs and perennials too close together, unaware of their mature size or just plain impatient for a finished look. His answer to the waiting game? Each year, Tim selects a different group of annuals to fill in the big gaps that are left when new plantings are properly spaced. The annuals give the whole composition fullness. Choices include 'Sensation' cosmos in white, pink, and burgundy; dark crimson snapdragons; parsley; *Verbena bonariensis*; old-fashioned nicotiana; and sunflowers. If the annuals self-sow, just accept them wherever you like. "This may be a different look from the mature planting composition," says Tim, "but it's a wonderful evolution and an excellent role for annuals." It provides immediate color and gratification, too.

tion, Tim didn't just consider the views visitors would enjoy from the pond. Whenever he planted, he'd look at it from as many angles as possible to get just the effect he was looking for. He looked for views he could enhance from one part of the garden to the other, as well as into his property from the road. For this reason, the pond and surrounding groves shape a handsome vista into the property from the road—across the pastoral valley to the house nestled into the crest of the hill. From his front porch, Tim looks out across the lawn and perennial border, over the meadow to the pond, which is framed by groves of conifers and deciduous trees.

There is a wealth of detail to enjoy close up throughout the stroll garden. Lightning bugs are profuse at night in areas that aren't heavily mown. During the day, there are wildflowers, birds, and butterflies to enjoy. Tim also added drifts of moisture-loving plants along the damp edges of the pond, including ornamental rhubarb (*Rheum palmatum*), dwarf forget-me-nots (*Myosotis scorpioides* var. *semperflorens*), Joe-Pye weed (*Eupatorium purpureum*), and a variety of primroses (*Primula* spp.).

Looking to the Future

This is a garden that will change continuously over the years as the trees and shrubs grow and Tim adds more plants.

Over the years, he'll watch to make sure the views he wants to keep will remain open, and prune accordingly. He'll also be on the lookout for new features to highlight—such as striking combinations of plants—that will make walking through the landscape even more enjoyable. Acquiring the plants he wants may take a lifetime, but since he developed his property almost like an arboretum, he'll be able to collect to his heart's content and still be able to find room.

Tim plans eventually to add a paved path from the house to the parking area that he can shovel in winter and use when the ground is muddy without tracking mud into the house. He'd like to add a small conservatory onto the summer kitchen, so he'll be able to grow plants as well. He would use the space as a cool greenhouse for cool-flowering plants such as camellias and bulbs, as well as to overwinter tender perennials, herbs, and fruits. Finally, he would sometime like to add a slate terrace to expand the entertaining room available on the narrow front porch. If so, it would be laid in sand for a handmade effect, similar to the edging around the lily pool. ✦

SHARING SPACE: TURNING TWO YARDS INTO ONE GARDEN

Margaret and Steven are good neighbors who own small, adjoining lots in a modern townhouse development. Both lots face south, and neither boasted anything but a plain strip of lawn when Margaret and Steven purchased them. Yet both neighbors wanted gardens filled with flowers, trees, and good things to eat. Together, they came up with an unusual solution to developing outdoor living spaces they could enjoy: They decided to remove the fence that divided their two properties and pool their resources to create one larger garden for both to enjoy. Landscape architect Michael McKinley helped them plan a garden that satisfies their needs, both in style and content.

The Place and the People

Margaret and Steven's townhouse plots lie in North Marin County, California, in the hot, dry Sacramento Valley. The Sacramento Valley is a rich agricultural area, but since there is little rainfall, irrigation is necessary to grow nearly any non-native plants.

The development Margaret and Steven live in is a planned community, sometimes called a "pedestrian pocket," designed so all its residents live within walking distance of basic neighborhood services. People live closer together in such developments than they would in the suburbs, and they have much less private space at

---

KEY CONCEPTS FOR A SUCCESSFUL DESIGN

Sharing space and views. Although many gardeners take advantage of scenery beyond their property lines, this design takes the concept one step further. These gardeners share their lots and create views for one another to make the small space seem larger. In the process, they also get to share the abundant produce of their combined garden.

Creating privacy in a small garden. Not all the space in these small adjoining gardens is in full view of the neighboring residence. Each garden features a small private patio near the back door and a completely secluded "secret garden" surrounded by walls composed of shrubs and trees.

Making a small space seem larger. The designer used a handful of tricks to make these gardens seem larger than they really are. These tricks include paths that narrow toward the back of the property, gates that aren't the size they seem to be, and smaller plants in paler colors along the back lot line.

Edible landscaping. Almost all the plants in this design produce food, but it's a beautiful garden, too. Fragrant, flavorful herbs and colorful fruit trees form the backbone of the design.

---

their disposal. On the other hand, the community offers many of the benefits that residents of small towns and older neighborhoods enjoy. These include access to nearby public spaces like parks and plazas, proximity to services, and the potential for a close-knit community.

The front doors of Margaret and Steven's townhouses face north, so the south-facing backyards get lots of sun. Each house has a sun room at the back, and when they first moved in there were no nearby trees to provide much-needed shade. The lots also are open to the southern sky, because the land falls off just past the rear fence. There is another terraced area below their back lot line, which is filled with commercial buildings that are also part of the development in which Margaret and Steven live.

Two Gardeners, Two Styles

Margaret looked upon her new home and garden as an oasis for her retirement from teaching French and history. She also wanted a lush, romantic garden that overflowed with flowers and fragrances that would remind her of those she enjoyed abroad during years of touring with student groups. Her neighbor Steven is about 20 years younger and is a financial manager for a local manufacturer. He likes to entertain formally and has a buttoned-down style. Despite their differences, the new neighbors hit it off when they met at their front doors and soon began consulting each other about home improvements. From there it was just a short step to talking about sharing their outdoor space.

Landscape architect Michael McKinley showed them how one design could satisfy both their needs—without sacrificing either's individuality. Now, not only do they both have a wealth of plants to enjoy, the design also makes the combined space, which is still small, seem much larger. McKinley did this by including secluded areas, using forced perspective, and employing other design tricks.

One Ingenious Design

For a design such as this one to succeed, it had to meet the needs of both gardeners. Margaret wanted the view from the patio outside her sun-room doorway to be soft and informal. Flowing lines and curving spaces lushly filled with plants appeal to her. Steven, on the other hand, wanted a crisply formal view, with tidy edges and straight lines.

Both wanted a sense of a large garden in what was, admittedly, a tiny lot. They agreed that it made sense to share a utility area. But each wanted both a semi-private entertaining area next to the house and a completely private place to retreat to. They also both wanted the garden to produce a variety of vegetables, fruit, and herbs: Margaret, to save money, since she is on a fixed income; Steven, to satisfy his gourmet palate.

Sharing the garden solves one problem that many single gardeners face: overabundance. For example, in this garden Margaret and Steven share the bounty from each orange or apple tree. And since they have twice the land to work with, they can plant a wider variety of foods than each could have alone. Another advantage in combining the plots is that both

Margaret and Steven will be able to borrow the view across the other's property. This is one of the main features that makes both spaces appear larger.

McKinley started the design by selecting two diagonal "view lines," which were eventually developed into pathways, from each patio. One extends from the patio to the back corner of the original lot, close to where the fence once stood. The other crosses the neighboring garden and leads to its far rear corner. These diagonals draw the longest possible line across the space available, which helps the area appear larger.

By using different paving, hedging styles, and plants along the pathways, the styles of the two different gardens—romantic and formal—overlap. But from each patio, only one style is visible: Margaret has her romantic garden; Steven, his formal one. And almost every plant in the design produces food.

As a crowning touch, McKinley used a variety of design tricks to make the pooled property appear larger than it actually is. From cleverly contrasting leaf and fruit size to gates of different dimensions, this garden design explores the many ways to pull off the illusion of greater space.

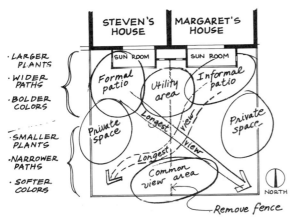

Even before neighbors Margaret and Steven had removed the fence that separated their two yards, landscape architect Michael McKinley sketched in a rough plan of their garden design. This not only helped locate the long "view lines"—one formal and one informal—that would make the yard appear larger, it also identified where the shared utility area would be. In addition, the plan provided for a completely private retreat in each garden and a patio just outside each house.

Getting from Fantasy to Fact

Once McKinley selected the view lines of the gardens—two from Margaret's home and two from Steven's—the design fell into place easily. Each garden is a mirror-image of the other, but features a contrasting style. Margaret's romantic garden has a loose and natural look, characterized by irregular curves, free-form paving, and unsheared plants. Steven's formal garden has a neat, tailored look with straight lines, angular paving, and strictly sheared plants.

In addition to including plenty of food plants, the design also has water-saving features. McKinley used drought-tolerant plants wherever possible. There is also an efficient drip irrigation system for plants that require supplemental water in this desert region. There is absolutely no lawn: It just uses too much water.

Margaret and Steven did all the work of installing the garden themselves. The first year they dismantled the dividing fence, planted the trees, and installed the gates and trellis-wall frameworks. They also planted the drought-resistant rosemary and thyme plants that form the edges of the view-line paths. These low hedges of herbs outline all the beds defined by the pathways and define the character of the two sides of the garden. The hedges Margaret can see from her patio are flowing and natural looking; those Steven can see are clipped and formal. At first, Margaret and Steven filled the beds with annuals. Over the years, they gradually replaced them with perennial herbs.

The Grand Illusion

McKinley used a variety of design tricks to make all four paths seem longer than they actually are. The diagonal paths are a key element in making the space seem larger. The first glimpse visitors get of the garden is from indoors. As they wander out into the sun room near the back of each townhouse and onto the patio, they look down the path that leads on a gentle diagonal toward the center of the property, where the fence once stood. Once they've walked to near the edge of the patio, they're surprised by the view down the second path in each garden. The second path follows the longest diagonal line McKinley could draw in the space available—from the corner of the patio outside the sun-room door to the far corner of the garden. It's a surprisingly long view for such a small space, which gives the illusion of a larger garden.

McKinley was careful to screen views of neighboring properties to make sure the illusions he was creating would work on all levels. To do this, he surrounded both properties with a fence and trees. Since the land drops away beyond the back lot lines, the buildings on the terrace below aren't visible. As a result, the trees at the back of the property are set against the sky and draw it down to the garden.

Each of the four paths leads to an ornamental gate at the rear of the property. To heighten the illusion that the paths are long, McKinley designed them so they gradually become narrower toward the back of the property. To reinforce the illusion of depth, he designed gates that are smaller than normal at the end of each path. McKinley also used plants to further exaggerate the perspective. For example, the hedges of herbs that outline the beds become shorter toward the back of the property.

Although both yards are nearly flat, there is a gentle downward slope toward the center of each property—no more than 1 to 2 feet. The land then slopes up again to the back lot lines. This gentle contour helps exaggerate the illusion of depth. The paths that cross the properties seem to dip out of sight near the middle and then re-emerge beyond. As a result, the eye reads the space as larger than it actually is.

Pairs of Plants to Fool the Eye

McKinley also used carefully chosen pairs of plants with similar characteristics to help emphasize the illusion of depth in this garden. As a general rule, bright colors and coarse textures appear closer; pale colors, such as grays and blue-greens, and fine textures tend to recede. Even

GARDEN SLEIGHT OF HAND

This design makes good use of the old painter's trick of "false" or "forced" perspective. Using perspective in this manner takes a bit more planning, but it's not a hard technique to apply to a garden plan.

It's easy to visualize how perspective works in terms of your own experience. Imagine you're looking down a railroad track: the parallel tracks come together and seem to meet in the distance. Your eye composes what it sees into a picture. From experience, it reads the tracks that converge in the distance as parallel, and it perceives the point where the tracks seem to converge as being very far away.

Painters use this knowledge to transform a flat canvas into what seems to be a three-dimensional scene. For example, roadways that recede into the distance are narrower in the background than they are in the foreground. Gates and houses in the background are smaller than ones in the foreground, too.

In a landscape, the principle works much the same way. Designing a path that gets narrower toward the back of a lot will trick the eye into reading the distance as farther than it actually is. This property doesn't just feature paths that get narrower: At the back of the property, the gates, the herb hedges, and the trees are smaller than those near the house. Even the colors of the plants near the back of the property fade as if into the distance.

In order for the illusion to be effective, it's important that all elements of the design work together. For example, narrowing paths with full-size gates at the end wouldn't be as effective. Too much exaggeration, on the other hand, won't trick the eye. Instead, it will read the illusion of greater depth as farcical rather than believable.

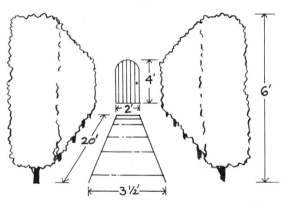

To exaggerate the perspective, and thus make the garden seem larger, landscape architect Michael McKinley diminished the height of the hedges toward the back of the garden. The paths narrow toward the back and terminate at smaller-than-normal gates to support the illusion of great distance from one end of the yard to the other.

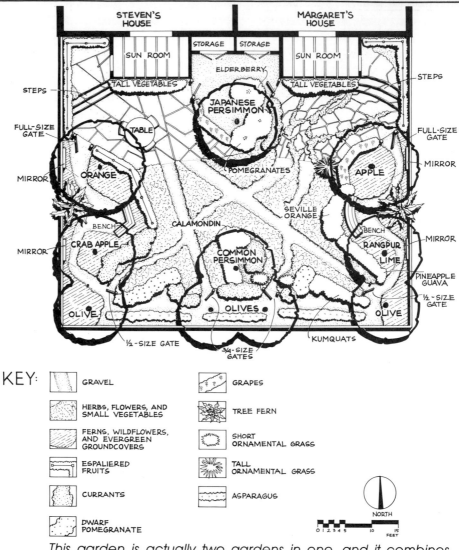

STEVEN'S HOUSE

MARGARET'S HOUSE

SUN ROOM

STORAGE STORAGE

ELDERBERRY

SUN ROOM

STEPS

TALL VEGETABLES

JAPANESE PERSIMMON

TALL VEGETABLES

STEPS

FULL-SIZE GATE

TABLE

FULL-SIZE GATE

MIRROR

ORANGE

POMEGRANATES

APPLE

MIRROR

SEVILLE ORANGE

BENCH

CALAMONDIN

BENCH

RANGPUR LIME

MIRROR

MIRROR

CRAB APPLE

COMMON PERSIMMON

PINEAPPLE GUAVA

½-SIZE GATE

OLIVE

OLIVES

OLIVE

½-SIZE GATE

¾-SIZE GATES

KUMQUATS

KEY:

GRAVEL

HERBS, FLOWERS, AND SMALL VEGETABLES

FERNS, WILDFLOWERS, AND EVERGREEN GROUNDCOVERS

ESPALIERED FRUITS

CURRANTS

DWARF POMEGRANATE

GRAPES

TREE FERN

SHORT ORNAMENTAL GRASS

TALL ORNAMENTAL GRASS

ASPARAGUS

NORTH

0 1 2 3 4 5   10   15
FEET

This garden is actually two gardens in one, and it combines formal and informal styles in a unique way: Each homeowner sees only a single view from his or her house. Steven's view is formal: The patio is paved with clean-edged, angular stone, the paths are straight, and the hedges that line them are neatly clipped. His neighbor Margaret's view is informal and romantic: The paving and paths are flowing and irregular, and the hedges that line them are soft and unsheared. Although the paths cross, shrubs and trees control the views. It's not until visitors walk out into the garden that the real design is revealed.

174

PLANTING NOTES

Edible landscapes like this one do double duty—they produce food and are attractive at the same time. They're perfect for anyone who loves to garden and eat fresh-picked produce. In this design, food-producing plants do double duty as ornamentals; they're used as hedges to create privacy, to mark paths, and to heighten the illusions of depth and space that make the garden seem larger than it is.

Above all, an edible landscape is convenient. Margaret and Steven merely need to step out their doors to clip fresh herbs for sauces or soups, to harvest fresh fruit in season, or to pick a ripe tomato or pepper for a salad. Their garden also features such well-known edibles as currants (*Ribes sativum*), elderberries (*Sambucus canadensis*), and grapes.

Because Margaret and Steven's gardens are located in the balmy Sacramento Valley, they're able to grow many plants that aren't hardy in the north. These include citrus trees and olive trees (*Olea europaea*), as well as the Mexican tree ferns (*Cibotium schiedei*) that adorn the private space in each garden. Other unusual fruits include calamondins (× *Citrofortunella mitis*), which produce tiny orangelike fruits that are excellent in iced tea or preserves, kumquats (*Fortunella japonica*), and pineapple guava 'Coolidgei' (*Feijoa sellowiana* 'Coolidgei').

shades of a single color can be used to exaggerate the feeling of depth in a garden. For example, brilliant blue morning glories would appear closer than pale blue ones.

McKinley used this principle when he choose the plants for this garden. He used large-leaved and large-fruited plants along with bold colors near the patios. Toward the back, he selected plants with smaller leaves and fruit and more subdued colors to make them seem farther away. For example, he planted olive trees (*Olea europaea*) along the rear property line, because their fine texture and faded gray-green color help suggest greater distance.

But he took it one step further: He selected pairs of plants throughout that would echo one another. He would match a taller plant with large leaves and fruit to a similar one with smaller leaves and fruit, planting the tall one near the house and the smaller one farther away.

For example, the tallest tree on the property is centered between the two patios. It is a Japanese persimmon (*Diospyros kaki*), a species with large, bright-orange fruit and shiny dark-green leaves that are 10 inches long and 3 inches wide. It is echoed at the back of the garden by a common persimmon (*D. virginiana*), which has dull-surfaced leaves and small dull-orange fruit. Under the Japanese persimmon are two 'Wonderful' pomegranate trees (*Punica granatum* 'Wonderful') with full-size fruit and leaves, while dwarf pomegranates (*P. granatum* 'Nana') with tiny fruits and leaves are massed in the distance under the common persimmon. Similarly, large strawberries near the patio

(continued on page 178)

The irregular paving of Margaret's patio is softened by clumps of sprawling herbs—Corsican mint and mother-of-thyme—that she planted in the cracks between the stones. The stones seem to flow toward the paths that lead to the gates at the back of the property. The gates are not all they seem to be: To make the garden seem larger, those at the back of the property are

smaller than the two that lead directly off it. The door on the right of the patio leads to a utility area that Margaret shares with her neighbor, Steven; the door on the left is a gateway to a completely private sitting area and "secret garden." The garden is an edible landscape through and through. It overflows with herbs, apples, grapes, persimmons, and a host of other edibles.

177

are echoed by alpine strawberries (*Fragaria vesca* 'Alpine') near the south gates.

McKinley used pairs of plants throughout the garden. An 'Anna' apple tree by the patio in Margaret's garden, is echoed by a 'Chestnut' crab apple at the end of the long diagonal path that leads from her patio to the far corner. A clump of blue oat grass (*Helictotrichon sempervirens*) in the foreground is paired with blue fescue (*Festuca caesia*, formerly *F. ovina* var. *glauca*), which is somewhat smaller and has more-bluish foliage, at the far end of the short path that leads to the center of the property.

Steven's more formal view is deepened by pairing a sweet 'Valencia' orange tree (*Citrus sinensis* 'Valencia') next to the patio with a rangpur lime tree (*Citrus* × *limonia*) at the end of the long diagonal path—the rangpur's fruits look like small oranges.

Paving Patterns

Both patios are paved with reddish brown Arizona flagstone. Margaret's is romantic in style, with irregularly shaped flagstones. Corsican mint (*Mentha requienii*) and mother-of-thyme (*Thymus serpyllum*) sprawl along the cracks between the stones to soften the edges. The stones seem to flow like a stream toward the curving, irregularly edged cottagey garden paths that wander along the view lines toward the back of the property.

Steven's patio is paved with clean-cut, angular stones. The joints between flagstones line up so they extend the edges of the arrow-straight pathways that lead from his patio. Unlike Margaret's soft, romantic-looking patio, Steven's has cemented joints so no plants will grow in the crisp and formal paving.

The paths that begin beyond the edges of both terraces are made of fine decomposed granite. The dusty red-brown color of the granite is very close to that of the Arizona flagstone used for the patios. Using the same color in both paths and patios helps link the two areas together.

The change in texture from the patios to the paths is another factor that helps make the garden seem larger. It contrasts the large pavers in the foreground with the fine texture of the pathways, giving the illusion of greater depth. The decomposed granite also made it easier to decrease the width of the pathways toward the back of the garden.

Games with Gates

This garden has a total of eight gates, four of which can be seen from each patio. Although all the gates appear to be perfectly matched in size, McKinley designed them to help make the garden seem larger. The gates next to the patios are full-size, but those in the distance are not: The illusion depends on the fact that visitors will tend to see them as full-size, so they seem farther away than they really are. The two gates at the end of the shorter paths near the center of the property are only shoulder-high (three-quarter size). Those at the end of the long diagonal pathways are only waist-high (half size).

McKinley scaled each gate according to its location along the forced-perspective lines. He reinforced the illusion that the gates are full-size but far away by designing free-standing green "walls" made out of shrubs and trellised plants that slope down from the height of the patio gates to the height of the distant gates, as well as by narrowing the pathways that lead to the gates.

Each set of four gates reflects the style of the garden from which they can be seen. The four gates Margaret can see from her romantic patio have curved tops and a handcrafted, rustic look. Steven's gates are squared-off and modern looking.

Separating Public and Private Spaces

In this design, the gates aren't just used to provide a focal point for the view lines to the back of the property. They're used to provide access to and privacy from the shared utility area. Better yet, each garden features a gate that opens into a completely private "secret garden" shielded from the rest of the world.

Steven's patio features a formal view. The angular lines of the stone paving direct the eye toward straight, neatly edged paths and small-size gates that seem farther away than they really are. Unlike the rustic-looking gates that his neighbor Margaret can see on her side of this shared garden, Steven's gates are square-edged and formal. The door on the left of Steven's patio leads to a shared utility area; the one on the right to his formal, private sitting area.

The gates to the shared utility space between Margaret and Steven's gardens are full-size and lead directly from each patio. By enclosing this shared space, McKinley automatically created privacy for each patio. The common area is a place where Margaret and Steven can meet, exchange news, share tools, and offer advice.

McKinley also used the outside edges of the garden to advantage. On the outside of each patio, a second full-size gate opens into a shady, completely private sitting garden—a tiny garden within a garden. From Steven's patio he can see a low hedge of sheared common boxwood (*Buxus sempervirens*) through the open gate. From Margaret's, a pleasing medley of ferns and wildflowers is visible. Trellises covered with espaliered fruits serve as walls for the private nooks and make the most of the space. Benches inside each space invite visitors to sit and enjoy the lush Mexican tree fern (*Cibotium schiedei*). Fence-mounted mirrors on either side reflect back the greenery and make the space seem twice as large.

Looking to the Future

Margaret and Steven have found that they enjoy sharing the ins and outs of this design with visitors. Although the illusion of forced perspective works best from the patios, it's also interesting to walk into the garden to appreciate the interplay of formal and informal styles and the structure of crossed diagonal lines. At each intersection with a crossing path, they discover a garden gate that wasn't visible from the patio, because it was concealed by intervening plants. This gives the garden an element of surprise and discovery.

IN ANOTHER PLACE

There are lots of ideas in this design that can be used on a single property. Selecting view lines is a good place to start any design, because it simplifies the design process and provides you with a ready-made focal point. In a very small space you may have room for only one view line—from the back of the house to a far corner of the lot, for example. Once you've selected the view line, consider what would make an effective focal point at the end of it. Adding a gate, a piece of sculpture, a bench or arbor, or a specimen plant are just some of the possibilities.

To create the illusion of a garden that's bigger than it really is, try to use the longest line across the garden that you can. Then consider using some of the tricks that landscape architect Michael McKinley used in this garden.

These tricks aren't just for small gardens, either. Some are just plain fun to play with, but even in a large garden there are many places where a sense of greater depth or space would be effective.

Don't forget, too, that you can borrow an interesting view beyond your property line, such as nearby scenery, a striking plant, or a distant church or other building. Once you've identified an interesting view to highlight, you can either clear away plants that block it, or add plants to frame it. You may want to link the view to the garden by repeating shapes or colors that help connect the two. For example, you can use small mounds of natural-looking rock to mimic nearby mountains and link them to your own landscape.

NOTES FROM THE DESIGNER

According to Michael McKinley, consistency is all-important in a design that uses forced perspective—or any kind of illusion, for that matter. All the elements of the design must support the illusion you're trying to achieve. For example, if a narrowing path leads to a full-size gate, the two will tend to cancel each other out.

McKinley uses lots of subtle detail to support the illusions he is trying to create. This garden features many of those details—foliage, flower, and fruit colors that seem to fade into the distance as well as smaller specimen plants, gates, and hedges in the far reaches of the garden. According to McKinley, using colors and textures in gardens like these is subjective: You have to decide what works for you. He warns, however, "You can push it too much, so that you get too great a contrast, as in a giant-leaved gunnera in the foreground and a delicate hosta in the background." In this case the illusion no longer will be effective.

Illusions are most effective when the outside world is excluded entirely. Disneyland is an ideal example: Each part is a world unto itself, and all the details are consistent with the illusion. Says McKinley, "If you want to get in here and play this game, you have to be willing to go all the way. One item out of context, or out of scale, absolutely destroys the whole effect."

"Getting started working with illusion takes a degree of playfulness with spatial relationships, seeing what you can get away with and what you can't," says McKinley. He recommends doing lots of simplifying, scaling back, and toning down, as your design develops.

This design took some patience before it reached its full effect. It was five years before the forced perspective in the design became apparent, and nearly ten before visitors could really appreciate the full effect. But in the meantime, Margaret and Steven found that the garden was still attractive, productive, and an enjoyable place to spend their time.

The most obvious question about a garden like this one is "What will happen if one of the two gardeners moves away?" It's altogether possible that a new resident would be just as taken as Margaret and Steven were with the idea of having a garden that seems larger than it really is.

Even if a new resident wanted to replace the fence, the efficient use of utility space, patios, and secret sitting gardens could remain unchanged. The slight diagonal line drawn by the shorter of the two paths, which terminates near the center of the two properties, would still give the illusion of depth. The long path, which would be cut off by replacing the fence, could remain, perhaps with a bench against the fence looking back along the view line that was originally part of the neighboring garden. The style of the perennial and groundcover plantings along this view line could easily be converted to conform to the style of the garden. ◆

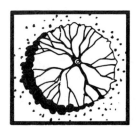

CREATING YOUR OWN OUTDOOR LIVING SPACES
A Step-by-Step Guide

In this section you'll learn how to design your own garden and how to create outdoor living spaces that you and your family can use and enjoy. Garden design is a creative process that can be intimidating; it's certainly complicated. After all, there are unlimited choices of plants and materials, not to mention the many ways in which you can combine them. And add to that the fact that plants change from hour to hour, day to day, season to season, and year to year.

But designing your own garden is also an enjoyable, deeply satisfying process

This welcoming entranceway, which provides an attractive streetside face in author Susan Frey's garden, features redbud trees underplanted with daffodils and tulips. The white picket gate at the end of the path effectively divides the more public area near the street from private spaces behind the house without being unfriendly.

that can have untold rewards. Once they get started, most gardeners thoroughly enjoy every aspect of it—from listing ideas and possibilities to tinkering with plant combinations.

In the chapters that follow, you'll find a framework to guide you as you design your garden. The framework will show you how to discover ideas and landscape elements that have special meaning for you—and how to use them in your garden. You'll learn how to do an in-depth investigation of your property, including how to map it. Then you'll find out how to take your ideas and translate them into garden spaces that you can use, how to connect different areas in your garden, and how to select plants and materials.

Throughout, you'll find suggestions and principles to guide you, along with lots of ideas and examples designed to help you see the possibilities. You'll also find loads of questions to ask yourself.

183

That's because only you can decide what kind of garden you want and what design would best fit your yard.

Garden design isn't as linear a process as it may seem. In real life, you'll probably find yourself working on a variety of steps—making notes about favorite places you'd like to use as inspiration, listing ideas for ways you'd like to use your garden, and investigating the character of your property—all at the same time.

You may find that you want to complete one step before attacking the next, or that one aspect—such as analyzing your site—may become a long-term process that you pursue as you design. It depends on how much you enjoy the process and whether or not you view it as a means to an end or as an enjoyable activity in and of itself. You also may find that your plans for different spaces are at various stages of design—from rough-sketched to nearly complete.

That's okay, because there is really no right way to do this process. You can plan your garden down to every last detail on paper before you start or leave most of the plan as a rough sketch in favor of developing a single area. Just try not to get bogged down in the process looking for the one right answer—there isn't one. Instead, you'll discover a number of solutions and then choose the one that is the best fit for you.

Set Up a Design Center

Before you go any further, find a spot in the house where you can collect information and let ideas simmer. You'll need a bookshelf and a bulletin board, with a stock of pencils and blank paper. Your design center is a convenient place to store plant catalogs, garden books, pages torn from magazines, and photographs or postcards of scenes you love, as well as inventory lists and drawings. Other supplies like files, sheet protectors, notebooks, and ring binders will depend on your penchant for organization and how much room is available.

Locate the design center in a place that's convenient to all members of the household, where it will be seen daily. Most important, establish that it is for everyone to use—and encourage them to use it. Anybody can write or sketch an idea and post it for the others to review. That way, for example, you can pin up alternative designs for a new fence and leave them there for days or weeks while family members consider them and pencil in suggested changes. As your family goes through the design process, your design center will support collaboration and demonstrate the project's importance.

Write It Down

If you haven't already started a garden journal as recommended in part 1, start one now. Gardens are complicated places where change is the only constant. Without good garden-journal records of your ideas, natural cycles, plants, purchases, and criticisms, you'll be working in the dark, ill-equipped to mull over new design ideas that may solve problems and add value to your outdoor living spaces.

Once you've drawn your base plan, clip a copy of it to the front or back cover of your journal, so it's handy for notations. You may find that unlined paper will allow you to switch back and forth between sketching and writing, lists and sentences, so that you are always using the form of documentation that suits your purpose. It's easier to write about the lovely sound when a winter breeze lifts the dried leaves of a clump of ornamental grasses than to draw it. On the other hand, it's easier to sketch your idea for a new gate design than to describe it with words. And then you have an image to show your spouse or a carpenter, as well as a visual idea that you can use when looking into questions such as the kind of wood to use or whether you could have it made out of wrought iron.

Journal entries that include rough sketches and notes of garden designs and details are invaluable throughout the process. They'll help you remember your ideas and build on them and also communicate ideas to family, friends, and anyone you hire to implement them. When you develop your design, you'll be working from your notes, sketches, plans, and photographs. If you haven't written down your ideas, sketched out possibilities, or collected photographs to inspire you, you'll quite possibly forget some of your best ideas. So, to make your job easier, take time to write things down: The more information you've collected, the better your plan will be.

Keep Looking

Once you start looking at landscapes from a garden designer's point of view, you'll find you never look at them the same way again. You'll begin to notice more of the details of a garden than you did before—the texture of paving patterns, effective plant combinations, and interesting ways to mark boundaries and pathways, for example. In natural areas, you'll notice everything from subtle combinations of plants to the way rocks or water works in a landscape.

All your observations will bring a richness to the designs you develop in your own garden. You'll also discover that garden design isn't a destination, it's a process. There will always be decisions to make, ideas to try out, and new plants to grow. Along the way, you'll fine-tune your skills, as both a designer and a gardener. Your outdoor living spaces will continue to evolve, as will your vision of what you want your garden to be. This is part of the joy of gardening—the anticipation of what is to come.

IDEAS FOR YOUR GARDEN: RECALLING FAVORITE LANDSCAPES

By now you know that design is the key to making a truly wonderful garden for yourself and your family. But how do you come up with all the ideas you need to make a design? And once you do that, how can you tell which ones are right for you? In this chapter we'll help you do just that. In the pages that follow, you'll find exercises that will help you uncover ideas and landscape elements that have special meaning for you.

You'll find that this chapter asks more questions than it answers. That's because you're the only one who can decide what kind of garden is right for you. Coming up with a list of what you truly want and really need in your garden takes thought. And it means asking yourself a lot of questions. But it's also a process that's great fun, and one that can give you new insight into yourself.

For now, set aside all the dreams and schemes you have for your garden. We'll come back to them later. First, let's explore where some of your likes and dislikes come from. The results may surprise you and suggest new and exciting garden ideas that are perfect for your outdoor living spaces.

Remembering Favorite Places

Ever wonder why some places touch a responsive cord while others leave you unmoved? The clues may hide in your subconscious. Memories of special childhood places—how they looked, felt, sounded, or smelled—can be very strong influences, but you may not recognize them. By delving deep into early memories, it's possible to uncover the reason certain places are special to you as an adult. This is a way of rediscovering those "sacred places" of your childhood—places where you delighted in nature and felt part of it.

Because the spaces you remember from your childhood are so charged with your emotions, they give valuable clues to your present-day desires. You can use the places you discover from your childhood memories to create extremely satisfying elements in your outdoor living spaces today. That's why your early memories of the outdoors are such a rich source of ideas for your garden. They're also clues to your personal style.

Leading teachers of landscape architects (including Clare Cooper Marcus and Randolph T. Hester, Jr., at the University of California, Berkeley campus, and Anne Whiston Spirn at the University of Pennsylvania) use the exercises that follow to help students become more aware of the ▶

Water strikes a responsive chord in many gardeners, whether it be in a placid pond that reflects the landscape around it or in a bubbling brook that plunges down a hillside. The sound of water—from a waterfall, fountain, or stream—adds life to a garden. It creates atmosphere and also can block out the sounds of the outside world.

Karen Bussolini

▲ *A path that dips out of sight somehow awakens the explorer in us all, pulling us along to discover what's beyond the bend. This narrow, leaf-mulched path threads its way into the forest between beds of naturalized ferns. Whether inspired by someone's childhood memories, the result of conscious planning, or just a happy accident, it is an effective and memorable design.*

kinds of spaces they value, and may tend to design. As you explore remembered places, you, too, will discover how to make spaces that satisfy you, because they're rooted in the values you formed as a child.

Return to Childhood Haunts

First, let's take an imaginary journey into your childhood. Get a pencil and some paper and find a quiet place where you can spend at least a half hour uninterrupted and alone. Close your eyes and breathe deeply and steadily. What is your earliest memory of the outdoors? One friend, for example, recalls escaping his nursery crib to a secret haven under a flowering shrub, where he felt more happily alive and safe. What are you doing in your memory? How are you feeling? What details do you notice? Was the place hot and sunny or cool and shady?

Was it high off the ground, or protected and enclosed? Was it wild-looking and home to animals, or clipped and formal? Was it colorful, fragrant, or full of good things to eat? Try to remember all the details you can.

Open your eyes and begin writing down your memory. Use the "free-writing" method, where you keep the pencil moving. Don't stop to reread or think, and don't cross out. Write as big and as sloppily as you wish: Don't worry about the lines or margins. Keep writing until you have written down the memory completely. You can sketch it, too, if you like.

Repeat this exercise at different stages of your life; don't restrict yourself to just your childhood years. Everyone has moments they remember of the outdoors when their perceptions were especially heightened. Think of times when you felt especially happy or content. Were you sitting in a field with tall grasses waving overhead, exploring a woodland trail, or playing along the edge of a pond? As you explore each memory, ask yourself the following questions: What are you doing? What makes it memorable? What about the memory stimulates you or gives you comfort?

Map Your Old Neighborhood

For even more information—and, more important, ideas for your garden—tap into your memory of the neighborhoods where you spent a lot of time outdoors as you were growing up.

Many childhood territories are a patchwork of areas that are dangerous and safe, wild and civilized. The settings you remember might be city alleys, the backyards of a subdivision, an uncle's farm, or a remote woodland surrounding a summer camp. You may recall areas where you played fantasy games—like a huge fallen log in a woods where you played "Viking ship," or a field you loved to explore again and again. Think, too, about areas where you played sports, sought solitude, or spent time with friends and family.

Begin again, with closed eyes, and focus on how your neighborhood looked,

Balthazar Korab

▲

Childhood memories of the outdoors are a rich source of ideas for garden designs. Use them to remember beloved plants you'd like to grow or as inspiration for outdoor rooms or special features to design—perhaps a tree-fort-like deck or gazebo.

felt, smelled, and sounded to you when you roamed your territory. Now take a blank sheet of paper and sketch a map, starting perhaps with the back door of your childhood home, that locates all your favorite childhood activities and places. You can draw your map like a beeline from place to place or perhaps as a series of connected "bubbles." Jot down a description of each place, and note what activity you did there and how you felt about it. Be sure to note highlights that you passed along the way as you went from place to place. These might include a bridge you had to cross, a marsh you had to detour around, or a path you traveled over.

You may want to draw several such maps, representing different times in your life or places in which you lived. Take all the time you like with this exploration. Remember, both positive and negative memories offer significant clues to what you are searching for in your adult landscape. Every piece of information you uncover may be a valuable piece of the puzzle. Remember, too, that there are no wrong answers! A friend finds walking through tall grass or brush very threatening because of an admittedly irrational fear of snakes. But she enjoys the look of a meadow. Her solution to these conflicting feelings is mown walking paths, winding through a sea of tall, rippling meadow.

Look at What You've Learned

Once you've finished writing down as many of your childhood memories as possible, spread the papers on a big table or tack them up on a wall so you can see them all at once. Look for the strongest feelings and what particular things about each place evoked them. On a new sheet of

Susan's Journal

Notes from My Outdoor Autobiography

I have a very strong memory of lying in a hammock with my mother, running my thumb and index finger down the mimosa twigs to pop off the tiny leaves. We are swinging lazily, Mother singing "Waltzing Matilda," and the light streams down in a thousand fragments through the feathery pink plumes of the mimosa flowers.

Climbing up on the garage roof at age six gave me a wonderful command of the world below.

Swinging on vines over gullies made me feel like Tarzan at age eight.

Plucking the luscious grapes from overhead and savoring their sweetness as we sat on Grandmother's porch gave me a wonderful sense of bounty as a 14-year-old.

This list and map in my journal show me that I resorted to the landscape both for sanctuary and adventure. As a child, my imagination was always in play, whether I was trying to walk silently like the Indians, or nestling in the trampled tall grass where I dreamed the deer slept at night.

Writing this as an adult, I realize that it's time to get a hammock, and that it needs to be secluded and beneath a tree. I'd also like to have some part of my garden that I can explore—that offers an element of surprise each time I visit, whether it be a new flower in bloom, or signs of a bird building a new nest.

Favorite Places

I'd love to have a water garden inspired by Slippery Rock State Park in Georgia, where water sheets over huge flat rocks. The sound of rushing water

triggers other good memories, too, like the stream behind my house where we caught crayfish when I was a child.

I can imagine a pool and waterfall that would remind me of these feelings. I would need very large, flat rocks that overlapped that the water could be pumped over. They could be set upon a bed of smooth gravel or river rock, with water-loving plants like bulrushes and irises at the edges. The water would collect at the bottom of the sloping rocks, to be recirculated to the top by a pump. I'd also need a pool liner underneath it all to contain the water.

An idea like this is something I'd mull over for quite a while: It would be a major project and new feature, and would require considerable changes in my current garden plan. But what fun it would be to work out the design, build it, and live with it!

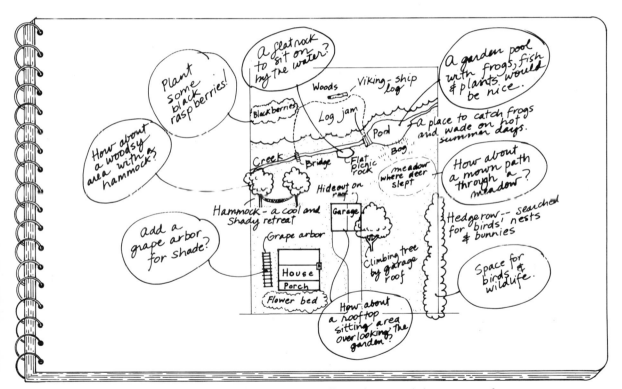

Places you remember from your childhood are a rich source of ideas for your garden because they have such a strong influence on the settings that you appreciate as an adult. Drawing a map of your childhood neighborhood is one way to uncover places that have special meaning for you. Who could resist a landscape that incorporates ideas and garden features linked to memories of their happiest times as a child?

paper, start a list of words that recur. Does a pattern emerge? Circle similar items in the same color so they stand out. Then think about what you could do in your outdoor living space that would give you the same good feelings. Start a list of these spaces. "Susan's Journal: Notes from My Outdoor Autobiography" on page 190 gives some examples of themes that appeared when she looked at early memories and the garden elements they inspired.

Visit Favorite Present-Day Spaces

Now that you've looked back into your childhood for clues to the outdoor places that most appeal to you, take a look at places that appeal to you today. Close your eyes and let your mind wander at will through your favorite outdoor places. You might think of a neighbor's garden that you particularly enjoy, a bench along a path in a park, or a corner of a public garden you visit time and again.

After you've explored each place in your mind, write down everything about it on a piece of paper, using the "free writing" method, as you did with your early memories. Jot down what you especially like about the place. How does it make you feel? Do you like the colors? The fragrances of the flowers? The privacy? Again, any clues you uncover about what most appeals to you will help you when it comes to designing your own garden.

Finally, add these writings to those about your childhood places, and compare the two. Do your favorite adult places have common themes with the places and moods you found in your early childhood memo-

ries? If so, what are they? Ask yourself again what words and themes recur and what ideas they suggest for your garden. Write them down as well.

Make a Master List

As you compare all your memories and notes, a list of things you want and need in a landscape will begin to emerge. Your list of favorite places is probably quite diverse. It may include a wooded glen, a meadow, a pond, an elevated deck, or a tree fort. Your list of favorite activities is probably equally varied. It may include activities like hiding out, watching fish swim, catching frogs, swinging, sleeping out under a full moon, growing vegetables, picking berries, tending flowers, or building castles. You might have learned that it's important to create a wild place where you can tread lightly as an explorer, an open meadow to run through, or a shiny pond to watch cloud reflections in.

Now that you have a better idea of just what appeals to you in a landscape, you're ready to make a list of all your dreams, schemes, ideas, wants, and needs for the outdoor living spaces you want to create. Start by making a list of all the possible elements and activities you could possibly do outside. It's time, too, to get

▶

Look to gardens owned by friends and neighbors for ideas you'd like to try as well as style and garden accents that appeal to you. They're also an ideal place to look for examples of effective plantings that work in your region. This border, which bisects a lawn and leads toward the house, features the colorful blooms of lilies.

Balthazar Korab

Pamela Harper

▲ *A list of what you want in your own garden—and how you want it to look—will emerge as you learn what landscapes appeal to you. If you prefer wild, natural-looking spaces, you may want a garden with mown grass paths and rustic gates and fences. Here, beds of oxeye daisies (Chrysanthemum leucanthemum), daylilies, and poppies create an informal modified meadow.*

out all the dreams and schemes for your garden you set aside at the beginning of this chapter, so add them to the ideas you have gathered while exploring your child-hood memories and favorite places. Write them all down in a column along the left-hand edge of the biggest sheet of paper you can find.

Don't limit yourself to practical or sensible ideas, but don't forget to include things like taking the recycling containers

▶

This garden room has instant appeal for anyone who loves plants. Heat-tolerant flow-ers and herbs, including lavender, santolina, and thymes, fill the cracks between blue-stone pavers. A rose-covered arbor provides a quiet spot to enjoy the sights, scents, and sounds of the garden, while evergreens form a dramatic background.

Karen Bussolini

out to the curb or hanging out the sheets to dry. List anything that could possibly take place out-of-doors. Think in terms of how you live through a normal day, from taking out the garbage to relaxing after work or cooking dinner. Don't forget to include special events, like family parties, volleyball games, or monarch butterfly migrations.

Chances are, you have at least one other family member who will be using the outdoor living space. What does your family need? A pow-wow can be a fun way to find out everyone's desires. One family's desires included playing horseshoes, doing paperwork and reading, cutting and arranging flowers, washing the dog, growing herbs for cooking, relaxing on a porch swing, pressing apples for cider, eating meals outdoors in summertime, and entertaining their church group at a yearly barbecue.

Or encourage everybody to make his or her own list and compile all the items into a single list, eliminating the duplicates. It's likely that the ideas will keep coming for a day or two, or even a few weeks, so you might want to post the list on a bulletin board where anyone can read it and add to it.

Fine-Tune Your List

Once you have made the master list, write each idea on the top of a separate 4 × 6-inch index card. Under the idea, jot down any additional information it would take to carry it out. Items to note include how large a space it would require; what it should be near; whether it needs sun or shade; and what utilities (water, electricity, gas), equipment, furniture, and storage would be needed.

Walk through the activity in your mind to discover the conditions you'll want to provide, making notes as you go. Does it need to be a quiet space, free from distraction, or is it a place from which to supervise children playing while planning the grocery shopping? Also note what time of day and season of the year the activity would happen and who would be involved and what their special needs are.

To do reading and paperwork outdoors, for example, would require seating with good back support and a smooth work surface for writing. The workspace would require good light but not direct sun, and protection from wind and rain. You'll also have to decide what size the work surface needs to be. An outdoor dining area would be most convenient within easy reach of the kitchen for example, and for an outdoor shower, you'll certainly want a place protected from winds and the neighbors' view.

Jot down any locations you may be already considering for a particular activity, but try to avoid assigning a concrete location or design for any of your ideas at this stage. Later on, when you've mapped your property, you can begin to locate specific places for each activity or element. For now, try not to limit your thinking or to rule anything out.

What's Your Style?

The next step is to see which of the ideas on your master list fit your style.

If you're considering including a pond in your design, choose a ▲
site in full sun. You'll need a power source, too, if you're planning
on having a pump to power a fountain or an artificial waterfall.
This pond is surrounded by ornamental grasses, thymes, ajuga,
and sedums, including 'Autumn Joy' sedum and October daphne
(Sedum sieboldii).

Susan A Roth

But before you can do that, you need to know just what your style is.

Most books on garden design try to show you how to duplicate specific garden styles—a formal or informal garden, for example, or an English cottage garden, a Japanese garden, or a New American Garden. That's not what we mean in this book when we say style, however. *Outdoor Living Spaces* is about finding your own personal style. It's about discovering what you want and need in your garden—what *you* will enjoy most—and then crafting a garden with that as a guide.

Your personal style is unique. It's what makes you, your home, and your outdoor living spaces special. Remember that where style is concerned there is no right and wrong. One person's collectibles are another's clutter. Although your preferences

Jerry Pavia

▲ *Don't forget to think about what you want utilitarian spaces to look like. Although this driveway is decidedly a practical area, it's also attractive. Brick edging along the pavement, pretty window boxes, climbing vines, a white picket gate, and groundcovers on either side of the drive create a friendly appearance without getting in the way.*

might go against what's currently popular or "in style," you need never apologize for your taste and way of doing things: Your style is yours, and you have a right to express it!

Choosing a set style can be a trap. There are as many "fashion victims" in the garden world as there are walking down Fifth Avenue. Usually it happens when you don't trust your own taste, or when

the glamorous magazines seduce you, or when you're railroaded by what's available at the local garden center. Doing the exercises in this chapter will help you avoid falling into this trap.

One good place to start learning more about your personal style is to take an honest look at the stylistic choices you've already made in your home, your wardrobe, and your car. The things you like to surround yourself with, and the mood they create, are clues to your personal style — your unique way of doing things. They are also clues to what style of garden would best suit you. While we can all point to mistakes we've made in these areas, there will be some things that are really "you." Start a list of words and phrases that say things about your personal style. Use some of the questions below to help guide you.

Think about the color, fit, and feel of your favorite pieces of clothing. Are they loose and relaxed, or tailored and imposing? What about the parts of your house that say who you are to first-time guests? Are they classic and formal or modern and informal? Do you love country-style decor? Think, too, about where you feel most comfortable. Do you love crowds or open spaces? Or is your idea of paradise a private retreat secluded from all the world?

Think, too, about how you like to do

Marilyn Stouffer/Rodale Stock Images

Only you can decide what style of garden is best for you. This ▲ lively and eclectic patio area is quite informal and clearly expresses its owners' personal style. Raised beds overflowing with plants, twig furniture, pots of colorful flowers, and rustic baskets and other ornaments all add up to a unique and appealing display.

Karen Bussolini

▲ *In this garden a white picket fence divides formal areas from the less formal ones beyond its boundaries. The areas inside the fence feature beds planted with peonies, a formal pool, and a potted dwarf Alberta spruce* (Picea glauca 'Conica'). *Outside it, the white blooms of kousa dogwoods* (Cornus kousa) *and a variety of evergreen and deciduous trees reign supreme.*

things. Are you casual and laid back, or formal and somewhat persnickety? Do you tend to be subdued, contemplative, and quiet, or are you boisterous, playful, and adventuresome? What colors and textures do you like? All these are clues to your personal style.

Look at the notes you've made about your personal style, and see what patterns emerge. Summarize the most important points on a sheet of paper.

Combining Styles

You may like more than one style, and almost surely members of your family will have very different likes and dislikes. There are ways to accommodate different styles in the same outdoor living spaces. Look back through the gardens in part 2 of this book for examples of how different parts of a garden can express different styles. Elizabeth and Matthew's garden in "Reclaiming a Suburban Ranch House" on page 118 incorporates private areas for dining outdoors, spaces for active play, and room for vegetable and flower gardening. In "Joining Forces: Perennial Gardens and Prairie Plantings" on page 89, Susan and David's garden design combines conventional vegetable and flower

Jerry Pavia

▲
Your style undoubtedly will be influenced by the region in which you live. This austere desert garden features a path defined by contrasting colored gravels. It flows between two rocks that form a gateway, and it has a decidedly streamlike quality. Clipped shrubs mirror the shape of pots set on simple benches.

MEMORIALS

Your garden, like your home, is the repository of many memories. Your antique roses may have come from rooted cuttings given to you by your grandmother; an arbor may represent the place where you were first kissed; a sundial or piece of garden sculpture may commemorate a particularly wonderful trip or other event. You may also use a corner of your lot to bury a particularly beloved pet. Using your garden as a place to remember adds a new layer of meaning to it, which will make it that much more satisfying.

gardens, lawn where their children can play, and areas of wild prairie that can be explored at will.

You may also want to look into your past for ways you have made creative compromises, where you and your family are satisfied with an outcome that none of you would have arrived at on your own. Remembering how you were able to work those compromises out can reawaken skills that you'll use to develop a garden design that will satisfy everyone.

Start from Strength

As you generate all these ideas about your emotional and practical needs, and personal and family style, you'll no doubt begin to think about the capabilities you bring to the garden project. Making a list of these is the last step in your self-assessment.

Whenever you undertake do-it-yourself projects, it simply makes sense to begin with your strengths. They will guide you and give you the confidence to get started. If you are an inexperienced gardener, for example, you probably shouldn't start off with a plan that calls for all the finicky, difficult-to-grow plants you can find. There are plenty of attractive, tough plants to choose from, and planting them will give you both a beautiful garden and the opportunity to learn and hone your skills. If you are an inexperienced carpenter, you probably don't want to start out with a plan that calls for a rustic gazebo, boardwalk, and decks—that is unless you can afford to hire someone to build them. If you cherish your freedom and don't like to follow schedules, you probably wouldn't enjoy a plan that calls for frequent trimming and pruning to keep things in shape.

Inventory Your Knowledge and Skills

What are your personal resources? On a new sheet of paper, make an inventory of your knowledge and your skills. Focus first on what you most enjoy and what you do best. Do you have a gift for organization or art? Are you an expert cook, or do you like to create gifts and

◀

When you begin your design, consider your strengths. If you're an expert carpenter, for example, it's easy to incorporate home-built raised beds, decks, and other structures. Low rock walls, on the other hand, aren't too hard to build. These contain a bed filled with snapdragons, cleome, petunias, and sweet alyssum.

crafts from your garden? Do you like to tackle projects that take some sweat and effort—like digging beds or building terraces—or would you rather let someone else do the heavy work? Would you like to build what someone else has planned for you? What do you know about growing different kinds of plants? Do you enjoy woodworking or know about electricity? Also make a note of activities you don't enjoy. Lawn mowing and trimming are probably on many people's list of least-favorite activities.

Look over your list, and jot down ideas about how these abilities could help to achieve your garden design. Do they suggest additional activities that the plan might accommodate? Think, too, about how much of the work you want to do yourself.

What's Your Budget?

Finally, bring the same realism to your financial considerations. How much can you afford to spend on materials, plants, and labor? Can you set up a savings account that is earmarked for special, long-term projects? It's certainly possible to develop a plan for your yard that you can phase-in over the years. Several of the gardens in part 2 of this book were phased-in over time, whether to accommodate the owners' budgets for plants and materials or to keep the work load manageable.

It's so tempting to buy healthy field-grown perennials at the nursery, but what if you can't afford to spend the money to plant your whole garden? Better in that case to buy fewer plants and fill in with annual seed, or even to start your perennials from seed. And if you do get tempted into buying a hundred dollars' worth of plants one balmy spring afternoon, what if you can't afford to buy the irrigation system that will water them? Better to have a realistic plan and budget for your garden to guide you.

Incidentally, most designers prefer designing for an honest budget. Any garden they plan can be implemented in phases, with furnishings and plants upgraded as budget allows. Furthermore, the design itself is often better when you can't have everything at once—it attains a richness that's hard to duplicate in a one-shot installation. For ideas on how to fit your design to your budget and to set priorities and break a design into phases, see "Phase-In Your Design" on page 296.

Plan for Change

Style does change over time, and the type of garden you want will undoubtedly change, too. You probably don't have the same hairstyle or clothes you wore ten years ago, so why should your garden become fixed in time? Your interests change, children are born or grow up and want different play areas, pets come and go, shade and sun change as trees grow up or die, and people move. You find that the orderly garden beds that once pleased you are now a bother, or that the lawn is eating up all your spare time.

As you've performed the exercises and compiled the lists described in this chapter, you've probably made notes about what you want your garden to become. Take time to think about any changes you anticipate in your life, and keep them in mind

Susan's Journal

Change in My Garden

My garden plan was inspired by Williamsburg and other historical town gardens, as well as by the tutoring of landscape architect Norman Johnson. Now, ten years later, with reading, travel, and lifestyle changes under my belt, I want the garden to express who I am now. The garden still functions perfectly well and elicits compliments, but I find it so tame. I want more freedom in my garden—fewer enclosed spaces, more color and varied texture in the plants, room for working on art projects, and room to live more out-of-doors. I also need privacy from noisy new neighbors and their barking dog.

I've wanted to develop a little water garden for some time now—it would be pretty and would also attract more birds. I should add some trees and shrubs that will supply the birds with food, too.

And I want to grow some vegetables. I didn't grow them until now because they were a chore when I was a kid. Dad gardened, and I had to pick the beans before dinner—a task that I hated. They were always past their prime because we grew much more than we needed. Now I'll only grow what I need, but I want to take responsibility for the quality of my nutrition as well as the state of my purse—organically grown vegetables can be hard to find, and expensive when you can get them.

Even the simplest objects can introduce drama and change in a ▲ landscape. Here, four wooden spools form a sculpture in a meadow that can be rearranged at will to change the composition. However they're arranged, they add movement to an otherwise quiet landscape. But perhaps they have a deeper meaning as well: At first glance, they may resemble round haybales awaiting collection. Or, they echo the shape of the wagon wheels that carried settlers across the prairies.

Balthazar Korab

as you work on your plan. Look for ways to have your plan stay flexible enough so that it can continue to grow and change as you do. Jeanne and Bill's garden in "The Small Garden: Rooms to Grow In" on page 33 is a perfect example of a garden that's planned to accommodate change—each of the garden rooms they've created can be developed and modified independently of the others.

You can even develop a plan that allows you to incorporate change whenever you wish. It's easy to change the color scheme of a garden from season to season if that's what suits you. Just plan on beds of brightly colored annuals and plant different ones each year. As you move through your daily life, you may encounter things that appeal to you and that you can accommodate in your garden. For example, you might discover an amazing piece of driftwood and bring it home to serve as a sculpture in your garden. You may come across a plant or fragrant blossom that appeals to you enough to identify it and consider using it in your garden. How could things that smell divine or are fascinating find their way into one of your garden projects? And how can you use an old millstone or a limestone lintel salvaged from a demolished hotel? Mull it over and see what you come up with.

Mulling is an essential part of the design process. It's great fun to play through the options before committing to carrying one out. Mulling keeps you on the lookout for materials—old weather vanes, statuary, birdhouses, plant containers, perennials, you name it. You can discover inspirations in everything from a painting to a wild corner of a garden that you particularly admire. As the philosopher Bertrand Russell observed: "Chance favors the prepared mind." Being on the lookout for ideas will encourage you to look at other gardens with a keener eye. You may find out how they have solved a challenge like one you're facing in your own garden or created an effect you've been striving for. Mulling can be shared, too. Talk over issues and ideas with friends and family—more to clarify your thinking than to get advice.

Things to Do Right Now

Now that you've developed loads of ideas for your garden, and are impatient to get started, it can be frustrating to wait

EARLY ACTION PROJECTS

Do whatever will bring a smile to your face right away. It can be useful or whimsical or both. A birdhouse, a new color for the gate, a compost bin, a garden ornament, or a colorful new bed of annuals can be a real pick-me-up. Here are some other suggestions for early action projects:

• Add something that looks permanent but will be easy to dismantle when you decide on a final design. A flagstone walkway laid in sand will serve for a few years, but can be taken up without special equipment. You can then recycle the stones into a permanent terrace.

• Complete unfinished projects (don't we all have some?) or do short-term spruce-ups, like painting a fence or replacing cracked spots in a concrete walk with crazy-quilt brick pieces or smooth river pebbles.

• Rearrange things that are easy to move, like a table and chairs. Move them to where you can sit in the sun or watch the birds feed and flit. Or use them to light up another distant corner of the garden as a charmingly inviting focal point.

• Transplant perennials to a new location, or into a holding area where they can thrive until you decide on their final home. Or do some thoughtful pruning to bring out the sculptural qualities of a tree. Just be sure it is the correct season before starting either project. Pruning is something constructive that you can do to dormant plants in the winter to balance dreams about what you'll do when the growing season arrives with warmer weather.

Joanne Pavia

While you're working on your design, don't neglect early action ▲
projects that will bring a smile to your face and a feeling of
accomplishment. It's easy to dress up a corner of your yard with
pots that overflow with flowering annuals. This exuberant group-
ing of red, pink, and white geraniums—some with variegated
foliage—and purple-flowered heliotropes creates a welcoming
front entrance.

until you've thoroughly planned the over-all design. It may even dampen your enthusiasm. Since by now you have a good idea of the kind of garden you will be working toward, you can start to make little changes without worrying that they won't fit the eventual garden design.

After all, your outdoor living spaces will change continually anyway, so it's fine to do some little projects right now. "Early Action Projects" on the opposite page lists just a few of the things that needn't wait until you have a complete design in hand.

ANALYZING YOUR SITE: WHAT DO YOU HAVE TO WORK WITH?

Now that you have a good idea of what attracts you to a landscape and what you want and need in a garden, you're ready to take a close look at your property. Although you may have used your garden daily for years, how well do you really know it? The first step in your site analysis is to take time to look at your yard with fresh eyes. Just as you put together your own outdoor autobiography, you need to observe and record the details of your land: In a sense, you'll be composing its biography.

By taking a close look at your property—its topography, features, plants, pathways, and even its history—you'll learn more about it and undoubtedly discover things you never noticed before.

Ideally, observing and learning about your property is a continuous process. It will help you notice more of the things that make it unique. The longer you live with curiosity in a place—observing it, keeping records about how it changes, and just taking the time to enjoy it close up— the more you respond to it and the more interesting it can become. Such observation will bring you in touch with the true character of the site. This search for insight will help lead to a creative design that's based on the landscape's own personality.

The Site at a Glance

Begin your examination with a stroll through your property. Take a notebook and pencil with you to jot down all the things that you like and don't like about the site and the current landscape. Here are some questions to guide you: What areas and objects are you drawn to? Which plants bring you the most pleasure? Where do you like to go when you are alone or with friends? What areas do you dislike or never visit? What parts are awkward or inconvenient? Is there a view that you especially enjoy, or something you hate looking at? Are there things that must be fixed immediately because they are unsafe, or things you need to add for security? Does anything remind you of the ideas, elements, and general themes that emerged when you explored your early outdoor memories?

Look at your property from many locations and directions. Do it as often as you can, at many different times of the day and seasons of the year. How does the look of the garden change through the day? Where does the sun move, and do you want to be able to follow it or escape it? You'll notice the angle of light, patterns of shadow, and general atmosphere ▶

Developing a design that fits its site takes careful observation and thought. You'll find invaluable design ideas by looking at the architecture of your home and the site's topography, plants, history, and features. Here, a stone wall and rustic, vine-covered gate complement the shapes of the cottage they surround.

will change from hour to hour and season to season. Try to see how the features of the garden change accordingly. For example, if you're trying to create a cool outdoor retreat under a tree, it's important to know exactly where it casts its shade on hot summer afternoons. Notice, too, how the sounds in your garden shift from bird songs in the very early morning to power tools in the afternoon. See "Take a Fresh

▶

When you're analyzing your site, take time to consider how visitors might see your house and front entranceway. This front planting, which features a brick walk and fence that curve along a steep slope, welcomes visitors and provides an attractive setting for the house.

Karen Bussolini

▲ *Magnificent old trees like the ones in this largely green garden provide ready-made inspiration. Their sinuous, sculptural trunks and branches add movement to the landscape. The designers of this garden have wisely reserved the shaded spaces beneath their branches for ferns and other groundcovers; sun-loving roses grow in beds beyond the reach of their branches.*

Jerry Pavia

TAKE A FRESH LOOK

It's fun to poke about in the far corners and byways of your garden. You may discover secret blooms, interesting new views, or a new route for a stroll path. Or you could find a place that would be ideal to add a bench so you can enjoy a particular view. See what you can find out by getting off the beaten path. Below are some ways to take a fresh look at a seemingly familiar place, or a close look at someplace new.

Look in from outside. Drive, cycle, or walk by on the street to see what you notice at certain speeds. What does the entryway look like? Is it well marked and welcoming? Are the plantings around the house attractive? Ask your neighbors' permission to walk around the perimeter of your property so you can see the positives and negatives from their vantage points. You'll see what feels friendly, what looks out of place, and what needs screening for privacy.

Look out each window. What do you see from places indoors where you spend a lot of time? To get a complete picture, look out when you're both sitting and standing. Does the window frame a special view? Or is the view nondescript or downright unattractive? How does the view differ through the upstairs and downstairs windows? Does the landscape out the street-side windows give you privacy without making you feel boxed in? Looking out each window will point out areas where you could design a beautiful scene to be enjoyed from an important window, or changes you'd like to make.

Look out each door. Is there a destination that beckons you out away from the house? When you step outdoors, is there a comfortable transition space? Looking from each exit can show you areas where changes would make the outdoor living spaces more comfortable and accessible.

Walk through and look. Walk the garden as thoroughly as possible: Walk along the boundary, around the house, on major and minor paths, and off the beaten track into the plantings. Where do you feel misled or thwarted from going where you wish? How do the ground and paving feel underfoot? Is there much variety from hard to soft surfaces? This will show you things you could add or change.

Sit down and look. Sit quietly in all possible places—porch, fence rail, patio furniture, the grass—and consider how comfortable that spot is and how you feel in it. Are you exposed or embraced? Are there interesting things to look at, to smell, or to touch? You might write a note in your journal, a letter, or a poem,

Look" above for suggestions on what to look for as you begin your examination.

However you choose to explore, be on the lookout for associations with the memories and ideas you uncovered in the exercises described in "Ideas for Your Garden: Recalling Favorite Landscapes" on page 186. Are there special places or attributes that could correspond to your dreams and ideas?

or draw pictures, to describe what you see and feel. If you can, select a piece of music or art that expresses your feelings. Play it for someone, or show it to them, and explain how you feel it represents the place as you know it. Think about how you would like your garden to stay the same or change.

Look beyond your property. Views beyond the edges of your yard often provide clues to your garden design. Wander into every area, and look over your land and beyond your boundary line to see how the outer world is part of the garden. Which scenes do you enjoy and why? What time of day do you tend to notice them? Are you usually doing the same thing, like walking in from the garage or basking in the sun? How much of the sky can you see or would you like to be able to see? What are the elements and attributes of each view that play a role in your enjoyment? Is it the movement of boats on the water, the sensuous line of distant hills, the neighbor's wellhouse, or a beautiful shade tree? How could you frame a view to bring out its best qualities? Does anything take away from the view, such as overhead wires or a rusting shed? There may be ways to screen part of it, not unlike cropping a photograph.

Take a Critical Look

After you've taken the time to appreciate what you already have, begin to study your property with a more objective and critical eye. If you just bought your home, this may be easy to do. If you're evaluating a place where you've lived for years, on the other hand, it may be a little more challenging. It's perfectly normal to see only what you want to—to perceive selectively—or to become so accustomed that your perceptions are glazed. Nevertheless, you should try to make your assessment as honest as possible.

Unless you feed the data into a computer program, your evaluation is inevitably a subjective sum total of all the things you've found out and filtered through your interests, values, and tastes. But that's not a bad thing. After all, you're trying to design a garden that *you* will enjoy, and your likes and dislikes are what make that enjoyment possible. For example, depending on your personal likes and dislikes, you might consider a bog on your property to be either beguiling or annoying. Either assessment would lead you to assign a very different value and design treatment to that particular area.

How can you see a place with new eyes? *Site analysis* is the term professional designers use when referring to the process of looking objectively at a property. This chapter serves as a primer for doing your own site analysis—from drawing a map of your property to locating the features on it. Doing a careful site analysis is your key to discovering the true character of your property.

Throughout the process, it's important to keep written records and plans: Maps, diaries, sketches, photographs, and lists will help you keep track of what you are finding out as you go along. They're a boon to your objectivity, not to mention your memory, because they will help balance the natural human tendency to make judgments and notice only negative features. Garden notes and plans are fascinating to look back at in future years, too. They're valuable reminders that a garden has changed over time, and they also yield interesting clues to its origins.

Mapmaking Made Simple

Obviously, having a map of your property is necessary if you're going to develop a garden design. As a preliminary step, or warm-up exercise, sketch a bird's-eye view of your property based only on your memory of it. Make the sketch as rough as you like, but try to include as much detail as you can. Be sure to indicate major parts of the garden, pathways, and any other features. Your memory sketch shows how you perceive the parts of your yard and the relationships between them.

Once you've drawn the accurate base plan and the plan of existing conditions described later in this chapter, it can be revealing to compare them to your rough sketch. What did you make bigger or smaller than it actually is? Did you draw any elements that are closer or farther away than they actually are?

Think about how you feel about the discrepancies. This exercise can uncover additional pieces of knowledge for you to use in planning the final design. For example, did you draw your vegetable garden far larger than it really is? Does that mean the work it requires is a burden? In your drawing, is the clump of trees in the far corner of your lot smaller and more remote than they really are? Does that discrepancy reflect the fact that you'd like more shade and trees closer to your house?

Types of Plans

This chapter will discuss three kinds of plans or maps—all of which are useful for getting your design down on paper: a base plan; an existing conditions, or "before," plan; and a topographic map. You'll also learn two basic ways to draw plans—using a grid and using triangulation.

The Base Plan

The base plan is one of the most useful maps you can have of your property. It shows your boundary lines, indicates which way is north, and maps the size and location of the house and other buildings. In addition, it also indicates the location of important, semi-permanent features such as utility lines, rights-of-way, wells, septic tanks and fields, walls, driveways, and paved areas. It can also indicate changes in elevation.

A base plan is a useful tool at all stages of creating a landscape design. Once you have your base plan, it's best not to

▶

When making a base plan of your property, it's important to note features you like as well as those you don't. That way, it's easier to deal with them in your plan. This design incorporates an informal fence constructed of ocotillo sticks and a clump of prickly pear cacti to screen the view of a neighbor's house.

write directly on it. Instead, make photocopies. That way, you can use a copy to make an existing conditions plan and another draw out the final design. If you're working on a copy, you'll also feel free to sketch out rough ideas as often as you like without worrying too much about making mistakes, because you'll able to start again fairly easily.

Existing Conditions Plan

An existing conditions plan—or a "before" map, if you prefer—begins with your base plan. So, it includes everything on the base plan, but it also shows trees, shrubs, and features like fences, paths, and flower beds that were there when you started the project. It also includes notes on such things as the height of fences, the materials used in paths, or other features like views you'd like to exploit or cover up, and other notations you think would help you arrive at a final design.

You'll also want to make notes on the slope of the land to remind yourself where the ground is flat, gently sloping, or steep. If you plan to add solid features such as walls, terraces, or steps to areas where the ground slopes, you'll probably want to make a plan of those areas that shows the exact changes in elevation. Appendix A on page 307 explains one method for drawing sloping land on flat paper.

Ideally, an existing conditions plan includes some features outside your property. It could indicate trees or buildings that cast shade onto you property, for example, or interesting views of neighboring lands and what season they are at their peak. Using it to mark the approximate location of unsightly objects or views

beyond your boundaries is helpful, because you can then use your existing conditions plan to help you screen them from sight when you make your design. In short, the more information you can include on your plan, the better your final design can be. For examples of existing conditions plans, look through the gardens in part 2, "A Gallery of Gardens: Ten Designs for Outdoor Living," which begins on page 29.

As with your base plan, it's a good idea to make a photocopy of your existing conditions plan for making notes and sketching out ideas. Enlargements of either type of plan are inexpensive and are easy to obtain from your local copy center, and they can be great to work with if you want to add lots of detail.

Topographic Map

A topographic map—called a topo map for short—details the physical features of your property, both natural and man-made. These include slopes, hills, low-lying areas, retaining walls, steps, and any other changes in elevation. If your property is relatively flat (or if you are not planning on altering a sloping site to any extent), you may not need a topo map at all. But one can be extremely useful if you are designing a series of terraces to make gardening space on a hillside, or building a deck on a sloping site. A topo map is also a valuable tool in solving water-drainage problems, because it can show you why water drains where it does. It's also a useful tool if you are planning on recontouring the land. For step-by-step directions on drawing your own topo map, see Appendix A on page 307.

Getting Started

If you're lucky, you may not have to start the maps of your property from scratch. For many properties, a survey may be available. A survey, which is essentially a map of the boundaries of your property, may be attached to your copy of the deed, or you may be able to get a copy of one from your mortgage holder, the city planning office, county courthouse, or the local property tax office. These plans usually locate structures, large trees, paved areas, and utility and drainage easements. Your builder or architect also may have plans that show details of the house as well as the boundaries of the property.

You can easily take information from these plans to make your own base plan. Often, you can simply trace the information you want from the copies of the maps onto a large sheet of tracing paper to form your base plan. Or just a large photocopy—or several smaller ones taped together—can do for a start. You can then use one of the drawing methods explained later in this chapter starting on page 218 to add the features for an existing conditions plan.

Drawing Your Own Plans

If you don't have access to any ready-made plans, you can draw a base plan and an existing conditions plan from scratch. All you need is some time, a few simple tools, and a helper. "Drawing Plans Using a Grid" on page 218 and "Drawing Plans Using Triangulation" on page 221 describe two ways you can picture your property accurately on paper. You can also hire a surveying firm to draw the plans for you, but this can be a costly option.

Locating the Property Line

Whether you have ready-made plans or will be drawing them yourself, you will need to locate the exact boundaries of your property on the ground. If you plan to add or remove plants or fences near the edges of your property, it's important to know if you are on your land or someone else's. Neighbors can get irate, and you might even end up defending yourself in court, if you are off by even a few inches. So locate your property lines before you do anything else. If you don't plan to make any changes near the perimeter of your property, you can probably get away with not locating the exact boundaries.

Start your search armed with a copy of your survey—or at least a written description of the boundary from the deed. Some property lines, such as those of a yard in a new condo development, are quite easy to locate. Others may be less obvious. Many properties are marked with permanent metal corner pins. If you have a survey map that shows existing buildings or features, you may be able to measure from them to find the location of the corners. Unfortunately, you cannot assume fences and other seemingly obvious markers are on the boundary.

Neighbors may have ideas (right or wrong) or more information to help you locate the corners or the lines. If you cannot locate property boundaries, it is often worth getting a surveyor in to do it for you. Despite the cost, it can save you from making enemies and expensive mistakes.

Once you have located your property lines and corner markers, mark them so you will be able to find them again easily. Metal stakes or piles of rocks work well and last for many years.

Now you are ready to draw plans of your property. The following pages describe two ways to draw plans. You can use either method to draw your base plan from scratch, to add features to an existing survey of your property, or to convert a base plan into an existing conditions plan. The grid method (see below) is time-consuming but foolproof. The triangulation method (see page 221) involves making a series of measurements and transferring them to paper. You can use it to draw your plan from scratch or to add features to an existing map, such as a survey map or one drawn by the grid method. Keep in mind that you can use either the grid or the triangulation method to draw your entire property, but you can also use them to map a particular portion of it.

Design Shorthand

Even if you have a small property, it will save later confusion on your base and existing conditions plans if you use a key instead of labeling each feature directly on the drawing. Many of the drawings in part 2 of this book have keys to simplify them, for example. You can use the typical symbols designers use on their keys; see page 299 for examples of some symbols. You can also page through part 2 to look for ideas on the garden plans in that section. Or develop your own system.

Drawing Plans Using a Grid

If you like seeing things spread out in front of you, this method is for you: It involves constructing a string grid over your property that you can use to locate all the important features you need to develop your plans. It is time-consuming, but you can see your plan growing before your eyes.

Because it involves covering your yard with stakes and strings, it's not a process you'd want to repeat. Work carefully, and be sure you've pinpointed *all* the features you want to include on your plans before you dismantle the string grid you've constructed. (Once you've dismantled the string grid, you can use triangulation to locate additional features.)

Laying the Groundwork

For starters, you'll need a clipboard with some scratch paper and a few sheets of graph paper, a pen or pencil, a 100-foot tape measure, lots of strong non-elastic string, a bundle of 2-foot-long, 1 × 2-inch wooden stakes, and a small sledgehammer. You'll also need a patient and willing helper.

In addition, you'll need a rough sketch of your property (or the portion of it that you are mapping). On it, note all the features you want to include on your plans. Before you start, double-check to make sure you don't forget any of them. If you need both a base plan and an existing conditions plan, list all the features for both, so you won't have to go through the entire mapping process a second time in order to locate them on a plan. You may want to make two rough drawings, one for the base plan and the other for the existing conditions plan. See the illustration on the opposite page to help you visualize this process before you get started.

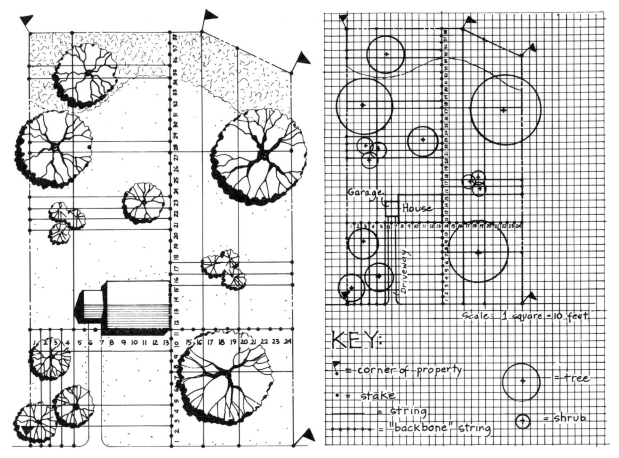

From above, it's easy to see how the grid system works. All the strings run parallel to the backbone strings, and these correspond to the graph paper of the final plan. From there, it's a relatively easy matter to determine which square a tree, shrub, or other feature belongs in.

Establishing the Backbone

The first step is to establish a backbone for the grid. The backbone is a pair of main strings that run perpendicular to each other and cross at a corner of your house. You'll use these two strings as a framework for "drawing" the rest of the grid.

1. "Draw" a visible boundary line around the perimeter of your property by pounding a stake into the ground at each corner of the lot and stretching string between the stakes.

2. With assistance from your helper, measure the length of the outside walls of your house and make a sketch of your house on one of your sheets of scratch paper as you work. Note these lengths, along with the exact location of ground-floor windows and doors, on the sketch of your house.

3. Choose one corner of the house from

219

which you can see straight along each wall to the property boundary. Stretch a string from one boundary to the opposite boundary along one of these walls. (The string should serve to extend the line of the house wall all the way across the property.) Insert stakes where the string meets the boundaries, and tie the string tight.

4. Stretch another string along a second, adjacent wall from boundary to boundary to extend that wall, as you did with the first. The second string line should cross the first at a right angle, and this intersection should occur at the corner of the house. Again, insert stakes and tie the second string tight.

5. Measure the distance from boundary to boundary along each of the two strings. Measure the distance along the strings from the boundaries to the point where the strings intersect. Write this information on your notepad.

6. Drive stakes at regular intervals, such as every 10 feet, along the two string lines. The string lines and stakes now form the backbone of a grid on which you can locate features of the property.

Making the Grid

The backbone strings divide your property into quarters. When you begin to fill out the grid, extend the strings over one quarter of your property at a time. As you and your helper work, be sure to keep your strings and measuring tape taut and as level as possible while you are laying out the grid and taking measurements. Tie the strings just a few inches off the ground, so they will be easy to step over later.

To establish the grid, use the following procedure.

1. Tie one end of a piece of string to one of the stakes nearest the intersection of the backbone strings. Walk parallel to the other backbone string, stretching the new string out until you reach the boundary line. Cut the string here, and tie the end to a loose stake. Use your tape measure and measure between this new string and the original grid backbone string in several places. Adjust the new string until the strings are the same distance apart all the way along, then pound in the loose end stake.

2. Now tie a string to the stake next to the one you just worked on, and repeat the procedure. Continue tying strings to stakes until you have covered that quarter of the property. Keep in mind that in areas of your property where there are no features you need to locate—such as expanses of lawn—there is no need to complete the grid; just skip a few strings.

3. Repeat the procedure described in steps 1 and 2, but extend strings perpendicular to the set you laid out in those steps. (This step is also good exercise, since you'll have to repeatedly step over the existing strings as you extend the new ones.) When you finish, one quarter of your property with be covered with a net of string squares.

Sketching Your Grid

Before you can draw a final plan, which is most easily accomplished indoors, you'll need to make a sketch of your grid to work from. To do this, draw the backbone strings on a blank sheet of graph paper. Make the squares on the paper equal to the interval of the stakes. If your property is large, for example, you may want one square to equal one 10- or 20-foot-interval; if it's smaller, two squares or more could equal an interval.

Next, note the position of each feature in its string square on the corresponding square of the graph paper. Make notes about the overall size of objects so you will be able to draw them on the final plan. Be sure to measure the broadest spread of the canopy of shrubs and trees and sketch them in as an outline on the final plan.

After you have located all the features, you can remove the grid from that quarter. (You may want to wait to remove the grid until you've drawn the final plan.) Whatever you do, don't remove the backbone strings or the boundary line until you have finished all four quarters. To finish mapping your entire property, repeat steps 1 through 3 under "Making the Grid" on the opposite page for the three remaining quarters of your property.

Drawing the Plans

To draw your final plan, take your notes and sketch plans inside. You'll need a table to spread out on and a large sheet of graph paper.

1. From the length and width measurements of your property and the number of squares on your paper, decide what scale will let you put the whole plan on one sheet of graph paper. For example, if your property is roughly 100×200 feet, and your graph paper has 45 squares the long way, make one square equal 5 feet. Make a note of the scale you are using in the corner of the plan.

2. Use a pencil to lightly draw the backbone lines on the graph paper. Although these will help you locate other features on your plan, you'll probably want to erase them once you've finished.

3. Use the sketch of your house and its dimensions to locate it on the graph paper plan. Draw a double line through the walls of the house to show where windows are, and leave openings for doors.

4. Transfer the locations and sizes of all of the features from your rough sketches to your final copy.

Drawing Plans Using Triangulation

Triangulation is a process you may have learned about in high school geometry. It involves measuring the distance from two distinct reference points to each of the features in your landscape. Then, using a drafting compass, you translate your list of measurements into an accurate, detailed landscape plan on paper.

Laying the Groundwork

To draw a plan of your property by triangulation, you'll need a clipboard and some scratch paper with a rough sketch of your property on it. You'll also need two pens or pencils of different colors, a 100-foot tape measure, and some thumbtacks or a piece of chalk, as well as a patient and willing helper to help you take the measurements.

All the features you want to include on your plans should be indicated on your rough sketch of the property. If you are drawing both a base plan and an existing conditions plan, locate all the features for both, so you only have to go through the process once. You may want to make two rough drawings, one for the base plan and the other for the existing conditions plan. Be sure to note the corners of your property so you will remember to measure the distance to each of them and be able to draw the boundary line on the final plans.

Before you begin, choose two reference points to measure from throughout the process. Corners of your property are good, as are corners of your house. You can also use stakes driven into the ground especially for this purpose, as long as you can leave them undisturbed until you are done mapping. It's best to select two points that are about as far apart from each other as half the width of the area you are mapping. Ideally, you should be able to see all of the area you want to map from both reference points. If this isn't possible, you can establish a new reference point or points when you need them anytime during the process. Just measure from the original two using the basic steps outlined below.

Collecting Measurements

In the steps that follow, you'll circle each reference point on your rough sketch in a color, and write all the measurements from that point in the same color. Using the correct color throughout the process is very important. The colors serve as a code to link the measurements on your rough sketch to the correct reference point. When you actually draw your plans, if your mea-

surements get mixed up and aren't coded correctly, the objects will not end up in the right places.

1. Measure the exact distance between the two reference points, and write it on your sketch.

2. Pick one of the reference points and circle it on your sketch with one of the two colored pens or pencils. You will write all the measurements you make from this point with the same color.

3. Measure the distance from the circled reference point to one of the features on your property—a large tree, for example. Mark the exact point on the object to which you measured with a colored thumbtack, or chalk mark. For example, put a small chalk X on the trunk of the tree. Using the correct color, make a note of this distance next to the feature on your rough sketch.

4. Continue measuring distances from the circled reference point to features on your property, marking the point to which you've measured, and writing down the measurements with the proper color. Be sure you measure the distance to all the features you plan to include on your base plan and existing conditions plan.

5. Circle the other reference point with the second color. Following the procedures described in steps 3 and 4, measure from the second reference point to each of the features of the property. Be sure to measure the distance to the spot you marked with chalk or a tack. If you measure to two different sides of the trunk of a tree, or any other large feature, your final plan will be less accurate, although not hopelessly wrong. Make a note of the distance

next to the feature on your rough sketch, again using the correct color.

6. Make other notes on the sketch so you will be able to draw each feature on the final plans. For example, note how wide tree trunks are or how wide the branches of a tree or shrub spread so that you can draw it in accurately in your final plans.

7. Once you've finished collecting measurements, you're ready to take your notes inside and draw the finished plans.

Additional Reference Points

You may need to have more than one set of reference points in order to locate all the features on your property. For example, if you have a hedge or blackberry bed in one part of your yard, it would be difficult—and perhaps painful—to stretch your measuring tape through it to measure distances to points on the far side. Or if your property is very large, your tape measure may not be long enough to reach from your reference points to the most distant features.

Any point that you have located from the original reference points can become a new reference point. Choose new reference points as far away as you can measure from the first reference points. Again, solid features or sturdy stakes are suitable. You can write the measurements from the new pair of reference points on a second sketch map. Mark the new reference points clearly on your rough sketch and circle them with two additional colors. That way you won't get them mixed up with those from the first set of reference points—which could really mess things up when you try to draw your plan.

Measure the distances from these new reference points to the features in the farther reaches of your property.

Drawing the Plans

It's hard to imagine that you can convert a rough sketch and a bunch of color-coded numbers into a finished map of your garden, but it's not as hard as it seems. You'll need a pencil, a large drawing or drafting compass (one that draws circles, not one that points north), and a ruler—preferably an engineer's rule with a choice of scales on it. It's best not to try to get away with one of the small compasses you used in school, for they often won't reach the distances you need when drawing a large property. The sample plan on page 224, for example, requires a compass that will reach 10 inches. See Appendix C on page 330 for a list of suppliers of drafting supplies.

Spread out a large sheet of clean paper on a table, and tape it down. You will probably want to put a sheet of smooth cardboard or poster board down first so that the point of the compass won't scar the surface of the table.

Decide what scale will let you fit the whole plan on the sheet of paper, and write it on the corner so you won't forget it. For example, if your property is 235 feet long and 150 feet wide, and you have an 11 × 17-inch sheet of paper, you can use 1 inch equals 20 feet. The resulting plan boundary will be roughly 8 × 12 inches.

Locate and mark the two reference points on the paper. Be sure to make them the correct distance apart. If your reference points aren't property corners, use the measurements you took from the reference points to the property corners to make sure the whole lot will end up on the paper when you draw it. If your reference points are about in the middle of the property, then they will be about in the middle of the paper, too.

Pencil in a note next to each one to remind you what color it is on your notes. This will help you keep the measurements from getting mixed up as you transfer them to the plan. Use the following steps to locate all the features on your plan. See "Triangulation Made Easy" at right for an illustration of this process.

1. Select a feature to draw. (It's a good idea to locate all the corners of the property first, just to make sure the whole property will fit on the paper.) Use your ruler or the scale on your engineer's rule to set the compass to the scaled distance from the first reference point to that feature. For example, if you are using the measurement from a reference point on one corner of your house to one corner of your garage, the distance is 50 feet, and your scale is ½ inch equals 10 feet, the scaled distance to set on your compass is 2½ inches.

2. Rest the point of the compass on the reference point, and use the pencil end of the compass to make a faint arc in the approximate location of the feature (in this example, the corner of the garage).

3. Next, set the compass to the scaled distance from the other reference point. (In this example, if the distance from the second point is 100 feet, you'd need to set your compass to 5 inches.)

4. Place the point of the compass on the second reference point, and make an arc that crosses the first arc. The point

TRIANGULATION MADE EASY

Triangulation isn't as confusing as it seems. Here's an example to help illustrate the process.

In this example, the two reference points are the east and west corners of the house. By measuring around the outside of the house, it's easy to determine its shape and draw it on the plan. To use triangulation to locate the tree in the backyard from these points, start with the measurements on the rough sketch. In this case, the tree is 50 feet from the west corner of the house and 100 feet from the east corner.

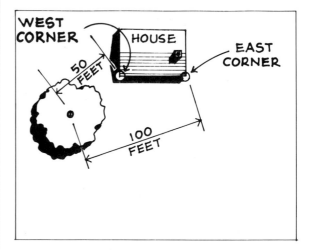

Next, set the compass according to the scale, in this case 1 inch equals 10 feet. To mark the distance between the east corner and the tree, set the compass to 10 inches.

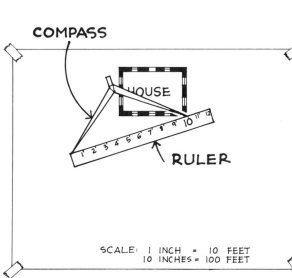

SCALE: 1 INCH =   10   FEET
         10 INCHES = 100 FEET

Set the point of the compass on the first reference point (the east corner of the house), and use the pencil end to make a faint arc on the paper.

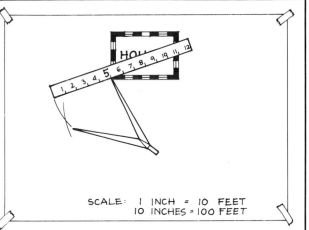

SCALE: 1 INCH =   10   FEET
         10 INCHES = 100 FEET

Set the compass to measure the distance from the west corner of the house to the tree—5 inches. Put the compass on the reference point corresponding to the west corner of the house and draw another arc. The point where the two arcs cross is the tree.

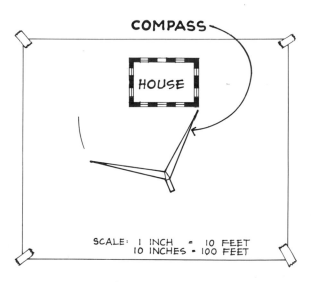

SCALE: 1 INCH   =   10   FEET
         10 INCHES = 100 FEET

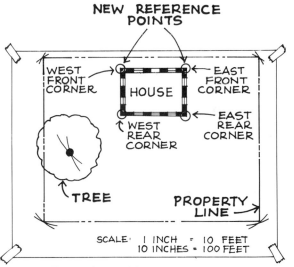

SCALE: 1 INCH   =   10   FEET
         10 INCHES = 100 FEET

From there, it's easy to see how to fill in additional features using the two points.

where the two arcs cross is the exact location of the feature.

5. Draw in the shape and description of the feature from your notes.

6. Repeat steps 1 through 5 for each pair of measurements to locate all the features on the property.

Studying the Shape of the Land

Unless your property is absolutely flat, another important step is to look carefully at the lay of the land. Why? A slope of only a few inches can make rainwater drain away from your house—or into your basement. And low-lying places tend to be wetter than high points, which can affect your choice of plants.

Start by taking a general look to see how the ground undulates. It's a good idea to take a photocopy or rough sketch of your base or existing conditions plan—along with a clipboard and pencil—out with you to make notes. Ask yourself some of the following questions. Where are the high and low points? Where does water tend to pool? Are there any visible drainage features such as gullies or deposits of washed-down soil? Where does the ground slope steeply, and where does it level off or slope gently?

Next time it rains, take a stroll with your boots and umbrella and see where water runs or collects. Note where it comes from. Your neighbors may give you funny looks, but you'll gain a wealth of information. You may even solve the mystery of where all that water in your basement comes from on rainy days. Water can pool up in even a slight depression near the house and seep through walls. Sometimes,

just a few wheelbarrows of soil is all it takes to encourage the water to flow away from your house instead of into it.

3-D Maps

You may also want to try re-creating the shape, or topography, of your land indoors. This may help you visualize the shape of the land and how you might enhance it with plantings, terraces, retaining walls, decks, or other structures. You can also experiment with ways you might like to change the shape of the land or its features without actually moving a shovelful of earth.

What you are looking for is an effective way to represent your property so that you can plan your projects confidently and determine the amount of plants and materials it will require. A design on paper is the most common way to do this. One obvious advantage of a paper plan is that you can use photocopies of it for sketching design changes, or you can overlay it with tracing paper upon which you can try different ideas. For more on this technique, see "Using Overlays" on page 299.

But not everyone is comfortable with drawing, or seeing three-dimensional shapes from flat paper drawings. Perhaps you would like to build a scale model, or miniature, of your property instead of (or in addition to) drawing a map. Try making the "ground" out of soil, plaster, clay, papier-mâché, or layers of cardboard. See "Scale Models" on page 228 for directions on how to make two different types of scale models.

A distinct advantage of a scale model is that it can help you see where the shadows will fall as the sun moves over your property. Put the model outside and place

The way your property is shaped—its topography—can play an important role in your design. Knowing where water collects or runs off has obvious importance, but topography can help you decide where to locate garden features like paths, which can disappear around a hillock. This backyard design spotted with trees, shrubs, sculptures, rocks, water, and places to rest makes the most of a rolling landscape.

Balthazar Korab

it so that its north/south line corresponds to that of your property, or shine a desk lamp across the box to represent the sun. This will reveal patterns of sunlight and shadow, and can help you locate and exploit areas that are hot and bright, or cool and dim, at different times of the day.

Topographic Maps

A topographic, or contour, map (called a topo map, for short) shows hilly land on flat paper. It's made up of a series of lines connecting all the points that are exactly the same elevation. To visualize how one works, imagine a lake. The edge where the water meets the land is a line—a contour line. Now, if the water level would drop a foot every night there will be a series of new lines, each one exactly 1 foot lower than the one before. The water lines would correspond to a topo map drawn of the exposed lake bottom.

The space between the lines on a topo

SCALE MODELS

If you have trouble seeing the shape of the land and how you might change it when looking at a flat piece of paper, don't despair. Here are two easy ways to make miniature models of your property:

Sandbox Maps

You can make a fine temporary map by molding damp fine builder's sand. Build a wooden frame the shape of your property with 2 × 4's and plywood. Fill the frame with a few inches of clean sand. Use your hands and other implements such as a spoon or a small brush to move the sand around. Mist the surface of the sand with water when you want it to hold its shape.

Here you can consider reshaping the ground for drama, drainage, or privacy, and explore many different shapes and solutions with ease. Before you erase the sand and shape new contours, take pictures (Polaroids are best) of forms that you want to remember.

Salt-and-Flour Models

For a more permanent record of the topography, you can make an old-fashioned salt-and-flour map. This option is best for recording the final features of your land. Because the maps harden when they dry, it's not as easy to experiment with changing the land forms as it is with a builder's sand map.

To make a salt-and-flour map, mix 2 cups white flour and ½ cup table salt in a bowl, then gradually add ¾ cup water. Knead the dough until it's thoroughly mixed, and then roll it out on a piece of plywood or very heavy cardboard. Cut the edges of the rolled piece so they conform to your base map. Then use the excess dough to shape the surface to match your property as closely as possible. Let the map air dry, then use an acrylic or polyurethane sealer to keep the moisture out. You can use acrylic paints to color areas such as lawns or driveways.

Adding Details

Adding a scale model of your house will make either type of property model more realistic. You can add miniature trees and other features, too, if you like. If you're crafty you can form all the elements yourself. Improvise structures from pieces of scrap wood or cardboard. Shape trees of twisted wire, tissue paper, or cotton balls. You can put dried plant materials such as moss, twigs, and flowers from your garden to use, too. Use small pieces of dried flowers and foliage to make trees, shrubs, and other plantings. Another option is to visit hobby, toy, and art stores for the fixings. Model railroad stores have a wealth of landscape elements from which to create fantasy countrysides.

Whether you make or buy your landscape features, stick them into the sand or arrange them on the salt-and-flour map. Move the features around as you think through design options. On a salt-and-flour map, you can eventually glue features in place once you're sure you've positioned them where you want them.

map represents regular changes in elevation, such as 1 foot or 10 feet, and is known as the contour interval. The interval is chosen depending on how large an area the map covers, and what the map is to be used for.

Although topo maps are extremely time-consuming to draw, there are reasons you might want to take the time to draw one of your property. Here are a few:

• To study and correct water-drainage problems.
• To design a series of terraces to transform a slope into flat growing beds.
• To design a deck on a sloping site.
• To design steps or wheelchair ramps.
• To find a natural depression that could form an attractive outline for a pond.
• To plan retaining walls.
• To lay out the path for a new driveway or walkways.

If you decide you do want to draw a topo map of your property, see Appendix A on page 307 for detailed instructions.

Looking Even Closer

Site analysis doesn't necessarily stop when you've finished drawing your maps of the property. There are still many more interesting and useful things your property can tell you. You'll also want to take stock of essential details such as the style of your house and other structures on your property. It will also help you uncover clues to the character of your property that you may have overlooked. Climate and soil have obvious effects on all the gardening decisions you make—from plant choices to soil improvement plans. You may also want to investigate the history of the property as well as plants and animals that are found there.

Once you have a base plan and an existing conditions plan, take a copy of each outside on a clipboard. Walk around and see what information your plans are lacking. By this point in the process, you're undoubtedly seeing details in your garden that you had never noticed before. You may want to indicate sites where you've never been able to grow an attractive lawn, pathways you and your family use to walk to the neighbors' house, and problems you hadn't noticed before. Add these notes to your plans.

Style and Architecture

The style of your house and other buildings on your property will have a great effect on your garden design. Take time to look carefully at the exterior of your house and record what it looks like. Notes about its style and exterior features will help you integrate house and garden in your final design.

Sketch, write notes, or attach photos to describe what the exterior looks like from all angles. What distinctive details are there? How would you describe the style and mood of the architecture? Is it historic, somber, ornate, heavy, exotic, or as comfortable as an old shoe? Perhaps it dates from a particular period—such as Victorian. You can use this information to develop a design that is linked to the architecture of your house.

Also look for new opportunities for outdoor rooms that you hadn't thought of. Could you make an appealing sitting area in an unused alcove or beside a door

John P. Hamel/Rodale Stock Images

▲ *This clapboard house and small formal garden blend together nicely. Both are traditional in style. The shape of the round boxwood hedges is echoed by the pea gravel paths and beds of neat groundcovers. The result is a private courtyard garden with plenty of textures, shapes, and colors to keep even this small space interesting all year round.*

that currently just features a utilitarian path?

What about the outbuildings? Anything from a garage to a doghouse counts, as long as it is freestanding, or "out," in the landscape. How does the building relate in style and material to the house? What is its relationship to the house or other features?

Finally consider all the other features in your yard—walls, fences, gates, pools, fountains, barbecue pits, swing-sets, walk-

▶

Angular lines and stark contrasts characterize this entrance planting. The design complements the modern wood-sided house that the garden encloses. Using natural materials for the front walk and walls helps link the landscape to the house. The shaded beds are filled with hostas, lilyturf (Liriope spp.), and pachysandra.

M. Catherine Davis

▲ *Always be on the lookout for the chance to create an outdoor room you hadn't seen before. This sitting area proves that with a little planning it's even possible to create an appealing space in the front yard. As the two shade trees grow, they'll provide shelter from the sun, and the free-form planting of grasses and viburnums will one day enclose the front yard.*

ways, steps, cold frames, planter boxes, birdbaths, and sculptures. What do they look like? How do they fit in to your style? Attach sketches or snapshots to illustrate important features. Consider whether each feature has sentimental, aesthetic, or utilitarian value, or whether you would rather be without it.

You now have a very good written picture of what exists on your property. It will be an invaluable reference as you begin to develop your design.

Consider the Climate

The climate of an area is determined by all the forces of nature: the amount of sunshine it receives, the strength and direction of winds, the quantity and distribution of precipitation throughout the year, and the changing temperatures. Microclimate is the term used for the climate of a very small area—such as your yard. It is also used to describe conditions found in even smaller areas—such as a spot against a south-facing wall, a protected alcove, or a frost pocket.

For gardeners, climate is often defined by a hardiness zone number. You probably already know which zone you live in (if not you can find out from the map on page 336). These zones are published by the U.S. Department of Agriculture and are based on the average low temperatures of each region.

However, your hardiness zone is only the beginning. Your property is affected by many other factors, and the sum of these factors determines its microclimate. The microclimate governs what you can and cannot grow there. It also can affect your design decisions. For example, if you get lots of snow, you'll want to have paths that are easy to shovel and keep ice-free.

You'll find that the best place to make notes about the microclimate of your property is in your garden journal. That's because you'll only really learn about it by making observations throughout the year. Use the following discussions to help you identify what types of observations you'll find most useful.

Sunlight and Exposure

The most critical of all the factors is the sun. How much of it do you get, and when? Its height in the sky (actually its angle in relation to Earth) changes throughout the year, thus changing how much

sunshine comes into the garden and the house as well as where it falls. If you know your property's latitude (the measurement that tells how far you are between the equator and the north or south pole), you can get a sun path chart from a book on solar house or greenhouse construction and design. The amount of sun your property receives is also affected by how many overcast days there are on the average in a year. By knowing the sun's yearly pattern, you can design to take advantage of it.

Your site's altitude above sea level, orientation to the sun, exposure to prevailing winds, and proximity to cities or bodies of water all also influence its microclimate. The higher the elevation, in general, the colder the climate. South-facing sites tend to be warmer than north-facing ones (in the northern half of the globe anyhow) because they collect more sunshine. Windy sites tend to be colder than sheltered sites.

Because of the heat-storing capacity of their buildings and paving, cities tend to be warmer than the surrounding countryside. Lakes, rivers, and oceans act as a buffer, keeping summers a little cooler and winters a bit less harsh. If you live near a river or lake, you may notice that spring flowers tend to bloom earlier and autumn frosts tend to be later than they are in the nearby countryside.

Even within the boundaries of your property there are likely to be variations. A south-facing wall can create a protected pocket with its own microclimate by storing and reflecting the sun's heat and blocking cold winds. Plants that are normally not quite hardy in your region may thrive there. On the other hand, leaf scorch is a common problem on broad-leaved ever-

Jerry Pavia

greens such as hollies or rhododendrons planted on south-facing sites. Such sites warm up on sunny winter days, and the plants' leaves begin transpiring water. Since the ground is still frozen, the roots can't replace the water the leaves lose, and yellow or brown scorched areas appear. A location on the north side of a wall or building doesn't present these problems. North-facing sites don't receive direct winter sun, so plants growing there will start to grow later in the spring. This may help prevent frost damage to tender flower buds such as those of apricots. North-facing sites tend to be cooler in summer, too.

Frost Pockets

Frost pockets are undoubtedly features you'll want to note on your plans and take into consideration. In spring and fall, cold air sinks to the bottom of a slope, creating a localized area of below-freezing temperature called a frost pocket. Buildings, hedges, and trees on a slope will stop the flow of cold air and create frost pockets on their uphill side.

Plants growing in frost pockets are more susceptible to frost damage in both spring and fall. Fruit trees with tender flower buds—peaches, for example—are

A garden that's suited to its climate will generally require less maintenance and have fewer problems than one that's not. The cacti and bright pinkish purple verbenas in this desert garden are right at home in the harsh conditions. Cobblestones and pea gravel serve as a groundcover, which helps link the garden to the larger landscape.

KNOW YOUR MICROCLIMATES

Identifying the microclimates on your property is a valuable exercise. It will help you do more than locate your vegetable garden or site plantings of fruit trees, too. Knowing your microclimates will help you design outdoor living spaces. On a cold winter day, a sheltered, south-facing alcove can be quite a pleasant place to sit when the sun is shining. Spring bulbs planted there will bloom delightfully early. In hot climates, thick walls and shaded paving can hold the cool of the night air and provide a haven from the heat of the day and the sun.

To verify your hunches about warmer or cooler pockets that would be especially hospitable for certain plants or uses, take temperature readings at different times of day throughout the year, in various locations in the garden. You can also design features that will create microclimate pockets for specific uses. Walls or plantings of shrubs can create sheltered areas, for example.

prone to spring damage if planted in spots where frost collects. And a vegetable garden planted in a frost pocket will have a shorter growing season than one that isn't.

Rainfall, Drainage, and Water

Annual rainfall, drainage patterns, and springs or other water existing on your

property also will influence your design. These factors affect the plants you choose, whether or not you plan a garden that needs to be watered, or just how you handle rain draining off your property.

When it comes to studying the precipitation your property receives, the annual measurement of total rainfall is only the beginning. It's also important to know how it is distributed throughout the year. Are some parts of the year dry, while others are wet? Many plants are intolerant of damp soil around their crowns during the winter months, for example. If you get lots of winter rain, they probably aren't good choices. Do you get rainfall daily, or once in a while in a big storm? If the latter is the case, you'll probably want to incorporate a plan for storm-water runoff in your design. Or you may decide to develop a system for saving the water for use in dry periods.

How much of the precipitation comes in the form of ice and snow? Many plants will overwinter just fine under a blanket of snow that stays in place all winter, but succumb if left exposed to the elements.

If you're new to an area, you may want to find out about the local history of weather extremes, including wet and dry cycles, periodic floods, and catastrophic storms such as hurricanes and tornadoes.

◄

Walls create a variety of microclimates you can take advantage of. A south-facing one may create warm-enough conditions year-round to provide a site suitable for growing plants that wouldn't normally be hardy in your area. A protected north-facing one is perfect for preventing windburn on broad-leaved evergreens.

Barbara's Journal

Managing Runoff

On rainy days the water just sheets off the hillside above the house on its way to the valley below. The path between the garage and the house becomes a muddy quagmire, and water floods the area in front of the house, eventually running into the basement. It also runs along the foundation of the new garage, which is built into the slope. That certainly can't be good for it.

Water drainage is an unexpected problem on our property, which is located halfway up a steep hillside. Garage construction left soil so compacted that weeds will barely grow in it, and water runs off, spreading mud everywhere. Water also runs down our long driveway and pools at the low point, which is between the house and garage. Building a series of terraces along the garage will slope the surface of the ground away from the garage. Double digging the beds and covering them with a thick layer of mulch will encourage water to soak in, rather than run off. Then we need to reduce the quantity of water that's reaching the area between the house and the garage. Low drainage swales of soil along the driveway should help deflect some of it onto the field below instead of letting it all pool up near the house. Adding a rock-and-gravel-filled trench under the wettest area should help carry the water away.

Your neighbors and other gardeners are a good source for this information, as is your local extension agent, a nearby botanical garden, or the local weather service.

In the previous chapter, we discussed the importance of knowing where water flows over your property after it rains. If you skipped that step, see "Studying the Shape of the Land" on page 226, and take time to learn where water runs or collects on your property. Make notes on your plans about these patterns. It's only sensible to accommodate these natural patterns when you make your design, and having them written down will make it easier to do so.

Unless you live on a perfectly flat landscape, you will already have discovered that some areas of the garden are wetter than others. This has to do with factors such as downspout drainage, natural springs, and storm water runoff from neighboring properties. For example, the margin of ground under the eaves of a house is usually much drier than the ground a few inches farther away. Look for places on your property where water collects. Or does it seem to rush right across your property without sinking in to soak the soil?

Drainage can make or break a garden design. Inventive design can turn a liability into an asset, simply by accepting the condition. Turn a low, wet spot into a bog garden, or contour sloping ground so that the water is channeled to where it's needed. Poor drainage can make a walk unusable or undermine a stone wall. In "A Country Garden: Privacy and Pathways" on page 151, owner Timothy Steinhoff turned a wet valley into a pond. This transformed a problematic site into an asset.

Sensible Water Management

The first choice in good water management is to have as much rainfall stay on your property as possible. If you keep your soil in good condition, it will be able to absorb any water it gets. Mulched, well-aerated soil will absorb water the best so it will be there when your plants need it. (Double digging soil greatly increases the amount of water it will absorb.) If your soil is compacted, water will tend to run off very quickly and not percolate down to plant roots. Large expanses of concrete also encourage water to run off rapidly.

The second choice is to manage water by collecting it quickly and redistributing it across the ground to plants that need it. In fact, some municipalities with flooding problems or overdevelopment have regulations that stipulate how much rainfall you are required to keep on site. Others regulate how to handle runoff that crosses your land. Check with your local public works or water department for local regulations. Drainage swales are one option for controlling the movement of water. They can be used to keep water away from pathways, for example, and move it to growing beds where plants can benefit from it.

Are there any springs, brooks, ponds, or other water features on your property? Do they flow year-round, or do they dry up in certain seasons or years? You'll want to be aware of how high the water rises when a stream or pond floods. If they flow through or out of your property, where do they go? How will you take care of the places where land meets water? Water-loving plants are an obvious choice for pond-side gardens.

Along a stream, however, you'll need plants that can occasionally withstand rushing floodwaters.

You'll also probably want to look into the health of the region's water reservoirs and underground aquifers, in terms of both water quality and quantity. What conservation practices are recommended, if not required legally, in your area? For example, you may not be able to water plantings during summer droughts that occur every few years. In that case, you may want to plan a garden that does not require any supplemental watering.

A Soil Primer

Knowing about your soil—what type it is and its pH—will help you select the best plants for your site and learn ways to

T. L. Gettings/Rodale Stock Images

Raised beds may be the perfect answer if the soil in your yard is ▲ terribly compacted or extremely clayey, or if there is a hardpan layer that prevents deep root penetration. Here, a whimsical horse sculpture feeds at a grouping of raised beds filled with flowers for cutting, including snapdragons, dahlias, petunias, and cosmos.

improve it so they will thrive. Soil is a mixture of particles of rock, organic matter, living organisms, water, and air. The volume of an ideal soil is nearly 50 percent space that holds air and water between soil particles. If the soil particles are very fine, it is a clay soil. Soils with very high clay content hold too much water and not enough air. They're sticky when wet, and when dry, they harden like concrete. Soils with some clay content are good, however, because clay helps hold nutrients in the soil for plants. Sandy soils have very coarse particles. They tend to be droughty because they hold little water, and nutrients tend to wash down out of the soil.

Here's a simple test you can do yourself that will give you an idea of what the mineral content of your soil is. Pick up a handful of moist soil, one that doesn't drip water when squeezed, and make it into a ball. Sandy soil won't hold together enough to make a ball. A sandy loam will hold its shape but will crumble into large chunks with even gentle pressure from your thumb. Clay soil will hold its shape—you may even be able to roll it into a little sausage. It's very likely that there are different types of soil in different areas of your property. So you may want to look at samples from several places in your yard.

The organic matter content of the soil is very important. Humus particles, which are decayed organic matter, hold lots of water, but also have lots of air spaces at the same time. Organic matter is nature's time-release fertilizer: As it decomposes, it slowly releases nutrients into the soil to feed the plants. Making and using compost—as a mulch or dug into the soil—is an easy way to ensure

WHAT SHAPED THE LAND?

If you choose to study your site's geology, you can learn how the land was formed and shaped. In the process, you may find inspiration for creating a rock garden, uncover why your soil is so alkaline, or decide on using a particular native rock for building retaining walls.

Depending on where you live, expect to find out about the earth's shifting wrinkles and faults, volcanic explosions, glacial littering, inland seas, and upstart rivers. All are factors that determine the lay of your land. You'll learn what forces brought your piece of the landscape to its present state, and you may even have clues about its future. You'll also develop a sympathetic eye for the character of the local landscape, with its slopes and flats, and be able to guess what type of soil you will find where. And what type of plants will thrive. Start your investigation with a trip to your local library to look for books on local or statewide geology.

that there is plenty of organic matter in your soil.

Acid or Alkaline?

Soils can be acid or alkaline. This characteristic is expressed as a number and referred to as the pH of the soil. The pH scale runs from 0 (very acid) to 14.0 (very alkaline); 7.0 is considered to be neutral. Most plants will grow better in a certain range of pH than they will outside that range. Soils below 5.0 or above 8.0 are not very good for growing most plants, because the nutrients plants need to grow tend to be tied up by the acidity or alkalinity of the soil.

You can test your soil pH and nutrient levels with a kit. Or you can send a sample to your local extension agent or soil conservation officer for a complete evaluation. Be sure to ask for organic recommendations for fertilizers and soil amendments. Adding organic matter, such as compost, to your soil will tend to raise the pH of acid soils and lower the pH of neutral ones.

The type of soil you have and its characteristics will give you an idea of what types of plants to include in the final design. Of course, you can add amendments to any soil to make it suit the plants you want to grow. But it can involve lots of cost and effort both initially and in maintenance. Why not find out which plants would like your soil the way it is, and go from there? See Appendix D on page 333 for books that discuss, in more detail, soils and soil tests you can perform.

Plants and Animals

There's a lot you can learn by identifying the plants already growing and living on your property—and the animals that live there, too. Taking time to learn about them will give you clues to how healthy the area around your house really is. The more diverse the populations of plants and animals, the healthier the system. For example, if you have only a handful of different types of plants—say, lawn grass, lawn weeds, and silver maple trees—you don't have a rich, healthy ecosystem that can support beneficial insects, songbirds, and other animals you may want to attract. Adding a variety of plants will provide food and shelter for wildlife and help enrich the habitat around your home. It will make it much more interesting for you, too. On the other hand, you may discover a staggering number of plants, and more interesting insects, birds, and other animals each time you look. If that's the case, you may need do nothing more than nurture them and help them thrive.

Know Your Plants

Knowing what plants thrive naturally on your property will help you discover what plants and landscape features are suited to your site. You have already located the current plants on your existing conditions plan. Now take time to identify as many of them as you can. You can use field guides to identify native plants on your property or photographic horticultural encyclopedias to identify cultivated ones. As you search through reference books you'll also come across new plants that seem just right for your property. Plants that require the same conditions that your site has to offer will be the best design choices. These include species that are native to the site, or ones that are native to an area with a similar climate and conditions. If you can't identify all of them, take samples of twigs, buds, leaves, and flowers to a local nursery, a master gardener from a local garden club, or a professional horticulturist or botanist for identification.

Take a close look at existing plants to see how healthy they are, too. You'll want to take steps to improve the health of the

Karen Bussolini

▲ *If your property is shaded by trees—or even nearby buildings that let in little light—wildflowers, perennials, shrubs, and small trees that grow naturally in the shade are the perfect choice. They'll thrive in sites where lawngrasses and other sun-loving plants would just barely survive. Here, a grouping of rhododendrons and viburnums brighten up a woodland edge.*

plants you'd like to save. Find out what they need, how they grow, if pruning can help them be stronger and more pleasing to look at, and how you can grow new plants from old ones. Look at them closely, studying their colors, textures, and forms through the seasons. These plants are veterans of your microclimate. They can form a safe backbone for a design because you know they will perform well on the site year in and year out. You'll want to give

them the care they need to remain healthy and happy.

Animal Evidence

What animals can you find evidence of on your property? You may see birds of various species, squirrels, insects, toads, and more. You also may find deer or raccoon tracks and see mole tunnels. What wildlife do you want to attract or encourage? And what types do you want to discourage? Whether an animal is a plus or pest depends on your point of view. For example, some gardeners want their gardens to become a virtual aviary, while others take steps to discourage birds such as starlings, pigeons, and blue jays. Some people trap squirrels and release them miles away, while others feed them peanuts by hand.

Where do the animals you find fit in the ecosystem? They depend on their habitat—part of which is your outdoor living spaces—to satisfy their needs for food, water, and shelter. The wildlife population of your garden is an important indicator of ecological health. More gardeners are waking up to this fact. One sign of the times is that people are beginning to put out bat boxes to attract these efficient insect controllers. Another sign is the growing awareness of chemical danger to wildlife (and people, too) from synthetic chemicals that can poison living creatures.

Jerry Pavia

You can turn dry, sunbaked slopes into plantings that are beauti- ▲
ful and easy to care for—it's all a matter of picking plants that will thrive in the conditions available. This sloping site boasts a set of informal stone steps and clumps of sun roses (Helianthemum spp.), *moss pinks* (Phlox subulata), *yuccas, and the greenish yellow spikes of* Euphorbia wulfenii.

Barbara's Journal

Nature Notebook

April: Bluebirds have definitely set up housekeeping in the new house we installed late last fall. Each time we walk along the driveway they swoop out of their house and across the driveway to perch in the sassafras trees in the hedgerow that runs along the south side of the driveway.

I've gotten so much enjoyment from keeping a nature notebook about our property—even though I don't always keep as complete notes as I'd like. I have a list of birds spotted on the property, which I do keep up-to-date. Best sightings thus far are a great blue heron hunting along the hedgerows—far nearer than I thought they ventured. We also had a great crested flycatcher investigate our old martin house for a nesting site. And each spring northern orioles sing their hearts out in an attempt to attract mates. They love to weave their hanging nests in the willow trees near the springhouse pond.

My notes about birds and other animals have also given rise to a list of plants I'd like to add to the garden—all will provide added food and shelter. Tops on the list are hollies, hawthorns, crab apples, and viburnums.

marauders or decide to restore a stream or pond to provide access to water. You may need to clear out underbrush that provides cover for undesirable critters such as poisonous snakes—at least in areas you plan to frequent.

You may also choose to use your outdoor living spaces as a private reserve to provide habitat for rare plants and animals that are native to your area. Bird-watching clubs, local parks, natural history museums, state agencies, and native wildflower associations are a few places you can find out about rare species. If you devote even a small portion of your landscape to providing habitat for animals and plants, you will be helping to preserve a small part of our natural heritage. Just be sure that you obtain rare wildflowers from a reputable nursery that has propagated the plants from nursery stock, not collected them from the wild. You can also propagate wildflowers by dividing ones on your own property without destroying the original stands. Or grow them from seed.

Previous Inhabitants

Have you ever wondered who has lived on the land before you? Every piece of land has its own genealogy, with generations of human life leaving traces for the ▶

Architectural style, regional history, and neighborhood character can all provide strong design clues. This Victorian-style house is complemented by a grouping of tidy geometric-shaped beds inspired by the gardens of the era. Solid plantings of ground-hugging plants like junipers and vinca contrast nicely with brick walks.

The creatures you already have and the ones you wish to attract will affect your final design. You may see a need for fencing to protect certain areas from

future to discover. Digging into the history of your property may uncover ideas to inspire your design, features on your lot that you can highlight, or just a better understanding of who once lived in the region. It may inspire your choices of plants, too. For example, you may decide on a garden that features plants historically grown in the period when your house was constructed.

The story of human habitation begins with the various tribes of Native Americans that once lived in your region. By looking at the ways they used native plants for food, medicine, clothing, dyes, and shelter, you'll discover a whole new dimension to the trees, shrubs, wildflowers, and other plants that grow—or once grew—where you live. Perhaps you will choose to include native medicinal plants in your garden design. Or perhaps you will draw from the colors and patterns they used to design your own outdoor living spaces.

Who has lived on your property since the European settlers began expanding across North America? Where did they come from, and how did they live on the land? Wave upon wave of people have added their layer of history to your town or region. Along with family treasures, they brought distinct traditions of building, gardening, cooking, clothing, society, and language that you may use to inspire your design. Perhaps a traditional Colonial herb garden is for you, or a Victorian planting scheme with beds of colorful annuals.

You may learn quite a bit by looking back at the property deed. Old property maps may show shifting boundaries and "improvements" such as the building of your house. The date your house was built and its style can give you clues about what kind of garden landscape it may have had at one time.

Your Neighborhood and Beyond

You will want to find out where your house, whether old or new, fits into the growth of the neighborhood or town or into the settlement of the countryside where you live. How was it meant to be lived in? (And how is your pattern of living different?) What does it tell you about the people who built it—their tastes, achievements, and aspirations?

Look around your neighborhood as it is today. You'll probably notice that it has a prevailing style of its own. It reflects design values that are, or were at some time, widely shared. Traditions such as broad front lawns and foundation plantings, or signature elements such as dogwood trees, picket fences, or holy shrines will emerge. Some local traditions will inspire you to continue or update them, others you will probably want to forget. There are often ways to create the landscape you want while satisfying your neighbors' unconscious needs, if you are creative.

Get to know the region's craft traditions in everything from furniture and fences to birdhouses and weather vanes. House museums, historical societies, antique stores, and craft expositions are good sources for inspiration, where you can get ideas for everything from handmade rustic furniture to patterning your garden after an Amish quilt.

Susan's Journal

Using Oral History

Oral history is an often-overlooked source of lore about how previous people used your landscape. For two years I puzzled over a concrete ring, 12 feet in diameter. When I first began to garden, it was filled with grass. My initial idea was to plant a tree in the middle (and therein lies a lesson about digging holes before you get the trees) until my shovel discovered a steel rod rooted so deeply that I could not remove it. Instead, I improvised my first perennial bed and went on my gardening way.

Eventually I met an elderly resident of the neighborhood who remembered being fascinated as a child by a goldfish pond there in the 1920s. The concrete ring was the basin's lip, of course. Our garden also teems with earthworms. I like to think got their start in the bait shack which once did a tidy business next door, perhaps 30 years ago.

Whether you decide to create a historically accurate garden design, or to just add a traditional plant or two, research into previous inhabitants is a rich source of inspiration. The more you know about the people who have lived on your land in its past, the more ideas you'll have.

Some of the local conventions may reflect local ordinances. You'll want to find out about any that govern what you may or may not do. Things like fence height, setbacks, pool safety, height-of-lawn limits, satellite dishes, clotheslines, and water use may be regulated. Regulations are designed to protect people, but they often lead to mass-produced solutions with little appeal. If you take the time to look for the creative opportunities within a restriction, you sometimes find a solution that truly supports and expresses your design intentions.

Studying your site will inevitably lead to questions about the larger region; how far to go is, of course, up to your own curiosity and time. You might want to start a separate notebook for information about the region. It can be handy to tape or paste in photocopies of maps or plant lists, brochures from local nature preserves, and so on. You'll be surprised at how much is easily available from local historical and environmental institutions, as well as sources in local, state, and federal governments.

Many garden makers and naturalists find that exploring their region becomes a lifetime pursuit and an enjoyable focus for recreational sports, art, vacations, and even volunteer activities. No matter how earnest or easy-going is your approach to this kind of research, you're likely to arrive at the same conclusion: Each layer in the natural history of the region creates the conditions that shape the next layer. You stand in your corner of the world, peeling back the layers to discover how each is connected to and reflected by the next. In the process, you'll develop a wealth of information and ideas for outdoor living spaces that suit both your site and you.

BRINGING IT ALL TOGETHER: MAKING YOUR LANDSCAPE DESIGN

Now that you've learned about your style and studied your property in detail, you have the tools you need to design your own outdoor living spaces. The creative process isn't over yet, though. In this chapter, you'll find out how to go about putting all you've learned together into a workable design.

By now, you undoubtedly have more design ideas than you ever imagined. You also know what activities you'd like to have room for and how you would like to be able to live outdoors. Where do you go from here? How can you put all these ideas together into a series of outdoor living spaces that are as livable and specialized as the rooms and hallways of your home? And how will you recognize the right design when you see it?

In this chapter, you'll use your new understanding of what landscapes can mean to decide how your landscape will work. Don't fall into the trap of just trying to copy or recreate favorite scenes, such as those from your childhood, in your design. Instead, use your feelings to inspire you and combine them with practical considerations about what you want and need in your garden today. For instance, a cherished memory of a campfire raises possibilities about how you might design a barbecue for family cooking. This approach will allow you to break out of preconceived ideas about what a garden element should be or should look like, and help you design a garden that is yours alone.

Keep in mind that the creative process described in this book rarely delivers a single correct answer. There is no one perfect design for your garden. Instead, you'll discover there are a number of possible designs. What you are seeking is the best fit between your own needs and the character of your property. Your garden will take shape from the way you weave together the ideas and information you gathered in previous chapters. It will be your designer original.

Identifying Your Key Concepts

So how can you use all the information you've gathered, instead of letting it use—or just confuse—you? The key to success is to come up with key themes or concepts that will guide your design, not just today and tomorrow, but five and ten years from now.

Your themes or key concepts essentially are simple statements that summarize what your garden will be—phrases or

▶

An effective design you'll enjoy for years to come incorporates what you want and need in your garden and also makes the best use of your property's character. A garden like this one, which combines a free-form water garden and terrace, takes planning and thought, but there's no doubt that it would provide a lifetime of enjoyment.

248

Walter Chandoha

▲ *It doesn't take much to create an outdoor room. This one would be little more than a wide spot along a woodland path without the flagstones and furniture. The paving helps establish the fact that this is more than just part of the path. Comfortable furnishings complete the effect and undoubtedly will lure visitors back to this casual sitting area again and again.*

sentences that describe its essential character, motive, and meaning. You may decide on one overriding theme and several key concepts that help shape how you accomplish it. Or you may have a handful of key concepts that will help you accomplish different goals or solve unrelated problems.

For examples of key themes and concepts—and how they relate to the people and the property—scan back over the ten garden stories in part 2. You'll find that all have overriding themes and/or key concepts that shaped the design. For example, the theme that guided Karen and Henry in "A Woodland Garden: Spaces for People and Wildlife" on page 74 was that they wanted to share their space with friends and family, as well as birds, butterflies, and other wildlife. On the other hand, the factors that guided Sheila and Terry's design in "From Bare to Beautiful: Foresting a Courtyard" on page 60 were small space, a tight budget, and an overriding need for shade—both for themselves and for their beloved dog, Emma.

Take Your Time

To begin the process of identifying *your* key concepts, start by looking over

▲
Don't forget that outdoor living spaces don't have to be permanent. You can create "instant" spaces for a party or a quiet afternoon of reading or conversation by just rearranging furniture you have on hand and perhaps adding some temporary shade. Such "instant" spaces are also a good way to try out ideas for more permanent ones.

the master list of ideas you developed and transferred to index cards. Also take a close look at the information you gathered about your property from your observations. The best key concepts for your garden may be obvious right from the start. Or you may need to mull over all that you've learned before you decide on them. Key concepts are a shorthand for your garden ideas. They'll help you make a garden that is an expression of your most personal interests and values, as well as a unique celebration of your landscape.

Here are a few reminders and suggestions to help you discover your key concepts.

Mull it over. Don't rush through this process: It can take a while to identify the best concepts for you and your property. Take your time to think things over—you'll be more satisfied with the results.

Look for connections. What are your most important needs? What themes came out of looking into your early outdoor memories? Does the site itself suggest obvious design concepts? For example, perhaps privacy tops your list of important things you need in your backyard, and you've always loved watching birds. You can easily make a connection between these two elements by developing plantings of shrubs and trees that provide shelter and food for birds as well as privacy for you.

Imagine using your new garden. Close your eyes and imagine being in your garden. What colors do you see? Is it shady or sunny? Also think about what you hear, feel, smell, and taste. What are you doing? Perhaps you are alone reading a book, harvesting herbs, or picking flowers for drying. Or maybe you are visiting with friends or family.

Let your garden talk to you. This may seem odd at first, but consider what your garden "wants to be." Some of the best designers talk about a place as if it were a person with desires of its own. Try imagining your landscape as a person. What would it thank you for? What problems is it having that you should be aware of? Is there something it needs for its well-being? How does it experience you? Turn the tables. Listen for its voice in your imagination, write a dialogue, or enlist someone to role-play with you. Have fun with this game. Many people believe that a living landscape of plants and animals has rights of its own, based on its intrinsic worth—its own values apart from human use. Try to approach your design as a relationship of equals, and respect the rights and needs of your land and the plants and animals that live there. Make your garden a place where both can fulfill their potential.

▲ *There's no doubt that this striking design is closely linked to the desert landscape around it. The walls that enclose the garden echo the shapes of the mountains, and the terrace features areas with both sun and shade. The drought-tolerant plantings include a variety of cacti, succulents, and other desert natives, which will grow well in the conditions available.*

Jerry Pavia

Clarify Your Concepts

To develop and refine your key concepts you may want to try an exercise called clustering. Writers and designers often use it to see how their thoughts cluster together and connect. Get a big sketch pad from an office supply or art store—a pad of cheap paper like newsprint is ideal, so you'll feel free to scribble, cross out, and use lots of pages.

Write down an idea or key concept in the center of a sheet of paper and circle it—just a word or two is fine. Now let your thoughts about that idea roam freely. As each new thought forms, jot it down, circle it, and draw a connecting line back to a previously circled thought. You needn't use every thought that occurs to you, only the ones that have strong connections to the key concept and to each other.

Allow 10 minutes for this exercise; if your thoughts run dry, just retrace the lines, circles, and words until another thought arrives—it will. At some point, this map of your idea and all its parts will seem complete. It will come together in your mind as a picture of your garden.

Now, write a description of the web of circles and lines you just drew. Use the present tense, and follow the rules of free writing—keep your hand moving, don't stop to think or reread, don't cross out— but be selective. Then summarize what you have written into a phrase or sentence that states the key concept.

Continue this process until you've identified the concepts that will guide your design. Throughout, always give your ideas the respect they deserve—note what pops to mind, and don't reject anything out of hand, no matter how implausible or unaffordable it might seem. Sometimes the silliest ideas contain the germ of brilliance. Even a little idea will have ripple effects on your landscape. Each choice you make, from where to plant the gift rose that came on Mother's Day, to how big the potting shed should be, makes a difference to your design.

Using Your Key Concepts

Before drawing a final design, you'll need to organize your list of possible features and activities—and undoubtedly narrow it down, too. This is where your key concepts are invaluable. They'll help you identify the most important elements for your final design. For this process, you'll once again need your set of index cards that list all the possible garden elements and activities.

Look at each card again. As you recall, you listed what the activity or element was, and what it would take to carry it out. As you look at the cards, consider your property and write down possible locations on each card. For example, if a card lists "space for active sports," an existing lawn area is an obvious choice. Also add any new notes or ideas you have on each feature—how you might create it, materials required, possible designs, and so forth.

As you work, you may discover new uses for spaces that already exist in embryo. The ells on either side of Jeanne and Bill's house in "The Small Garden: Rooms to

Pamela Harper

▲ *As you develop your design, you'll find that certain areas and activities fit together naturally. In this informal garden, a path that meanders through the landscape wraps around a pond outfitted with a small fountain. The fountain adds movement and sound to the otherwise quiet scene, and a bench overlooking the pond provides a spot for sitting and sunning.*

Grow In" on page 33 are a good example. They all too easily could have remained empty, unused space. Instead, they're used to create attractive views from inside the house. One is transformed into a tiny area that will attract birds; the other a utility area and scene to enjoy from the kitchen. Such spaces-in-waiting offer a very efficient and effective way to get your plan started. All you need to do is learn to recognize the opportunity.

Rank Your Cards

Now, spread your idea cards out on a big table next to your list of key concepts. Review each card and consider how it relates to your key concepts. Move cards that are very important toward the center of the table. Place ones that are less important toward the outer edges.

You'll end up with a cluster of cards in the center surrounded by rings of cards.

If you end up with a few cards that don't relate to any of your key concepts but still seem important to you, you'll need to go back and add to or refine your key concepts. Then rearrange the cards accordingly.

Connecting Elements and Activities

Next, look at each of the cards again. Consider how the elements or activities on them would or could impact one another. What activities could occur close together? For example, you could use the same space for visiting with friends, dining outdoors, reading, and relaxing. Which would conflict and need to be separated? Space for active sports like football would need to be far away from plantings of perennials or the vegetable garden, for example. As the relationships get clearer in your thinking, rearrange your cards accordingly.

Jerry Pavia

What better place to enjoy a garden than on a bench set right ▲ *among the flowers? Shrubs and the branches of a nearby tree shelter the site and add a bit of shade. A variety of perennials— including a large thistle and clumps of brightly colored poppies— provide color and texture. The result is a pleasing nook in which to sit and rest from a morning's gardening chores.*

As you work, consider what time of day or season of the year each activity takes place. You may find that two or more activities can take place in the same space without conflicting with each other. The warm sunny bench where your spouse enjoys a morning cup of coffee outdoors may, with the passing of the sun, become a cool and shady spot where you can read the mail after work, for example.

When you're finished with this process, you should have several stacks of cards—each with activities that can occur in the same place. Arrange each pile so that the most important activity or element is on top. The piles should be arranged with the ones most important to your key concept near the center of the table.

Make Rough Designs

Now you're ready to start making rough designs by assigning possible locations on your overall plan to the elements and activities on your cards. To do this, you'll need a copy of your base and/or existing conditions plan along with some large sheets of tracing paper. To make your rough designs, you'll lay the tracing paper over your plan and sketch ideas on it. The tracing paper makes it easy to work on several rough designs at the same time, as you'll be doing here. It also makes it easy to start over or incorporate ideas from several sheets of paper. When you want to start fresh, all you need do is add another sheet, trace the ideas you'd like to keep, and go from there.

Start with the cards in the center of the table—those that are most important to your key concepts. Pick up the first card—or stack of cards—and consider the requirements for location and equipment that you've listed. Does it need to be close to the house, the road, or the storage shed? Or does it need to be tucked away from sight and sound in the back corner? Look at your base plan and find the possible sites that fill the requirements. Consider how large an area you want or need as well.

To start a rough plan, sketch in the first feature—a circle and a label or a scribbled drawing is fine for now. At this stage, it's best to develop several rough designs at the same time. To do this, use several sheets of tracing paper and sketch in the first activity or element in the possible locations you identified on different sheets. Then pick up a second central card, or stack of cards, and find possible locations for that feature. If there's only one suitable place for an activity, sketch it in on the same place in each rough plan.

Throughout the process, remember to consider the relationships between the activities and elements on the cards. Can a single area be used for several activities? Do activities or elements need to be close together or far apart?

Once you have located each of the features on the central cards, move on to the ones of intermediate importance, and finally to those of least importance. You may run out of space before you run out of ideas, of course. If you do, perhaps you can think up creative ways to make spaces serve more than one function. Don't compromise the space you've allocated to your most important elements in an effort to cram in all of your ideas. Not only will you end up with a cluttered-looking design, you also may end up with a garden full of spaces that are all too small for the activities they've been designed for.

To narrow down the number of rough designs you develop, you may want to limit the number of sites you consider for each activity—by either identifying the best possible sites or setting an arbitrary limit. (You can always go back and consider new ones.) Of course, you'll give priority to the most important elements and activities so that they'll end up in the best sites. You may need to make compromises on less important ones. When you finish, you will have a number of possible garden designs rough-sketched on paper.

Weigh the Design Options

Spread your rough designs out and look at them closely. Since each of them grew out of your personal needs and your

Small gardens can be especially difficult to plan since the space needs to be used so efficiently. This small city garden has it all—a terrace for sitting or dining, a water garden, and a wild area to enclose the back of the garden. Plantings on either side of the lot link house and garden and provide privacy. Evergreens add year-round color and texture.

John P. Hamel/Rodale Stock Images

John P. Hamel/Rodale Stock Images

▲ *A low-maintenance garden doesn't need to be a boring mono-culture of English ivy or pachysandra. The plantings that edge this patio and pool provide interesting color and texture every day of the year. Herbs, evergreens, liriope, ophiopogon, and a large clump of porcupine grass* (Miscanthus sinensis *var.* strictus) *combine to form an attractive but easy-to-maintain garden.*

site's attributes, they'll probably all appeal to you to some extent. But each makes certain elements more important than others. Try to weigh their strengths and weaknesses as carefully as you can.

The amount of space you've allocated to each element will affect its importance in the overall landscape. It may also affect the amount of maintenance the design would require. For example, an herb knot garden may be high on your list of priori-ties, but it's a high-maintenance element that requires frequent trimming. A design that features a knot garden that takes up much of your backyard would need lots of maintenance. Selecting a design that moves it from center stage, reduces its size, and combines it with other lower-maintenance plantings of herbs may be the best solution for you: You'll have the knot garden, but also a design that needs less maintenance.

Another thing to look for is how the location and proximity of one element to another affects the overall feeling of the design. Here, your personal preferences come into play. One design may seem to favor relaxation; another, exertion. Elements may fit together better in one design than another. Proximity of elements can have a concrete effect on how easy a design is to maintain, however. For example, locating the compost pile far away from the vegetable garden, one of the primary places you'll want to use the compost, has an obvious effect.

Try to decide which design really pleases you. It can be helpful to look at a design as though you're telling a story. Does it have a beginning, a middle, and an end? What do its characters (you and others) do in each "scene" or space? What do you get out of it when all is said and done? Of course, a garden is never a finished place with pat endings, and the designs you're evaluating are quite rough, but perhaps this approach will help you weigh the options you've created.

Professional designers usually offer several options, all viable, to clients, and expect to be surprised at the choices their clients make. You may be surprised by your preferences, too. That's because good choices help to clarify what you really want but may not be able to express.

You may well find yourself combining parts of the different rough designs and resketching to come up with a new one you like better. You'll also undoubtedly end up with elements in one design that you couldn't find room for in another. That's fine. Just keep sketching until you have one or two rough designs that please you.

Consider Your Resources

Before you make a final decision, it's important to compare the overall cost of your designs. This doesn't just mean cost in terms of money. In this case, it means cost in terms of your resources—your time, the amount of physical labor you want to devote, and money you want to spend, as well as the water, fuel, and electricity the design would require. Most of us have only a certain amount of each available. How you choose to spend your resources is up to you, but setting a realistic budget for them is crucial to developing a successful—and satisfying—design.

If you aren't working from a realistic plan, it's easy to get overwhelmed or be disappointed. If you design a garden that you can't finish installing because you don't have the money or skills it requires, you'll invariably be disappointed. A plan that requires more time in upkeep than you have available will be equally frustrating: The garden will never look its best, you'll never get to relax in it, and you'll be permanently frustrated. Fitting your design to your resource budget will avoid this problem.

It may help to look back to the notes you made about your strengths and the budget you have available during the early stages of this process. Consider which of the rough designs makes the most of your strengths. Which uses your abilities to best advantage?

Consider, too, how each option uses the other resources you have available. If money is the issue, you may want to consider the options for phasing-in a plan before eliminating it in favor of a less expensive one. (See "Phase-In Your Design" on page 296 for ideas.) Do consider factors such as how much water is available and how you want to use it. Also consider how much gasoline, electricity, and time you want to spend in keeping things mowed, trimmed, or lighted. Any or all of these may throw the balance in favor of one rough design or another.

Consider Your Time

For most of us, time is probably the most limiting and inflexible resource. It makes sense to plan a landscape that fits the time you have to spend. It's nearly as important that you plan a design that will let you spend as much of that time as possible doing things you enjoy.

So forget for a moment your fantasy of garden life and consider how you actually spend time outdoors. How much time do you spend in your yard on a weekly basis throughout the year? Are there certain days of the week and times of the day you're likely to be out in your garden? Do you work in it during some seasons but avoid being outdoors in others—the dog days of August, perhaps? Your garden journal is a good place to keep a log of the time you spend in your garden.

How much of that time do you spend working as opposed to relaxing? What proportion of time would you really like to spend relaxing or working? Do you even distinguish between the two activities?

Once you know about how much time you have to spend working in your garden, write it down. Weigh the amount of time you'd like to spend on your garden against each rough design. Decide if the rough

designs you've drawn are workable or not. If not, go back and develop some designs that might be more in keeping with the time you have available.

Think, too, about what tasks you enjoy doing. Which do you do only out of obligation? Be sure to consider these preferences in your design. You may enjoy fussing over perennials or herbs, or find weeding relaxing. If you hate mowing the lawn, see what you can do to reduce the size of it or the time it takes to mow it.

In the best of all worlds, someone else in your household enjoys doing the tasks you dislike, making it easy to cover all the bases. More likely, though, you'll find tasks in some of your design options that no one wants to do or is able to do. In this case, you can decide to eliminate the task by choosing a design that doesn't require it, reduce the size of the area to minimize the problem, or bite the bullet and plan on doing the task anyway. Or you can hire someone else to do the work for you.

Compare the Costs

A line-by-line comparison of the costs of different options you're considering can be invaluable when it comes to making final decisions. It's important to consider both installation and maintenance costs—in terms of both money and time. Installation jobs are usually once and done, but maintenance must be done again and again.

Start by listing what will be involved in installing and maintaining each feature. How many hours will it take? Do you have the skills to do the tasks involved yourself? Do you enjoy or want to do the tasks that are required? Talk to other gardeners

TIME-SAVING IDEAS

Few of us have as much time as we need or want. Choosing design features, materials, and plants with care can help you get the most accomplished in the time you have to spend. Here are a few ideas to keep in mind while you plan your design:

• Use edgings. Edgings can keep grass out of flower beds, prevent gravel from scattering over a flagstone walk, and cut down on trimming. Brick or plastic mowing strips, which are set flush with the soil around lawn areas, make it much easier to maintain a neat edge. One wheel of your mower rides on the strip, so the mower can cut the grass right at the lawn's edge. This eliminates hand-trimming.

• Confine high-maintenance features such as lawns and rose gardens to small areas.

• Install drip irrigation systems for areas that you have to water; plant most of your landscape with plants that can grow well without supplemental water.

• Replace lawn areas with groundcovers or mulch—or even decks or patios. You'll eliminate some mowing, trimming, and watering.

• Replace any hard-to-mow lawn-covered slopes with terraces, or plant them with easy-care groundcovers.

• Mulch under trees, shrubs, and plants. It reduces weeding, watering, and trimming.

• Use a mulching lawn mower. As you mow, it finely chops the grass clippings and scatters them on the lawn, so your lawn gets mulch and you don't have to deal with grass clippings. Grass clippings are also a free source of nitrogen for your lawn!

• Choose hedges, shrub borders, and specimen plants that have natural-looking, informal shapes. Sheared hedges and other plantings require frequent trimming to keep them looking neat.

• To save pruning time, choose slow-growing plants and plants that won't outgrow their site.

• Set pavers in mortar, or plant something like creeping thyme between them to keep weeds from growing between them. It saves tedious weeding.

• Choose plants that don't make a mess by dropping seedpods, sap, or lots of large leaves. Also avoid plants that are prone to problems in your area. They will look messy and take up your time as you try to keep them healthy.

• Choose plants suited to your site and climate, so you won't need to spend time cosseting finicky plants.

• Make a few large beds around a number of trees and shrubs, rather than dozens of little planting islands that take lots of time to mow and trim around.

• Choose the best—not necessarily the most expensive—materials possible; they will last longer and require less maintenance, and you won't have to replace them so soon.

or local nursery owners about how much time things really take to install and maintain. "Comparing Short- and Long-Term Costs" on the opposite page shows a sample comparison between two options.

It's important to remember that a botched job can cost more in the long run, so try to be realistic about the match between your skills, your ideas, and your need to save money. Hiring someone to do the job for you or someone to assist you and renting special equipment that will make the job easier are options to consider.

Use your lists to help you make your final choice. As you can see in "Comparing Short- and Long-Term Costs," costs can be deceptive. An element that is costly to install may save loads of time and money in the long run. On the other hand, one that's inexpensive to install or leave unchanged may be quite costly to maintain in the long run.

Of course, there are intangible benefits to each option, too. Fine-tuning a design involves trade-offs. Which ones are you comfortable making? Which design can you accomplish and enjoy living in? You may be willing to spend a little more on something that is deeply satisfying to you.

Establishing the Framework

Once you have made a final decision on which rough design you'd like to work with, sketch it out either on a fresh copy of your base plan or on a new sheet of tracing paper. The rough design establishes the framework of your garden—the elements that it contains and where they are located.

At this point, your design is probably little more than a rough sketch with some notes. Your next challenge is to fit all the elements together into a series of living spaces that feel like one connected whole. A garden that overemphasizes individual elements at the expense of how they fit together will be less comfortable than one that works as a single unit.

In the following sections, you'll learn how to hold the parts of your garden together by planning its structure and establishing boundaries between spaces. Use the examples and the photographs in the rest of this book to help guide you in making decisions about how you'll use these principles to develop your own design. You may want to read through this entire section first to get the general idea, and then read it again while you sketch notes and spaces on your base plan or a series of tissue overlays. By the time you start on the step "Connecting the Spaces," which begins on page 271, you should have a drawing of the spaces and how they fit together, along with an idea of how they are divided.

Plan the Bones

Well-designed gardens are said to have "good bones." That means they have a strong structure that holds the garden together to make it a unified whole rather than a collection of random parts. An effective structure—good bones—will hold the garden together no matter what the season or how neglected the garden may be. In fact, you can learn a lot about good garden structure by visiting gardens during the winter. That's when you can see what's really there unifying all the parts of the garden.

COMPARING SHORT- AND LONG-TERM COSTS

You may be surprised at what you find when you compare the short- and long-term costs of design options that you are considering. In the example below, we'll assume you have a moderately steep, lawn-covered slope that's in partial shade and the grass is not very happy. The area is only about 1,000 square feet, but mowing and trimming around trees that grow on the slope is a tedious, time-consuming chore. You are considering replacing the grass with ferns, bulbs, and other groundcovers but are not sure whether it is worth the expense in time and money.

When comparing landscape options, add a dollar cost for your time, even if you are going to do the work yourself. That way, even if you don't have any out-of-pocket expenses, you can weigh the options more evenly. Here we've used $5 per hour for labor. You can use more or less than that, depending on how you value your time. Also, if you hate one job but love another, you might want to value them differently—if you hate mowing and trimming, you could use $20 per hour and put a lower value on an activity you love, like planting. Here's what the breakdown of costs might look like.

Leave Existing Lawn

If you leave the existing lawn, installation costs are zero, but you do need to consider annual maintenance. If it takes 2 hours a week to mow and trim, that's about 35 hours a year. Plus you'll have yearly cleanup chores such as raking leaves, fertilizing, and reseeding, which may add another 5 hours. At $5 per hour, that would mean the lawn would cost $200 a year to maintain, plus the cost of grass seed and organic fertilizer, if you don't have enough compost to apply.

Replace the Lawn

Weigh that option against replacing the grass with ferns, bulbs, and other groundcovers. It would take about 20 hours to dig up the lawn, prepare the soil, plant the plants, and mulch the area. At $5 an hour, that's $100. Plants would cost $300, mulch and soil amendments $100, for a total first-year cost of $500. After that, you'd have to spend about 2 hours a year weeding and mulching the area.

While the initial cost of replacing the lawn is high, it will pay for itself in about 2½ years. There are other considerations you might weigh as well: For example, say you hate mowing and trimming but enjoy planting, and prefer ferns and flowers to lawn. Then when you add in the fact that the renovated area will be an attractive addition to your home, it makes sense to replace the lawn.

Anything that helps establish the visible framework or structure of the garden can be part of its "bones." That includes walls, paved areas, pathways, fences, hedges, trellises and other structures, plus permanent plantings of shrubs, trees, evergreen groundcovers—even ornamental grasses. A repeated or echoing shape can

PLAN FOR PRACTICALITY

There are some basic practical considerations to keep in mind while you're designing the framework, and later the connections and pathways, in your garden. A variety of people need to have access to your property. Oil or gas delivery people need to get to the tank or inlet. Meter readers need to get to the meters. Be sure to accommodate their needs when you plan. An element as simple as a short stepping-stone path through a flower bed to a meter can make it easy for a meter reader to get in and out without damaging your plantings.

Electric, telephone, and cable television service people may trim trees that grow near their lines: It pays to design plantings that they will be able to work around.

Don't forget to consider your own everyday needs either. Have you planned your paths so you will be able to get your mower and garden cart where you need to go? Is it easy to take out the garbage? What about someone delivering bulky garden supplies like mulch—is there a place for that?

And of course, don't plan, and certainly don't dig, before finding out where underground utilities run. Not only do you want to avoid injuring them or yourself, but you may not even be allowed to build or plant permanent features over them.

also be used to define the bones of a garden and help unify its parts.

You may see the framework of a garden in its boundaries or walls or in the paths or doors that connect elements. For example, hedges can be used to divide a garden into rooms, with brick pathways connecting them. Or the unifying frame-

Karen Bussolini

▲
The bones of a garden are most evident in winter, when tree trunks and branches, walls, walkways, garden furnishings, and evergreens shine without competition from bright flowers and the lush green hues of summer. With a little planning, it's possible to create a garden that will have features that are attractive all year.

also be part of the structure—such as free-form beds that fit together. A signature material—like piled stone, landscape ties, or a particular pattern of brickwork—can

Karen Bussolini

The bones of this formal garden effectively pull it together to ▲
*create a unified whole. The white picket fence and curving
terrace wall echo the shape of the pool, while pairs of lamp
posts, perennial beds, gate posts, and shrubs emphasize the
symmetrical design. White-flowered kousa dogwoods (Cornus
kousa) and evergreen and deciduous trees form a dramatic
backdrop.*

work may be part of the spaces themselves—a shade tree in the center of a
terrace whose branches define the shape
of the space (the terrace). For a good example of a garden with a very clear framework,
see "The Small Garden: Rooms to Grow
In" on page 33. You'll find that a variety
of different materials—including walkways,
trellises, and plants—serve as the bones.

Your key concepts may already contain clues to a suitable material or theme.
For example, in "Celebrating a Desert Landscape" on page 104, Patrice and John used
pinkish cinder block, from which their house
was constructed, throughout the design
to tie the landscape to the house. They
also used natural boulders to tie the landscape to the mountains nearby. These ele-

ments establish the framework of their garden and help link all the parts together. In "A Woodland Garden: Spaces for People and Wildlife" on page 74, plants that feed birds and other animals play an important role in establishing the structure of the garden.

Try to decide what you'd like to use to establish the framework of your garden. You'll find some suggestions on how to select plants and materials that you can use when you design your framework later in this chapter (see "Plants for Your Garden" on page 279 and "Selecting Materials" on page 285). Is there a theme or themes that would tie all the spaces together? An obvious material? Are there plants you especially want to have in your garden? Deciding how you'll establish the garden's structure will help guide you when it comes to choosing the boundaries and walls of the outdoor living spaces. It will also help you choose materials and plants to build and decorate each space.

Frame the Spaces

Now that you're armed with your key concepts, a framework for your design, and an idea of how to establish your garden's structure, you're ready to fill in the design.

To start framing-in the garden, you'll need to begin deciding on the boundaries between different outdoor spaces. Boundaries give shape to individual spaces the way a cup gives shape to water. In a garden, boundaries can be as solid as a two-story brick wall, or as ephemeral as the line between sunlight and shade under a tree's branches. There's no such thing as a gar-

den with a single, simple exterior boundary. Even a city courtyard with walls on all sides will have a variety of spaces. For example, Sheila and Terry's tiny garden in "From Bare to Beautiful: Foresting a Courtyard" on page 60 features a variety of spaces that have boundaries that range from formal to informal and can be used for a variety of activities.

Susan A. Roth

▲

A whimsical gate forms the front door of this appealing cottage garden, separating public areas from private ones. Passers-by can catch a glimpse of orange lilies and yellow and orange calendulas along the brick path that leads into the garden.

WATER IN THE GARDEN

Water adds life to a garden throughout the year. It reflects the sky and the colors of the garden around it. It also adds movement and sound as well—at least when it isn't frozen. In a design, water features such as water gardens, ponds, and streams function as part of the bones of the garden, because they play such an important role in unifying the overall design. If your site already has a stream or pond, you have undoubtedly already considered it in your design. But even tiny gardens can feature a small pool.

Large permanent water features require careful planning. See Appendix D on page 333 for books on how to plan and plant a water garden. You'll also find that several of the gardens in part 2 of this book feature water in their designs. They may give you some ideas about how you might include water in your design.

The most common mistake gardeners make when planning a water feature is that they design ones that are too small for the setting. The result is a garden that's overwhelmed by the surrounding landscape and ends up looking puny and a bit unkempt. In general, the best rule to follow is "when in doubt, make it bigger." It helps to think of the water as a space in its own right: One exercise that may help you design a water garden that's big enough to be effective is to try imagining the space the pool will occupy as filled with lawn rather than water. On the other hand, in an arid climate, too much water may seem like overkill. A large pool may look uncomfortable in such a setting, while a trickle of precious water is powerfully refreshing in its subtlety.

Swimming pools are simply large water features with a special use. You can design a swimming pool to complement any garden since pools can be almost any size, shape, or color as long as they are large enough and deep enough for the kind of swimming you want to do. Dark blue-gray paint inside the pool is most effective for reflecting, but other colors have their merits, too. You can bring plantings right up to the edge of the pool in some places to tie it into the garden and to make use of its surface for reflections. Paving doesn't need to be oppressive; a 3-foot-wide strip of paving is plenty for access.

The way a swimming pool looks in the off-season is a factor to consider when making your design. If winter views from the house are important, then you will probably want to locate the pool slightly out of sight or screen its view from the house's windows. Exposure to the sun and protection from the wind are usually desirable.

Of course, the boundaries you draw will depend on the type of design you have. Your design may be open and unstructured—with a large space that accommodates many different activities—or it may be structured in a more formal way, with many small rooms clearly separated by walls or tall plants and connected by pathways. An interesting garden design often combines some of each. If you're having trouble envisioning the types of boundaries you can use, look back through part 2 to see how the spaces in the gardens are divided from one another.

Planning Boundaries

To plan the boundaries between spaces in your garden, you'll need to decide what each section of the boundary needs to do for you. Boundaries function differently depending on how you want to use each of the garden's spaces. Look around your property and consider the functions of your outdoor living spaces. What spaces are public, semi-public, and absolutely private? To create a welcoming front entrance, yet separate your front yard in a friendly way from the sidewalk, you may want to use a low retaining wall or picket fence, for

▲ In a garden, boundaries don't have to be solid to effectively create an outdoor room. This space is created by a soft screen of foliage that encloses the area and provides dappled shade and protection from the hot sun "outside." Because of the soft screening, the room has a bright, open atmosphere. Flowers and low benches complete the effect.

example. You could use low shrubs or small trees to partially screen a semi-private terrace, yet leave the area open to a view beyond. If an outdoor room that provides absolute privacy is the objective, a tall fence or a dense planting of mixed evergreens and deciduous shrubs may be the best choice.

It's surprising how little it takes to create a recognizable boundary. Anything that stops or trips the eye, whether it's vertical or horizontal, can be a boundary between two outdoor spaces. You can establish a boundary with as little as a single large boulder, a low-growing shrub, or a clump of ornamental grasses. An open area that narrows at one end, or a single step up or down along a pathway can mark the boundary between two spaces. You can use a turn in a path or a subtle change underfoot, such as from brick to gravel, to create the perception that you have entered another space. Even changes in temperature can tell your skin where the boundaries of a space are: the gentle warmth radiating from the sun-soaked walls of a sheltered patio, or the cool shade under a vine-covered arbor.

Of course, you may want more concrete boundaries between spaces. If you need to confine pets or small children safely, you'll want fences or walls—perhaps around your entire property—to keep them in. When keeping strangers out is an issue, consider using hedges of thorny plants, locking gates, lighting, pointy-topped fences without footholds, and walls.

The way your neighbors are using their property will affect the kinds of boundaries you draw as well. If you need to block the sights and sounds of a nearby swimming pool, for example, you'll want a hefty

LIGHT IN THE GARDEN

You can use light to create subtle boundaries in a garden and set the mood of individual outdoor living spaces. Whether you use natural sunlight, artificial light, or a combination of the two, light functions in your outdoor spaces much as it does in the different rooms of your house. As you design your garden, try to think about how you can use light to add interest and appeal. Here are some factors to consider.

Areas that are in full sunlight, dappled shade, and deep shade all have different feeling or moods. As the sun moves across the garden, the shadows it casts move with it, bringing different features and colors to the fore across the hours of the day. The sun also casts a myriad of patterns from leaves, awnings, latticework, and woven screens that can add texture and interest.

As the sun sinks in the West, a whole new variety of lights fill the garden. Twilight, moonlight, starlight, torch light, gaslight, electrical light—every source has its individual quality and value. Even a single pool of light can make a space, claiming it from the enveloping night.

hedge or a shrub border that will absorb some of the noise. If, on the other hand, you want to "borrow" an attractive scene from next door, you'll want a less solid boundary that you can enjoy the view through—perhaps a shrub border with strategic openings. Other obvious choices for marking boundaries are low hedges, rows of trees or shrubs, flower borders, and vine-covered trellises.

Susan A. Roth

▲ *Perennial borders and a low rock wall divide up the front yard of this house, and add interest and color as well. The borders feature white clouds of baby's-breath blooms* (Gypsophila paniculata), *white Shasta daisies* (Chrysanthemum × superbum), *and pink bee balm* (Monarda didyma). *Hedges in front of the house provide an effective dark backdrop to the scene.*

When you are planning your boundaries, keep in mind that layers of screens can provide the complete privacy of a solid wall, but they are far more interesting and less forbidding. That's one reason borders of shrubs and small trees are so effective.

Don't be surprised to learn that the boundaries you draw today will change over time. That's because your whole garden will change and evolve, as will your interests. In addition, neighbors come and

go, and views change. Perhaps you'll want to create a new outdoor space, or you'll decide you need more privacy in one part of the garden. You'll also see new opportunities as your garden grows and develops. Perhaps looking at the spaces and boundaries that you draw as flexible and not cast in stone will make it a bit less intimidating to create them. After all, you'll have plenty of time to refine them as your garden develops and as you change with it.

SEASONAL BOUNDARIES

Sometimes you'll find you need a boundary only at certain times of the day or seasons of the year. Perhaps an open view from your living room across neighboring properties is pleasant in the winter, but in summer when you are outdoors more, you want privacy on your terrace. You can use fast-growing flowers, clumps of tall ornamental grasses, container plants, or a lattice covered with flowering vines to create a temporary summer screen. Bamboo curtains or fabric shades on the sides of a porch or deck are an even more flexible way to provide privacy when needed.

Connecting the Spaces

Now that you've designed the boundaries of your outdoor living spaces, you're ready to design connections between them. Here is where you consider how each living space is connected to the others, as well as to the house and the outside world.

Connections in a garden can be designed to get you from one place to another. Such obvious connections include steps, paths, gates, and arbors. But that's not the only kind of connections you can have. Connections can be visual as well: They're part of your aesthetic experience of being in an interesting, satisfying landscape. It's often your imagination, intrigued by a glimpse of some distant focal point or inviting space, that compels you to get up and walk into a garden and use its spaces. For example, a visual connection can be a view

over a hedge or a glimpse of a bench at the end of a winding path.

Sounds can also be used as connections. Hearing the splash of a fountain can lighten your load as you bring groceries in from the car. Pleasant and pungent scents can connect spaces. A fragrant plant outside a window can connect inside to outside. The cool air wafting from a shaded courtyard can connect it to a sunny space just outside the gate.

Depending on your design, a space in the garden may relate not only to the one that's right next to it, but to more distant spaces. Connections between spaces, whether they join two areas that are right next door to one another or over a greater distance, introduce mystery and enticement into the garden. They lure you from one space to the next. Borrowed scenery, such as of a view into a neighboring property, is an example of a connection outside the garden that will make it seem larger than it is.

As you read through the sections that follow, think about what types of connections you would like to make in your garden. Keep in mind that interesting and livable gardens provide a variety of connections between spaces—including obvious ones like paths and less obvious ones like fragrance that are designed to entice your senses. Draw in your ideas on your plan and make notes as you go.

Pathways for Your Feet

Paths connect spaces in a garden just like the string of a necklace connects the beads. They organize the outdoor living spaces into a coherent design. A good "cir-

Karen Bussolini

▲ *There's a compelling link between the formal and informal parts of this garden. The formal garden in the foreground, which features boxwood, junipers, and rock-rimmed raised beds of herbs, is bounded by a latticelike fence that divides formal from informal. Beyond the arch at the back of the garden, an informal grass path leads through a small meadow and into the woods.*

culation system" of pathways pumps human energy through a garden. Without them, you'd have only a pretty picture, to be admired from an armchair or a passing car. With them, you have a landscape that's inviting, efficient, and effective. Even a driveway can be a positive element in a design rather than an unfortunate interruption, if it seems to flow through the spaces. (For examples of effective driveway designs, see "A Country Garden: Privacy and Pathways" on page 151 and "Reclaiming a Suburban Ranch House" on page 118.)

Use the following ideas to help you plan the pathways in your garden. They will help you design ones that will play on your curiosity and help you get the most enjoyment out of your garden.

An effective path has a clear beginning. A pathway needs a clear beginning so that people know where to start. You can mark the beginning with a landmark such as a mailbox, a lamppost, a gate, the opening in a hedge, an interesting rock or pile of rocks, a sculpture, or a specimen plant like a tree or shrub. Or the beginning can be more subtle—a widened area at the start of a path that leads into the woodland, for example.

An alluring path has a destination. There's nothing more frustrating than a path that leads to a dead end with nothing to reward you for your journey. Even in a tiny garden with a single path, it's possible to provide a destination by adding a gate at the end of a path. Even if you can't really open it, or if it just leads to an alley, just the possibility adds to the garden. Or perhaps you could use a slightly widened turnaround with a bench or specimen plant to enjoy before retracing your steps. The landmark at the end of a pathway can actually be another space (or even the

Pamela Harper

Plants and paving complement one another in this fascinating rock garden. Paths consisting of round paving stones and rustic stone steps, along with a host of rock garden plants, encourage visitors to explore every inch of ground. The low seat at the center of the garden provides an added opportunity for observing the diminutive rock plants up close.

space you left at the beginning of the path, just viewed from a different angle). In fact, the beginning of a path can become a destination in itself. For example, the opening to a woodland path on the far edge of the lawn will lead you across the lawn.

An exciting pathway disappears from sight. Concealing parts of the landscape tickles the imagination and teases you into venturing farther, to satisfy your curiosity about what lies just beyond the bend or past the pyracantha. You can use shrubs, clumps of tall plants, or walls to hide the parts of a path. Even a very small garden can have a path that disappears out of sight—even if it's just around a tiny bend.

An interesting pathway keeps you guessing. An interesting path changes underfoot, perhaps from brick or gravel to wood chips. It also takes unexpected turns, may change in width, and passes through different spaces on the way to its destination. After all, getting there should be at least half the fun. Music would be very boring if it were made up of equal-length notes and all one pitch. Interesting music has various rhythms, many pitches, and variable speeds—so do interesting pathways.

An intriguing pathway is eventful along the way. Pathways are a delightful place to put all sorts of interesting plant combinations, curiosities, thingamajigs, details, and planned surprises. That way, you can pause to contemplate the flowers or foliage of plants in a bed along the way, to admire the sight of a child and bird cast in stone, or to laugh at a funny little sign. As you walk, you may suddenly notice the

sharp smell of creeping thyme as you crush it underfoot. The soft plumes of ornamental grasses that overhang the path may brush your arm as you pass them.

A pleasant pathway makes you feel cared for. It's okay to have an irregular path that keeps you focused on where you need to step next—in fact, this is an ancient technique used in Japanese gardens to keep visitors focused on the journey through the garden. But if you feel jeopardized at any point of the path, it will shatter your enjoyment as your attention shifts to protecting yourself from its dangers.

Problems may occur where water pools and freezes, where branches hang too low, or where plants encroach from both sides. Other problems to watch for include places where shadows or plants might conceal someone or something harmful, steep grassy slopes that might be slippery, and steps that are crooked, too shallow, or too steep. Stepping stones perfectly spaced to your tread might be difficult for an elderly aunt to traverse. Think out the possible problems of a route and who will be using it, and design the path accordingly.

Pathways for Your Senses

You can use all your senses to make imaginative connections between spaces—both indoors and out. Sight is the sense most commonly used to make connections. Glimpses of an interesting destination draw you out into your garden and from space to space within it. A scene "borrowed" from a distant landscape and carefully spliced into place as part of your garden's own scenery is one way to use sight to

Susan's Journal

Views to the Garden

How about a circular porthole window cut into the back porch lattice and softened with wisteria as a pleasant focal point for walking up the brick path toward the house? This would frame the view from indoors, too, and strengthen the connection between house and garden.

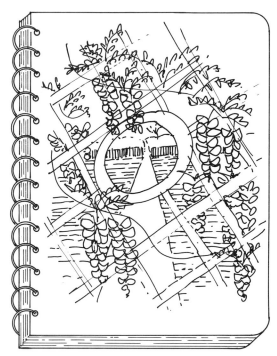

The back porch is a crossroads between the kitchen, the barbecue and storage area, the main garden gate facing the street, and the main center part of the garden. Plus, it's a place of its own, with a ceiling fan for comfort and a deck extension for more space.

Originally, the kitchen door lined up with a narrow set of steps and a brick walk that meandered through the center of the garden to the back gate. When we decided to screen the back door and widen the central steps, which had to be moved off-axis, the brick walk no longer met the porch steps: You had to make a jog along the terrace to get to the new steps. For months, I'd been wondering how to make a strong connection between the two.

After cutting out various-size circles of cardboard and holding them up against the lattice, my husband and I selected the size that looked best to use as a pattern for cutting out the lattice with a jigsaw. We finished the cutout with a 4-inch-wide frame of 1-inch-thick plywood.

The new window creates a very pretty and interesting focal point as you walk up the path toward the house. In addition, as you step out of the kitchen, it makes a wonderful picture frame for the crab apple at the far end of the path. The end result is a strong link between house and garden: Every time we walk out on the back porch, we can't help but look through the new window and the picture it creates.

Susan A. Roth

▲

Don't forget there are opportunities for effective paths in the front yard, too. This pea-gravel path leads through a planting of perennials—including buttercups, hostas, irises, and ferns. The design creates an intriguing and welcoming front yard.

make a connection. In that case, it may not be possible to physically travel along the path to the distant scene, but you can go there in your imagination, which can be nearly as enjoyable.

Another wonderful way to use sight to connect indoors and out is to design views from the windows of your house. Every window in your house has the potential to frame an outdoor scene, almost like a poster that changes with the seasons. At night, you can use outdoor lighting—such as along a pathway or up into the branches of a tree—to continue the connection.

Sound is another sense that can be used to connect spaces in a garden. Sounds like grasses rustling, wind chimes jingling, birds singing, or a fountain of water splashing can draw you into the garden as effectively as a glimpse of a view—like the sparkle of light on water. Things that make noise fill a space with life. Sound constantly reminds us that our garden is alive and is a part of the world around us.

Sometimes sounds can make unwelcome connections, and your design can screen them just as it can screen unpleasant views. The noise from a busy road or loud neighbors with a penchant for power tools can be screened or blocked with walls and plantings. Undesirable noises can also be covered by the "white" noise of a splashing fountain.

Fragrances can be used to make potent connections, because they often bring with them floods of memories. For example, you may catch the fragrance of honeysuckle and be seven years old again and hiding under a favorite thicket. The smell of the earth after a rain wakens feelings inside every gardener. Not only do fragrances trigger memories, they may also be potent mood-changers.

Our sense of touch is a vital but underappreciated sense that can be used to connect spaces as well. The feel of cool air spilling out of a shaded bower, or the warmth of a south-facing wall on a sunny winter day, can make an enticing connection between spaces. Or the sight of the

Carol F. Shuler, Landscape Architect

The plants, building materials, sculptures, and other features that ▲
*furnish the spaces of your garden help express your personality
and the ideas that inspired your design. They also add life to a
garden and can be used to surprise or amuse visitors who are
exploring its spaces. This simple sculpture adds character and
whimsy to a corner of a desert garden.*

soft, fuzzy leaves of lamb's-ears can make
you want to walk over and touch them.

Furnishing the Spaces

Now that you've designed the boundaries and connections of your living spaces,
what are you going to furnish them with?
Plants and building materials are the main
"clothes" of your design. Other elements
like small sculptures, whimsical signs, inter-

esting rocks, and basins of water for birds
serve as ornaments.

The plants and materials you choose
should fit in with your overall idea, so
your choices will depend to a large extent
on your key concepts. Other factors include
the way you decided to establish the "bones"
or structure of your design, and your
resource budget, which includes your
available time and money. Your choices
may also have to do with the context of

neighborhood and region—what plants will thrive there, or what styles of plantings fit in best, for example.

Review the Spaces

Before you select plants and materials, take time to review the index cards that relate to the spaces on your rough design. As you recall, each lists an element or activity you are going to accommodate in your final design. Ask yourself what the function of each space is and how you want it to feel. Some cards may already list ideas for possible materials and designs. Think, too, about your key concepts and the structure you want to use to unify your design. Try to decide how can they be expressed in each space. Think of a few different materials and designs for each living space and write them on the card.

Then compare the choices. You can weigh the options of one feature against another just as you weighed one complete design against another. Ask yourself how well each of the options matches your key concepts. Are you using the materials effectively and can you install them properly? Do they complement each other? Do they fit into your resource budget? How long will the elements last? If you plan to remove them and replace them with something else as money becomes available, can they be removed easily?

The bamboo screens and Oriental gate in this garden establish the style that's echoed throughout the garden. In addition, the use of stonework, the small pool, and the carefully selected plants are characteristic. The waterfall adds movement and also provides white noise to help hide the sounds of the outside world.

PICTURE DESIGN

It's true that a picture is worth a thousand words. Pictures of your garden are a great way to experiment with plantings and design. Take a photograph of your garden to a copy center and have inexpensive enlargements made. Then "go to town" sketching in plants you'd like to try or pasting down photographs of plants clipped from catalogs. Fill the copies up with notes and comments, too.

Such enlargements are a great study tool for standing back from the real garden and seeing it more objectively. Have you ever taken what you thought was a beautiful family picture only to find that your prints show that someone was making a face? Taking pictures is fun; studying them is revealing.

Plants for Your Garden

Plants, of course, are what a garden is all about. And choosing the right ones for your garden can be an intimidating task. By this point in the design process, though, you've probably made more decisions about the best plants for your garden than you realize.

You've already identified the plants growing on your property and evaluated how healthy they are. Before you start a list of new plants for your garden, however, you need to make some decisions regarding the ones already growing there.

Evaluating What You Have

Unless you're starting your garden on a bare lot that features nothing but

Pamela Harper

▲ *The style of your garden will greatly influence the plants you choose and the style in which you grow them. Shrubs and trees pruned in natural shapes are characteristic of informal gardens. Here, naturally shaped rhododendrons are an excellent choice to complement the rustic style of this zigzag fence; closely clipped yews in geometric shapes would clash with it.*

grass, there are probably existing plants that have influenced your design. It's not surprising that existing plants can lead you to a design just as a design can lead you to certain plants. A tree in just the right place can form an arch over a new walkway. A small patch of thriving daylilies might suggest a design strategy for the roadside. There may also be plants that are in the wrong place or that are simply not healthy or attractive.

Take a critical look at the existing plants in your landscape, and divide them into the three following categories.

Keepers. Plants that you like, that are in a good location and are thriving, are definitely keepers. Their shapes, locations, and groupings may create a structure for your design to build on. Plants that are in a good location but aren't healthy or attractive are marginal. Maybe you can rehabilitate them by renewal pruning or by

MISTAKES TO AVOID

Here are some guidelines to use when you select plants for your outdoor spaces.

Consider final size. Know the mature height and spread of each plant you choose, and fit them into your design accordingly. It's also good to know how fast they'll grow. You may want a fast-growing tree or shrub for quick privacy. On the other hand, a slow-growing one might fill the bill on a small terrace. This is especially important when selecting trees and shrubs. Why not select a plant that will mature at an ideal height rather than entering into a futile struggle to keep a plant in bounds by repeated severe pruning?

Don't overplant. It's tempting to fill up your garden with plants at the beginning, and all too easy to neglect moving or removing extra plants a few years down the road. The result is overcrowded, stressed plants. Instead, space plants so they can grow naturally, and fill in between them with annuals in the early years. If you are planting very slow-growing trees, take a cue from nature and interplant them with sheltering "nurse" trees that are fast-growing but short-lived.

Match plant to site. Avoid plants that won't be happy in the conditions you have to offer. Plants that won't grow well in the soil, amount of light, or exposure your garden has to offer won't do well. Instead, look for plants that will thrive, and you'll have fewer problems and a better-looking garden in the long run.

Consider maintenance. In the interests of low maintenance, try to select plants that can make do with the water that nature provides. Plants that are native to your area are obvious choices. Plants from other regions with similar climates can also be good choices for non-irrigated garden spaces.

Don't plant one of everything. Most successful garden designs avoid every plant lover's tendency to plant one of everything. Rarely does a spotty planting make a coherent display. Cottage gardens and meadow gardens are exceptions. Their charm is in the sheer abundance of bloom, while texture provides a strong overall effect. Usually it's best to use masses of the same plant, especially in the ground layer. Against these masses, you can plant individual specimens as exclamation points or sculpture.

Don't plant too many evergreens. If you are using evergreens, especially large ones, you'll probably want to limit them to no more than one-third of your total plantings. Too many evergreens can make a landscape seem darkly somber and changeless. You can add interest by planting evergreens with a variety of foliage colors.

providing better care, but maybe not. Be ruthless; if you have any doubts, treat them as nursery stock or replace them.

Nursery stock. Healthy, desirable plants can be in the wrong place as far as your design is concerned. An otherwise handsome yew, for instance, might be over-growing a walk or blocking a view. Or you may have crowded plantings of plants in dire need of more space. Regard plants that you can move as candidates for trans-planting to a nursery bed or to the right spot in your design. If they're too large for you to move, you have a couple of options: Hire someone to move them; rework your design to accommodate them where they are; live with them where they are; or take cuttings or divisions and eventually remove the parent plant.

Compost. Chances are, you have plants that are unhealthy, overgrown, too big to move, or just not to your taste. Don't let guilt make you keep them and cosset them at the expense of what you really want and need. Give them away if you can. Otherwise, chop them down, rip them out, shred them up, and put them in your com-post pile. After all, composting is part of the natural nutrient cycle of plants, too.

Selecting New Plants

By now you've probably realized that going to the garden center and loading up on whatever looks pretty isn't the best way to select plants for your garden. Instead it's best to do a little homework and pick plants that not only thrive in the condi-tions you have available but also fit in well with your design. To make your list, use plant encyclopedias and mail-order catalogs, talk to other gardeners, and visit gardens (both public and private) near your home. Appendix B on page 312 contains lists of plants for all kinds of garden sites and uses. You'll want to jot down the name of each plant (both botanical and common), the conditions it requires, and the seasons of the year when it's either in bloom or attrac-tive in the garden. Here are some catego-ries of plants to consider when making your plant list.

Favorite plants. You undoubtedly have plants that you've admired in other gar-dens or that you've grown before and espe-cially enjoy. Or perhaps you have a rose bush given to you as a gift, plants moved from a previous garden, or divisions of peonies from your grandmother's garden. Favorite plants add sentimental value to your garden; find out what conditions they require and try to find sites that will keep them happy.

Plants that support your key concepts. You'll find your key concepts point you toward many of the plants you should be considering. For example, if an herb or rose garden plays a major part in your design, you're already well on your way. If you want to build habitat for butterflies, you'll need to list plants that provide nec-tar for adults and food for caterpillars.

Plants that complement the frame-work. Repeating the colors or textures of plants that make up the framework of your garden is an excellent way to bring all the spaces together. For example, if huge clumps of ornamental grasses make up a part of the "bones" of your garden, perhaps clumps of low-growing grasses or sedges in the garden's spaces would link the two. You can also repeat foliage colors for the same effect—by planting both evergreens and herbs with gray-green leaves, perhaps.

Plants that complement key plants in the design. Although key plants or spec-imens in your design are in most cases part of its framework, there may be cases where a single specimen would give you ideas for other plants to include. You may want to replace the lawn under a magnifi-

Jerry Pavia

Silver-leaved plants are often a good choice for hot, sunbaked ▲
sites with well-drained soil. This sloping site features drifts of laven-
der cotton (Santolina chamaecyparissus), *pale-purple English*
lavender (Lavandula angustifolia), *and deep-purple Spanish lav-*
ender (L. stoechas). *Dark-green-leaved rosemary and a greenish-*
yellow-flowered euphorbia complete the picture.

cent shade tree with hostas or other shade-loving perennials just to keep it happy and eliminate the unhealthy lawn beneath it. Or you could complement a specimen tree or shrub with flowers that bloom at the same time—a crab apple underplanted with daffodils, perhaps.

Plants that add seasonal interest. Do you want your garden to be a mass of color just in spring, or all year long? If you haven't already done so, think about which seasons you'd like your garden to be at-

tractive. For winter interest, plants with handsome bark, evergreen foliage, or interesting habits (ornamental grasses, for example) are obvious choices. To extend the blooming season, you can look for plants that bloom during seasons when you'd like more color in your garden—nearby gardens, nurseries, and catalogs are all fine places to get ideas, especially if you look during seasons when your garden isn't in bloom. You can also extend the bloom season of many species—daylilies, daffodils, and peonies, for example—simply by selecting a variety of cultivars that bloom early, mid-season, and late.

Combinations for seasonal succession. Most plants change throughout the year, and some even change from morning to evening. Carefully planned seasonal succession is a kind of "time-sharing" that helps the drama of your outdoor living spaces to unfold all year long. Tall ornamental grasses, for example, get cut back in late winter, so they can share space with spring bulbs or early perennials. The spring perennials' foliage disappears completely by the time the ornamental grasses retake the stage.

Or you may want the garden to shine only at certain times of the year when you use it most. Choosing plants that are at their best at those times can focus your resources for maximum results. If you especially love autumn colors and weather, perhaps your garden design could feature sunny spaces and brilliant foliage and berries.

Native plants. Make a special effort to look at native plants that might fit in well with your design. Plants that require the same conditions that your site has to offer often are the best design choices— and require the least maintenance. These include species that are native to the site, or ones that are native to an area with a similar climate and conditions. You may be able to propagate them yourself by collecting seeds or taking cuttings. But don't dig native plants from the wild, and if you purchase them, make sure you're dealing with a reputable nursery that doesn't wild-collect.

Color. You'll also want to select plants with flower and foliage colors that will fit into your garden. You may have a color scheme in mind already—pinks, blues, and whites—for example. Don't forget to consider foliage color as well: Foliage comes in much more than just green. For maximum interest, select a mixture of evergreens and deciduous plants. Foliage colors can include silver-gray, gray-green, blue-green, and burgundy, as well as pale to deep green. There's also a host of plants with variegated foliage to consider.

Texture. Finally, there's texture. For maximum interest, you'll want to include plants with a variety of textures—from graceful clumps of ornamental grasses to the hard-edged, shiny leaves of holly.

Narrow Down Your List

If you're like most gardeners, by now you have far more plants on your list than you could possibly accommodate in your garden. Take time to go back through your list and eliminate any plants that won't be happy with the conditions your garden has to offer. That includes the amount of sunlight or shade, soil, exposure, and natural rainfall. Once you're done, you should have a great list of plants that's fine-tuned to your site.

Building Materials

Building materials include all the non-living elements that you can use to build your garden. These include soil, stone, brick, tile, concrete, wood, bamboo, glass blocks, metal, plastic, fiberglass, canvas, and rope.

Local designers, builders, suppliers, and gardeners in your area are probably the best source of information about which materials are best and what is available.

You'll also spare yourself some heartache by finding out what's available locally and getting cost comparisons on local and long-distance orders before you make any decisions. Certainly you can get material anywhere, as long as you can afford the time and expense. Local materials often have a unique regional character, which may be desirable in your design scheme.

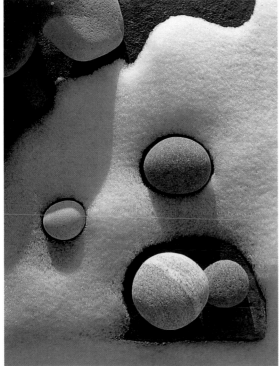

▲

Your choice of building materials should be guided by the overall style of your garden. For a natural-looking, informal garden, river rock, railroad ties, rustic fencing, and irregular paving blocks are good choices. A formal landcape, on the other hand, may feature brick or stone retaining walls, a painted picket fence, and rectangular paving blocks.

Balthazar Korab

Gardens built in the vernacular of a region—such as the brick houses and wrought iron trim characteristic of the South—can have a quality of fit and richness that's all too easy to miss if you take local materials for granted. Try taking a fresh look at what's readily available in the marketplace and using it in new ways.

Half the fun—and half the danger—lies in how you put various materials together, not unlike the composition of materials in a room of your house. Take a moment to look around the room you're sitting in right now. How many different materials are there? Do some stand out as being of a poorer quality, wrong color, or strange texture, for instance? What qualities do all the successful materials have in common? How might that apply to the outdoor room you're considering?

Regardless of what you choose, all these materials change with time, although some change far more slowly than others. Some materials become more beautiful as they age—copper develops a lovely blue-green patina and wood can turn silver-gray. Other materials take aging less kindly—plastics scratch and fade and sheet metal rusts, for example. In general, the longer a material lasts, the more it costs—though this is not a hard-and-fast rule. Good construction and maintenance will give any material its maximum life span.

Selecting Materials

The following list includes some common building materials, suggestions for their use, and some of the pros and cons of using them. Use this information, along with your evaluation of how the materials will fit in with your key concepts, to decide what to use to furnish your spaces.

Soil. You can use soil to reshape the natural contours of your property to fit them to your needs. Soil is to a gardener as clay is to a sculptor. You can design soil berms that will screen noise, protect your garden from a busy highway, block blowing dust, and generally shield unpleasant views. Trees, shrubs, and other plants growing atop soil berms can transform them into attractive and formidable barricades. Check local regulations and plan on having a heavy-equipment operator build any soil berms you design.

Adobe blocks are made of sun-dried soil and straw, and are one of the most ancient of all building materials. They're readily available in the Southwest and tend to be a bit unevenly sized. Completed walls built of adobe blocks are often covered with mud, plaster, or concrete. Rammed earth is another ancient form of building with soil. It is formed in place by pounding wet soil and straw into forms.

Wood. Wood is an easy material to work with. You cut it with a saw and put it together with nails or screws. If you understand wood's enemies, it's reasonably easy to keep wood in good condition for a long time. If not installed and cared for properly, however, wood will deteriorate rapidly.

Rot, caused by fungi, is wood's worst enemy. Since fungi need water to live, any type of wood will last a long time if you keep water away from it. Some woods are quite resistant to rot, including cypress, cedar, and redwood, but even they will rot eventually if they stay constantly moist.

Weathering is the second cause of wood deterioration, and all woods are susceptible to it. Sunshine breaks down the wood's surface, first turning it gray and then causing it to roughen and disinte-grate slowly. Moisture fluctuations inside wood are even more destructive. Wood is porous and soaks up water. The surface dries out faster than the center, which can cause cracking and curling. In winter, water trapped inside the wood will freeze and expand, often cracking the wood.

When you are planning your design, it's important to keep wood from staying in contact with water and soil (where fungi lurk), and to keep moisture from soaking into it. A naturally rot-resistant wood can be put directly in contact with soil, but make sure water doesn't pool on top of the wood.

Avoid using pressure-treated lumber, which contains arsenic-based compounds that are released as the wood breaks down. Choose naturally rot-resistant wood instead, or try wood treated with borax-based preservatives. Or use this recipe for non-toxic wood preservative developed by the USDA's Forest Products Laboratory:

> 3 cups exterior varnish or 1½ cups boiled linseed oil
>
> 1 ounce paraffin wax
>
> Enough solvent (mineral spirits, paint thinner, or turpentine, at room temperature) to make 1 gallon of mixture

Melt the paraffin over water in a double boiler (not over a direct flame). In another container, vigorously stir the solvent, then slowly pour in the melted paraffin. Add the varnish or linseed oil and stir thoroughly. Dip untreated wood into the mixture for 3 minutes or brush on a heavy application. If you wish, you can paint the wood when it is completely dry.

Wood can be used in almost any landscape. Generally speaking, the harder or more finished the surface, the more formal the wood looks. Unpeeled wood is informal and rustic; sanded and painted wood is much more formal.

Landscape timbers and railroad ties can be useful but are often overused. Beveling their exposed corners can upgrade their prefab look, and combining them with other materials can add interest to the final effect. They're good for edgings, steps, and retaining walls.

Soft, woodlike materials such as bamboo and rattan are less resistant to deterioration. Twig and wicker furniture needs to be sheltered over the winter. Woven mats of bamboo or reeds are short-lived but make effective and inexpensive shade screens.

Shredded or chipped wood and bark make good mulch. They break down quite slowly and are good choices for pathways and areas you don't plan to disturb often. Compost and leaf mold are better choices for a nutritious mulch under perennials and annuals.

Stone. Stone comes in a rich range of colors, surfaces, and shapes, from squared-off blocks to rough field stones. It is, of course, extremely durable and will last a long time. Depending on the size and shape, you can use it to pave terraces or walkways, build walls, edge driveways or paths, build raised beds, and much more.

Stone is usually referred to by its shape and surface characteristics. Here are some common types available: Fieldstone is dug out of the ground and may be all too available on your property. Cobblestones are rounded stones or large pebbles such as those found on a beach or in a river. Flagstones are thin, flat sheets of stone and are often used for paving. Rubblestone

is uncut quarried stone in random shapes. "Ashlar" refers to cut, shaped stone.

Stone is also known by what kind of rock it is. Limestone, sandstone, and slate are somewhat easier to shape than harder rocks like granite and marble.

Small bits of stone—like crushed rock, gravel, pebbles, sand, crushed limestone, and decomposed granite—can be used by themselves for pathways or as mulch. They can also be mixed into concrete for more permanent surfaces such as paths, walkways, and terraces.

Concrete. Concrete is a mix of portland cement, water, sand, and crushed rock. It can be poured and molded when first mixed but is quite strong after it hardens or sets. You can mix small batches of concrete yourself or have premixed concrete delivered in a truck.

Although its characteristic color is gray, you may be surprised to find that it's possible to color concrete by adding pigment or by using colored rock in the mix. You can also add surface textures and patterns by casting it in a mold, pressing objects into the surface to leave marks, or scraping objects across the surface of the almost-set concrete. You can also press loose objects such as seashells, pretty pebbles, or beach glass into almost-set concrete.

Precast concrete pavers, blocks, and bricks come in shapes, sizes, and designs for almost any application you can think of—walls, stepping stones, paving, edgings, and even furniture.

Concrete can also be laid in a solid slab to make a driveway or patio. If you have an old concrete slab, steps, or walls in your garden, you may want to consider giving them a quick and relatively inexpensive face-lift. Providing that the concrete is solid and uncracked, you can use it as a base for a thin covering of tiles, faux brick or stone, or any of a wide selection of attractive decorative cast products.

Brick. Bricks come in an astonishing variety of colors, shapes, sizes, and finishes. The two most important types of bricks are building bricks and paving bricks. Building bricks are smaller than paving bricks because they're designed to be laid with mortar between them, although they can be laid in sand. It's important to select a suitable type of brick for the job you have in mind, or the bricks may not hold up well.

Building bricks are graded by how hard they are, which depends on how long they were fired. In the North, where freezing and thawing of water is a factor, you'll want to use severe weathering (SW) building bricks to construct walkways and the like. If you are using them for a wall or making a walkway in a southern climate where the ground never freezes, you can use moderate weathering (MW) building bricks. Some building bricks have holes through them to lighten the weight, and are used for building walls.

Paving bricks are even harder than SW building bricks. They can be used for driveways, terraces, and walkways. They may have beveled edges, and some are textured for good traction.

Face bricks come in a wide range of colors, sizes, and finishes. They are more expensive, but they provide lots of choices for decorative walls and planters. Some have holes through them to reduce the bricks' weight.

If you want to use recycled, salvage, or "antique" brick for paving, be sure it's not old building brick that's too soft to hold up very long under foot traffic or freezing and thawing.

Tile. Tiles are thin sheets of fired clay. Frost-proof tiles can be used for patios, walkways, and wall facings. They are quite thin and designed to be glued onto a concrete slab with cement paste. Incorrectly installed tiles will pop or crack, so be sure to get exterior-grade materials, and seal them properly. Or have someone install them for you. Colored mosaic tiles are fragile but fascinating. They are usually used on walls, most often in frost-free areas. Patio tiles, more properly called pavers, are much thicker and should be used to pave walkways, terraces, and the like.

Metal. There are a wide variety of ways to use metals in a design, including lighting fixtures, sculpture, wrought iron, furniture, fencing, trellises, and more. Some metals offer long life and low maintenance outdoors. Iron is strong and relatively inexpensive but may rust if unprotected. Brass and copper can be sealed to retain a bright, shiny finish or allowed to develop a blue-green patina. Vinyl-, plastic-, or enamel-covered metal lasts as long as the coating. It can be used in fences, trellises, and furniture.

The care that metal objects require depends a lot on the way they were manufactured or created. You'll have to consult experts on the care of found metal objects that you'd like to use, such as ornamental wrought iron from demolitions. For newly made pieces you purchase, follow the manufacturer's recommendations for routine care.

Wire fencing makes a secure fence and is useful for trellising plants. Many different patterns of weave exist; you'll want to choose your pattern according to the size of opening that's appropriate for the job at hand. For long life, choose aluminum, which is rustproof; galvanized steel, which resists rust; or vinyl-coated wire. Vinyl coatings in shades of black, brown, and green are now available.

Any metal hardware you use outdoors, including hinges, nails, and screws, should be made of stainless steel or brass. Galvanized steel is somewhat resistant to weathering; the best type is triple-hot-dipped. Untreated steel hardware rusts easily. A rusting nail head or hook not only will eventually break, but also will stain the material below it.

Other materials. There are as many other possibilities as you can imagine. These include canvas, fiberglass, plastics, glass blocks, PVC pipe, mirrors, and Plexiglas. In short, almost any material that can resist the weather can be used outside. The only limits are your creativity and imagination. Old tires can get reborn in the form of a swing or as the core for a retaining wall. Heavy nautical rope strung through wooden posts can be used to safeguard the edges of a deck.

Plan for Utilities

Utilities—including water and electricity—are an essential but often forgotten part of a successful garden. Utility lines are usually buried or concealed in some way, and it's all too easy to forget how important they are. Although utilities can be added at any time, it's usually easiest to plan them and have them installed early in your garden renovation project. That way you don't have to tear up the garden after you've finished it.

Here are some general guidelines on what to consider when designing your garden. Be sure to mark your garden plan with the exact location of water and power lines that you have installed.

Water. Almost every garden needs some source of water. You may only need a single outside faucet, or you may want to install a complete, in-ground drip irrigation system. The average do-it-yourselfer can install irrigation systems since many of them are simply attached to an existing faucet. In areas where the ground freezes, they need to be drained in the winter unless the main pipes are installed below the frost line.

Another option to consider when planning your water needs is installing permanent faucets throughout the garden to shorten the lengths of hoses you need to drag around. An outdoor sink and/or water fountain can save lots of trips inside and cut down on tracked-in dirt. If your design includes a large pool, you may want to plan on a permanent water line for it. You can easily fill smaller pools and recirculating fountains with a hose as needed.

Electricity. Outdoor lighting is an important part of outdoor living. Most houses already have porch lights and perhaps other outdoor flood lights. Consider adding outdoor lights for security or to illuminate pathways or accent sculptures, trees, or other garden features. Lighting an outdoor terrace or other outdoor living space makes it possible to enjoy it at night.

There are other reasons you'll need electricity outdoors. Water gardens generally depend on electric pumps to power fountains and recirculating filters. Weatherproof outlets are useful for running electrical equipment, and they eliminate the need to run an extension cord out through a window.

▶

It's always a good idea to plan and install utilities like electricity and water before you put down permanent walkways. Then settle in your plants as a final step, so plantings won't get damaged during the construction process. This garden has stone pathways that are cemented in place. With the exception of roses, the beds feature heat-tolerant gray- and silver-leaved plants.

Susan A. Roth

There are three types of outdoor electric lighting. Standard 120-volt lights can create almost any effect you can imagine. These systems can be expensive since local codes generally require you to hire an electrician to do all the installation. They also use considerable electricity when in operation.

Low-voltage, or 12-volt systems are safe, can often be plugged into an existing outlet, and use less electricity. A number of self-contained systems are designed for do-it-yourselfers. But 12-volt systems have limitations: The current looses its oomph if the wire runs more than about 100 feet, and each line can only handle a few lights.

Self-contained photovoltaic lights require no wiring since they store the sun's energy and release it as light after darkness falls. They are simple to install and can be used anywhere. Some even come with the sun-gathering panel at the end of an extension so that it can be put where it will gather sunshine, while the light fixture can be placed under a porch or eaves. Solar lighting can be a very attractive alternative to conventional systems for your garden.

Other wires. You can run speaker or telephone wire with electrical wires. Stereo speakers or a phone jack can be a nice addition to an outdoor living space. Totally waterproof sound speakers are available for outdoor installation.

Gas. If you are building an outdoor barbecue area, you may want to have a gas line run from your main tank or house supply so you don't need to fuss with refilling and carrying tanks.

Drainage. Drainage is a consideration that doesn't fit neatly into any category.

But since drainage lines do make up part of the underpinnings of your garden, it's an easy matter to consider them when you plan conventional utilities.

As we discussed in "Rainfall, Drainage, and Water" on page 235, many drainage problems can be cured by grading the surface of the soil so that water runs in an appropriate direction. If surface grading can't correct the problem, you may want to install surface drains to collect the water. Such drains, which look like shallow trenches, sometimes with a grating over the top, can channel water to a natural watercourse or to a storm drain or gutter. You can line the surface drains with bricks or other paving materials. For severe drainage problems, you can install underground tile or drain lines. Drain lines are usually perforated pipe laid in gravel-filled trenches from one to several feet underground. They gather and direct water out of the area.

For localized wet areas, such as a spot under an outdoor faucet, you can install a dry well. A dry well is a small pit filled with crushed rock or stone that allows water to seep gradually into the surrounding soil without creating a mud hole in the meantime.

Draw Your Final Plan

Your final design is complete now, although the actual papers are probably a bit messy. Not only have you located all of the outdoor living spaces and designed their boundaries and connections, but you have also selected the plants and materials that will furnish each space.

Before you go any further, draw a neat copy of your final design. (If your

▶

Drawing out a final plan will help you envision your whole design. It will also help you decide where to start installing the garden. Perhaps most important, though, a final plan will give you courage and direction when you're halfway through the process and it's difficult to see how wonderful the finished garden will be.

J. Michael Kanouff/Rodale Stock Images

sketch copy is neat and clean, you don't need to redraw it.) Draw everything the way it would be if you could wave a magic wand and make it appear. This final design will let you see the whole picture. You'll use it to plan how you will actually go about installing your outdoor living spaces.

Look through the garden plans in part 2 of this book for ideas on how to tailor the size and detail of your plans to fit your property. If your property is quite small, it may fit on one plan easily with room for plenty of detail. If your property is very large, you may want to draw a simplified map that locates all the key features of your design. Then you can draw detailed plans for specific areas. You can use keys to simplify the drawing, like the ones you'll find throughout part 2 and in the illustration on page 299. If you don't want to plan out every last detail of the plantings that furnish the spaces—beds of perennials, annuals, and herbs, for example—just indicate the space you've allocated for them on your drawing. Then attach a plant list to your design to guide you when it comes to making the actual plantings.

Decide on Your Installation Strategy

The final step in the design process is to decide how you will get from a design on paper to a finished landscape. You still need to decide what spaces you'll develop first, which plants to install right away, and whether or not you can do all the work yourself or will hire someone to help you.

There are as many ways to install a garden as there are designers. You might

decide to lay out all the spaces and install the boundaries right away, then fill in the furnishings as resources permit. Or, perhaps you'll decide to complete a set number of outdoor living spaces this year, and plan on adding others in the following years as money and time become available.

Putting a complete design installation plan on paper is well worth the effort it takes, because you can gain some very real benefits from it. First, it helps you to communicate your plan to family members, neighbors, plant suppliers, and contractors—along with any local or city government officials you may need to contact for permits.

A complete plan is also your best friend. It is always there to remind you of your best ideas, to support you against all odds, and to point the way when you get lost. It helps you remember the big picture as you assemble each piece of the puzzle, each stage of the design. A plan is like a map that shows you how to get where you want to go. A plan is also the jumping off point for changes down the road.

Step-by-Step Planning

The easiest way to plan an installation project is to break it down into a sequence of steps. To do this, you'll decide what tasks you need to accomplish to install your garden and what order you need to do them in.

Although you can develop a plan and install your entire garden at once, more realistically, you'll probably want to plan on renovating a part of it at a time. Perhaps you'd like to develop a patio first so

▲ *Gardens that incorporate a large amount of permanent "hard" elements like stone or concrete patios and pathways require more careful planning to install than ones that feature simple mulched or grass paths. This garden features a swimming pool surrounded by a series of stone paths and rock-garden-style beds filled with azaleas, dwarf conifers, and perennials.*

T. L. Gettings/Rodale Stock Images

you can enjoy sitting outdoors, or you want to plan your vegetable garden and composting area. Another practical place to start is to plant trees and shrubs you'd like to have for shade and/or privacy. That way they'll have a chance to grow and you can get a head start on your design. Then when time and money allow, you can fill in the garden around them.

Whether you're renovating your entire garden or just a part of it, keep in mind that the realities of construction play a critical part in planning. Certain tasks must be done, or are better done, before others. Use the following list of steps or tasks as a guideline for developing your installation plan for each area. Skip ones that don't apply to your situation or design.

1. Move plants that are in the way. Transplant movable plants to a nursery bed where you can care for them until you have their final home ready. Or, transplant them permanently to another part of the garden if a suitable place is available. Dig up or cut down any plants you don't want.

2. Protect plants you can't move. If you'll need heavy equipment to accomplish your plans, fence off trees and shrubs that are too large to move. Heavy equipment can damage the roots by driving over them. It can also compact the soil. Changing the grade around large trees and shrubs, by either piling soil on the roots or scraping it away and exposing them, can damage or kill trees. Fences will help prevent this. On smaller-scale projects, you may be able to get away with just protecting them with wire cages or padding their trunks with cardboard tied on with string. It may be a good idea to mark each plant you'd like to save with a colored flag as a reminder.

3. Remove the "hard" elements that don't belong in the new design. Hard elements include paving, fences, and retaining walls. Stockpile the materials that can be recycled in the new garden, and get rid of the rest. Mark or protect any features you're saving that might be in the way and could be damaged by accident.

4. Reshape the land if the design calls for it. This is where the information about how water drains across your property comes into play. Regrade now to correct poor drainage patterns. It's also the best time to create earth berms or other interesting landforms. Depending on the size of your project, you may be able to do the regrading yourself. If you're not sure if you can tackle it, get an estimate and have someone do the work for you if possible. It will save hours of backbreaking work. You should also install any necessary surface or subsurface drainage and in-ground utilities at this stage.

5. Install the "hard" elements. These include stone or brick walls, terraces, retaining walls, driveways, and paved paths. Complete any shaping of the soil around the structures.

6. Install structures. Now's the time to build any structures like fences, sheds, and arbors that are called for in your design and would be hard to install after the plants are in place. Smaller structures can wait.

7. Plant large, slow-growing plants like trees and shrubs. If you aren't planning any major construction or regrading, you can plant trees and shrubs earlier in the process, anytime after you've removed "hard" elements that you're planning to replace.

8. Install the remaining pathways and edgings. In addition, at this stage you can prepare the surface of the soil by incorporating organic matter and other soil amendments and raking it smooth. Then you can plant groundcovers and sow or sod any lawn areas.

9. Add the details. Finally, you can dig and prepare garden beds, plant all those new plants you've been longing to see growing for so long, and move any transplanted specimens from their temporary homes in your nursery bed to their permanent places in the garden. After planting be sure to mulch the soil and water thoroughly.

Plan Your Attack

Now that you have an idea of the general order in which you'll accomplish the installation, take another look at your entire design, and at each of the outdoor spaces in it. Make a breakdown list of the steps and costs involved in installing each feature—or at least the ones you are considering attacking first. Be sure to note what order the steps need to be done in.

It's important to keep season constraints that may apply in mind while you do this. For example, if you set aside a weekend for shaping the land during the rainy season, you're more likely to compact the soil and turn yourself into a mud-baby than create the new contours you envision. Or, if you buy plants in August, you need to decide if you're going to be able to coddle them into surviving the hot weather. What's more, are you willing to take the risk of losing them?

Also check with suppliers to be sure you'll be able to get materials when you want them, especially things that must be ordered, or that are available seasonally. Plan ahead and make notes to yourself of when you will need to order things.

Once you have completed your lists of tasks and costs for each feature, step back and compare them to the resource budget you developed earlier. (See "Consider Your Resources" on page 259 for a refresher.) Be realistic, and ask yourself if the project is going to take more time or money than you have available, or exceeds your skill level. Now is a better time to plan an alternate attack than after you've torn up your entire yard and found you don't have time to finish the job. Plan on breaking the installation project into steps or phases that are within your resource budget.

Phase-In Your Design

Planning to phase-in your design to accommodate your available time and budget will make the installation easier and more enjoyable. In fact, the opportunity to "grow" a garden design by phasing it in over the years is your great luxury as owner-designer-builder. You are free to break the installation down into manageable pieces that fit your most pressing needs and suit your budget. You can also plan your strategy so that you can develop your skills along the way—tackling easy tasks at first, more difficult ones later on. You can also change your design whenever you want to fit your changing needs and to accommodate new ideas that you have along the way. In fact, the idea of developing a landscape in phases is a common practice when professionals "master plan" large landholdings for corporate and institutional clients who must raise funds and justify their expenditure on a landscape design.

There are a number of ways to break a design into phases. The first phase of building should focus on your highest priorities. Perhaps safety factors will point out things that must be completed first, such as replacing unstable old steps with new ones. Maybe you'll concentrate on developing the boundaries first—framing your spaces and screening out the undesired parts of the outside world. Or perhaps you'll just want to start by planting some strategically located shade trees. Most garden makers pursue a combination of strategies, with certain outdoor spaces and connections lying in wait

◀

Shade is a common short-term goal in many gardens—especially new ones that don't have large trees. An ideal way to create shady areas quickly is to plan a vine-covered pergola, arbor, or gazebo and then create a sitting area beneath it. There are many fast-growing vines to choose from, including ones that bear flowers and/or fruit.

Diane L. Petku/Rodale Stock Images

for resources to become availabe or for a good idea to strike.

Another strategy is to lay out the entire garden design at once, in its simplest form, using the least expensive, easiest-to-install materials available. Over time, as more money becomes available, you can upgrade the materials—for instance, replacing loose gravel with stone pavers. Sheila and Terry used this approach in "From Bare to Beautiful: Foresting a Courtyard" on page 60. During phase one, they planted trees to provide the framework of the design and covered the ground with inexpensive cobblestones and a single groundcover. Then, in phase two, they added more expensive pavers, a rich assortment of shade-loving groundcovers and perennials, and unique garden ornaments.

Another strategy is to develop the garden one space at a time. Jeanne and Bill installed their garden in this manner in "The Small Garden: Rooms to Grow In" on page 33. Their design will also be easy to change over time because each of the spaces in it works independently.

In "Rejuvenating an Older Garden: New Plants and Terraces" on page 134, Phyllis and Norman phased-in their garden by solving their most pressing problems first. In phase one, they eliminated the difficult-to-mow slopes on two sides of their lot and replaced the dangerous steps that led up from the sidewalk. Then they moved on and developed the rest of the garden.

Timothy Steinhoff's garden, "A Country Garden: Privacy and Pathways" on page 151, represents yet another approach. His garden is a lifetime project because of his love for collecting plants. Yet he phased-in his plans by concentrating first on plants that would solve immediate problems—too little privacy and too much noise.

Nature's own stages of landscape development can provide a natural basis for planning phases of design. The idea of woodland succession—that fast-growing trees are the first to populate a clearing—was another inspiration that guided Sheila and Terry's garden in "From Bare to Beautiful: Foresting a Courtyard" on page 60. On a much larger scale, in "Converting a Farmstead for Work and Play" on page 45, Bonnie and Charles planned on allowing old pasture land to return to woodland. Allowing this natural process to occur should create an effective screen by the time the neighboring property is developed.

Draw Each Phase

Once you have separated the installation of the design into phases, you need to draw a plan of what the garden will look like after each stage is complete. The intermediate plans may cover the entire property or just the area you will be working on.

One easy way to accomplish this is to start with a base plan and draw the elements each stage will include on a sheet of tracing paper taped over it. (See "Using Overlays" on the opposite page for an illustration of this technique.) These plans will help you concentrate on the tasks to be accomplished in each phase and help you communicate the tasks and requirements for materials to others.

Collaborators to Help You

Now that you finally have your finished design and your plan for implement-

USING OVERLAYS

For decades, landscape architects have been using the overlay technique to map different kinds of information about a site. You can use a simple version to map your garden; in fact, it's an especially useful technique for drawing out the installation phases you've planned. All you'll need are a stiff board that's large enough to tape your base plan to and sheets of tracing paper that are as large as your base plan.

Start with your base plan, and then draw out your ideas for your phase-one plantings and installations. Then add additional layers of tracing paper for each additional phase. The end result will show all the elements you've planned, and you'll be able to see how they work together on the landscape. Indicate which way is North to remind yourself of sun and shade conditions.

Assign a different color or pattern to each type of information, if you'd like. You could use different colored pencils or markers for each phase, or use separate colors for utilities, plants, and hard elements like paving. Using symbols or colors to indicate plants, or to mark elements, helps save space and keeps the design less confusing. Be sure to make a master key that explains in words what the symbols represent.

You can use overlays to indicate other types of information, too, including microclimates or possible alternate designs. Try not to put so much information on one sheet that it gets cluttered and can't be read at a glance.

Using overlays can stimulate new ideas for your design. You can take sheets out to see how the garden will work without certain elements and look for conflicts between areas, and you'll feel more in command of your information.

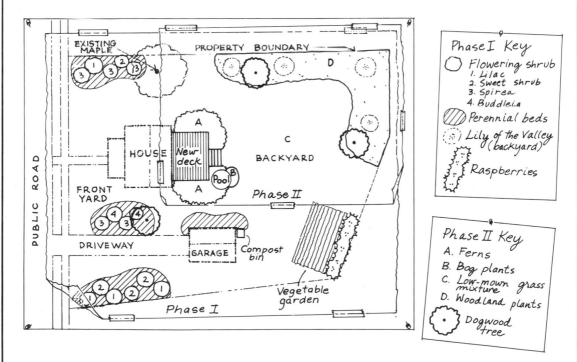

▲

Containers filled with bright flowers are a great way to dress up any corner of a garden—whether it's still in progress or long-since finished. Potted flowers are especially fun because they can be moved around and rearranged at will. Here, a small grouping of pots adds a touch of color to the front of a garden bed.

Jerry Pavia

ing it in hand, there's nothing to stop you from digging in and getting started. You might find it helpful, though, to consider how your plans will affect other people and where you might turn to get help you need along the way. You'll find that family members, neighbors, community associations, suppliers, and design professionals are all valuable resources.

The outcome of your work invariably affects family and friends, and has various impacts on your neighborhood. These people may need or want to have input—or at least be kept up-to-date with what's going on. You may want to seek professional assistance to help answer questions about design, securing permits, and ordering materials. Or you may need or want help in the actual building. Let's look at the people you can go to for help.

Family and Friends

Your outdoor living spaces have the best chance of flourishing when their design is based on the needs of all the people you expect to use the garden. That's why we recommended that you consider the needs of and consult all the members of your family throughout the design process.

If you involve family members from the start, you may discover that they have a wealth of good ideas and enthusiasm. You can use all the help you can get when it comes to building and planting your garden, and with luck you can turn their enthusiasm to your advantage. Everyone in the family can have a role to play in the garden's installation, provided you've thought through in advance the best ways to use their time, talents, and labor. If they're excited about getting to use the spaces they helped design, they'll be more enthusiastic about helping to install them.

To help ensure the survival of your outdoor living spaces, it's best to involve all family members in caring for them. If possible, try to avoid routinely assigning boring or dreaded chores, such as deadheading sticky petunia blossoms or mowing the lawn, to the same person. Who knows what kinds of lingering garden aversions and phobias have begun that way?

Friends, too, can be helpful when it comes to designing and implementing your garden. They may have interesting ideas that would add to your design, or you may be able to rely on their practical experience and advice—if not their actual labor—when it comes to installing it. And of course, gardeners always trade plants back and forth. You may have friends who'd love a division of one of the plants you're removing, and they may have plants to contribute to your garden in return.

Neighbors and Community

No garden is an island, to paraphrase the poet John Donne. As you are designing, look at your plans from the point of view of your neighbors. How will the design affect sunlight conditions and drainage, for instance, on adjacent properties? Might it create unsightly views from outside vantage points? How will the sound of a fountain be perceived from your neighbor's patio? Questions such as these will help you fine-tune your design so it works within the larger context of your community.

At the outset, perhaps the best step you can take is to tell your neighbors about your intentions, long before any plans are in place. Find out about their attitudes, plans, and dreams for their own landscapes. If they are going to put a satellite dish in the backyard, you might need to rethink your approach to screening a terrace. Are there problems along the common boundary that they have noted, and can you

agree on what is theirs and what is yours along that line? Are there views into your property that they especially value? These kinds of questions will yield useful input and help to defuse future problems. You may even decide to join some spaces as a common area that you can design, use, and care for together. "Sharing Space: Turning Two Yards into One Garden" on page 169 illustrates an ambitious way two gardeners are sharing areas and views.

Try to overcome any negative feelings about particular neighbors and their tastes and habits so you can continue to informally consult all your neighbors throughout the development of your outdoor living spaces. It's a good idea to show them a rough plan and invite them over to see the results as each phase or individual project is completed. You'll head off many negative responses just by being open.

Some neighbors may be experienced gardeners who can tell you about plants and materials. You can also benefit greatly by making contact with local garden clubs and community gardeners. These people will gladly offer advice, wisdom, and even plants or other materials.

Another benefit is the strength that each new gardener brings to the gardening community. Together, you can lobby local suppliers to carry native plants and regional products. You can work together to add or change local legislation. Your collective actions can speak strongly on behalf of a more healthful and beautiful environment.

Professional Designers

At some point in the process, you may decide that you'd like to consult an

BUDGET-STRETCHING IDEAS

There are many ways to stretch your gardening dollar. Here are a few to consider:

• Learn a new skill and install features yourself. Check your local library for how-to books, or attend a workshop (often free) at your local building supply store.

• Renting can be much less expensive than buying tools or equipment you may need, especially large power equipment such as shredders and tractors that you may need only occasionally. Renting also may make the difference between being able to do a job or having to hire someone to do it for you.

• For a soil-enriching boost of almost-free fertilizer and organic matter, plant a green manure crop like annual ryegrass, soybeans, or buckwheat and till it under before planting lawn or garden beds.

• Make compost. It saves money on purchased mulch and soil amendments, makes great free fertilizer, and recycles valuable nutrients. Some municipalities have leaf and yard waste composting facilities, and often give away the results.

• Ask your local utility company who does their tree work, and give them a call. Many will dump chipped-up brush on your property for free mulch.

• Spend your money on the best— not necessarily the most expensive— materials possible; they will last longer and be a better investment.

• Propagate plants from existing plants or buy a few new ones and propagate them. You may want to have a nursery bed just for this purpose. Other gardeners often love to give out cuttings—just ask!

• Start with smaller plants. Small plants are easier to plant and less expensive.

• Buy from reputable nurseries.

---

expert to help you. You may want to consult with a professional with experience in any number of fields. If your design calls for a large deck, you may want someone to design and install it for you. Or you may want to hire a landscaper to install a network of terraces and pathways—or a designer to design one. In some cities if you need special permits to implement your design, you may have to hire a licensed landscape architect to review and submit the design.

Approach finding a professional as carefully as you would when hiring any

employee you need to work closely with. Most designers will be happy to show you examples of their garden designs and even arrange for you to visit some of them. Be sure to ask questions about their education and areas of specialization and expertise. It's also good to get a list of clients as references and call and/or visit them without the designer present. Ask questions about how easy the designer was to work with, how well and how promptly the work was accomplished, and how close the final bill was to the estimate.

If you're looking for someone to help

You'll find healthier plants, often for little more than those found at bargain-basement sales. Reputable nurseries will often replace plants for free if they don't thrive.

• Order plants with a friend or group to take advantage of volume discounts.

• Plan before you shop, and buy only what you need. Impulse shopping is costly.

• Include some edibles in your design. You'll harvest tasty food and save money on your food bill. Many edible plants are ornamental, too.

• Consider your homeowner's insurance policy when something happens to your landscape. Call your agent when a car sideswipes your fence or an ice storm destroys your favorite cherry tree. It may be covered.

• Recycle what you have, use found materials, and make the best use of existing plants and features.

you design your whole garden, you want someone who not only understands design but can create spaces in a garden that you will enjoy and want to return to again and again. That means that your designer must want to understand your dream. They must also be able to put your ideas first. It's important that you are able to communicate your personal vision or ideas to one another. The ideal is to develop a design relationship in which you share your problems and ideas without being embarrassed or feeling like your ideas are being discounted.

To facilitate communication, try visiting a gallery or leafing through books together. You can join forces to develop basic objectives and design strategies. Perhaps the greatest benefit in consulting a professional designer is the new perspective it will bring to your design thinking. Someone who has been through the process before with other clients—and ideally with their own garden as well—will bring their experiences, failures, and successes to the project, along with well-reasoned and knowledgeable advice.

Parting Thoughts on Gardening and Design

The creative process works from hand to heart to head and back to hand, and garden design is very much a creative process. Working with the soil and the plants that spring from it can only stimulate the growth of your own ideas. You'll find that simple tasks—like taking the dog out or plucking a few wild onions—is often enough to get your creativity flowing. Soon you will get absorbed in just being in your garden, enjoying its sights and sounds, daydreaming, and just generally feeling alive as a creature of the garden. This is the time to follow your heart to shape the landscape. Let one thought lead to another, one act lead to the next, and your life in the garden will ebb and flow with a joyful rhythm all its own.

To get better and better at the art of garden making, you also need to learn to stand back and criticize your work objectively. As you look at what works and

what doesn't, you'll find that the practical experience you've gained by installing and fine-tuning your design is invaluable.

The more you garden, and the more you think about design, the more creative you'll become. You'll also begin to notice details in your garden that you hadn't seen before—the light sparkling off holly leaves or sunlit water, the warm colors and rich texture of ornamental grasses backlit by the setting sun, or the rich fragrances of an herb garden on a hot summer day. Your heightened awareness will be an invaluable asset as you create plant combinations and fine-tune your design.

Let Change Be Your Partner

Probably the most challenging aspect of making gardens is to be always alert to change and opportunity. To treat a garden as a museum piece that will never change is to go against its natural grain. Change is inevitable: Each change can be the starting point of delightful new features and layouts in your garden. Some changes come from you, others come from the garden or its environs. Plants grow and fade, climates fluctuate, and your interests change, too. Spaces designed for life need to respond to life's changes.

◀

Effective, satisfying gardens don't happen overnight. They're the result of planning, puttering, and experimenting—but that's half the fun. This charming shed shows the creative process that's so important in a good garden. Roses, hostas, herbs, and climbing vines link it closely to the garden, and the result is a memorable place you'd want to explore and enjoy again and again.

Sometimes changes are forced on us unexpectedly; other times they creep up while we are looking the other way. Don't get so fixed on a perfect image of your garden that you can't adapt creatively to change. Even a loss can stimulate positive change in your garden's design—a tree falls in a storm, and you have new space for a sunny garden. A new house is built in the center of your favorite view, and to screen it you develop the shrub border you've always wanted. Or you find you just can't manage the work you could a few years back, so you redesign some areas to leave you with more time to relax or enjoy other activities. Your garden will always be evolving, and it exists as much in your own mind's eye as it does on the ground.

Trying new things gives you the chance to experiment, and possibly to make mistakes and then correct them. Trying a new design in your garden is sort of like getting a haircut. Taking a chance on bangs, for instance, is an easy and relatively non-risky change to make in your style, because hair soon grows out no matter what. So, too, the garden grows in or can be replanted.

If you're making big changes, it's a good idea to think them through and then try them out one step at a time if possible. In our rush to finish projects, we often don't give ourselves the chance to live with our ideas before making them permanent. Sometimes building and living with a temporary mock-up will lead the way to a different and even better idea.

Just remember that the goal is progress, not perfection, and you'll enjoy designing spaces for outdoor living all the more.

APPENDIX A
Drawing Your Own Topo Map

You can draw your own topo map with a few simple tools, but you'll also need lots of patience, for it's not a small undertaking. Laying it out is a major operation, but it's not difficult—just time consuming. If you really have a use for a topo map, it will be time well spent. Because of the time and patience they take to prepare, you'll probably only want to draw a topo map of a portion of your property. You can have a surveyor prepare one for you, but it might be quite expensive, depending on the size of the area you want surveyed.

Before you start, there are a few special terms mapmakers have for features of a topographic map that you need to know:

Elevation. The height of a point relative to some reference point. On official topographic maps, the reference point is sea level. On your topographic map, the reference point will be the highest point on your property, or some other convenient point of reference.

Contour Line. A line on the map that connects a series of points that are all the same elevation.

Contour Interval. The change in elevation between two contour lines.

Getting Started

To measure out and draw your map, you'll need a clipboard with a copy of the base plan of your property on it; a 100-foot tape measure; at least 50 feet of strong non-elastic string; a bundle of 2-foot-long, 1 × 2-inch wooden stakes; and a small sledgehammer. You'll also need a wide permanent marking pen, a line level, a 6-foot pole marked in 1-foot (or smaller) incre-

ments, and a patient helper. You can also rent a transit and a surveyor's pole and use them instead of the line level and the measuring pole. Ask the person at the rental office to give you a brief lesson on how to use them.

Before you start, decide how much of your property you need to map. Outline it roughly on the ground so you'll know how far to measure. (Lime sprinkled on the ground makes an easy and self-erasing mark.)

Pick a Reference Point

Step one is to pick a single reference point that will serve as "zero" elevation on your map. It's best to choose the highest point of the area you are mapping as your reference point. (If you can't choose the highest point for some reason, see "Working Uphill" on page 310.) A corner of your house, or some other permanent feature, also makes a great zero point. If you don't have a permanent feature to work from, pound a sturdy stake into the ground at the highest point, but be sure you choose a point where the stake can be left undisturbed until your proposed landscape changes are completed. For example, if you're planning to put in terraces on a slope, don't position the stake where you'll be digging or filling soil. It's important to have the zero point to refer to while you install the terraces.

Place the end of your measuring pole firmly on the ground next to your zero reference point. Draw a line 1 foot above the ground on the zero reference point. This will be your working level. Working above ground level is important for accurate measurements. If you try to work at ground level, every stone or

307

clump of grass will interfere with your ability to obtain accurate measurements.

Choose Your Contour Interval

The contour interval you choose may vary depending on the size and slope of your property. If you are mapping a small area or a very gently sloping site, you may want to choose a smaller interval for greater accuracy. For a large area or a very steep slope, a larger interval may save time yet still give you enough information. The example that follows uses a 1-foot interval; if you use a smaller or larger one, substitute your interval for 1 foot in all the directions that follow. Keep in mind that you will still work 1 foot off the ground, regardless of the interval.

Working Down the Slope

1. Tie the end of a long piece of string to the working level—the 1-foot mark—on your reference point. Stretch the string toward the downhill edge of the area you're mapping. When it's taut, hang the line level on the string.

2. Here's where your helper plays a role. One of you will hold the string, while the other reads the line level and takes measurements. Raise or lower the far end of the string until the bubble in the line level is centered (see illustration below). If you happen to have a tree handy, you can tie the end of the string to it; otherwise one person keeps holding the end of the string.

3. Once the line is level, the string-holder's job is to stay perfectly still. The measurer proceeds as follows: Place the measuring pole straight upright against the string and move it down the slope. Find the point where the 2-foot mark on the measuring pole is exactly even with the string when the pole is firmly on the ground. Check the line level to make sure the string is still level. Replace the measuring pole with a stake and pound it in firmly.

4. Write "−1" on the top of the stake to identify this level as 1 foot below "zero." Place the end of your measuring pole firmly on the ground next to this stake. Draw a line 1 foot above the ground on the stake you just put in to mark the working level.

5. Repeat step 3, but move the measuring pole until the string is level with the 3-foot mark. Then repeat step 4, noting that this stake is marked "−2" since the elevation is now 2 feet below zero.

6. Continue working down the slope using the steps above to mark the elevations.

Once you have pounded in five or six stakes (4 or 5 feet below zero) the string-holder may not be able to hold the string up high enough at the down-slope end to keep it level. When this happens, untie the string from the zero stake. Tie it firmly to the 1 foot mark of the last (lowest) stake you just put in (see illustration on opposite page). Then repeat the procedure until you have inserted stakes all the way down to the lowest point of the area you are mapping. (Continue numbering from

To level your string, raise or lower the end of the string that is not tied to the working level on your reference point. The line is level when the bubble in the line level is exactly centered between the lines.

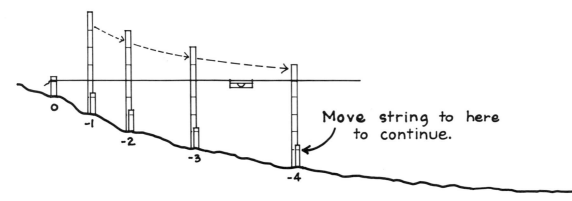

When the string-holder can't hold the line-level string high enough to keep it level, untie the string from the zero stake and tie it firmly to the 1-foot mark of the last (lowest) stake you just put in. Then repeat the procedure until you reach the end of the area you're mapping.

the point you left off, though, not from −1 again.) If the area you are mapping is a valley, to map back up the other side of a slope, see "Working Uphill" on page 310.

You've now established a line of stakes that marks 1-foot changes in elevation down the slope—each with a mark at the 1-foot working level. The next step is to work across the slope to mark off the contour lines.

Working Across the Slope

In order to lay out the contour lines across the slope, you'll need to first tie one end of a string firmly to your measuring pole at exactly the 1-foot mark. Put a small slip knot loop, just large enough to slip over a stake, in the other end. A length of string that's roughly 10 feet is fine, but you may want to use a longer length if the area you're mapping is very smooth and/or very large—such as a wide sweeping stretch of lawn. A shorter length will produce a more accurate map if the ground is very bumpy or if there are lots of trees or other objects to work around. In fact, you can use different lengths for adjoining parts of the same contour line. Having the string a set length just eliminates untying and retying.

To map out the contours across the slope, use the following procedure:

1. Put the slip knot loop of the string over the reference stake that marks your "zero" elevation and tighten it around the 1-foot mark.

2. Have your helper pull the string taut by walking away with the measuring pole. Since you are laying out lines that are level and run across the slope's contours, your helper should try to stay at the same elevation.

3. Hang the line level in the center of the string. Again, one of you will hold the string, while the other reads the line level and takes measurements.

4. Have the string-holder keep the measuring pole straight up and the string taut while he or she moves around until the bubble in the line level indicates that the string is level (see illustration at top of page 310).

5. When you locate a point where the bubble is centered when the pole is placed firmly on the ground, you know the point is exactly the same elevation as the reference point that marks zero elevation. Mark the spot by pounding in a stake exactly where the pole rested.

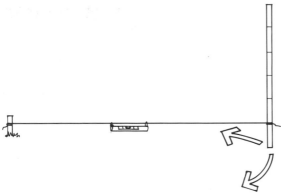

When working across the slope, the string-holder must keep the measuring pole straight up and the line-level string taught while he or she moves around until the string is level.

6. Write a "0" on the top of the stake to identify it as part of the zero contour line.

7. Place the end of your measuring pole firmly on the ground next to this stake. Draw a line 1 foot above the ground on the stake you just put in.

8. Take the loop of string off the original stake, put it around the one you just pounded in, and tighten it around the 1-foot mark.

9. Repeat steps 1 through 7 until you come to the edge of your mapping area. Then go back to the stake you started from on that level, and work in the opposite direction to the other edge of the area you are mapping. When the contour line is complete, you can use string or brightly colored yarn to connect the stakes. This will help you see the line if you have a hard time imagining it.

10. Repeat the procedure with each of the interval stakes that mark the elevations. Be sure to mark each stake with the number of the level you are currently working on: The correct number is on each stake marking the elevation interval.

When you have finished, you will have the whole area peppered with stakes. If you opted to "draw" each contour line with string, you will also have a life-size topo map spread out over the land. To draw the map, use triangulation to locate each individual stake on your base plan. (First, you'll probably want to take down any strings you used so you don't trip over them.) Pencil in the level number of each stake next to its location on the plan so you will know which marks belong to each contour line. Then draw a freehand curve to connect all the "0" points. This step is much like playing "connect the dots." Now you have the zero contour line. Repeat for all the sets of numbered points. You now have a contour map of your land (see illustration below).

CONTOUR MAP

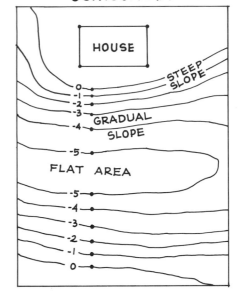

Working Uphill

You can modify the method previously described to work uphill, too; you'll just need a second measuring pole and another helper to hold it. The second pole is used to make the interval stake taller so the line level string can be tied 5 feet off the ground.

When you need to work uphill, use the following procedure:

1. Have your additional helper hold the second measuring pole upright next to the last interval stake you put in, with the end of the measuring pole firmly on the ground. Tie the end of a long piece of string to the 5-foot mark of that measuring pole. (This "stationary" measuring pole will not be moved until four new interval stakes have been installed.)

2. Your original helper stretches the string toward the uphill edge of the area to be mapped. When it's taut, hang the line level on the string.

3. Raise or lower the far end of the string until the bubble in the line level is centered. If you happen to have a tree handy, you can tie the end of the string to it; otherwise one person keeps holding the end of the string. Once the line is level, the string-holder's job is to stay perfectly still.

4. The measurer proceeds as follows: Place the "free" measuring pole straight upright against the string and move it up the slope. Find the point where the 4-foot mark on the measuring pole in your hand is exactly even with the string when the pole is firmly on the ground. Check the line level to make sure the string is still level. Replace the free measuring pole with a stake and pound it in firmly.

5. Write a number on the stake that is 1 foot *higher* than the one before it. (If the last interval stake was −4, this one is −3.) Place the end of your free measuring pole firmly on the ground next to this stake. Draw a line 1 foot above the ground on the stake you just put in to mark the working level.

6. Repeat steps 4 and 5 three more times, but move the free measuring pole until the string is level with the 3-foot mark, 2-foot mark, and 1-foot mark (see illustration below).

7. If you have more "uphill" to map, move the stationary measuring pole to the last interval stake you put in, and repeat steps 1 through 5 as many times as needed. When you reach the end of the area you are mapping, return to "Working Across the Slope" on page 309. If the land slopes down again, return to "Working Down the Slope" on page 308.

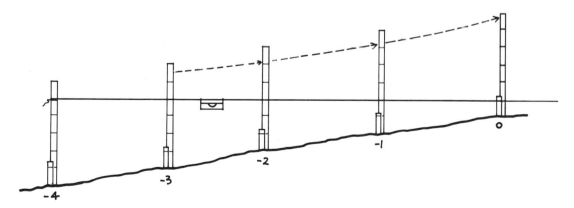

When working uphill, use a stationary measuring pole to make the interval stake taller so the line-level string can be tied 5 feet off the ground. Move the "free" measuring pole up the slope until the string crosses the 4-foot mark on the measuring pole. Place a stake at this point, and label it −3. Continue the process until you reach the end of the area you're mapping.

APPENDIX B
Plants for Every Purpose

Annuals

Annuals (plants that flower and die in one season) have a place in every garden. Use these adaptable, easy-to-grow plants to add color all season long in beds, borders, or containers. Annuals are invaluable for making a new garden look established: Use them to help fill the gaps in young perennial borders or to fill in between newly planted shrubs. Tall annuals can even be used to create a temporary screen. And because you can replace annuals every year, you can experiment with different plant forms and color schemes each year.

While most annuals will thrive in a wide range of garden conditions, some are more tolerant of hot-summer or cool-summer areas; you'll find these listed below. Also listed are annuals that have particularly interesting foliage. Use foliage annuals to complement annuals grown for flowering display, or as accents on their own.

Heat-Tolerant Annuals

Amaranthus tricolor (Joseph's-coat): Large leaves in brilliant shades of red, yellow, bronze, and green on erect plants to 6' tall.

Begonia Semperflorens-Cultorum Hybrid (wax begonia): Showy flowers in shades of white, pink, and red, or blended or edged combinations. Plants may reach 15'' by autumn.

Catharanthus roseus (Madagascar periwinkle): Open pink or white flowers over glossy green foliage. Plants grow 6''-18'' tall.

Celosia cristata (cockscomb): Crested or plumed flowers in cream, yellow, orange, red, or red-purple shades. Plants grow 6''-24'' tall.

Coreopsis tinctoria (calliopsis): Single, broad-petaled daisies in yellow, gold, red, brown, or combinations on erect 1'-2' plants.

Euphorbia marginata (snow-on-the-mountain): White bracts over bright green leaves edged in white on plants that can reach 2' tall.

Gomphrena globosa (globe amaranth): Rounded white, pink, magenta, orange-red, or lavender flower heads on 1'-2' plants.

Helianthus annuus (common sunflower): Single or double daisies in cream, yellow, orange, or red-brown on 2'-10' plants.

Mirabilis jalapa (four-o'clock): Fragrant trumpet-shaped red, pink, white, or yellow flowers on 1'-3' plants.

Petunia × hybrida (common garden petunia): Single or double trumpet-shaped flowers in white, pink, red, yellow, blue, or purple on plants to 1'.

Portulaca grandiflora (moss rose): Single or double roselike flowers in white, pink, red, yellow, orange, or magenta on 4''-6'' plants.

Ricinis communis (castor bean): Large, deeply lobed green or reddish leaves on plants that can reach 5'-8' tall.

Rudbeckia hirta 'Gloriosa Daisy' (gloriosa daisy): Single yellow, dark-centered daisies on 3' plants.

Salvia splendens (scarlet sage): Dragon-mouth blooms in white, pink, purple, or brilliant red on 8''-34'' plants.

Sanvitalia procumbens (creeping zinnia): Yellow daisylike flowers with dark centers on sprawling 6''-tall mats of foliage.

Tithonia rotundifolia (Mexican sunflower): Daisylike reddish orange flowers with yellow centers on 3'-4' plants.

Verbena × *hybrida* (garden verbena): Dense clusters of white, pink, red, or blue flowers (often with white centers) on 8"-12" plants.

Zinnia elegans (common zinnia): Single or double flowers in white, pink, orange, red, or yellow on 6"-36" plants.

Cool-Growing Annuals

Brachycome iberidifolia (swan river daisy): Small blue, pink, or white daisies over feathery foliage on 18" plants.

Chieranthus cheiri (wallflower): Fragrant four-petaled flowers in red, orange, yellow, or white on 8"-24" plants.

Clarkia amoena (farewell-to-spring): Single or double pink or white flowers on 2' plants.

Consolida ambigua (rocket larkspur): Dense spikes of blue, purple, pink, or white flowers on 1'-4' plants.

Lathyrus odoratus (sweet pea): Fragrant, butterflylike flowers in white, pink, red, purple, or bicolors on 6' vines or 15" mounds.

Matthiola incana (stock): Spikes of fragrant white, pink, red, or lavender flowers on 12"-30" plants.

Mimulus × *hybridus* (monkey flower): Showy flared tubular reddish, orange, or yellow blooms with spotted faces on 6"-24" plants.

Nemesia strumosa (nemesia): Trumpet-shaped white, pink, red, orange, yellow, or purple flowers on 8"-18" plants.

Papaver nudicaule (Iceland poppy): Single white, pink, red, or orange blooms on 2' stems.

Salpiglossis sinuata (salpiglossis): Trumpet-shaped red, yellow, orange, or blue flowers, often with contrasting veins, on 1'-2' plants.

Schizanthus pinnatus (butterfly flower): Showy butterflylike flowers in pink, purple, or yellow, often with yellow centers, on 1'-3' plants.

Tropaeolum majus (garden nasturtium): Fragrant, cup-shaped flowers in yellow, orange, or red on short vines or 1' mounds.

Viola × *wittrockiana* (pansy): Flat blooms in a wide range of solid colors and combinations. Plants are usually less than 1'.

Annuals with Attractive Foliage

Amaranthus tricolor (Joseph's-coat): Large leaves in brilliant shades of red, yellow, bronze, and green on erect plants to 6' tall.

Begonia Semperflorens-Cultorum Hybrid (wax begonia): Bright green or purple-brown, rounded, waxy leaves on stems 15" tall.

Beta vulgaris (Swiss chard): Large green leaves with 18" white or red stalks.

Brassica oleracea (ornamental kale): Thick blue-green leaves with white, pink, red, or purple centers in 1' rosettes.

Caladium × *hortulanum* (caladium): Large heart-shaped leaves marked with white, pink, red, and green. Clumps may reach 2' tall.

Coleus × *hybridus* (coleus): Pointed, scalloped, lacy, or oaklike leaves marked with hues of green, white, pink, red, and yellow. Plants grow 8"-30" tall.

Euphorbia marginata (snow-on-the-mountain): White bracts over bright green leaves edged in white on plants that can reach 2' tall.

Foeniculum vulgare 'Redform' ('Redform' fennel): Feathery reddish brown licorice-scented leaves on plants that can reach 6' tall.

Hypoestes phyllostachya (polka-dot plant): Dark green leaves dotted with red, pink, or white on 24"-30" plants.

Impatiens New Guinea hybrid (New Guinea impatiens): Pointed green leaves marked with red, pink, or yellow on 12″-18″ plants.

Ipomoea spp. (morning glories): Heart-shaped green leaves on 8′-10′ twining vines.

Iresine herbstii (bloodleaf): Rounded purplish red leaves on 2′ plants.

Kochia scoparia (summer cypress): Feathery clumps of narrow, bright green leaves that turn red in autumn. Plants grow to 3′ tall.

Ocimum basilicum (sweet basil): Smooth or ruffled aromatic green or purple leaves on mounding or upright 1′-2′ plants.

Pelargonium × *hortorum* (zonal geranium): Fuzzy rounded, scalloped, or lobed green leaves often marked with white, red, or yellow on 1′-4′ plants. Some have fragrant leaves.

Perilla frutescens (common perilla): Aromatic reddish purple leaves on 2′ plants.

Ricinis communis (castor bean): Large, deeply lobed green or reddish leaves on plants that can reach 5′-8′ tall.

Senecio cineraria (dusty miller): Hairy, lobed, silvery gray leaves on 1′ plants.

Silybum marianum (holy thistle): Spiny, deeply lobed green leaves with white marbling in 1′ rosettes.

Tagetes filifolium (Irish lace marigold): Dense 1′ mounds of delicate, lacy foliage.

Zea mays var. *japonica* (ornamental corn): Long, narrow green leaves marked with white, yellow, and pink on 3′-6′ plants.

Perennials

Perennials add beauty and permanence to any outdoor living space. The endless variety of heights, colors, and habits means that you can always find a perennial to fit your needs. While many perennials are easy to grow throughout the United States, listed below are some that are particularly well adapted to warmer or cooler regions. "Perennials for the North" suggests plants that flourish in the cooler summers of northern zones and withstand cold winters to Zone 3. Species of *Campanula*, *Delphinium*, *Eryngium*, *Hemerocallis*, *Papaver*, *Penstemon*, *Phlox*, *Thermopsis*, and *Veronica* are hardy to Zone 2. Many of these same plants will grow as far south as Zone 9, but only a few prosper under hot, humid conditions. "Perennials for the South" lists plants that stand up to the heat and humidity of southern summers, although most benefit from partial shade in the hottest months. Species of *Achillea*, *Baptisia*, *Boltonia*, *Coreopsis*, *Echinacea*, *Helianthus*, *Hemerocallis*, *Hibiscus*, *Iris*, and *Rudbeckia* will tolerate full southern sun. "Perennials with Striking Foliage" suggests dual-purpose perennials that have especially interesting foliage when not in flower. In all the lists below, the botanical name is followed by the common name, characteristics, and zones.

Perennials for the North

Achillea spp. (yarrows): Flat clusters of yellow, white, or red flowers in summer. Zones 3-8.

Aquilegia spp. (columbines): Starry spurred flowers in a wide range of colors in spring and early summer. Zones 3-9.

Campanula spp. (bellflowers): Star- or bell-shaped blue, white, or purple in late spring and summer. Zones 3-8.

Cimicifuga racemosa (black snakeroot): Spikes of small white flowers in late summer. Zones 3-8.

Delphinium spp. (delphiniums): Spikes of single or double blue, pink, violet, or white flowers in summer. Zones 3-7.

Dianthus spp. (pinks): Single or double flowers in pink, red, white, or yellow in spring or summer. Zones 3-8.

Dicentra spp. (bleeding hearts): Heart-shaped rose-pink or white flowers in spring. Zones 3-8.

Eryngium amethystinum (amethyst sea holly): Rounded silver-blue flowers in summer. Zones 2-8.

Gypsophila spp. (baby's-breaths): Airy clusters of tiny white or pink flowers in summer. Zones 3-8.

Hemerocallis spp. (daylilies): Trumpet-shaped flowers in all colors except blue in summer. Zones 3-9.

Hosta spp. (hostas): Spikes of trumpet-shaped violet, lilac, or white flowers over heart-shaped leaves in summer or fall. Zones 3-8.

Papaver orientale (Oriental poppy): Bowl-shaped scarlet flowers in early summer. Zones 3-7.

Penstemon barbatus (common beardtongue): Spikes of tubular pink or white flowers in spring. Zones 2-8.

Phlox stolonifera (creeping phlox): Clusters of blue, pink, or white blooms in spring. Zones 2-8.

Rudbeckia spp. (coneflowers): Yellow dark-centered daisies in summer. Zones 3-8.

Sedum spp. (sedums): Clusters of starry yellow, pink, or white flowers in spring, summer, or fall. Zones 3-10.

Thermopsis spp. (false lupines): Spikes of pealike yellow flowers in spring. Zones 3-8.

Veronica spp. (speedwells): Narrow spikes of blue or white in spring to summer. Zones 3-8.

Perennials for the South

Achillea spp. (yarrows): Flat clusters of yellow, white, or red flowers in summer. Zones 3-8.

Armeria maritima (common thrift): Rounded clusters of pink or white flowers in spring. Zones 4-9.

Asclepias tuberosa (butterfly weed): Flat clusters of starry orange flowers in summer. Zones 3-9.

Baptisia spp. (baptisias): Spikes of pealike blue or white flowers in summer. Zones 3-8.

Belamcanda chinensis (blackberry lily): Loose spikes of orange flowers in summer. Zones 5-9.

Boltonia asteroides (boltonia): Small daisylike white or pink flowers in late summer. Zones 4-9.

Coreopsis spp. (coreopsis): Daisylike yellow flowers in summer. Zones 3-8.

Echinacea spp. (purple coneflowers): Daisylike purple or white flowers with large centers in summer. Zones 3-8.

Gaura lindheimeri (white gaura): Loose spikes of white flowers in summer. Zones 5-9.

Helianthus spp. (sunflowers): Yellow daisylike flowers in late summer to fall. Zones 3-8.

Hemerocallis spp. (daylilies): Trumpet-shaped flowers in all colors except blue in summer. Zones 3-9.

Hibiscus moscheutos (common rose mallow): Large open white, pink, or red in summer. Zones 5-9.

Hosta spp. (hostas): Spikes of trumpet-shaped violet, lilac, or white flowers over heart-shaped leaves in summer or fall. Zones 3-8.

Iris spp. (irises): Narrow- to round-petaled flowers in a wide range of colors in spring to summer. Zones 3-8. (Hardiness varies among species.)

Liatris spp. (gayfeathers): Narrow spikes of magenta or white flowers in summer. Zones 3-8.

Liriope muscari (blue lilyturf): Spikes of violet-blue or white flowers in late summer. Zones 6-10.

Perovskia atriplicifolia (Russian sage): Open spikes of small light blue flowers in late summer. Zones 5-9.

Platycodon grandiflorus (balloon flower): Rounded buds open to blue, purple, or white blooms in summer. Zones 4-8.

Rudbeckia spp. (coneflowers): Daisylike yellow flowers with dark centers in mid- to late summer. Zones 3-8.

Salvia spp. (sages): Thin spikes of blue, purple, or red flowers in summer to fall. Zones 4-7.

Sedum spp. (sedums): Clusters of starry yellow, pink, or white flowers in spring, summer, or fall. Zones 3-10.

Stokesia laevis (Stokes' aster): Daisylike blue flowers in summer. Zones 5-9.

Perennials with Striking Foliage

Acanthus spp. (bear's-breeches): Shiny, spiny, lobed, or heart-shaped leaves in basal rosettes. Zones 7-9.

Achillea spp. (yarrows): Clumps of ferny green or gray-green leaves. Zones 3-8.

Aegopodium podagraria 'Variegatum' (variegated bishop's weed): Lobed green leaves edged in white. Zones 4-9.

Ajuga reptans (ajuga): Low rosettes of green, bronze, purple, or variegated leaves. Zones 4-8.

Alchemilla mollis (lady's-mantle): Pleated round yellowish green leaves. Zones 4-8.

Amsonia tabernaemontana (blue star): Narrow willowlike green leaves turn yellow in fall. Zones 3-9.

Anemone vitifolia (grape leaf anemone): Vigorous clumps of dark green lobed leaves. Zones 5-8.

Arabis caucasica (wall rock cress): Spreading clumps of fuzzy light green leaves. Zones 4-7.

Armeria maritima (common thrift): Spreading clumps of grasslike evergreen foliage. Zones 4-8.

Artemisia spp. (artemisias): Mounds of ferny, silver, or gray aromatic leaves. Zones 3-8. (Hardiness varies among species.)

Asarum spp. (wild ginger): Rounded glossy dark green leaves. Zones 3-8.

Astilbe spp. (astilbes): Clumps of shiny fernlike foliage. Zones 4-8.

Baptisia australis (blue false indigo): Dense clumps of cloverlike blue-green leaves. Zones 3-8.

Bergenia spp. (bergenias): Glossy evergreen leaves often turn burgundy in fall. Zones 4-8.

Cerastium tomentosum (snow-in-summer): Spreading mats of silvery leaves. Zones 2-7.

Dicentra eximia (fringed bleeding heart): Mounds of fernlike bluish green leaves. Zones 3-8.

Epimedium spp. (epimediums): Clumps of heart-shaped red-brown leaves that mature to light green. Zones 3-8.

Geranium spp. (cranesbills): Spreading, mounded, or slightly upright clumps of scalloped to deeply cut leaves. Zones 3-8.

Helleborus spp. (hellebores): Mounds of deeply lobed evergreen leaves. Zones 4-8.

Heuchera spp. (alumroots): Clumps of green to dark purple, lobed or heart-shaped leaves. Zones 3-8.

Hosta spp. (hostas): Wide mounds of smooth or puckered green, blue, or yellowish leaves, often variegated or edged with yellow or white. Zones 3-8.

Houttuynia cordata (houttuynia): Heart-shaped shiny green leaves often marked with red and yellow. Zones 3-8.

Iberis sempervirens (perennial candytuft): Spreading mounds of narrow, dark green evergreen leaves. Zones 4-8.

Iris spp. (irises): Clumps of long, flat green swordlike leaves. Zones 3-8. (Hardiness varies among species.)

Kniphofia uvaria (common torch lily): Clumps of spiky, grassy green leaves. Zones 6-9.

Lamiastrum galeobdolon (yellow archangel): Heart-shaped green- and white-variegated leaves. Zones 4-9.

Lamium spp. (lamiums): Heart-shaped green-, yellow-, or white-variegated leaves. Zones 3-9.

Lavandula spp. (lavenders): Narrow gray-green fragrant leaves. Zones 5-8.

Ligularia spp. (ligularias): Mounds of dark green, kidney-shaped leaves. Zones 5-7.

Liriope muscari (blue lilyturf): Evergreen grassy clumps of green leaves often striped with white or yellow. Zones 6-10.

Lupinus spp. (lupines): Large clumps of deeply lobed, palmlike leaves. Zones 4-7.

Nepeta × *faassenii* (catmint): Spreading mounds of fragrant, gray-green scalloped leaves. Zones 4-8.

Paeonia lactiflora (common garden peony): Mounds of dark green lobed leaves. Zones 3-8.

Polygonum odoratum 'Variegatum' (variegated Solomon's seal): Clumps of dark green leaves edged in white. Zones 3-7.

Pulmonaria spp. (lungworts): Clumps of dark green heart-shaped leaves, often with gray or silver spots. Zones 3-8.

Rodgersia spp. (rodgersias): Huge, maple- or buckeye-like green or bronze leaves. Zones 4-7.

Santolina spp. (lavender cotton): Dense clumps of woolly silvery white aromatic leaves. Zones 6-8.

Saxifraga stolonifera (strawberry geranium): Rosettes of rounded silver-veined green leaves with reddish undersides. Zones 6-8.

Sedum spp. (sedums): Fleshy pointed or rounded leaves in many colors. Zones 3-10.

Sempervivum spp. (hens-and-chickens): Fleshy rosettes of green or red-tinged leaves. Zones 3-10.

Stachys byzantina (lamb's-ears): Soft, fuzzy oblong gray-green leaves. Zones 4-8.

Thermopsis caroliniana (false lupine): Dense clumps of cloverlike blue-green leaves. Zones 3-9.

Tiarella cordifolia (Allegheny foamflower): Evergreen clumps of heart-shaped leaves. Zones 3-8.

Verbascum spp. (mulleins): Rosettes of fuzzy gray-green leaves. Zones 4-8.

Yucca spp. (yuccas): Evergreen clumps of dark green swordlike, sharply pointed leaves. Zones 4-9.

Bulbs for Naturalizing

Bulbs are a natural addition to any garden. A planting of carefully chosen bulbs can provide color all season long with little or no maintenance. Listed below are some of the most desirable bulbs for low-maintenance areas. They will come up year after year, and often multiply and spread to form large clumps. Try these easy-care plants in a perennial or shrub border, woodland garden, or meadow. You can even plant some of the smallest bulbs right in your lawn—they will have finished flowering by the time your lawn needs its first spring mowing. (Note: Many of these small bulbs are collected from the wild, which can endanger their natural populations. Check with your supplier, and buy only bulbs that are produced in cultivation, not wild-collected.) In the list below, the botanical name is followed by the common name, bloom color, season of bloom, growing conditions, and zones.

Allium moly (lily leek): Clusters of bright yellow flowers on 10″ stems in spring. Sun; well-drained soil. Zones 3-9.

Anemone blanda (Grecian windflower): Daisy-like white, pink, or blue flowers on 6″ stems in spring. Sun or partial shade; well-drained soil. Zones 5-8.

Camassia quamash (common camass): Spikes of purple-blue or white flowers on 3′ stems in early summer. Sun or partial shade; moist but well-drained soil. Zones 4-8.

Chionodoxa luciliae (glory-of-the-snow): Loose clusters of blue or pink flowers on 6″ stems in early spring. Sun or partial shade; well-drained soil. Zones 4-9.

Colchicum autumnale (autumn crocus): Large clusters of pink or white flowers on 6″ stems in fall. Sun; well-drained soil. Zones 5-9.

Crocus spp. (crocuses): Nearly stemless, goblet-shaped white, yellow, or purple flowers reach 2″-6″ tall in spring or fall. Sun or partial shade; well-drained soil. Zones 4-8.

Cyclamen hederifolium (hardy cyclamen): Nodding pink or white flowers on 4″ stems in fall. Shade; dry soil. Zones 5-9.

Eranthis hyemalis (winter aconite): Bright yellow buttercup-like flowers on 4″ stems in early spring. Partial shade; well-drained soil. Zones 4-9.

Fritillaria meleagris (checkered lily): Nodding, bell-shaped white or maroon flowers on 10″ stems in spring. Sun or partial shade; moist but well-drained soil. Zones 3-8.

Galanthus nivalis (common snowdrop): Nodding white flowers on 6″-9″ stems in very early spring. Sun or partial shade; moist but well-drained soil. Zones 3-8.

Iris reticulata (reticulated iris): Narrow-petaled, blue or purple, yellow-marked flowers on 6″ stems in very early spring. Sun; well-drained soil. Zones 5-8.

Leucojum aestivum (summer snowflake): Pendulous, bell-shaped white and green flowers on 2′ stems in mid-spring. Sun or partial shade; moist but well-drained soil. Zones 4-9.

Lilium spp. (lilies): Bowl- or trumpet-shaped, white, pink, red, orange, or yellow flowers on 2′-7′ stems in summer. Sun or partial shade; moist but well-drained soil. Zones 3-8.

Muscari spp. (grape hyacinths): Dense clusters of tiny rounded purple-blue flowers on 8″ stems in spring. Sun; well-drained soil. Zones 3-8.

Narcissus spp. (daffodils): Open, white, red-cupped flowers on 1′ stems in late spring. Sun; well-drained soil. Zones 4-9.

Ornithogalum umbellatum (star-of-Bethlehem): Loose, flat clusters of starry white flowers on 9″ stems in late spring. Sun or partial shade; well-drained soil. Zones 5-9.

Puschkinia scilloides (striped squill): Spikes of starry, light blue flowers on 6″ stems in early spring. Sun or partial shade; well-drained soil. Zones 3-9.

Scilla sibirica (Siberian squill): Clusters of bell-shaped blue, pink, or white flowers on 6″ stems in early spring. Sun to partial shade; well-drained soil. Zones 4-8.

Tulipa clusiana (lady tulip): Red- and white-striped cup-shaped flowers on 12″ stems in mid-spring. Sun to partial shade; well-drained soil. Zones 3-8.

Trees and Shrubs

Trees and shrubs form the backbone of any landscape. They add height and a sense of permanence to the garden throughout the seasons. Because these plants *are* relatively permanent (not to mention expensive), you should choose and site your trees and shrubs carefully. A well-chosen plant in the right spot will give you years of pleasure with little maintenance. Listed below are plants for foundation plantings; these shrubs usually stay below 5 feet with minimal trimming, so they won't grow up to block your windows. There are also lists of special tree shapes to help you select a tree for a particular site or effect. And the list of trees and shrubs with multi-season interest suggests plants you may want to consider for adding seasonal or year-round interest.

Foundation Plantings

Berberis thunbergii (Japanese barberry): Deciduous. Egg-shaped green leaves turn reddish in fall. Zones 4-8.

Buxus sempervirens 'Suffruticosa' (edging boxwood): Evergreen. Dark green foliage may bronze in winter. Zones 6-8.

Cotoneaster horizontalis (rockspray cotoneaster): Deciduous or semi-evergreen. Tiny white flowers in spring, followed by bright red berries. Zones 5-8.

Daphne spp. (daphnes): Evergreen or semi-evergreen. Clusters of pale pink, purple, or white flowers in spring. Zones 4-8.

Deutzia gracilis (slender deutzia): Deciduous. White flowers in summer. Zones 5-8.

Euonymus fortunei (wintercreeper): Evergreen. Glossy evergreen leaves may bronze in winter. Zones 4-8.

Fothergilla gardenii (fothergilla): Deciduous. Clusters of fragrant white bottlebrush-like flowers in spring. Zones 6-9.

Hypericum calycinum (St.-John's-wort): Evergreen. Yellow flowers in summer. Zones 6-9.

Ilex crenata 'Compacta' (dwarf Japanese holly): Evergreen. Small glossy green leaves. Zones 6-8.

Itea virginica (Virginia sweetspire): Deciduous. Long, densely packed clusters of small white flowers in late spring. Zones 5-9.

Juniperus horizontalis (creeping juniper): Evergreen. Needlelike green, blue-green, or gray-green foliage. Zones 2-10. (Hardiness varies among species.)

Kerria japonica (Japanese kerria): Deciduous. Bright yellow flowers in spring; green stems all winter. Zones 4-8.

Lavandula spp. (lavenders): Evergreen. Fragrant purple or white flowers in summer. Zones 5-8.

Leucothoe fontanesiana (drooping leucothoe): Evergreen. Clusters of fragrant white flowers in spring. Zones 5-9.

Mahonia spp. (mahonias): Evergreen. Spiky clusters of drooping yellow flowers in spring. Zones 6-8. (Hardiness varies among species.)

Myrica pensylvanica (northern bayberry): Deciduous or semi-evergreen. Fragrant dark green leaves and small, waxy, gray fruits. Zones 2-6.

Paxistima canbyi (paxistima): Evergreen. Small dark green leaves may bronze in winter. Zones 3-7.

Pinus mugo var. *mugo* (dwarf mugo pine): Evergreen. Medium to dark green needle-like leaves. Zone 3-7.

Potentilla fruticosa (shrubby cinquefoil): Deciduous. Yellow flowers in spring and summer. Zones 2-7.

Prunus laurocerasus 'Otto Luyken' (cherry-laurel): Evergreen. Spikes of fragrant white flowers in spring; glossy dark green leaves. Zones 6-8.

Rhododendron 'P.J.M.' ('P.J.M.' hybrid rhododendron): Evergreen. Lavender-pink flowers in spring; dark green leaves turn purplish in fall. Zone 4-8.

Sarcococca hookerana (Himalayan sarcococca): Evergreen. Tiny fragrant white flowers in spring; glossy dark green leaves. Zones 6-8.

Skimmia japonica (Japanese skimmia): Evergreen. Clusters of fragrant white flowers in spring; females produce red berries. Zones 6-8.

Spiraea bullata (crispleaf spirea): Deciduous. Rosy red flower clusters in summer; crinkled blue-green leaves. Zones 4-8.

Spiraea × *bumalda* (Bumald spirea): Deciduous. Clusters of white or pink flowers over dark green leaves. Zones 4-8.

Stephandra incisa 'Crispa' (lace shrub): Deciduous. Small white flowers in spring over mounds of finely cut leaves. Thrives in shade. Zones 3-8.

Taxus baccata 'Repandens' (English yew): Evergreen. Dark green foliage. Seeds and leaves are poisonous. Zones 4-7.

Trees with Rounded Form

Acer spp. (maples): Deciduous. 20'-70' tall. Zones 3-9. (Height and hardiness vary among species.)

Aesculus hippocastanum (common horse chestnut): Deciduous. 50'-75' tall. Zones 4-6.

Amelanchier spp. (serviceberries): Deciduous. 15'-40' tall. Zones 3-7. (Height and hardiness vary among species.)

Betula spp. (birches): Deciduous. 30'-70' tall. Zones 3-8. (Height and hardiness vary among species.)

Chionanthus virginicus (white fringe tree): Deciduous. 12'-25' tall. Zones 4-9.

Cornus mas (cornelian cherry): Deciduous. 20'-25' tall. Zones 4-8.

Cotinus coggygria (smoke tree): Deciduous. 10'-15' tall. Zones 5-8.

Crataegus phaenopyrum (Washington hawthorn): Deciduous. 20'-25' tall. Zones 4-8.

Fagus spp. (beeches): Deciduous. 50'-70' tall. Zones 4-8. (Hardiness varies among species.)

Fraxinus spp. (ashes): Deciduous. 50'-80' tall. Zones 4-9.

Halesia carolina (Carolina silverbell): Deciduous. 30'-40' tall. Zones 5-8.

Magnolia × *soulangiana* (saucer magnolia): Deciduous. 20'-25' tall. Zones 5-8.

Magnolia stellata (star magnolia): Deciduous. 15'-20' tall. Zones 4-8.

Malus spp. (apples, crab apples): Deciduous. 12'-25' tall. Zones 3-8. (Height and hardiness vary among species.)

Prunus spp. (cherries): Deciduous. 15'-25' tall. Zones 4-9. (Height and hardiness vary among species.)

Quercus spp. (oaks): Deciduous. 40'-80' tall. Zones 2-8. (Height and hardiness vary among species.)

Syringa spp. (lilacs): Deciduous. 6'-30' tall. Zones 3-8. (Height and hardiness vary among species.)

Tilia spp. (lindens): Deciduous. 50'-80' tall. Zones 2-7. (Hardiness varies among species.)

Trees with Spreading Form

Albizia julibrissin (mimosa): Deciduous. 15'-25' tall. Zones 5-9.

Cedrus libani (cedar-of-Lebanon): Evergreen. 40'-60' tall. Zones 5-7.

Cornus alternifolia (pagoda dogwood): Deciduous. 15'-20' tall. Zones 3-7.

Cornus florida (flowering dogwood): Deciduous. 20'-40' tall. Zones 5-8.

Cornus kousa (kousa dogwood): Deciduous. 15'-25' tall. Zones 5-8.

Crataegus crus-galli (cockspur hawthorn): Deciduous. 20'-30' tall. Zones 4-7.

Prunus serrulata (Japanese flowering cherry): Deciduous. 20'-25' tall. Zones 5-7.

Trees with Weeping Form

Betula pendula 'Youngii' (weeping European birch): Deciduous. 10'-15' tall (if staked when young). Zones 3-6.

Fagus sylvatica 'Pendula' (weeping European beech): Deciduous. 50'-60' tall. Zones 5-7.

Malus floribunda (Japanese flowering crab apple): Deciduous. 20'-25' tall. Zones 4-7.

Malus sieboldii (Toringo crab apple): Deciduous. 10'-12' tall. Zones 4-7.

Prunus subhirtella 'Pendula' (weeping Higan cherry): Deciduous. 15'-25' tall. Zones 5-8.

Salix alba 'Tristis' (golden weeping willow): Deciduous. 50'-70' tall. Zones 2-8.

Tsuga canadensis 'Sargentii' (weeping Canada hemlock): Evergreen. 10'-15' tall. Zones 4-7.

Ulmus glabra 'Camperdownii' (weeping Scotch elm): Deciduous. 20'-30' tall. Zones 5-7.

Trees with Columnar or Pyramidal Form

Carpinus betulus 'Fastigiata' (upright European hornbeam): Deciduous. 30'-40' tall. Zones 4-7.

Cedrus atlantica 'Glauca' (blue atlas cedar): Evergreen. 40'-60' tall. Zones 6-8.

Chamaecyparis lawsoniana 'Columnaris' (columnar Lawson false cypress): Evergreen. 40'-60' tall. Zones 6-8.

Chamaecyparis obtusa (Hinoki false cypress): Evergreen. 50'-80' tall. Zones 4-8.

Cupressus glabra 'Pyramidalis' (smooth Arizona cypress): Evergreen. 30'-50' tall. Zones 7-9.

Juniperus scopulorum 'Skyrocket' (Rocky Mountain juniper): Evergreen. 20'-25' tall. Zones 4-7.

Liquidambar styraciflua (sweet gum): Deciduous. 60'-80' tall. Zones 5-8.

Magnolia grandiflora (southern magnolia): Evergreen. 50'-75' tall. Zones 6-9.

Oxydendron arboreum (sourwood): Deciduous. 30'-40' tall. Zones 5-9.

Pseudotsuga menziesii (Douglas fir): Evergreen. 50'-80' tall. Zones 5-7.

Styrax obassia (fragrant snowbell): Deciduous. 20'-30' tall. Zones 6-9.

Taxus baccata 'Fastigiata' (upright English yew): Evergreen. 15'-30' tall. Zones 6-7.

Deciduous Trees and Shrubs with Multi-Season Interest

Abelia × *grandiflora* (glossy abelia): Lightly fragrant pale pink flowers in spring through summer; glossy green leaves turn reddish in fall. Zones 5-8.

Acer spp. (maples): Many species have outstanding red to yellow fall color; some have striped bark. Zones 3-9. (Hardiness varies among species.)

Amelanchier spp. (serviceberries): White flowers in spring; red to black berries in summer; yellow to red fall color. Zones 3-8.

Berberis spp. (barberries): Small yellow flowers in spring; red to black berries in late summer into winter. Zones 4-8. (Hardiness varies among species.)

Betula spp. (birches): Many species have bright yellow fall color and peeling bark. Zones 3-8. (Hardiness varies among species.)

Callicarpa spp. (beautyberries): Pinkish purple flowers in late summer; bright purple berries in fall and winter. Zones 6-8.

Chionanthus virginicus (white fringe tree): White flowers in early summer; females produce blue berries in summer; yellow fall color. Zones 4-9.

Cladrastis lutea (American yellowwood): Fragrant white flowers in late spring; yellow fall color; smooth gray to tan bark. Zones 4-8.

Cornus florida (flowering dogwood): White flowers in spring; red berries in late summer to fall; reddish fall color. Zones 5-8.

Cornus kousa (kousa dogwood): White flowers in late spring; red fruit in late summer; red fall color; peeling bark. Zones 5-7.

Cornus mas (cornelian cherry): Yellow flowers in early spring; red berries in late summer; peeling bark. Zones 4-8.

Cotinus coggygria (smoke tree): Airy masses of pinkish flowers in summer; yellow, orange, or reddish purple fall color. Zones 5-8.

Crataegus phaenopyrum (Washington hawthorn): Reddish purple new leaves turn dark green in summer; persistent bright red fruit. Zones 3-8.

Eucalyptus spp. (eucalyptus): Yellow, red, or white flowers in summer to fall; aromatic bluish leaves; peeling bark. Zones 8-9.

Fagus spp. (beeches): Smooth gray bark; dark green leaves turn coppery in fall. Zones 4-8.

Fothergilla spp. (fothergillas): White flowers in spring; bright yellow to orange-red fall color. Zones 6-9.

Hamamelis spp. (witch hazels): Yellow, orange, or reddish flowers in fall or early spring; yellow to orange fall color. Zones 4-8.

Hydrangea quercifolia (oakleaf hydrangea): White flowers in summer; burgundy-red fall color. Zones 5-8.

Itea virginica (sweetspire): White flowers in late spring to early summer; bright red to purplish fall color. Zones 5-9.

Jasminum nudiflorum (winter jasmine): Yellow flowers in late winter to early spring; bright green stems. Zones 6-9.

Lagerstroemia indica (crape myrtle): White, pink, red, or purplish flowers in summer; peeling bark. Zones 6-9.

Liquidambar styraciflua (sweet gum): Lobed leaves turn red in fall; deeply ridged bark. Zones 5-8.

Magnolia stellata (star magnolia): White flowers in spring; red seeds in summer. Zones 4-8.

Malus spp. (crab apples): White or pink flowers in spring; red or yellow fruit in summer. Zones 4-7.

Oxydendrum arboreum (sourwood): White flowers in late summer; bright red fall color. Zones 5-9.

Prunus serrulata (Japanese flowering cherry): Small white flowers in spring; yellow fall color; peeling reddish brown bark. Zones 5-7.

Rosa rugosa (rugosa rose): Fragrant white, pink, or red flowers in summer; orange-red fruits in late summer. Zones 3-8.

Stewartia spp. (stewartias): White flowers in summer to fall; yellow, red, or purplish fall color; peeling bark. Zones 6-9. (Hardiness varies among species.)

Viburnum spp. (viburnums): White flowers in spring or summer; red or blue berries; red to purple fall color. Zones 3-9. (Hardiness varies among species.)

Vines and Climbers

Don't overlook the value of vines and climbing plants in your outdoor living spaces. These versatile plants can help you to merge the boundaries between different areas or to soften the harsh edges of new walls and fences. Use vines and climbers on an arbor as a decorative entrance or on a pergola to provide shade.

Listed below are some particularly useful vines. Choose a fast-grower to cover a space quickly. Or select a flowering vine for an added benefit to an already useful landscape plant.

Fast-Growing Vines

Actinidia spp. (kiwis): Deciduous. Woody-stemmed vining climbers need a strong support. Zones 4-9. (Hardiness varies among species.)

Ampelopsis brevipedunculata (porcelain ampelopsis): Deciduous. Variable dark green leaves; bright blue berries. Climbs by tendrils. Zones 4-8.

Aristolochia durior (Dutchman's-pipe): Deciduous. Twining vine with dark green heart-shaped leaves and pouched flowers in summer. Zones 4-8.

Bignonia capreolata (cross vine): Semi-evergreen or evergreen. Woody vine with orange summer flowers. Climbs by tendrils. Zones 6-9.

Clematis maximowicziana (sweet autumn clematis): Deciduous. Twining woody vine with fragrant white blooms in late summer into fall. Zones 4-9.

Cobaea scandens (cup-and-saucer vine): Annual. Bell-shaped blue or white flowers from summer to fall. Climbs by tendrils.

Humulus lupulus (hops): Annual. Twining vine with lobed green leaves.

Ipomoea spp. (morning glories): Annual. Twining vine with trumpet-shaped blue, white, or pink flowers from summer into fall.

Passiflora spp. (passionflowers): Dramatic purple, pink, or white flowers from summer to fall. Climbs by tendrils. Zones 7-9. (Hardiness varies among species.)

Phaseolus coccineus (scarlet runner bean): Annual. Twining vine with bright red pea-like flowers in summer.

Thunbergia alata (black-eyed Susan vine): Annual. Twining vine with heart-shaped leaves and orange-yellow flowers in summer.

Vines with Attractive Flowers

Aristolochia durior (Dutchman's-pipe): Tubular, pouchlike greenish to purple-brown flowers in early summer. Zones 4-8.

Bignonia capreolata (cross vine): Trumpet-shaped orange flowers in summer. Zones 6-9.

Campsis radicans (trumpet vine): Trumpet-shaped red or orange flowers in late summer. Zones 4-9.

Clematis spp. (clematis): Saucer-, star-, or bell-shaped flowers in a wide range of colors and bloom times. Some are fragrant. Zones 3-8. (Hardiness varies among species.)

Cobaea scandens (cup-and-saucer vine): Annual. Bell-shaped blue or white flowers from summer to fall.

Gelsemium sempervirens (Carolina jessamine): Trumpet-shaped fragrant yellow flowers in spring. Zones 7-9.

Hydrangea anomala subsp. *petiolaris* (climbing hydrangea): Wide, flat clusters of white flowers in summer. Zones 4-7.

Ipomoea spp. (morning glories): Annual. Trumpet-shaped white, blue, or pink flowers from summer to fall. *I. alba* is fragrant and only open at night.

Jasminum officinale (common white jasmine): Clusters of fragrant tubular white flowers in mid- to late summer. Zones 7-9.

Lonicera × heckrottii (goldflame honeysuckle): Showy, trumpet-shaped magenta flowers with yellow interiors, in late spring and summer. Zones 4-9.

Lonicera sempervirens (trumpet honeysuckle): Showy, trumpet-shaped scarlet or yellow-orange flowers in summer. Zones 4-9.

Passiflora spp. (passionflowers): Spectacular purplish, pink, or white flowers from summer into fall. Zones 7-9. (Hardiness varies among species.)

Phaseolus coccineus (scarlet runner bean): Annual. Bright red pealike flowers in summer.

Rosa spp. (climbing roses): Flowers are available in a wide range of colors, forms, and fragrances. Zones 4-9. (Hardiness varies among species.)

Thunbergia alata (black-eyed Susan vine): Annual. Narrow, trumpet-shaped, flat-petaled orange-yellow flowers in summer.

Wisteria spp. (wisterias): Pendulous clusters of pealike purple-blue or white flowers in early summer. Zones 5-9.

Plants for Erosion Control

Gentle slopes can add a lot of interest to a landscape, but steep slopes can be maintenance nightmare. Mowing these areas is often difficult (if not impossible) as well as dangerous. If you can't reshape the area with walls or terraces, an attractive, low-maintenance groundcover could solve your problem. Listed below are some of the best plants to use on a sloping site. Unless noted, these plants all tolerate full sun and well-drained soil.

Aegopodium podagraria (bishop's weed): Deciduous. Green or variegated leaves. Prefers partial shade. 6″-12″ tall. Zones 4-9.

Ajuga reptans (ajuga): Deciduous. Spikes of blue, pink, or white flowers over rosettes of green, purple, or variegated leaves. Prefers partial shade. 4″-6″ tall. Zones 4-8.

Arctostaphylos uva-ursi (bearberry): Evergreen. White bell-shaped flowers in spring, followed by red berries. 6″-12″ tall. Zones 2-6.

Coronilla varia (crown vetch): Deciduous. Pink flowers in summer over ferny green leaves. To 2′ tall. Zones 3-9.

Cotoneaster spp. (cotoneasters): Deciduous or semi-evergreen. Tiny white flowers in spring, followed by bright red berries. 1′-3′ tall. Zones 5-8.

Euonymus fortunei (wintercreeper): Glossy evergreen leaves may bronze in winter. 4″-6″ tall. Zones 4-8.

Hedera helix (English ivy): Dark green or variegated leaves. Prefers partial shade. 6″-10″ tall. Zones 6-9. (Hardiness varies among cultivars.)

Hemerocallis spp. (daylilies): Deciduous or evergreen. Trumpet-shaped flowers in a range of colors in summer. 1′-3′ tall. Zones 3-9.

Hypericum calycinum (St.-John's-wort): Evergreen. Yellow flowers in summer. 12″-18″ tall. Zones 6-9.

Juniperus horizontalis (creeping juniper): Evergreen. Needlelike green, blue-green, or gray-green foliage. To 18″ tall. Zones 2-10. (Hardiness varies among species.)

Pachysandra terminalis (Japanese pachysandra): Evergreen. Spikes of white flowers in spring. Prefers partial shade. 6″-10″ tall. Zones 4-9.

Phlox subulata (moss pink): Evergreen. White, pink, or lavender flowers in spring. Shear after bloom. 1″-6″ tall. Zones 3-8.

Potentilla fruticosa (shrubby cinquefoil): Deciduous. Yellow flowers in spring and summer. 2′-4′ tall. Zones 2-7.

Spiraea bullata (crispleaf spirea): Deciduous. Rosy red flower clusters in summer. 12″-15″ tall. Zones 4-8.

Stephandra incisa 'Crispa' (lace shrub): Deciduous. Small white flowers in spring over mounds of finely cut leaves. Thrives in shade. To 2′ tall. Zones 3-8.

Vinca minor (common periwinkle): Evergreen. Blue or white flowers in spring over glossy green leaves. Prefers partial shade. 4″-8″ tall. Zones 5-8.

Plants for Hedges and Screens

Plants are often a wonderful alternative to a solid fence for dividing a property or blocking an unpleasant view. All of the plants listed below tolerate close planting, so they form an effective barrier or screen. Tall, fast-growing plants are ideal for windbreaks. A flowering hedge of one or more types of shrubs can provide seasonal or year-round interest. Or for a formal look, you may choose a sheared hedge of plants that tolerate regular pruning.

Trees and Shrubs for Windbreaks

× *Cupressocyparis leylandii* (Leyland cypress): Evergreen. Dense, dark green leaves. 60′-70′ tall. Zones 6-10.

Juniperus virginiana (Eastern red cedar): Evergreen. Medium to dark green foliage. 40′-50′ tall. Zones 3-8.

Picea abies (Norway spruce): Evergreen. Bright green foliage when young; darker green when older. 40′-60′ tall. Zones 2-7.

Pinus spp. (pines): Evergreen. Medium to dark green or bluish green foliage. 30′-60′ tall. Zones 3-8. (Height and hardiness vary among species.)

Tsuga spp. (hemlocks): Evergreen. Dark green, fine-textured foliage. 40'-70' tall. Zones 3-8. (Height and hardiness vary among species.)

Plants for Flowering Hedges

Abelia × *grandiflora* (glossy abelia): Semi-evergreen. Lightly fragrant pale pink flowers in spring and summer. 4'-6' tall. Zones 5-8.

Chaenomeles speciosa (flowering quince): Deciduous. Single or double, red, pink, or white flowers in spring. 4'-8' tall. Zones 4-8.

Deutzia spp. (deutzias): Deciduous. White flowers in summer. 2'-8' tall. Zones 4-8. (Height and hardiness vary among species.)

Forsythia spp. (forsythias): Deciduous. Yellow flowers in early spring. 6'-8' tall. Zones 4-8.

Hibiscus syriacus (rose-of-Sharon): Deciduous. White, pink, red, or violet flowers in summer. 8'-12' tall. Zones 5-8.

Hydrangea paniculata var. *grandiflora* (peegee hydrangea): Deciduous. Creamy white flowers in late summer. 4'-8' tall. Zones 4-9.

Lavandula spp. (lavenders): Evergreen. Fragrant purple or white flowers in summer. 1'-3' tall. Zones 5-8.

Lonicera fragrantissima (winter honeysuckle): Semi-evergreen. Fragrant white flowers in very early spring. 6'-10' tall. Zones 5-9.

Philadelphus coronarius (sweet mock orange): Deciduous. Fragrant white flowers in late spring. 10'-12' tall. Zones 4-7.

Potentilla fruticosa (shrubby cinquefoil): Deciduous. Lemon-yellow flowers in late spring and again in summer to fall. 2'-4' tall. Zones 2-7.

Prunus cerasifera (Myrobalan plum): Deciduous. Fragrant pale to deep pink flowers in spring. 15'-25' tall. Zones 4-8.

Prunus laurocerasus (cherry-laurel): Evergreen. Fragrant white flowers in spring. 10'-20' tall. Zones 6-8.

Rosa spp. (roses): Deciduous. Shrub, grandiflora, and floribunda roses come in a range of colors. Height and hardiness vary among species.

Spiraea spp. (spireas): Deciduous. White flowers in spring. 6'-10' tall. Zones 4-8. (Height and hardiness vary among species.)

Syringa spp. (lilacs): Deciduous. Fragrant white, pink, or purplish flowers in spring. 5'-30' tall. Zones 3-8. (Height and hardiness vary among species.)

Viburnum spp. (viburnums): Deciduous or evergreen. White flowers in spring or summer. 6'-15' tall. Zones 3-8. (Height and hardiness vary among species.)

Shrubs for Sheared Hedges

Berberis thunbergii (Japanese barberry): Deciduous. Thorny stems make an impenetrable hedge. Red berries in winter. Zones 4-8.

Buxus sempervirens (common boxwood): Evergreen. Dark green foliage may bronze in winter. Zones 6-8.

Carpinus betulus (European hornbeam): Deciduous. Dark green leaves that are usually pest-free. Good for tall hedges. Zones 5-7.

Fagus sylvatica (European beech): Deciduous. Green leaves turn golden brown in fall. Good for tall hedges. Zones 5-7.

Ilex crenata (Japanese holly): Evergreen. Shiny, dark green leaves. Very adaptable. Zones 6-8.

Ligustrum spp. (privets): Deciduous. Glossy dark green leaves. Needs frequent trimming. Zones 4-9. (Hardiness varies among species.)

Lonicera nitida (boxleaf honeysuckle): Evergreen or semi-evergreen. Shiny dark green leaves. Zones 6-9.

Photinia spp. (photinias): Evergreen. Reddish new leaves turn dark green when mature. Zones 6-9. (Hardiness varies among species.)

Pyracantha coccinea (scarlet firethorn): Evergreen or semi-evergreen. Dark green leaves, spiny stems, and persistent red fruit. Zones 6-8.

Taxus spp. (yews): Evergreen. Dark green foliage. Seeds and leaves are are poisonous. Zones 4-7. (Hardiness varies among species.)

Tsuga canadensis (Canada hemlock): Evergreen. Glossy, dark green fine-textured foliage. Zones 3-8.

Plants for Edible Landscaping

You don't have to have a separate herb garden, vegetable garden, and orchard to enjoy fresh-picked produce from your yard. Many plants that provide edible leaves, flowers, or fruits are also quite ornamental. Tuck a few of your favorite edibles into your garden, or plan a whole landscape around these attractive and productive plants. In the lists below, the common name is followed by the botanical name, the plant's edible parts, and its cultural requirements.

Annuals

Basil (*Ocimum basilicum*): Leaves. Sun; well-drained soil.

Borage (*Borago officinalis*): Leaves, flowers. Sun; well-drained soil.

Cardoon (*Cynara cardunculus*): Stems. Sun; well-drained soil.

Chard, Swiss (*Beta vulgaris*): Leaves, stems. Sun to partial shade; well-drained soil.

Dill (*Anethum graveolens*): Leaves, seeds. Sun; well-drained soil.

Fennel (*Foeniculum vulgare*): Leaves, seeds. Sun; well-drained soil.

Kale, ornamental (*Brassica oleracea*): Leaves. Sun; moist but well-drained soil.

Marjoram, sweet (*Origanum majorana*): Leaves. Sun; well-drained soil.

Nasturtium (*Tropaeolum majus*): Flowers. Sun; well-drained soil.

Okra (*Abelmoschus esculentus*): Pods. Sun; well-drained soil.

Parsley (*Petroselinum crispum*): Leaves. Sun to partial shade; moist but well-drained soil.

Savory, summer (*Satureja hortensis*): Leaves. Sun; well-drained soil.

Sunflower (*Helianthus annuus*): Seeds. Sun; well-drained soil.

Perennials and Bulbs

Angelica (*Angelica archangelica*): Stems. Sun to partial shade; moist but well-drained soil. Zones 4-9.

Anise hyssop (*Agastache foeniculum*): Leaves, flowers. Sun to partial shade; moist but well-drained soil.

Artichoke, Jerusalem (*Helianthus tuberosus*): Tubers. Sun; well-drained soil. Zones 3-9.

Bee balm (*Monarda didyma*): Leaves, flowers. Sun; well-drained soil. Zones 4-8.

Catnip (*Nepeta cataria*): Leaves. Full sun to partial shade; moist but well-drained soil. Zones 3-9.

Chives (*Allium schoenoprasm*): Flowers. Sun to partial shade; well-drained soil. Zones 3-9.

Lemon balm (*Melissa officinalis*): Leaves. Partial shade; moist but well-drained soil. Zones 4-9.

Mints (*Mentha* spp.): Leaves. Partial shade; moist but well-drained soil. Zones 3-9.

Oregano (*Origanum heracleoticum*): Leaves. Sun; well-drained soil. Zones 6-9.

Prickly pears (*Opuntia* spp.): Fruit. Sun; well-drained soil. Zones 5-10. (Hardiness varies among species.)

Rhubarb (*Rheum rhabarbarum*): Leaf stalks only (leaves are poisonous). Sun; well-drained soil. Zones 3-8.

Rosemary (*Rosmarinus officinalis*): Leaves. Sun; well-drained soil. Zones 7-9.

Saffron crocus (*Crocus sativus*): Orange stigmas (floral parts). Sun to partial shade; well-drained soil. Zones 5-8.

Sage (*Salvia officinalis*): Leaves. Sun; well-drained soil. Zones 4-9.

Salad burnet (*Poterium sanguisorba*): Leaves. Sun; well-drained soil. Zones 3-9.

Savory, winter (*Satureja montana*): Leaves. Sun; well-drained soil. Zones 5-9.

Sorrel, French (*Rumex scutatus*): Leaves. Sun to partial shade; well-drained soil. Zones 4-9.

Strawberry, Alpine (*Fragaria vesca*): Fruit. Sun; well-drained soil. Zones 3-9.

Violets (*Viola* spp.): Flowers. Partial shade; moist but well-drained soil. Zones 4-8.

Groundcovers

Chamomile (*Chamaemelum nobile*): Flowers. Sun; well-drained soil. Zones 5-9.

Cranberry (*Vaccinium macrocarpon*): Fruit. Sun; moist, acidic, humus-rich soil. Zones 3-8.

Lingonberry (*Vaccinium vitis-idaea* var. *minus*): Fruit. Sun to partial shade; acidic, well-drained soil. Zones 1-6.

Strawberry (*Fragaria* × *ananassa*): Fruit. Sun; well-drained soil. Zones 3-9.

Thymes (*Thymus* spp.): Leaves. Sun; well-drained soil. Zones 5-9.

Shrubs

Bay, sweet (*Laurus nobilis*): Leaves. Sun to partial shade in well-drained soil. Zones 8-9.

Blueberries (*Vaccinium* spp.): Fruit. Sun; moist but well-drained acidic soil. Zones 3-9. (Hardiness varies among species.)

Brambles (*Rubus* spp.): Fruit. Sun; well-drained soil. Zones 3-9. (Hardiness varies among species.)

Calamondin (× *Citrofortunella mitis*): Fruit. Sun; moist but well-drained soil. Zone 9.

Cranberry, highbush (*Viburnum trilobum*): Fruit. Sun to partial shade; moist but well-drained soil. Zones 2-7.

Currants (*Ribes* spp.): Fruit. Sun to partial shade; moist but well-drained soil. Zones 3-6.

Elderberries (*Sambucus* spp.): Fruit, flowers. Sun; moist but well-drained soil. Zones 3-9. (Hardiness varies among species.)

Fig (*Ficus carica*): Fruit. Sun; well-drained soil. Zones 8-10 (can be grown in colder areas with winter protection).

Filberts (*Corylus* spp.): Nuts. Sun; well-drained soil. Zones 2-8.

Gooseberries (*Ribes* spp.): Fruit. Sun to partial shade; moist but well-drained soil. Zones 3-6.

Pineapple guava (*Feijoa sellowiana*): Fruit. Sun to partial shade; well-drained soil. Zones 8-10.

Pomegranate (*Punica granatum*): Fruit. Sun; well-drained soil. Zones 8-10 (best in hot, dry climates).

Rose, rugosa (*Rosa rugosa*): Fruit (hips). Sun; well-drained soil. Zones 2-7.

Tea (*Camellia sinensis*): Leaves. Partial shade; well-drained soil. Zones 7-9.

Trees

Almond (*Prunus amygdalus*): Nuts. Sun; well-drained soil. Zones 7-9.

Alpricot (*Prunus armeniaca*): Fruit, nuts. Sun; well-drained soil. Zones 5-8.

Apples, crab apples (*Malus* spp.): Fruit. Sun; well-drained soil. Zones 3-8. (Hardiness varies among species.)

Beechnut (*Fagus grandifolia*): Nuts. Sun to partial shade (especially when young); moist but well-drained soil. Zones 2-8.

Cherry, cornelian (*Cornus mas*): Fruit. Sun (for best fruiting) to partial shade; well-drained soil. Zones 4-8.

Cherry, sweet (*Prunus avium*): Fruit. Sun; moist but well-drained soil. Zones 5-8.

Cherry, tart (*Prunus cerasus*): Fruit. Sun; moist but well-drained soil. Zones 5-8.

Citrus (*Citrus* spp.): Fruit. Sun; well-drained soil. Zone 9.

Hickory, shagbark (*Carya ovata*): Nuts. Sun; well-drained soil. Zones 3-8.

Jujube (*Ziziphus jujuba*): Fruit. Sun; well-drained soil. Zones 6-10.

Medlar (*Mespilus germanica*): Fruit. Sun; well-drained soil. Zones 5-8.

Olive (*Olea europea*): Fruit. Sun; well-drained soil. Zone 9.

Pawpaw (*Asimina triloba*): Fruit. Sun to partial shade (especially for young plants); well-drained soil. Zones 5-9.

Pears (*Pyrus* spp.): Fruit. Sun; moist but well-drained soil. Zones 3-8.

Pecan (*Carya illinoinensis*): Nuts. Sun; well-drained soil. Zones 6-9.

Persimmons (*Diospyros* spp.): Fruit. Sun; well-drained soil. Zones 5-9. (Hardiness varies among species.)

Pines (*Pinus* spp.): Nuts. Sun once established (young trees benefit from some shade); poor, well-drained soil. Zones 2-9.

Quince (*Cydonia oblonga*): Fruit. Sun; moist but well-drained soil. Zones 5-9.

Serviceberries (*Amelanchier* spp.): Fruit. Sun to partial shade; well-drained soil. Zones 3-8.

Walnut, Persian (*Juglans regia*): Nuts. Sun; well-drained soil. Zones 5-9.

Vines and Climbers

Grapes (*Vitis* spp.): Fruit. Sun; well-drained soil. Zones 4-9. (Hardiness varies among species.)

Hyacinth bean (*Dolichos lablab*): Pods. Sun; well-drained soil. Annual.

Kiwis (*Actinidia* spp.): Fruit. Sun to partial shade; well-drained soil. Zones 4-9. (Hardiness varies among species.)

Passionflowers (*Passiflora* spp.): Fruit. Sun to partial shade; moist but well-drained soil. Zones 7-9. (Hardiness varies among species.)

APPENDIX C
Sources

Look for interesting garden ornaments, lighting fixtures, and useful materials like stone paving or landscape ties at local nurseries and garden centers, as well as stone or landscaping materials dealers. For more mail-order sources, look on your local newsstand for magazines such as *Garden Design, Architectural Digest, Horticulture, Fine Gardening, Sunset, Southern Living,* and *Better Homes and Gardens:* The advertisements in these magazines will lead you to interesting suppliers.

Unless otherwise noted in the lists below, catalogs or brochures are free.

Drawing Supplies

If you live near a college or university, the bookstore is often a useful source of drawing supplies. Large art stores and drafting supply stores are also good sources. If you don't have ready access to a store, here are some mail-order companies that carry a wide selection.

Art Station LTD
144 W. 27th St.
New York, NY 10001
(212) 807-8000

Dick Blick
P.O. Box 26
Allentown, PA 18105
1-800-723-2787

Weather Instruments

You can monitor the weather with a simple thermometer and rain gauge, or a computerized weather station. These sources carry basic and more advanced instruments.

Davis Instruments
3465 Diablo Ave.
Hayward, CA 94545
1-800-678-3669

Maximum, Inc.
30 Barnet Ave.
New Bedford, CT 02745
(508) 995-2200

Wind & Weather
The Albion Street Water Tower
P.O. Box 2320
Mendocino, CA 95460
1-800-922-9463
Also carries weather vanes and sundials

Garden Furnishings

These companies offer garden furniture, accents, structures, and landscape installation aids.

Agri Drain Corp.
R.R. 2, Box 458
Adair, Iowa 50002
1-800-232-4742
In-ground drainage supplies

Bamboo & Rattan, Inc.
470 Oberlin Ave. South
Lakewood, NJ 08701
(908) 370-0220
Bamboo and reed fencing

Bamboo Fencer
31 Germania St.
Jamaica Plain, MA 02130
(617) 524-6137
Catalog $2 (refundable with order)
Bamboo fencing and structures

BowBends
P.O. Box 900
Bolton, MA 01740
(508) 779-2271
Catalog $3
Kits for arbors, gazebos; pre-built bridges

Carruth Studio, Inc.
1178 Farnsworth
Waterville, OH 43566
(419) 878-3060
Cast concrete and terra-cotta accents

Country Casual
17317 Germantown Rd.
Germantown, MD 20874
(301) 540-0040
Catalog $3
Furniture, planters, and trellises

Custom Iron Work, Inc.
P.O. Box 180
Union, KY 41091
(606) 384-4122
Catalog $1
Iron fencing

Earthworks
P.O. Box 67
Hyattville, WY 82428
Send SASE for brochure
Hypertufa (artificial stone) troughs

Florentine Craftsmen, Inc.
46-24 28th St.
Long Island City, NY 11101
(718) 937-7632
Catalog $5
Furniture, fountains, and accents

Garden Angel
P.O. Box 240
Mayfield, KY 42066
Catalog $2
Accents and furniture

Gardener's Eden
P.O. Box 7307
San Fransisco, CA 94120
1-800-822-1214
Accents

Granite Impressions
342 Carmen Rd.
Talent, OR 97540
(503) 535-6190
Hand-cast granite containers and accents

Haddonstone USA
201 Heller Place
Interstate Business Park
Bellmawr, NJ 08031
(609) 931-7011
Catalog $5
Stoneware ornaments and accents

Henri Studio, Inc.
2260 Rand Rd.
Palatine, IL 60074
(708) 359-8500
Cast stone fountains, waterfalls, pools,
planters, and accents

Kinsman Company, Inc.
River Road
Point Pleasant, PA 18950
1-800-733-5613
Trellises and planters

Lazy Hill Farm Designs
P.O. Box 235
Colerain, NC 27924
(919) 356-2828
Handcrafted accents

New England Garden Ornaments
38 E. Brookfield Rd.
North Brookfield, MA 01535
(508) 867-4474
Catalog $8
Cast stone and lead structures, accents, and
planters

Rockustics
15400 E. Batavia Dr.
Aurora, CO 80111
(303) 363-6161
Simulated rock outdoor music speakers

Smith & Hawken
25 Corte Madera
Mill Valley, CA 94941
(415) 383-2000
Furniture and accents

Stone Forest
Box 2840
Santa Fe, NM 87504
(505) 986-8883
Catalog $2
Hand-carved granite, Japanese accents

The Timeless Garden
P.O. Box 5406
Arlington, VA 22208
(703) 536-8958
Reproductions of historic gates

The Trellis Works
Box 1143
Barnstable, MA 02630
(508) 362-9813
Handcrafted, limited-edition trellises

Windsor Designs
37 Great Valley Parkway
Malvern, PA 19355
1-800-783-5434; in PA, (215) 640-1212
Wood and cast aluminum furniture

Outdoor Lighting

Local building centers may have a selection of wholesale catalogs that you can look at and order from. You can also look in the yellow pages under "lighting fixtures" and call around to see if they sell to retail customers.

Classic & Country Crafts
5100-1B Clayton Rd., Suite 291
Concord, CA 94521
(510) 672-4337
Copper, lily-shaped light fixtures

Doner Design, Inc.
2175 Beaver Valley Pike
New Providence, PA 17560
(717) 786-8891
Handcrafted copper light fixtures

Gardener's Supply Co.
128 Intervale Road
Burlington, VT 05401
(802) 863-1700
Solar yard light with automatic on/off

Idaho Wood-Lighting
Box 488
Sandpoint, ID 83864
1-800-635-1100
12-volt lighting

Landscape Lighting by Outdoor Gardens Inc.
1961 NE 147th Terrace
North Miami, FL 33181
(305) 947-7000
12-volt lighting

Liteform Designs
P.O. Box 3316
Portland, OR 97208
1-800-458-2505
Wooden and metal light fixtures

Northern
P.O. Box 1499
Burnsville, MN 55337
1-800-533-5545
Discounter; sale-priced solar lights often included in catalog

Vista Landscape Lighting
7459 Laurel Canyon Blvd. #4
North Hollywood, CA 91605
1-800-766-VISTA

APPENDIX D
Recommended Reading

A great many books have been published on garden design and landscaping. They range from pictorial essays on great gardens to do-it-yourself guides packed with ideas and plans. Spend an afternoon at your public library skimming the books and magazines they have. Here are a few books to look for.

Garden Design and Landscaping

Brooks, John. *The Book of Garden Design.* New York: Macmillan Publishing Co., 1991.

————. *The Small Garden.* New York: Crown Publishers, 1989.

Chan, Peter. *Peter Chan's Magical Landscape: Transforming Any Small Space into a Place of Beauty.* Pownal, Vt.: Storey Communications, 1988.

Collins, John F., and Marvin I. Adleman. *Livable Landscape Design.* Ithaca, N.Y.: Cornell University Press, 1988.

Crowe, Sylvia. *Garden Design.* London: Packard Publishing in association with Thomas Gibson Publishing, 1981.

Environmental Design Press Staff and Gary Robinette. *Home Landscaping to Save Energy.* New York: Van Nostrand Reinhold Co., 1986.

Fairbrother, Nan. *The Nature of Landscape Design: As an Art Form, a Craft, a Social Necessity.* New York: Alfred A. Knopf, 1974.

Fell, Derek. *Garden Accents.* New York: Henry Holt and Co., 1988.

Jellicoe, Geoffrey and Susan, Patrick Goode, and Michael Lancaster. *The Oxford Companion to Gardens.* New York: Oxford University Press, 1986.

Leighton, Phebe, and Calvin Simonds. *The New American Landscape Gardener: A Guide to Beautiful Backyards and Sensational Surroundings.* Emmaus, Pa.: Rodale Press, 1987.

Loewer, Peter. *Gardens by Design.* Emmaus, Pa.: Rodale Press, 1986.

Ortho Books Staff. *Creative Home Landscaping.* San Fransisco: Ortho Books, 1987.

Roth, Susan A. *The Weekend Garden Guide.* Emmaus, Pa.: Rodale Press, 1991.

Smaus, Robert. *Planning and Planting the Garden.* New York: Harry N. Abrams, 1989.

Taylor's Guide Staff. *Taylor's Guide to Garden Design* (Taylor's Gardening Guides). Boston: Houghton Mifflin Co., 1988.

Whiten, Faith and Geoff. *Creating a New Garden.* New York: W. W. Norton & Co., 1986.

Drawing and Planning

Austin, R. *Graphic Standards for Landscape Architecture.* New York: Van Nostrand Reinhold Co.

Blandford, Percy W. *The Complete Handbook of Drafting.* Blue Ridge Summit, Pa.: Tab Books, 1982.

Robinette, Gary O., ed. *A Guide to Estimating Landscape Costs.* New York: Van Nostrand Reinhold Co., 1983.

Simonds, John Ormsbee. *Landscape Architecture: A Manual of Site Planning and Design.* New York: McGraw-Hill Publishing Co., 1983.

Tab Books' editors. *Surveying.* Blue Ridge Summit, Pa.: Tab Books, 1982.

Materials and Construction Techniques

Gabrielson, M. Alexander. *Swimming Pools: A Guide to Their Planning, Design, and Operation.* Champaign, Ill.: Human Kinetics Publishers, 1987.

Hylton, William, ed. *The Backyard Builder: Projects for Outdoor Living.* Emmaus, Pa.: Rodale Press, 1990.

The Portland Cement Association and the Editors of Rodale Press. *The Homeowner's Guide to Building with Concrete, Brick, and Stone.* Emmaus, Pa.: Rodale Press, 1988.

Snyder, Tim. *Decks: How to Design and Build the Perfect Deck for Your Home.* Emmaus, Pa.: Rodale Press, 1991.

Sunset Magazine and Book editors. *Swimming Pools.* Menlo Park, Calif.: Sunset Books, 1981.

————. *Garden Pools, Fountains, and Waterfalls.* Menlo Park, Calif.: Sunset Books, 1981.

Landscaping with Nature

Devall, Bill. *Simple in Means, Rich in Ends: Practicing Deep Ecology.* Layton, Utah: Gibbs Smith Pub., 1988.

Diekelmann, John, and Robert Schuster. *Natural Landscaping: Designing with Native Plant Communities.* New York: McGraw-Hill Publishing Co., 1982.

Hightshoe, Gary L. *Native Trees, Shrubs, and Vines for Urban and Rural America.* New York: Van Nostrand Reinhold Co., 1987.

Kormondy, Edward J., *Concepts of Ecology.* Englewood Cliffs, N.J.: Prentice-Hall, 1969.

Martin, Laura C. *The Wildflower Meadow Book: A Gardener's Guide.* Charlotte, N.C.: Globe Pequot Press, 1986.

Paulson, Annie. *The National Wildflower Research Center's Wildflower Handbook.* Austin, Tex.: Texas Monthly Press, 1989.

Shuler, Carol. *Low Water Use Plants for Southern California and the Southwest.* Tucson, Ariz.: Fisher Books, 1992.

Plant Propagation and General Care

Bradley, Fern Marshall, and Barbara W. Ellis, eds. *Rodale's All-New Encyclopedia of Organic Gardening.* Emmaus, Pa.: Rodale Press, 1992.

Ellis, Barbara W., ed. *Rodale's Illustrated Encyclopedia of Gardening and Landscaping Techniques.* Emmaus, Pa.: Rodale Press, 1990.

Ellis, Barbara W., and Fern Marshall Bradley, eds. *The Organic Gardener's Handbook of Natural Insect and Disease Control.* Emmaus, Pa.: Rodale Press, 1992.

Halpin, Anne Moyer, and the Editors of Rodale Press. *Foolproof Planting: How to Successfully Start and Propagate More Than 250 Vegetables, Flowers, Trees, and Shrubs.* Emmaus, Pa.: Rodale Press, 1990.

Hartmann, Hudson T., and Dale E. Kester. *Plant Propagation: Principles and Practices.* Englewood Cliffs, N.J.: Prentice-Hall, 1983.

Martin, Deborah L., and Grace Gershuny, eds. *The Rodale Book of Composting.* Emmaus, Pa.: Rodale Press, 1992.

McCullagh, James C., ed. *The Solar Greenhouse Book.* Emmaus, Pa.: Rodale Press, 1978.

Special Topics

Creasy, Rosalind. *The Complete Book of Edible Landscaping.* San Fransisco: Sierra Club Books, 1982.

Loewer, Peter. *Tough Plants for Tough Places: How to Grow 101 Easy-Care Plants for Every Part of Your Yard.* Emmaus, Pa.: Rodale Press, 1992.

Proctor, Dr. Noble. *Garden Birds: How to Attract Birds to Your Garden.* Emmaus, Pa.: Rodale Press, 1990.

Schneck, Marcus. *Butterflies: How to Identify and Attract Them to Your Garden.* Emmaus, Pa.: Rodale Press, 1990.

Uber, William C. *Water Gardening Basics.* Upland, Calif.: Dragonflyer Press, 1988.

USDA PLANT HARDINESS ZONE MAP

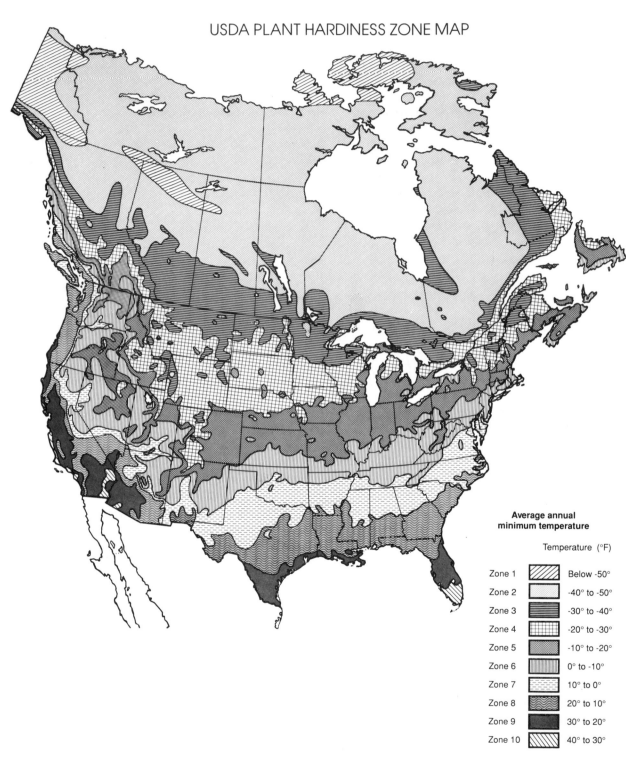

Average annual minimum temperature

Temperature (°F)

Zone 1		Below -50°
Zone 2		-40° to -50°
Zone 3		-30° to -40°
Zone 4		-20° to -30°
Zone 5		-10° to -20°
Zone 6		0° to -10°
Zone 7		10° to 0°
Zone 8		20° to 10°
Zone 9		30° to 20°
Zone 10		40° to 30°

INDEX

Note: Page references in *italic* indicate illustrations and photographs.

A